Internal Alchemy

Self, Society, and
the Quest for Immortality

edited by

Livia Kohn & Robin R. Wang

Three Pines Press
Magdalena, NM 87825
www.threepinespress.com

© 2009 by Livia Kohn & Robin R. Wang

All rights reserved. No part of this book may be reproduced in any form or by any means, electronic or mechanical, including photocopying, recording, or by any information storage and retrieval system, without permission in writing from the publisher.

9   8 7 6 5 4 3 2 1

First Three Pines Press Edition, 2009
Printed in the United States of America

⊗ This edition is printed on acid-free paper that meets the American National Standard Institute Z39.48 Standard. Distributed in the United States by Three Pines Press.

Cover art: "Aligned Body." © Marianne A. Kinzer 2008, watercolor on paper. Used by permission.

Library of Congress Cataloging-in-Publication Data

Internal alchemy : self, society, and the quest for immortality / edited by Livia Kohn & Robin R. Wang. -- 1st ed.
    p. cm.
Includes index.
ISBN 978-1-931483-11-7 (alk. paper)
1. Alchemy--Religious aspects--Taoism. I. Kohn, Livia, 1956- II. Wang, Robin. III. Title: Self, society, and the quest for immortality.
 BL1923.I58 2009
 299.5'1444--dc22
                    2008052960

Contents

Livia Kohn
    Modes of Mutation: Restructuring the Energy Body   1

Sara Elaine Neswald
    Internal Landscapes   27

Guangbao Zhang
    History and Early Lineages   53

Xichen Lu
    The Southern School: Cultivating Mind and Inner Nature   73

Stephen Eskildsen
    Neidan Methods for Opening the Gate of Heaven   87

Shin-yi Chao
    Summoning the Thunder Generals: Internal Alchemy
    in the Thunder Rites   104

Xun Liu
    Numinous Father and Holy Mother: Late-Ming
    Duo-Cultivation Practice   121

Elena Valussi
    Female Alchemy: An Introduction   141

Robin R. Wang
    To Become a Female Daoist Master: Kundao in Training   163

Michael Winn
    Daoist Internal Alchemy in the West   179

Stuart Sovatsky
    On Being Moved: Kundalini and the Complete Matura-
    tion of the Spiritual Body   203

Althea Northage-Orr
    Western Parallels: The Esoteric Teachings of Hermeticism   219

Index   243

Editors' Preface

Internal alchemy (*neidan*) is the culmination of several millennia of Daoist cultivation and transformation practices—physical, meditative, and alchemical. It combines numerous techniques and intricate philosophical concepts into a complex system, geared to allow adepts to refine accessible, tangible body energy into highly spiritual forms while awakening and activating subtle powers and connecting to ultimate reality. Perceiving the body as an intricate network of energy channels and centers, pervaded by flowing subtle vibrations, they utilize sexual energy as the starting point of their exploration and soon come to see themselves as layered levels of body-mind dimensions that grow increasingly finer and eventually merge with the divine.

This vision, which may be generically called "body energetics," is also present in Indian Kundalini yoga and Western Hermeticism. In many ways it matches the quantum physics understanding of the universe as consisting of fine particles that are simultaneously energetic waves. According to this, all matter is made up of vibrating energy and energy fields which change their state very rapidly and are constantly oscillating, arising and dissolving. Reality is thus not a combination of solid entities but an interlocking web of energy fields that each pulsate at their own rate. These interlocking fields of vibration—described in Daoism as patterns of *qi*-flow—can come into harmony with each other and mutually support and increase their amplitude. They can also interfere with each other and create disturbances; or they can be modified, refined, and transfigured into subtler and more divine levels.

The goal of internal alchemy is to identify, control, modify, and eventually transform subtle energies as they are present in the human bodymind. As scientists in biology and medicine increasingly come to see the body as an energetic system, a "living matrix" made up of bioelectricity and bioenergy, it has an important contribution to make. *Neidan* can inspire and guide theory and practice in rapidly developing new fields, such as energy medicine and energy psychology. The only obstacle to integrating millennia of traditional Daoist knowledge and experimentation into the modern discourse is the lack of accessible presentations on the subject.

This is changing with this volume. When the editors and several contributors met at the Third International Daoist Conference on "Cultivation in Theory and Practice," held in an ancient monastery on a Bavarian island in May 2005, they were amazed at the large number of excellent presentations on internal alchemy, most by recent graduates who had made this important aspect of the Daoist tradition the focus of their dissertations.

Getting together in the course of the conference, we realized that the time had come to integrate internal alchemy into the modern discourse on body energetics. Finally, there was enough scholarly information available to create an introductory volume that combined a presentation of basic *neidan* concepts with solid historical and doctrinal studies as well as with examinations of later developments and a comparison with cultivation systems in other cultures. Agreeing to pursue the project, we decided to meet again in a specialized workshop on the subject, with the goal of compiling such a work.

The workshop became a reality a year later, in 2006. Sponsored by Three Pines Press, it was held at a New Mexico mountain retreat over Labor Day weekend. The generous support of the Hong Kong Taoist Association made it possible to invite scholars from both the U.S. and China. In addition to many of the presenters in this volume, supporting participants included David Capco, Caryn Diel, Louis Komjathy, Wang Li, and Zhang Qin as well as Tong Wai-Hop and Andrew Law from Hong Kong. Everybody participated in a vigorous discussion of the various papers that had been prepared and distributed ahead of time. They identified key issues and contributed significantly to the specific vision of this volume, which consists of four main sections.

The first focuses on the overall system. It begins with an overview of the different cultivation methods that contributed to the complexity of internal alchemy by Livia Kohn, long-time scholar of medieval Daoism and professor emerita of Boston University. A specialist of immortality concepts and practices, she has most recently edited *Daoist Body Cultivation* (2006) and authored *Chinese Healing Exercises* (2008). Next comes a detailed examination of *neidan* body concepts with numerous charts and an explanation of key terminology by Sara Neswald, a graduate of McGill University and assistant professor at Mingchuan University in Taipei. Her dissertation focuses on the *Nüdan hebian* (Combined Collection on Female Alchemy), a key document of the Qing dynasty which she is currently translating in full. Third in this section is a substantial outline of the history of internal alchemy with a focus on distinguishing the major schools and tendencies. This is by Zhang Guangbao, a graduate of Beijing University who now serves as a research fellow at the Academy of Social Sciences in Beijing. He has authored numerous books and articles on the subject, including the standard volume *Tang Song neidan daojiao* (2001) and the recent *Jin Yuan Quanzhen jiao xin yanjiu* (2007).

The second major section deals with specific doctrines and practices in the formative phase of internal alchemy during the Song dynasty. Here we have a philosophical examination of the key concepts of inner nature, destiny, and mind as formulated in the Southern School. The author is Lu Xichen, a graduate of Hunan Normal University who currently directs the Institute of Religion at Central South University in Changsha and also serves on the faculty of the Chinese Daoist College. She has written many books and articles, focusing on an in-depth philosophical and psychological exploration of the tradition. Her presentation is followed by a detailed study of the final stages of the *neidan* process, the emergence of the spirit embryo through the top of the head, by Stephen Eskildsen, a graduate of the University of British Columbia and associate professor at the University of Tennessee in Chattanooga. He is the author of two important volumes, *Asceticism in Early Taoist Religion* (1998) and *The Teachings and Practices of the Early Quanzhen Taoist Masters* (2004). Last but not least in this part is an examination of the role of internal alchemy in ritual practice, notably the important Song method of the Thunder Rites, by Shin-yi Chao who also graduated from the University of British Columbia and now serves as assistant professor at Rutgers University in Camden. Her main focus is the deity Xuanwu, Dark Warrior, and the legends and rituals surrounding him.

The third major section of the volume concentrates on later developments during the Ming, Qing, and contemporary periods, especially as related to women. Here we have first a study of duo-cultivation practice, an adaptation of sexual techniques into internal refinement that necessitated specific social and physical settings. The presentation is by Liu Xun, a graduate of the University of Southern California who now teaches at Rutgers University in New Brunswick. His dissertation on the life and career of Chen Yingning (1880-1969) and the transformation of Daoist practice in early 20th-century Shanghai is in press with the Asia Center of Harvard University under the title *Daoist Modern*. His current research focuses on the social and cultural history of Complete Perfection institutions in central China.

The next contribution in this section is an introduction to women's alchemy which emerged powerfully during the Qing dynasty and involved new techniques as well as detailed formulations of how women's bodies are different from men's and necessitate unique methods. The author is Elena Valussi, a graduate of the School for Oriental and African Studies at the University of London who now teaches at Columbia College in Chicago. Her dissertation (2003) was the first English study on women's alchemy; her work has appeared in various scholarly journals. This is followed by a report on the understanding of Daoism and its practices among graduates of the elite Daoist women's academy on Nanyue in Hunan, founded in 2005 and representative of the new dimensions Daoism is about to enter. The work represents field research undertaken by Robin R. Wang, a graduate of Beijing University who now serves as philosophy professor and director of Asian and Pacific Studies at Loyola Marymount University in Los Angeles. She is the author of *Images of Women in Chinese Thought and Culture:* (2003) and *Chinese Philosophy in an Era of Globalization* (2004) and conducts active fieldwork on Daoist mountains.

The final part of the volume is dedicated to modern adaptations and comparative perspectives. It begins with an insightful examination of *neidan* as transformed by transmission into a Western and specifically American context. Its author is Michael Winn, founder of Healing Tao University in the Blue Ridge Mountains, North Carolina. The editor and co-author, with Mantak Chia, of seven books on internal alchemy, he is also the producer of ten Daoist *neidan* home study courses in audio and video format and in great demand as a teacher all over the world. Next we have a survey of the complex theoretical system and practical techniques of the Indian counterpart of internal alchemy, Kundalini yoga by Stuart Sovatsky, a graduate of Princeton University and long-term practitioner and teacher of the system. He is also the author of *Eros, Consciousness and Kundalini*, which focuses on celibate practices, and of *Your Perfect Lips*, a poetic rendition of Indian *pariyanga* erotic yoga in a modern context. The volume concludes with an analytical and comparative description of Western alchemy and its philosophical foundation in Hermeticism by Althea Northage-Orr, a Hermetic initiate and priestess since 1973 who served as the spiritual director of the Hermetic Order of Chicago for many years. Also a practicing acupuncturist and inspired herbalist who grows all of her own materials and is in the process of compiling an herbal encyclopedia, she not only teaches Hermeticism but has been involved in the practice of Daoist women's alchemy for the past ten years.

Taken together, the volume presents internal alchemy in many different dimensions and from a variety of different perspectives in its endeavor to raise awareness of this important tradition among humanities scholars and scientists alike. We hope that, thanks to the unfailing efforts of the contributors and the generous support of the Hong Kong Taoist Association, this book will open a door for many to a world so far shrouded in mystery.

Modes of Mutation

Restructuring the Energy Body

Livia Kohn

Internal alchemy has been the dominant system of Daoist spiritual practice since the Song dynasty, when it was first defined as the complex integration of multiple forms of Daoist self-cultivation (Baldrian-Hussein 1990, 187). Working through the meditative transformation of body energies into subtle levels of spirit and pure cosmic being, internal alchemy is "a method of finding illumination by returning to the fundamental order of the cosmos" and can be characterized by the active reconciliation of physiological training and intellectual speculation (Robinet 1989a, 299-300). Internal alchemy combines operative alchemy as described by Ge Hong of the fourth century; the visualization of body gods central to Highest Clarity; the transformation of bodily energies through systematic guiding of *qi*; absorptive meditations in the *zuowang* and insight traditions; and a cosmological reorientation on the basis of yin and yang, the five phases, lunar and solar cycles, and the *Yijing* (Pregadio 2006a, 210, 219; 2006b, 123).

Developed into different schools and technical variations over the centuries, the alchemical process generally begins with an encompassing moral and physical readiness, which provides a safe setting for the Great Work. From this basis, adepts work through three distinct stages, refining essence (*jing* 精) into energy (*qi* 氣), energy into spirit (*shen* 神), and spirit into the formless purity and vast emptiness of Dao. In this process they consciously and actively reverse human gestation and cosmic creation (Robinet 1989a, 317-19; Skar and Pregadio, 488-90). The actual practice, moreover, actively combines the various forms of Daoist self-cultivation: guiding the *qi*, visualization, absorptive meditation, operative alchemy, and cosmological speculation (for conscious reorientation). However, this does not occur in a linear fashion, one after the next. Instead, adepts weave an intricate network, using the different modes in a spiraling, twisting, and ever turning movement.

What, then, exactly are the different modes of Daoist cultivation that combine into internal alchemy? When do they originate and what major developments have they undergone? How are they transformed in alchemical practice? How exactly do they access the energy body and transform the mind? And, finally, what similar or parallel methods are there in other traditions to better understand the nature and workings of internal alchemy? To answer these questions, I will discuss the modes of mutation one at a time—in the linear fashion of academic writing, yet never forgetting that in actual reality there is nothing linear about the activation and effect of these practices.

Bodily Refinement

Bodily refinement is at the root of all advanced spiritual and mystical practice, in Daoism as much as in other religions. Most traditions begin by demanding the adept's complete dedication through surrender to the system and obedience to the master. They require that adepts leave their ordinary life, vow to observe fundamental ethical principles, and change their garb, diet, and habits. Only in a pure life that is free from tension, guilt, and bodily cravings—all traditions agree—can spiritual attainments flourish. Thus Buddhists have five precepts, monk's robes, shaved heads, and vegetarian diets. Yogis follow the five *yamas* and five *niyamas*, join an *ashram*, eat simple food, sleep on hard cots, and learn to obey their master. Christian monks and nuns take vows of poverty, obedience, and chastity, and spend their lives in nondescript clothes working and praying. In all cases, the person leaves his or her ordinary surroundings, embraces a simple life to prevent distractions, and submits to an ethical code that protects against inner tension and opens pathways to the divine.

Daoists are no exception to this rule, with the main difference that they place a somewhat stronger demand on physical cultivation. But they, too, begin with ethics, commonly requiring the observation of the four great moral rules that are universal to all traditions: to abstain from killing, stealing, lying, and sexual misconduct (Kohn 2004, 28-29). In addition, they insist on the proper observation of social virtues as defined in the Confucian canon (e.g., filial piety and political loyalty), advise the conscientious avoidance of cosmic taboos to prevent any tension in the larger universe, and promote fundamental kindness, effectiveness, and moderation (Ni 1992, 34).

Internal alchemy inherits the full ethical system of medieval Daoism with its numerous rules and regulations. As an essential foundation of cosmic oneness, it requires its practitioners to be in harmony with the forces of nature and to exercise goodness in society. A clear and distinct outline of *neidan* ethics appears in the *Laojun wai riyong miaojing* 老君外日用妙經 (Lord Lao's Wondrous

Scripture of Exterior Daily Practice, DZ 646).[1] Clearly focusing on "exterior practice," the text specifies forty-seven rules of conduct that facilitate the dissolution of desires and establishment of harmony necessary for the great work:

> Respect Heaven and Earth; honor the sun and the moon.
> Fear the law of the land, follow the king, and obey your parents.
> To superiors be honest and humble; to inferiors be gentle and kind.
> All good things do; all bad things eschew.
> From perfect people learn; debauched people avoid.
>
> High knowledge is dangerous; deep knowledge is enriching.
> Be calm and always at peace; be restrained and always content.
> Be cautious without worrying; be patient without shame.
> Give up all luxury and devote yourself to perfection.
>
> Conceal others' flaws; praise others' virtues.
> Practice skillful means and teach your neighborhood
> Befriend the wise and the good; keep away from sounds and sights.
> In poverty, stick to your lot; in wealth, give to charity.
> In action, be even and deliberate; in repose, rely on others.
>
> Always battle your ego and never give in to jealousy and hate.
> Reduce stinginess and greed; give up cunning and craftiness.
> Those oppressed help to liberate; those who hoard try to change.
> Never break your promises and always speak the truth.
>
> Support the poor and orphaned; aid the homeless and indigent.
> Save those in danger and trouble so you accumulate hidden merit.
> Always practice compassion and never kill any beings.
> Listen to words of loyalty and be free from a scheming heart.
> Follow these rules and you can ascend to the beyond.

Another dimension of physical preparation is the weaning of the body from ordinary pleasures to effect a return to simplicity that makes it ready for spiritual cultivation (Ni 1992, 31). Daoists, as much as Buddhist and Christian adepts, remove themselves from society—either permanently as monastics or temporarily for intense practice—to wear uniform clothes, avoid decorations or embellishments, and eat a simple vegetarian diet. All this creates what Marcel Mauss (1979) and Pierre Bourdieu (1990) call *habitus* or "body techniques." These are "ordered, authorized, tested actions" sanctioned by a community that serve to shape the reality and identity of its members (Mauss 1979, 102).

Ranging from body movements (walking, squatting) through ways of caring for the body (washing, grooming) to consumption techniques, body techniques include attitudes to food, authority, sexual relations, nakedness, pleasure and pain, medicine and healing, and the use of "body metaphors" (Coakley

---

[1] Texts in the Daoist canon are cited according to Schipper and Verellen 2004.

1997, 8; Bourdieu 1990, 53). The various body techniques, therefore, learned and habituated in a culturally determined and structured manner, create a specific set of feelings, conceptions, and expressions that reflect the culture and society that instilled them and gives them enduring structure.

In the case of internal alchemy, the various new ways of being in the body free it from outside concerns and create an increased awareness of interior energy patterns. They include:

—physical exercises called *daoyin* 導引 (today continued in qigong) which involve simple moves in conjunction with deep, intentional breathing and a subtle guiding of intention, especially to places where there are pain, tension, or blockages (see Kohn 2006; 2008a);

—specific ways of breathing to warm or cool the body, usually undertaken in the form of intentional exhalations known as the Six Breaths or Healing Sounds (*liuzi jue* 六字訣) (see Despeux 2006);

—a reduced vegetarian or raw food diet that may involve periods of fasting, often referred to as "abstention from grain" (*bigu* 辟穀) (see Arthur 2006);

—and the supplementation of the diet with herbal remedies to create overall physical harmony, which results in a free flow of *qi*, a vibrant sense of health, an increased vigor, and an extended longevity (see Akahori 1989).

All these methods—documented in Chinese sources since before the Han dynasty—played an important role in the medical tradition and entered Daoism in the early middle ages. Tang Daoists combined them into an integrated system and formally acknowledged them as the backbone of advanced Daoist cultivation (Kohn 2008a, 128). Following this, practitioners of internal alchemy too begin by creating a safe working environment: externally in society and nature through ethical conduct; internally in their bodies through the conscientious application of longevity techniques. Doing so, they establish the body formally as the main arena of the Great Work that will lead to cosmic oneness.

Guiding *Qi*

Guiding *qi* (*xingqi* 行氣) is a uniquely Chinese exercise, although it does have some similarities with the conscious sending of breath into specific areas of the body in yoga and with the observation of subtle vibrational body patterns in Buddhist insight meditation.[2] It involves the subtle awareness of body energies together with the careful noting and directing of *qi*-vibrations through energy channels. To engage in the guiding of *qi*, adepts have to be stable physically and calm mentally. With the body properly strengthened and the joints opened, they can sit completely still and turn their intention inward. They then use sim-

---

[2] On yogic breathing while holding postures, see Farhi 2003, 97-99. On the body scan and observation of energetic flow in mindfulness meditation, see Kabat-Zinn 1990, 75-93.

ple observation of breath to calm the mind, bringing it from a state of constant agitation and racing thoughts—often described as the "monkey mind" or "a mind like wild horses"—to a level of stability and calm. As Sun Simiao 孫思邈 describes it in his *Cunshen lianqi ming* 存神鍊氣銘 (Visualization of Spirit and Refinement of *Qi*, DZ 400):

> Stage Five: The mind is turned entirely toward purity and tranquility. Whether involved in affairs or at leisure, there is no agitation at all. From an efficiently controlled mind, firmness and solidity of concentration develop. (1b)

This, of course, matches the deep restful state of mind acquired in Buddhist concentration on breathing (*ānapāna*; see Rosenberg 1999), the mental stability of yoga reached in the stages of one-pointedness and absorption (*dhārana* and *dhyāna*; see Hewitt 1977), and the pervasive serenity attained in Christian contemplation. To become open to the divine and ready for in-depth spiritual exploration, the mind has to be restful and at peace, untroubled by sensory distractions and ordinary thoughts.

On this basis of concentration, Daoists engage in the practice of guiding *qi*. The first mention of this appears in an inscription on a dodecagonal jade block of the Zhou dynasty that dates from the fourth century B.C.E. The original function of the block remains uncertain (Chen 1982), but the inscription in forty-five characters has been studied by several scholars (Wilhelm 1948; Li 1993, 320-23). It reads:

> To guide the *qi*, allow it to enter deeply [by inhaling] and collect it [in the mouth]. As it collects, it will expand. Once expanded, it will sink down. When it sinks down, it comes to rest. After it has come to rest, it becomes stable.
>
> When the *qi* is stable, it begins to sprout. From sprouting, it begins to grow. As it grows, it can be pulled back upwards. When it is pulled upwards, it reaches the crown of the head.
>
> It then touches above at the crown of the head and below at the base of the spine. Who practices like this will attain long life. Who goes against this will die. (Harper 1998, 126)

According to this, to guide the *qi* people first inhale deeply and allow the breath to enter the chest and the mouth. They mix it with saliva, another potent form of *qi*, by moving their tongue around the mouth. Next, they swallow, allowing the *qi* to sink down and feel it moving deep into their abdomen, where they let it settle in the central area of gravity, known in Chinese medicine as the Ocean of *Qi* (*qihai* 氣海) and in Daoism as the cinnabar or elixir field (*dantian* 丹田). There the *qi* rests and becomes stable.

As adepts repeat this practice, the *qi* accumulates and becomes stronger. Eventually it does not remain in the lower abdomen but begins to spread through the body or, as the inscription says, it "sprouts." Once this is felt, adepts can consciously guide it upwards—a technique that usually involves seeing it flow down to the pelvic floor and then moving it gradually up along the spine in coordination with deep breathing. Guiding it all the way up the back, adepts eventually feel it reach the top of the head. When the entire passage between the head and the pelvic floor is opened, the Penetrating Vessel in the center of the torso is activated: this is the first energy line in the human embryo and the central channel to connect people to Dao. With this pervading line open, adepts can attain long life and reach for transcendence.

The method in this early description, which also matches healing techniques in early medical manuscripts (Harper 1998, 125), is essentially identical with the *neidan* practice of the Microcosmic Orbit (*xiao zhoutian* 小周天), in which adepts circulate the *qi* around the two channels in the front and back of the torso, the Governing and Conception Vessels. Their goal is to prevent essence, which is felt as sexual energy (semen or menstrual blood), from being discharged and instead revert it back into *qi* (Chia and Chia 1993; Wik and Wik 2005). This strengthens the body and creates health, but it also activates a subtler awareness of internal energies and develops an energetic vibrancy.

Internal alchemy also uses the conscious guiding of *qi* in various other ways as, for example, when adepts isolate the warm energy of the heart (fire) and the cool energy of the kidneys (water) and intermingle them consciously for a greater level of refinement (Baldrian-Hussein 1984, 73; Winn 2006). Another concrete example is a *qi*-circulation exercise called the Eight Brocades (*baduan jin* 八段錦), a sequence of eight seated practices that stimulate *qi*-flow, rotate energies around the body, and encourage alchemical transmutations.[3]

Visualization

Visualization is the conscious use of imagery to alter or transform the mind and emotions. Although called "visualization" and often dominantly visual in nature—as opposed to the more kinesthetic mode of guiding *qi*—it involves all the other sense faculties: hearing, smelling, touching, and tasting. For this reason some translators prefer the rendition "to actualize" for the Chinese term *cun* 存 (Schafer 1978; Pregadio 2008, 287-89). The object of the visualization is to be made as real as possible, and while colors and shapes are important, they are not the sole mode of work.

---

[3] The meditative (seated) Eight Brocades—not to be confused with the martial, standing exercise of the same name—are first described in *Xiuzhen shishu* 修真十書 (Ten Books on Cultivating Perfection, DZ 263), a compendium linked with Bai Yuchan 白玉蟾 (1194-1227?) (Schipper and Verellen 2004, 946).See Kohn 2008a, 180-83.

Imagery as activated in visualization practice is universal and part of primary process thinking. In the development both of the individual and of cultures it is one of the earliest forms of cognition that connects to deep levels of the brain. Imagery creates a more immediate experience of a situation, memory, or vision than the more distant experience conveyed by verbal expression or abstract thinking. In addition, scientists have shown conclusively that internal images are just as real, emotionally and physiologically, as physical experiences in the external world. The body reacts in exactly the same way to an internal imagined experience as to an actual outside one.[4] Visualization is thus another major tool for accessing subconscious levels of the person and activating the subtle energy body within (Kohn 2008b, 130).

Chinese texts first describe visualization in the Han dynasty, when both medical and Daoist sources advise practitioners to envision their inner organs in specific colors to enhance their workings and thus create health. The *Daode jing* commentator Heshang gong 河上公 (Master on the River) thus describes organ *qi* in terms of spiritual forces or body divinities (*shen* 神). He says:

> Whoever is able to nourish the spirits within will not die. By spirits I refer to the spirits of the five organs: the spirit soul in the liver, the material soul in the lungs, the spirit in the heart, the conscious intention in the spleen, and the essence together with the will in the kidneys. When these five organs are exhausted or harmed, the five spirits will flee. (DZ 682, 6: 1.5a) (see Chan 1991)

Envisioning the spirits in the organs, therefore, helps with the maintenance of health and can lead to higher attainments.

A more detailed description of inner visualization appears in the *Taiping jing shengjun bizhi* 太平經聖君秘旨 (Secret Instructions of the Holy Lord on the Scripture of Great Peace, DZ 1102), a Tang redaction of a text associated with the *Taiping jing* of the Later Han. It advises adepts to begin with deep concentration, then notice the arising of a light that can appear in different colors: a clear radiance signals the energy of greater yang; a green light is that of lesser yang; a red light is a sign of transcendence; a yellow light indicates central harmony and "a potent remedy of Dao;" a white light, "as clear as flowing water," is the light of lesser yin; and a black light represents the energy of greater yin (2a). Adepts visualize their bodies pervaded by these lights, allowing them to pervade the entire structure and to settle in their matching organs. They then allow specific deities to appear in the halo of the lights, settling them into their bodies and increasingly create a network of divinity within (2b).

---

[4] On modern definitions of visualization and its uses as a medical and hypnosis tool, see Samuels and Samuels 1975; Korn and Johnson 1983; Epstein 1989. On its application in Neuro-Linguistic Programming, see McDermott and O'Connor 1996.

Highest Clarity
The same concept, expanded into a vision of the body as an internal landscape, complete with radiant gods and splendid palaces, became the backbone of Daoist practice in the medieval school of Highest Clarity (Shangqing 上清), which emerged on the basis of a series of revelations in the 360s (see Robinet 1989b; Bokenkamp 2007; Miller 2008). Visualization techniques appear first in a group of texts that slightly predate the school: the *Huangting jing* 黃庭經 (Yellow Court Scripture, DZ 263, 403, *Yunji qiqian* [DZ 1032, abbr. YJQQ] 11-12), the *Laozi zhongjing* 老子中經 (Central Scripture of Laozi, DZ 1168, YJQQ 18-19), and in Ge Hong's 葛洪 *Baopuzi neipian* 抱朴子內篇 (Inner Chapters of the Master Who Embraces Simplicity, DZ 1185).

According to these sources, the head is the celestial headquarters, matching the immortals' paradise of Mount Kunlun and described as a large, luscious mountain surrounded by a wide lake and covered with palaces and orchards. Between the eyes (sun and moon), one can move inside to the Hall of Light (*mingtang* 明堂), one of nine major palaces located there. Best reached by passing through the deep, dark valley of the nose, it is guarded by the two high towers of the ears. To attain entry one has to perform the physical/ritual exercise of "beating the heavenly drum": with both palms covering the ears, snap the index and middle fingers to drum against the back of the skull.

From the Hall of Light, one moves deeper into the head to reach the Grotto Chamber (*dongfang* 洞房), then goes on to the center and enters the upper Cinnabar Field, also known as the Niwan Palace 泥丸宮, the residence of the upper lord of the Three Ones, deities that represent the universe and occupy the elixir fields in the adept's body. The remaining six palaces are placed around the central three, housing further deities such as the lords of the Great Ultimate and goddesses of Highest Clarity. Taken together, the Nine Palaces symbolize the totality of the universe in the human being, matching the nine sectors of Earth and the nine provinces of China as established by the sage emperor Yu. Adepts thus gain access to the greater cosmos and its ruling divinities through internal visualization (see Kalinowski 1985).

The same pattern also holds true for the torso. Again beginning with conscious breathing at the nose, adepts may travel downward through its valley to find the mouth in the form of a small lake. Filled by divine fluid that is experienced as saliva, this regulates the water level of the upper lake in the head and raises or lowers it as necessary. Crossing the mouth-lake over a bridge (tongue) and moving further down, adepts reach the twelve-storied tower of the throat, then come to the Flowery Canopy (lungs), the Scarlet Palace (heart), the Yellow Court (spleen), the Imperial Granary (stomach), the Purple Chamber (gall bladder), and various other starry palaces transposed into the body's depth. Going ever deeper, another cosmic region is reached, with another sun and moon (kidneys). Beneath them, the Ocean of *Qi* extends with another Mount Kunlun in its midst. Various divine beings reside throughout, creating vitality and providing spiritual resources.

Even in these early visualization texts, a certain level of alchemical imagery is used to describe the internal dynamics of the body. Thus, for example, the desired goal is often formulated in terms of a divine elixir; a number of internal fluids match alchemical substances; and in some cases the deities are envisioned as emerging from alchemical cauldrons and stoves (Pregadio 2005, 208-11; 2006, 127-32).

Followers of internal alchemy commonly use visualization in conjunction with the guiding of *qi*. For example, they unite yin and yang energies by either feeling them as kidney water and heart fire in internal *qi*-circulation or by imagining them as two deities: the perfect father is a young man dressed in red, the color of fire, who stands above; the perfect mother is a young woman dressed in black, the color of water, and rests below. They move toward the Yellow Court in the center of the torso to encounter an old woman, the matchmaker, who invites them to enter the nuptial chamber where they become husband and wife. After their successful union, they separate: the young man returns upward while the young woman moves back downward, each enriched with the essence of the other, while leaving the pearl of dew—the core of the immortal embryo—behind in the center (Baldrian-Hussein 1984, 76-77).

Compared to ethical integrity, mental concentration, and the guiding of *qi*, visualization presents a yet subtler form of accessing the energy body and thus allows a greater degree of control. Through it one can purposely influence the structure and shape of subconscious content, rearranging patterns and creating new systems. Reorienting the body to hold heavenly palaces and deities, to become a cosmos in itself, adepts develop an intimate connection with the cosmic dimensions of the universe. As more and more parts of the body are transformed into divine entities and mutated into subtler levels of being, the very physicality of the adept turns into a cosmic network and becomes the celestial realm in which the gods reside. Visualizing and feeling the divinity of Dao within the bodily self, the Daoist becomes a more cosmic being, transforming but not relinquishing his physical, embodied nature.

Absorptive Meditation

In the Tang dynasty, the visualization techniques of medieval Daoism merged with methods inspired by Buddhism, notably of the Tiantai 天台 and Sanlun 三論 schools. These included methods of insight meditation, then called "inner observation" (*neiguan* 內觀), and the attainment of deep states of absorption, described in terms of forgetfulness and associated with a practice already mentioned in the *Zhuangzi* and known as "sitting in oblivion" (*zuowang* 坐忘). Both continue actively in the practice of internal alchemy, where states of intense concentration and an acute awareness of inner states are prerequisites for the successful creation of the immortal embryo.

Insight or mindfulness meditation guides adepts to develop a new dimension of the conscious mind by establishing a detached, objective observer or witness consciousness, a mental position of distanced seeing, a faculty of taking a step back from involvement with experiences and emotions. Learning to both feel an experience immediately and see it from a distance, they begin to identify, observe, and cleanse negative emotions while cultivating positive states, such as compassion and kindness, calmness and equanimity, peace and joy. They also come to see the world increasingly in Buddhist terms, understanding that neither mind nor self are immutable, firm entities; that life is constantly changing and essentially unsatisfactory; and that true contentment can only be found in the present moment (Kohn 2008b, 73).

In Daoist terms, the practice appears most prominently in the eighth-century *Neiguan jing* 內觀經 (Scripture on Inner Observation, DZ 641), integrating the insight practice of the Tiantai school. It describes "inner observation" or "inner vision" as the introspection of one's body and mind, instructing practitioners to see themselves in terms of subtler energies of life and varying body gods that all undergo dynamic and constant change. Doing so, adepts realize the law of universal impermanence (Buddhist: *anicca*) and understand that their living person and self are nothing but a vehicle of the spirit which reaches far beyond the individual and leaves no room for a personal self (Buddhist: *anatta*) (see Kohn 1989). They learn to work with the transformation of emotions and develop a detached attitude toward the flow of life, seeing self and body as a conglomerate of changing forces rather than solid entities. They also train themselves to pay close attention to spirit and strengthen the observing faculty in the mind. As the text has it:

> What makes the various joints of the body function together are the hundred manifestations of the spirit of life. As it pervades the whole of the body, spirit is not empty. When primordial *qi* enters through the nose and reaches the Niwan Palace in the center of the head, the spirit light radiates and the body is stable and at peace. For all movement and rest, however, it fully depends on the mind.
>
> When you observe yourself in detail and with care, beware of the mind. As the ruler of the self it can prohibit and control everything. It is responsible for the proper position of the body spirit [gods]. The mind is the spirit. Its changes and transformations cannot be fathomed. (2a; Kohn 1989, 213)

Working more with vacillating energies than with body divinities, this mode of practice integrates visualization but moves it into a subtler dimension: the body gods are still there, but rather than powerful individual entities they are manifestations of a universal spirit which pervades everything and is intimately connected to primordial *qi*, the root force of life. Spirit, moreover, is strongly present in the mind, activates it, and works through it. Keeping the mind focused and detached will allow spirit to radiate through the body, which is observed with detachment and perceived as the combination of vibrating energies of various kinds and intensities.

Sitting in oblivion takes this practice another step further into the formless appreciation of energies. Adepts using this method take great care to place the body into a specific posture and hold it in complete stillness, then open their awareness to the present moment and let go of everything. Doing so, they hope to overcome both the conscious and subconscious mind, to eradicate all sensory evaluation and dualistic thinking, and achieve an immediate presence in all activities (Kohn 2008b, 97).

The practice appears first in the *Zhuangzi*, which describes it as the systematic elimination of conscious and sensory perception in favor of a pure level of experience at one with Dao at the root of creation. It has Huizi say:

> I smash up my limbs and body, drive out perception and intellect, cast off form, do away with understanding, and make myself identical with the Great Thoroughfare. (ch. 6, Watson 1968, 90; Graham 1981, 95; Roth 2000, 37)

This, then, describes a state where all visceral awareness of emotions and desires is lost and all sense perception is cut off. Completely free from dualistic thinking or bodily self-consciousness, it represents a state of no-mind where there are no boundaries between things and where the person as person has "lost himself" (*Zhuangzi*, ch. 2).

In the early Tang dynasty, Daoists formalized this ancient method in the school of Twofold Mystery, combining it with Buddhist Mādhyamika (Middle Way) philosophy of the Sanlun school. They formulated a systematic approach to the practice that survives in Sima Chengzhen's 司馬承禎 (647-735) *Zuowang lun* 坐忘論 (On Sitting in Oblivion; trl. Kohn 1987). Based on this, the practice became part of internal alchemy and is still actively undertaken in Daoist monasteries today (see Shi 2006). Beyond that, Zhuangzi's vision also merged with fundamental tenets of Mahayana Buddhist thought and, in the sixth century, became the inspiration of Chan (Zen) Buddhism where the practice is called *zazen* or *shinkantaza*, with the goal of the overall "dropping off of body and mind" (Kohn 2008b, 99).

More specifically, Twofold Mystery works with the basic dichotomy of two levels of truth (worldly and absolute) and envisions the meditative process of discarding desires in two steps: making all mysterious and again mysterious; or decreasing and again decreasing (Kohn 1991, 189-96). As Cheng Xuanying 成玄英 notes in his commentary to the *Daode jing*:

> A practitioner must first discard all desires, then proceed to discard the level of no-desires. Only then can he truly accomplish twofold discard-

> ing of both sides and wondrously merge with the Dao of Middle Oneness. Beings and ego looked upon in equal fashion, mental states and wisdom both forgotten—when someone makes such a state his principle of government, then everything will be well ordered. (ch. 3; Kohn 1991, 191; Assandri 2008, 7)

The process thus consists of a twofold decrease, a double obscuring, which is also described as "double forgetfulness" (*jianwang* 兼忘). First all mental states have to go, i.e., mental projections constructed in the mind yet erroneously regarded as solid reality. Then wisdom and mind, the inherent functions of active consciousness, are discarded. Twofold Mystery thus aims at a reorganization of ordinary consciousness toward absolute consciousness and again from absolute consciousness to no consciousness at all, to neither consciousness nor no consciousness. Yet the sagely state aimed for is not a state of nothingness; rather, it is the "embodiment of Dao of Middle Oneness," a state of radiance and surging activity.

Building on this understanding of oblivion, the Highest Clarity patriarch Sima Chengzhen gave a series of lectures on the practice that—not unlike the "Recorded Sayings" of contemporaneous Zen masters such as the Sixth Patriarch—were first recorded in an inscription (dat. 931) and later compiled in the classic text on the method, the *Zuowang lun*. Integrating inner observation and adding ecstatic flight and ascension into the heavens as the ultimate goal of the practice, he provides a detailed outline in seven steps that eventually lead to a deep trance called "Intense Concentration," followed by an ecstatic celestial state described as "Realizing Dao."

In "Intense Concentration," even the inner agent that gave rise to the various mental states—the spirit that played such a prominent role in inner observation—is forgotten. Practitioners find themselves in deep, stable serenity, a restfulness within that needs no stimulation or outer action, but is at the same time accompanied by a radiant heavenly light, the pure energy of Dao shining through, the power of penetrating wisdom and sign of enlightenment. In "Realizing Dao" adepts attain oneness with Heaven and Earth, a life as long as the universe, and various spiritual powers. As perfected beings they can live among fellow men and spread the purity of Dao by just being themselves; or they can ascend spiritually to the heavens where they take up residence among the immortals (Kohn 1987, 104, 107).

Both states appear in internal alchemy during the third stage of the practice, when adepts go into deep absorption and become motionless, often for several days. Being immobilized in catatonic trance, they allow the immortal embryo to rise along the spine and exit through the top of the head—thus reaching ultimate ecstatic freedom and gaining various supernatural powers for themselves (Despeux and Kohn 2003, 238).

Cosmological Reorientation

While much of the *neidan* work takes place deep inside the body and serves to restructure its functioning and refine its subtlety, there is also an intellectual dimension to the process that creates a new understanding of self and world and relates the practice to the larger rhythms of nature. For this, adepts learn to appreciate the cosmological patterns of the universe and see the world in terms of interrelated patterns, calendar cycles, complex numerologies, and intricate networks of abstract symbols.

This, too, is typical for transformative traditions throughout the world. Adepts of Buddhist insight meditation, for example, are trained to see the universe as the ever changing interaction of flowing, swirling energies and to appreciate the key doctrines of suffering, impermanence, and no-self (see Brown and Engler 1984). Similarly, students of Western esotericism study the intricacies of Hermetic philosophy, following in the footsteps of Albertus Magnus, Thomas Aquinas, Jacob Boehme, and Robert Fludd, and work with the complex system of the Jewish Cabbala (see Atwood 1960; Stavish 2006). In all cases, the universe is reinterpreted to fit the new identity created through the practice and often intricate cosmologies and highly abstract symbols take the place of ordinary perception.

Internal alchemy works with three different cosmological systems. There is first classical Chinese cosmology, most prominently known from its application in Chinese medicine, that divides the universe according to the two forces yin and yang and understands their working in terms of the five phases (*wuxing* 五行). Next, there is the Chinese calendar and the understanding of the seasonal rhythms and patterns, the cycles of summer and winter, the sun and the moon, and the various phases of the Great Work associated with them. And third, there is the *Yijing* 易經 (Book of Changes), which serves not only to create a more detailed outline of alchemical timing but also provides the blueprint for the stages before and after creation and a powerful symbolism for internal energetic transformation.

Cosmology and the Calendar
Yin and yang are at the root of traditional Asian cosmology, commonly presented in the well-known circle with two black and white curved halves, plus a white dot in the black section and a black dot in the white section. The image

shows the balance and yet interlocking nature of yin and yang, the fluidity of their interchange. The two forces originated from geographical observation, indicating the sunny and shady sides of a hill. From there they acquired a series of associations: bright and dark, light and heavy, strong and weak, above and below, Heaven and Earth, ruler and minister, male and female, and so on.

The structure that underlies the yin-yang system is a form of correlative thinking, which is not unique to China but can also be found in other traditional cultures, such as ancient Greece (see Kuriyama 1999), and in the West is still used in occultism, magic, and alchemy. It represents a basic pattern of the human mind, forms the foundation of more elaborate forms of logic, and is clearly present in the way we acquire language. For example, to build the plural of *shoe*, we add the letter "s" to get *shoes*. The same applies to cat/cats, stone/stones, road/ roads. But then we learn that this correlative pattern when applied to the word *foot* is wrong and instead of *foots* we use another pattern and go from *foot* to *feet*, then apply the same to get goose/geese, and so on. In all cases, the organization of language is based on a simple pattern that is correlated and repeated in different concrete cases (see Graham 1986).

Developing an intricate set of correlative patterns, the yin-yang system provides a good basis for understanding the workings of *qi* in the world. To access its subtler movements, moreover, the system subdivides into five stages of development: minor yang—major yang—yin-yang—minor yin—major yin. These five are then associated with five organic substances that symbolize the different stages in the process: wood, fire, earth, metal, and water. These, then, are known as the "five phases" and appear in integrated cycles of mutual production or control. Thus, for example, water makes things grow and produces wood, wood dries and becomes fuel for fire in a productive sequence; water extinguishes fire, fire melts metal, and so on, in the controlling cycle.

In the early Han dynasty around 200 B.C.E. the five phases became the foundation of Chinese cosmology. They were associated with colors, directions, seasons, musical tones, smells, and flavors, and with all kinds of other dimensions, including various functions in the human body, such as storage organs, digestive organs, senses, emotions, body parts, and body fluids. The basic chart is as follows:

yin/yang	phase	direct.	color	season	organ1	organ2	emotion	sense
minor yang	wood	east	green	spring	liver	gall	anger	eyes
major yang	fire	south	red	summer	heart	sm. int.	exc. joy	tongue
yin-yang	earth	center	yellow		spleen	stomach	worry	lips
minor yin	metal	west	white	fall	lungs	lg. int.	sadness	nose
major yin	water	north	black	winter	kidneys	bladder	fear	ears

This complex correspondence system provides a vision of the universe that is relational and dynamic and places human beings in a world subject interaction patterns that can be orderly or chaotic. It both limits and empowers people. It limits them by placing them into a natural cycle which responds to their actions and demands total adaptation. Yet it also empowers them because it gives them a proactive role in connection with all things, the power to support or disturb the natural and political order. It also, as is most clearly the case in internal alchemy, forms the backbone of an understanding of self and world that lends itself to modification and mutation, allowing the subtle refinement of one aspect to carry over into all others and creating a conscious intellectual framework for the Great Work.

In addition to the five phases as a fundamental cosmological underpinning, adepts of internal alchemy are also very conscious about the structure and patterns of time. They work closely with the four seasons which are marked by the solstices and the equinoxes, often beginning the Great Work at the height of yin at the winter solstice. Following this, they observe the so-called Eight Nodes, the solstices and equinoxes plus the beginnings of the seasons—a system that roughly matches the festivals of Western pagan or Wiccan religion. In addition, they may work with twenty-four solar periods of about two weeks each that are named after weather patterns such as "great heat," "slight cold," "great rain," and "slight snow" and also include the solstices and equinoxes.

The *Yijing*

More than through the agricultural cycle, however, alchemists understand time with the help of *Yijing* hexagrams, using them to show the waxing and waning of yin and yang through the year. In particular they use a series of twelve hexagrams, beginning with the hexagram *fu*, which consists of five yin lines and one yang line, and moving through an increase first of yang, then of yin to the hexagram *kun*, which consists of all yin lines. Each hexagram stands for a particular phase in the energetic transmutation and growth of the embryo, allowing a subtle timing and cosmic patterning of the inner alchemical process.

The *Yijing* with its hexagrams goes back to the Zhou dynasty, when it served as the official dynastic divination manual and, along with astrology, numerology, and other methods of fortune-telling, helped to determine the inherent tendencies in the course of Heaven (see Smith 2008). Unlike other forms of divination which give yes-or-no answers, the *Yijing* is morally based and provides specific advice on optimal, usually ethical, behavior. As a result, long after the demise of the Zhou dynasty the *Yijing* is still around, providing personal readings on career decisions and family concerns.

As all of Chinese cosmology, the system of the *Yijing* is based on yin and yang, here symbolized by an unbroken (yang) and a broken (yin). The two lines, like the binary pattern at the base of computing, are then combined two by two into four symbols: double yang, yang over yin, double yin, and yin over yang. In addition, the lines form eight symbols of three lines each, known as trigrams. The Eight Trigrams (*bagua* 八卦) are as follows:

Heaven (*qian*, creative)	☰	Earth (*kun*, receptive)	☷
Fire (*li*, clinging)	☲	Water (*kan*, abysmal)	☵
Wind (*sun*, gentle)	☴	Lake (*dui*, joyous)	☱
Thunder (*zhen*, arousing)	☳	Mountain (*gen*, still)	☶

The hexagrams, then, consist of the combination of two trigrams in various permutations. They each come with an explanation of the image, a judgment, an explanation of the judgment, and a fortune for individual lines (see Wilhelm 1950). Rather than for fortune-telling, however, in internal alchemy the *Yijing* is used to symbolize timing and energetic transmutations. For example, the pure *qi* of the heart and kidneys (yang and yin), once transformed, becomes the *qi* of cosmic Fire and Water, then described as the trigrams Li and Kan. The central line of each trigram is seen as part of a higher purity; it has to be isolated to revert to the pure state of Heaven and Earth, symbolized by Qian and Kun. This, in turn, is achieved in practice by refining the energies further in the body, hoping to attain a level of cosmic creation that will then allow the attainment of immortality.

The Eight Trigrams are at the core of *neidan* thinking. They are arranged in two different patterns, laid out on a geographical grit, one representing the state before creation or "Before Heaven" (*xiantian* 先天), the other showing the forces of the universe post-creation or "After Heaven" (*houtian* 後天)—states that also apply to the human body as pre- and postnatal. Thus, before creation or birth in this body, Heaven (Qian) is due south, while Earth (Kun) is due north, Fire (Li) and Water (Kan) are to the east and west. In the course of creation, described as the union of Heaven and Earth, Kun desires to join with Qian and moves south. After connecting with Qian, it establishes itself in the southwest. Similarly, Heaven, in an effort to merge with Earth, begins to move north and eventually comes to reside in the northwest. Fire and Water in the meantime rotate by ninety degrees and end up on the north-south axis. As Fire is established in the south and Water in the north, they match the set-up of the five phases that governs the world as we know it (Baldrian-Hussein 1984, 63).

Understanding the body in energetic terms and matching its different functions with the patterns of nature and the greater universe, adepts of internal alchemy transform themselves and their concepts of the world to increasing levels of subtlety, coming to appreciate the abstract complexities of *Yijing* speculation and seeing themselves in terms of energetic combinations and interaction patterns, at any time on a different level of the continuous exchange and unfolding of yin and yang. The subtle energy body, already modified through various physical, breathing, and imagery practices, is mutated yet again in a different way, through the adjustment of the conscious mind, the critical and intellectual aspect of the self.

Alchemy

All of these mutations and transformations, last but certainly not least, are couched in the terms of the alchemical process, an active modification of substances and energies that allows the replication of cosmic evolution and leads to the root of cosmic oneness. Chinese alchemy goes back to the Han dynasty, when emperors hired magical practitioners to create an elixir of life that would allow them to bypass death and ascend to the isles of the immortals. It is described first and in most concrete detail in Ge Hong's *Baopuzi neipian*.[5] According to this, the alchemical process had to be undertaken in complete secrecy and only by carefully selected and fully dedicated individuals. After a number of exacting trials by a master, the disciple had to first make a pledge by "throwing a golden human statuette and a golden fish into an east-ward flowing stream," then "close a formal covenant with the teacher by smearing one's lips with blood" (4.6b; Ware 1966, 75; Benn 2000, 330).

Once ready for elixir concoction, the work had to take place at exactly the right time and in exactly the right place. Ideally, it should begin at the height of yin—at midnight of the winter solstice—then follow a cosmic time schedule reduced to a microcosmic level. In terms of place, it could only be performed in a carefully chosen spot with the right kinds of streams, hills, and trees for the proper flow of *qi*. The place further had to be completely secluded because the slightest contact with a nonbeliever could ruin the entire process. Before even the first ingredient could be placed in the cauldron, a proper furnace, typically a three-tiered brick oven, had to be set up and several ritual purifications had to be undergone, including bathing, fasting, and avoidance of sex and blood (see Pregadio 2000). In addition, the seeker had to set up protective talismans, offer a sacrifice to the gods, swear an oath of secrecy, and make a formal pledge (often involving substantial gifts) to the master alchemist.

Next, the concoction process commenced, a lengthy and complicated procedure that involved creating a chemical reaction on the basis of highly disparate and often poisonous substances, such as pine needles and resin, mushrooms, persimmons, apricot kernels, deer antlers, mother-of-pearl, mica, aconite, realgar, sulphur, mercury, arsenic, silver, and gold. These materials, which sometimes took years to collect, were cooked according to the revealed, cosmic instructions, placed in a cauldron coated with various luting compounds and surrounded by magical and protective devices to ensure the proper atmosphere

---

[5] On Chinese alchemy, see Sivin 1968; 1990; Needham 1980; Pregadio 2000; 2006a.

for the elixir to grow. Over months or even years, the right times of firing and cooling, stirring and burying had to be observed to the minutest detail.

The process was thought to imitate the growth of gold in the earth on a microcosmic scale, and accordingly followed the stages of cosmic creation as perceived at the time. Essentially the work of the alchemist occurred on three levels: the concrete concoction of the elixir for immortality, the creation of gold from base metals for personal wealth, and the replication of the cosmic processes of creation for insights into (and power over) the innermost secrets of the universe. Alchemy was, therefore, both a chemical and a mystical endeavor which led not only to chemically induced trances and visions but also to the high spiritual states necessary for immortal transformation.

If and when the elixir had been created successfully, the alchemist had to perform a thanksgiving sacrifice and give away large portions of his newly created gold to the gods and, anonymously, to the crowds. He then could take varying doses of the elixir, a gray-brown mud that was ingested either rolled into a pill or dissolved in liquid. Depending on the dose, he would attain various levels of magical powers, gain extensive divine protection (crowds of divine generals and supporters hovering over his every step), find a new level of lightness and radiance in body and mind, and have the choice of either extending his sojourn on earth indefinitely or ascend to Heaven in broad daylight.

The most commonly used drug was called cinnabar (*dan* 丹), which is also the generic word for "elixir." It is a mercury-sulfite that dissolves into its parts when heated, then reconstitutes itself back into cinnabar (i.e., "reverted cinnabar"). Mercury, of course, is highly poisonous: taken in small amounts it causes delusions and brain damage and in massive doses it is fatal. That Daoists at the time were well aware of this and yet still undertook these experiments shows again the strong spiritual dimension of their belief in immortality (see Strickmann 1979, 129. People set their hearts onto the otherworld, ready to give up their worldly goods and life for a goal greater than anything this planet had to offer.

Western Alchemy

Alchemy in China has numerous similarities with that practiced in the West, both sharing an emphasis on the transmutation of base metals into gold, the discovery of the elixir of life, and the creation of the Philosophers' Stone (Waite 1969, 1). Traced back in its earliest beginnings to the Greek mysteries, notably associated with the gods Hermes and Dionysus, and to practices in Egypt under Greek and Roman rule (see Lindsay 1970), Western alchemy began to flourish in the early Christian era, focusing particularly on the rather obscure figure of Hermes Trismegistos, who supposedly lived around 100 C.E. (Waite 1969, 22). He is linked with an early document, the *Tabula Smaragdina* or *Emerald Tablet*, which outlines the basic principles: as above, so below; all material entities are of one matter; the sun and the moon are the parents of all things; the wind brings them to gestation; and the earth is their great nourisher (Doberer 1948, 17-18). Realizing this truth in one's own body and self, one can find the essence of nature and realize perfection within.

The ultimate goal of alchemy—in the West as much as in China—was therefore not just the material transmutation of one substance into another, but the attainment of perfect self-knowledge and participation in the divine "through conscious and hypostatic union" (Waite 1969, 22), the "return to primordial chaos and reversal of the cosmogony" (Eliade 1962, 169). Employing multiple-layered symbolism, the philosophers' gold also meant absolute and supreme reason, perfect universal truth, the sun, and the concrete precious metal (Waite 1969, 33; Ploss et al. 1970, 19).

Similarly sulphur stood for organic nature and mercury represented the supernatural, connected within human beings through salt, the medium of chemical concoction and at the same time the germ of pure consciousness, of a higher divine faculty within (Waite 1969, 37). The color red was associated with the planet Mars and stood for the end of the Great Work, the Philosophers' Stone; the color green was connected to Venus and represented the beginning, the great base of Nature (Stavish 1997b). The Hebrew letter *shin* stood symbolic for divine light and universal love; it was visualized above the head and—like in the guiding of *qi*—was made to enter through the head, descend to the heart and engulf all, until practitioners would see themselves in an ocean of fire, burning up negativities and rising into the heat of divine love (Stavish 1997b).

Alchemy is less "an art in metals, but it is the Art of Life," for which "the dominant chemical phraseology is only a veil" (Waite 1969, 19). Similarly, operative alchemy in China was not the mere mixing of noxious substances in secret cauldrons, but involved extensive physical and ethical preparation, meditations and visualizations, and was generally geared to return to the origins of the universe and serve the self-realization of the practitioner (Pregadio 2006a).

Internal Application

Internal alchemy continues this tradition actively with the main difference that the various metals and minerals are now found in the body and that the concoction of the elixir takes place in the cinnabar field within rather than a sacred furnace in the wilderness. Thus the *Laojun nei riyong miaojing* 老君內日用妙經 (Lord Lao's Wondrous Scripture of Interior Daily Practice, DZ 645) matches the seven material treasures to aspects of the body:

>Essence is quicksilver [silver];
>Blood is gold [gold];
>Energy is jade [lapis lazuli];
>Marrow is crystal [crystal];
>The brain is numinous sand [agate];
>The kidneys are jade rings [rubies];
>And the heart is a glittering gem [cornelian]. (2a)

It then describes the alchemical process in meditative rather than chemical terms. Practitioners sit in deep quietude, immersed in a trance where "your eyes don't see a single thing, your ears don't hear a single sound" and where their "mind is unified and focused within" (1a). Then the essential fire and water—often also called lead and mercury or expressed through the trigrams *li* and *kun*—begin to circulate and combine:

> Naturally the fire of your heart
> Will sink down to the water of your kidneys
> And ascend to the cavern of your mouth,
> Where sweet saliva will arise of itself.
> Then the numinous perfected will support your body,
> And spontaneously you know the path to eternal life. . . .
>
> Harmonious energy becomes superb,
> And its sweet cream trickles to the top.
> Then with ease you can drink from the pure pinch
> And your ears will begin to hear the tunes of the immortals.
> They are melodies never plucked on strings,
> Sounding spontaneously without clapping,
> Reverberating of themselves without drumming.
>
> Spirit and energy then combine
> To form a boy child in the womb.
> If you can spot them in your interior realm,
> Spirit will start speaking to you
> From the true residence of emptiness and nonbeing,
> Where you can reside at ease with all the sages.
>
> Next, refine the combination in nine transmutations
> And you will produce the great cinnabar elixir.
> Spirit will leave and enter freely
> And your years will match those of Heaven and Earth.
> The sun and moon will join to shine on you,
> And you are liberated from all life and death. (1ab)

Alchemy thus provides the overall framework for the various forms of transmutation that make up the complex tradition and practice of internal alchemy. It goes back far in history and has numerous parallels in the Western tradition, always organically centered yet never mere chemistry and experimentation. The cosmological, transformative, and transcendent dimension is always at the forefront, however much intention, wealth, and effort are poured into the physical concoction of the elixir. Even internal alchemy does not let go of it completely but retains the concoction metaphor, the concept of transmutation, and the idea of the immortal embryo as the Golden Elixir.

Modernity

In China, operative alchemy came to an end in the Tang dynasty when several emperors died from elixir poisoning. The tradition was discontinued and went underground, so that there are practically no records left on experiments and activities involving chemicals and material elixirs. In its stead, internal alchemy arose and came to flourish. In the West, after its beginning in the early Common Era, alchemy was taken up by the Muslims, who created an extensive literature on the subject, and continued vigorously throughout the Renaissance and Enlightenment—notably in orders such as the Rosicrucians—until it fell into disrepute in the eighteenth century and was essentially extinct in the nineteenth (Ploss et al. 1970, 11).

Nonetheless, there is an active alchemical community in the West today, organized in the U.S through the American Rosicrucian Order (AMORC) in New York, Rose+Croix University (RCU) in California, and the Institute for Hermetic Studies in Pennsylvania (Stavish 1996). Like contemporary Daoists and *neidan* followers, its practitioners engage in a combination of religious rituals, herbal concoctions, cabbalistic speculations, and deep meditations. What is more, they have begun to reach out and acknowledge the similarities of their practices with Indian Kundalini and Chinese qigong (Stavish 1997b; 2006).

Like internal alchemists in China, they work with the energy body, described as subtle, astral, and etheric, and divide it into three layers or "levels of light": the spirit body which is closest to physical being (*jing*); the radiant body which is the medium through which we appreciate beauty and interact with nature (*qi*); and the resurrection body, the subtlest entity and the medium through which one can access higher realms (*shen*). The latter is also called the "pure body of light" or technically the *cowan*. It is so superior and strong that a large part of the practice is to control it. The advice is to go slow, remain secure in a sacred space or protected environment, prevent it from wandering too far off, and make sure it learns to obey conscious commands (Stavish 1997a).

They also recognize that the full development of the cowan can lead to supernatural powers—a common result of alchemical practice and a popular feature of qigong (Liang and Wu 1997, 87). Like Daoist internal alchemists, they emphasize the essential power of sexual energy, which they describe as the secret fire deep within the human being, the force that can be most easily transmuted into subtler energies and the body of light. They engage in cosmological speculation involving the cabbalistic Tree of Life and practice energy circulation exercises such as the activation of the Middle Pillar, the path of divine energy through the person (Stavish 1997b)—similar to the central *nadi* in Kundalini and the Penetrating Vessel in the Chinese system. In addition, they also perform elaborate initiations which in many ways match Daoist ordination ceremonies and engage in herbal concoctions (Stavish 2006), another feature Daoists excel in—although they think of them more as preparatory health measures than a part of the inner alchemical work proper. Most importantly, like inner alchemists, they are aware that their central work is the activation, conscious arousal, and sublimation of the energy body, its restructuring toward a being of light, an immortal embryo, an existence of pure spirit. The ultimate goal is oneness with the root powers of the universe, the underlying power of all existence, the greater divinity of eternal life. Health and longevity, physical vigor and mental acuity, supernatural powers and divine revelations are all part of the Great Work, undertaken through all five modes of mutation.

Bibliography

Akahori Akira. 1989. "Drug Taking and Immortality." In *Taoist Meditation and Longevity Techniques*, edited by Livia Kohn, 71-96. Ann Arbor: University of Michigan, Center for Chinese Studies Publications.

Arthur, Shawn. 2006. "Life Without Grains: *Bigu* and Daoist Body." In *Daoist Body Cultivation*, edited by Livia Kohn, 91-122. Magdalena, NM: Three Pines Press.

Assandri, Friederike. 2008. "Laozi's Eclipse and Comeback: The Narrative Framework of the *Benji jing*." *Journal of Daoist Studies* 1:1-27.

Atwood, M. A. 1970. *Hermetic Philosophy and Alchemy*. New York: Julian Press.

Baldrian-Hussein, Farzeen. 1984. *Procédés secrets du joyau magique*. Paris: Les Deux Océans.

_____. 1990. "Internal alchemy: Notes on the Origin and the Use of the Term *neidan*." *Cahiers d'Extrême-Asie* 5: 163-90.

Benn, Charles. 2000. "Daoist Ordination and *Zhai* Rituals." In *Daoism Handbook*, edited by Livia Kohn, 309-38. Leiden: E. Brill.

Bokenkamp, Stephen R. 2007. *Ancestors and Anxiety: Daoism and the Birth of Rebirth in China*. Berkeley: University of California Press.

Bourdieu, Pierre. 1990. *The Logic of Practice*. Stanford: Stanford University Press.

Brown, Daniel P., and Jack Engler. 1984. "A Rorschach Study of the Stages of Mindfulness Meditation." In *Meditation: Classic and Contemporary Perspectives*, edited by Deane N. Shapiro and Roger N. Walsh, 232-62. New York: Aldine.

Chan, Alan. 1991. *Two Visions of the Way: A Study of the Wang Pi and the Ho-shang-kung Commentaries on the Laozi*. Albany: State University of New York Press.

Chen Banghuai 陳邦淮. 1982. "Zhanguo 'Xingqi yuming' kaoshi" 戰國行氣玉銘考試. *Guwenzi yanjiu* 古文字研究 20:485-576.

Chia, Mantak, and Maneewan Chia. 1993. *Awaken Healing Light of the Tao*. Huntington, NY: Healing Tao Books.

Coakley, Sarah, ed. 1997. *Religion and the Body*. Cambridge: Cambridge University Press.

Despeux, Catherine. 1988. *La moélle du phénix rouge: Santé et longue vie dans la Chine du seiziéme siècle*. Paris: Editions Trédaniel.

_____. 2006. "The Six Healing Breaths." In *Daoist Body Cultivation*, edited by Livia Kohn, 37-67. Magdalena, NM: Three Pines Press.

_____, and Livia Kohn. 2003. *Women in Daoism*. Cambridge, Mass.: Three Pines Press.

Doberer, K. K. 1948. *The Goldmakers: 10,000 Years of Alchemy*. London: Nicholson & Watson.

Eliade, Mircea. 1962. *The Forge and the Crucible*. New York: Harper & Row.

Epstein, Gerald. 1989. *Healing Visualizations: Creating Health through Imagery*. New York: Bantam.

Farhi, Donna. 2003. *Bringing Yoga to Life*. San Francisco: Harper.

Graham, A. C. 1981. *Chuang-tzu: The Seven Inner Chapters and Other Writings from the Book of Chuang-tzu*. London: Allan & Unwin.

_____. 1986. *Yin-Yang and the Nature of Correlative Thinking*. Singapore: The Institute for East Asian Philosophies.

Harper, Donald. 1998. *Early Chinese Medical Manuscripts: The Mawangdui Medical Manuscripts*. London: Wellcome Asian Medical Monographs.

Hewitt, James. 1977. *The Complete Yoga Book*. New York: Schocken Books.

Kabat-Zinn, John. 1990. *Full Catastrophe Living*. New York: Bantam.

Kalinowski, Marc. 1985. "La transmission du dispositif des Neuf Palais sous les Six-dynasties." In *Tantric and Taoist Studies*, edited by Michel Strickmann, 3:773-811. Brussels: Institut Belge des Hautes Etudes Chinoises.

Kohn, Livia. 1987. *Seven Steps to the Tao: Sima Chengzhen's Zuowanglun*. St. Augustin /Nettetal: Monumenta Serica Monograph XX.

_____. 1989. "Taoist Insight Meditation: The Tang Practice of *Neiguan*." In *Taoist Meditation and Longevity Techniques*, edited by Livia Kohn, 191-222. Ann Arbor: University of Michigan

_____. 1991. *Taoist Mystical Philosophy: The Scripture of Western Ascension*. Albany: State University of New York Press.

_____. 2004. *Cosmos and Community: The Ethical Dimension of Daoism*. Cambridge, Mass.: Three Pines Press.

_____. 2006a. "The Subtle Body Ecstasy of Daoist Internal alchemy." *Acta Orientalia* 59.3: 325-40.

_____. 2006b. "Yoga and Daoyin." In *Daoist Body Cultivation*, edited by Livia Kohn, 123-50. Magdalena, NM: Three Pines Press.

_____. 2008a. *Chinese Healing Exercises: The Tradition of Daoyin*. Honolulu: University of Hawai'i Press.

_____. 2008b. *Meditation Works: In the Daoist, Buddhist, and Hindu Traditions*. Magdalena, NM: Three Pines Press.

Korn, Errol R., and Karen Johnson. 1983. *Visualization: The Uses of Imagery in the Health Professions*. Irvine, Calif.: American Institute of Hypnotherapy.

Kuriyama, Shigehisa. 1999. *The Expressiveness of the Body and the Divergence of Greek and Chinese Medicine*. New York: Zone Books.

Li Ling 李零. 1993. *Zhongguo fangshu kao* 中國方術考. Beijing: Renmin Zhongguo chubanshe.

Liang, Shou-yu, and Wen-ching Wu. 1997. *Qigong Empowerment: A Guide to Medical, Taoist, Buddhist, Wushu Energy Cultivation*. East Providence: Way of the Dragon Publishing.

Lindsay, Jack. 1970. *The Origins of Alchemy in Graeco-Roman Egypt*. London: Frederick Muller.

Mauss, Marcel. 1979. *Sociology and Psychology, Essays*. London: Routledge and Kegan Paul.

McDermott, Ian, and Joseph O'Connor. 1996. *NLP and Health: Using NLP to Enhance Your Health and Well-Being*. San Francisco: HarperCollins.

Miller, James. 2008. *The Way of Highest Clarity: Nature, Vision and Revelation in Medieval Daoism*. Magdalena, NM: Three Pines Press.

Needham, Joseph, et al. 1980. *Science and Civilisation in China*, vol. V.4: Spagyrical Discovery and Invention—Apparatus, Theories and Gifts. Cambridge: Cambridge University Press.

Ni, Hua-ching. 1992. *Internal Alchemy: The Natural Way to Immortality*. Malibu: Shrine of the Eternal Breath of Tao.

Ploss, Emil Ernst et al. 1970. *Alchimia: Ideologie und Technologie*. München: Heinz Moss Verlag.

Pregadio, Fabrizio. 2000. "Elixirs and Alchemy." In *Daoism Handbook*, edited by Livia Kohn, 165-95. Leiden: E. Brill.

_____. 2006a. *Great Clarity: Daoism and Alchemy in Early Medieval China*. Stanford: Stanford University Press.

_____. 2006b. "Early Daoist Meditation and the Origins of Internal alchemy." In *Daoism in History: Essays in Honour of Liu Ts'un-yan*, edited by Benjamin Penny, 121-58. London: Routledge.

———, ed. 2008. *The Encyclopedia of Taoism*. London: Routledge.

Robinet, Isabelle. 1989a. "Original Contributions of *Neidan* to Taoism and Chinese Thought." In *Taoist Meditation and Longevity Techniques*, edited by Livia Kohn, 297-330. Ann Arbor: University of Michigan, Center for Chinese Studies Publications.

———. 1989b. "Visualization and Ecstatic Flight in Shangqing Taoism." In *Taoist Meditation and Longevity Techniques*, edited by Livia Kohn, 157-90. Ann Arbor: University of Michigan, Center for Chinese Studies Publications.

Rosenberg, Larry. 1999. *Breath by Breath: The Liberating Practice of Insight Meditation*. Boston: Shambhala.

Roth, Harold D. 2000. "Bimodal Mystical Experience in the "Qiwulun" Chapter of *Zhuangzi*." *Journal of Chinese Religions* 28:31-50.

Samuels, Mike, and Nancy Samuels. 1975. *Seeing with the Mind's Eye: The History, Technique, and Uses of Visualization*. New York: Random House.

Schafer, Edward H. 1978. "The Jade Woman of Greatest Mystery." *History of Religions* 17: 387-98.

Schipper, Kristofer M., and Franciscus Verellen, eds. 2004. *The Taoist Canon: A Historical Companion to Daozang*. 3 vols. Chicago: University of Chicago Press.

Shi, Jing. 2006. "Sitting and Forgetting: An Introduction to *Zuowang*." *The Dragon's Mouth: Newsletter of the British Taoist Association* 2006/1:10-13.

Sivin, Nathan. 1968. *Chinese Alchemy: Preliminary Studies*. Cambridge, Mass.: Harvard University Press.

———. 1990. "Research on the History of Chinese Alchemy." In *Alchemy Revisited*, edited by Z. R. W. M von Martels, 3-20. Leiden: E. Brill.

Skar, Lowell, and Fabrizio Pregadio. 2000. "Inner Alchemy (*Neidan*)." In *Daoism Handbook*, edited by Livia Kohn, 464-97. Leiden: E. Brill.

Smith, Richard J. 2008. *Fathoming the Cosmos and Ordering the World: The Yijing and Its Evolution in China*. Charlottesville: University of Virginia Press.

Stavish, Mark. 1996. "The History of Alchemy in America." www.hermetic.com/stavish

———. 1997a. "The Body of Light in the Western Esoteric Tradition." www.hermetic.com/stavish

———. 1997b. "Secret Fire: The Relationship between Kundalini, Kabbalah, and Alchemy." www.hermetic.com/stavish

———. 2006. *The Path of Alchemy: Energetic Healing and the World of Natural Magic*. Woodbury, MN: Llewellyn Publications.

Strickmann, Michel. 1979. "On the Alchemy of T'ao Hung-ching." In *Facets of Taoism*, edited by Holmes Welch and Anna Seidel, 123-92. New Haven, Conn.: Yale University Press.

Valussi, Elena. 2003. "Beheading the Red Dragon: A History of Female Internal alchemy in China." Ph. D. Diss., School of Oriental and African Studies, University of London, London.

Waite, Arthur Edward. 1969. *The Secret Tradition in Alchemy: Its Development and Records*. London: Stuart & Watkins.

Wang, Li. 2004. "A Daoist Way of Transcendence: Bai Yuchan's Inner Alchemical Thought and Practice." Ph. D. Diss., University of Iowa, Iowa City.

Ware, James R. 1966. *Alchemy, Medicine and Religion in the China of AD 320*. Cambridge, Mass.: MIT Press.

Watson, Burton. 1968. *The Complete Works of Chuang-tzu*. New York: Columbia University Press.

Wik, Mieke, and Stephan Wik. 2005. *Beyond Tantra: Healing through Taoist Sacred Sex*. Forres, Scotland: Findhorn Press.

Wilhelm, Hellmut. 1948. "Eine Zhou-Inschrift über Atemtechnik." *Monumenta Serica* 13: 385-88.

Winn, Michael. 2006. "Transforming Sexual Energy with Water-and-Fire Alchemy." In *Daoist Body Cultivation*, edited by Livia Kohn, 151-78. Magdalena, NM: Three Pines Press.

Yao, Ted. 2000. "Quanzhen—Complete Perfection." In *Daoism Handbook*, edited by Livia Kohn, 567-93. Leiden: E. Brill.

Internal Landscapes

Sara Elaine Neswald

The body in internal alchemy partakes of the shape and logic of the cosmos. Just as magic squares such as the Hall of Light (*mingtang* 明堂) and Luo Chart (*Luoshu* 洛書) outline the cosmic landscape,[1] so the body could manifest as a magical landscape or an illustrated map. Like magic squares, the alchemical body may represent the entirety of creation and the processes of cosmic change. It manifests the hexagrams of the *Yijing* 易經 (Book of Changes) and the unfolding of cosmogenesis. The Daoist alchemical body is commonly inhabited by deities, palaces, sacred groves, and entire continents that interact in the processing of internal energies. In addition, it is also often described in the terms of Chinese medicine, using organs (*zang* 臟), viscera (*fu* 腑), and meridians (*mai* 脈). All these modes overlap and interact dynamically, finding their foundation in traditional cosmology that has pervaded Chinese culture.

It is a classic aspect of Chinese thinking that the body mirrors the cosmos: the head is round like Heaven; the feet are square like Earth. The four-plus-one seasons of the *Yueling* 月令 (Seasonal Ordinances) chapter of the *Liji* 禮記 (Book of Rites) correspond to the five phases and match the five organs (heart, liver, kidneys, spleen, and lungs). The nine orifices correspond to the directions: the eight standard directions plus the center; the number of joints matches the number of days in the traditional calendar. And various internal and external functions correspond to different categories of the cosmos.[2] The Confucian Dong Zhongshu 董仲舒 (ca. 195-115 B.C.E.) is generally credited with formalizing this integration of the five phases, yin-yang cosmology, *Yijing* hexagrams, and Confucianism, an integration that proceeds from cosmos and state all the way to the human body. Ever since the Han, moreover, these concepts have formed a storehouse of knowledge shared throughout Chinese culture:

---

[1] On ancient squares, see Kalinowski 1985; Neswald 2007, 7-15.
[2] For a summary of Daoist body concepts, see Kohn 1991. This concept is also presented in the *Neiye* (Inward Training) chapter of the *Guanzi* (Book of Master Guan) (see Yates 1994, 69; Roth 1999) and in the *Huainanzi* (see Kohn 1996a).

> The agreement of Heaven and Earth and the correspondence between yin and yang are complete in the human body. The body is like Heaven. Its numerical categories and those of Heaven are mutually interwoven, and therefore their lives are interlocked. Heaven completes the human body with the number of days in a full year.[3]
>
> Consequently the body's 366 lesser joints correspond to the number of days in a year, and the twelve larger joints correspond to the number of months. Internally, the body has the five organs, which correspond to the five phases. Externally there are the four limbs, which correspond to the four seasons. The alternating of opening and closing the eyes corresponds to day and night. . . The alternating of sorrow and joy corresponds to yin and yang." (Chan 1963, 281-82)

The correspondence systems developed in the Warring States and early Han, documented in texts such as the *Lüshi chunqiu* 呂氏春秋 (Spring and Autumn Annals of Master Lü, dat. 249 B.C.E.) and the *Huainanzi* 淮南子 (Book of the Prince of Huainan, dat. ca. 139 B.C.E.), and systematized by Dong Zhongshu, continued as part of Chinese medical and spiritual knowledge well into the Qing and are still alive in Chinese medicine today. According to this vision, all things in the cosmos are generated by yin and yang and their interactions, while the cyclic existence of people and things is measured by the five phases.

Correspondences of the Five Phases

	lesser yang	great yang	equipoise	lesser yin	great yin
phase	wood	fire	earth	metal	water
star	Jupiter	Mars	Saturn	Venus	Mercury
season	spring	summer	late summer	fall	winter
direction	east	south	center	west	north
wills	anger	elation	sadness	sorrow	fear
sense	eyes	tongue	lips	nose	ears
organ	liver	heart	spleen	lungs	kidney

This table presents the correlations of cosmic and individual bodies, and their transformative phases. Both cycle through repeated series of transformations governed by the phases and hexagrams. The yearly cycles of the seasons pass through a gradual progression from increasing yang and decreasing yin (i.e., qualities of dryness, heat, fire, purity, masculinity) until the summer equinox, when yang reaches its zenith moment and begins to decline. In the second half of the year, the proportion of yang gradually decreases while yin increases (i.e., enhancing wetness, cold, water, turgidity, and the female). When yin reaches its zenith and begins to fade, the cyclic progression begins anew.

---

[3] The notion of the body as being "interwoven with the number of days in a year" in Qing-dynasty interpretations is particularly associated with the *male* body.

Likewise the five phases rule over particular periods in the annual cycle. Cosmic processes such as the passage of the moon through the astral houses are paralleled in the body by the passages of *qi* through the channels. The five wills or emotions, the organs, and senses likewise parallel seasons and colors. The natural processes of cosmos and body thus correspond equally to the five phases and yin-yang polarities—a general understanding that persists throughout Chinese culture and forms the foundation of the Daoist vision.

The Cosmic Body

The Daoist concept of the individual embodiment of the cosmos appears first in descriptions of Laozi as the body of the cosmos. The *Laozi ming* 老子銘 (Inscription for Laozi, dat. 165 C.E.) says that he "is united with and then separates from cosmic chaos; he is coeternal with the Three Luminaries; he participates in the radiance of the sun and moon in harmony with the five planets" (Schipper 1994, 120; see Seidel 1969).

Soon afterwards, Laozi's cosmic embodiment develops: his organs, meridians, and even hair and whiskers are described as celestial bodies and elements;[4] he also maintains a place as initiator of the universe and the body of Dao and all its aspects (Pregadio 2006; Kohn 1998). "The incarnate [Laozi] is the image (*xiang* 象) of the world; the sun, moon, and stars, the whole heavenly clockwork, are all present in his body," summarizes the *Xiaodao lun* 笑道論 (Laughing at the Dao, T. 52.2060; Kohn 1995, 54). Here Laozi's body is transformed to fully associate with Dao and equals the cosmos. His left and right eyes are the sun and moon, his head is Mount Kunlun, his beard forms planets, his bones become dragons, his belly is the ocean, and his left and right kidneys transform into the true mother and father of all beings (Lévi 1989, 109; Seidel 1969). Lévi links this development to the ancient folk tale of Pangu 盤古, the Chinese adaptation of the Indian myth of Puruṣa (see Lincoln 1975), whose body transforms into the cosmos (Lévi 1989, 109). The cosmogonic body of Pangu, appropriated into the tale of Laozi's transformations, thus arises as an early manifestation of the ideal alchemical body.

Neidan adepts seek to inhabit the body of Laozi and Pangu. They embody the cosmos, complete with its sun, moon, planets, stars, continents, palaces, and deities. In the *Huangting jing* 黃庭經 (Yellow Court Scripture, DZ 331, 332),[5] the body consists of cosmic pathways and earthly paradises, and is inhab-

---

[4] E.g., *Laozi bianhua jing* 老子變化經 (Scripture of the Transformations of Laozi, ZW 737; dat. 186); *Laozi huahu jing* 老子化胡經 (Scripture of Laozi Converting the Barbarians, ZW 738; dat. 300). For more details, see Kohn 1998, 11.

[5] Scriptures in the Daoist Canon and its supplement are referred to by numbers found in Komjathy 2002: DZ – *Daozang*; JH – *Daozang jinghua*; JY – *Daozang* jiyao; ZW – *Zangwai daoshu*. The DZ numbers also match Schipper and Verellen 2004.

ited by astral gods. Nine palaces in the head match the immortals' residences on Mount Kunlun (Kalinowski 1985). Among them the Hall of Light is located between the eyes, which in turn are the home of the Queen Mother of the West (Xiwang mu 西王母) and the Lord King of the East (Dongwang gong 東王公). Behind it lies the Cavern Chamber and the Niwan Palace, also known as the upper cinnabar or elixir field. This internal landscape is paralleled by an outer landscape that describes the realities of Heaven, Earth, and Humanity. The system carries directly from the medieval tradition of Highest Clarity text into the alchemical traditions of Complete Perfection, where it remains a relevant and a continuing source of reference.

Fig. 1: Body gods in Highest Clarity. From *Dadong zhenjing* 大洞真經 (Perfect Scripture of Great Cavern, DZ 6).

Another important early source on bodily cosmogony is the *Laozi zhongjing* 老子中經 (Central Scripture on Laozi, DZ 1168), probably of the late second century. It provides a detailed description of the body, its dynamic effulgences, and their concretization as deities and heraldic animals. It begins by naming the essential gods of the cosmos and linking each to an associated moment of initiation (temporal locus), a space in the multi-layered heavens (cosmic locus), and a position in the body (physical locus). In addition, each god is associated with a specific kind of *qi* and with an emblematic creature. The body is mandala-like in organization, implying a political and divine arrangement, a compartmentalized, bureaucratic structure that rationalizes the dispersal of power throughout in the body. The body is a mandala of the cosmos, where each deity and divine attendants are located in their appropriate region and rule over it. As they are assigned a space and take up residence, their sectors become part of divine management, control, protection, and potency. For example, the deity know as Highest Great Unity (Shangshang Taiyi 上上太一) commands the head. As the text says:

> Highest Great Unity is the father of Dao and the predecessor of Heaven and Earth. He resides above the Nine Heavens within Great Clarity; he is also beyond the Eight Expanses the Four Subtleties. I do not know his proper name, but he is primal *qi*. The deity has a human head and the body of a bird. (*Yunji qiqian* 18)

The Lord King of the East and the Queen Mother of the West similarly reside in the head, in the earthly paradises of Penglai, and in Great Clarity among the heavens. Above, the Lord King sports a five-colored halo and controls the eastern quadrant; in the body, he inhabits the left eye, i.e. the internal sun. His essence and cosmic energy accordingly rise up as solar effulgence. The Queen Mother in turn inhabits the right eye, i.e., the internal moon; on Earth she resides in the paradise of Kunlun; in Heaven, she controls the Northern Dipper. When transformed to pure essence, she rises up as lunar effulgence.

Between the two resides their son Floreate Brilliance (Yingming 英明), part of whose name combines the characters for "sun" and "moon" (Lévi 1989). He thus represents a union of the aspects and essences of the yin-yang, sun-moon polarities, a theme that appears frequently in the literature, evoked in the number three as the symbol of ideal unity. The return to unity and the harmonization of opposites dominate throughout the *Laozi zhongjing*, just as threefold unities repeat throughout cosmic and human bodies in the Daoist tradition. In internal alchemy, the human body accordingly unites three cinnabar or elixir fields, located in the head, chest, and abdomen;[6] and traces of early descriptions remain in contemporary *neidan* bodyscapes.

Above all, the number one resounds. As the *Laozi zhongjing* has it, the Lord of Dao (Daojun 道君) presides over the numeral one and stands for oneness and unity. He and his two main attendants, Lord Lao (Laojun 老君) and Great Harmony (Taihe 太和), form a tripartite unity, which further divides into a nine-part oneness to form the Nine Heavens; the Lord and his attendants reside above, in the Purple Chamber. The Jade Maiden Dark Radiance of Great Yin (Taiyin xuanguang yunü 太陰玄光玉女) is a self-emanating female principle of the Lord. She gives birth to a perfected child in the womb, known as the Palace of Great Simplicity (Taisu gong 太素宮). This child is the being that will

---

[6] Already in the *Laozi zhongjing*, they are designated Purple Chamber 紫房, Scarlet Palace 絳宮, Yellow Court 黃庭, and Cinnabar Field 丹田 (*Yunji qiqian* 18).

eventually grow until it is the size of the adept's own body. Once again, the unity of a triad is replete.

The five phases demarcate another series of harmonizing divisions on the cosmic and human levels. They each have their own symbols and colors, are associated with seasons and directions, and in the body match the five organs, senses, wills, tastes, tissues, fluids, and many more. The *Laozi zhongjing* already has a set of five divine entities located in the chest, centered around the Jade Watchtower (*yuque* 玉闕): the gods Jun'a 君阿 and Wengzhong 翁仲—minister and elder—below it at the left and right nipples and the two starry constellations known as Heavenly Dog and Heavenly Chicken above. The vision of a fivefold division of powers in the center of the body is actively retained in modern *neidan*.

Also matching later patterns, the *Laozi zhongjing* makes distinctions between men and women. Women's breasts are like the spouts of yin and yang. Below their left and right nipples are the sun and moon, the residences of the Lord King and Queen Mother, while male breasts have the minister-elder duality. Also, it seems that alignments typical for men's elixir fields appear in other registers of the female body, notably between the breasts—later called the breast chamber and defined as the main female elixir field.

In addition to numeric values of ones, threes, and fives, an eight-part division repeats on levels designating space and time, corresponding to the eight hexagrams, directions, winds, calendrical interstices (seasons, equinoxes, solstices), and ministers. The unity of all is replicated in the navel, where the numeric equivalencies of all things in the universe come together: the eight ministers, five directions, three primes, and so on. The value of these multipartite unities lies in their ability to function and transform in the human body as in the cosmos, creating a powerful unity among multiplicity.

Body as Mountain

Above and beyond being an energetic network in terms of Chinese medicine and a residence of multiple, complex deities as described in early Daoism, the body in internal alchemy also often appears as a mountain and is thus a potent internal pilgrimage site. The notion of mountains as mysterious, hidden, and dangerous places, where strange creatures dwell and different laws apply, goes back far in Chinese history (see Hahn 1988; 2000). In the course of the middle ages, Daoists not only enhanced this vision of mountains as retreats and mysterious centers but also absorbed the Buddhist multi-valent concept of the mountain as sacred pilgrimage site, fortress of the gods, sacred reliquary (*stūpa*), and cosmic symbol (*mandala*; see Gyaltso 2000; Huber 2004).

The oldest surviving image of the body as pilgrimage mountain is found in the *Duren jing neiyi* 度人經內意 (Internal Meaning of the Scripture on Salvation, DZ 91, dat. 1227), a Song commentary on the *Duren jing* (DZ 1), a key text of the Numinous Treasure school that was vastly expanded under Emperor Huizong (r. 1101-1125).⁷ As shown (Fig. 2), the image draws on the concept of

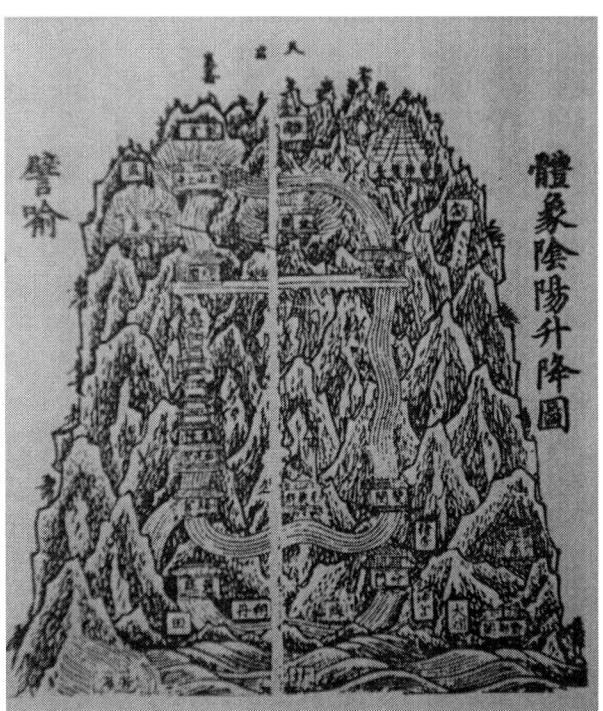

circumambulation. The route is shown in the oval shaped river that *qi* takes through the body during internal practice. At the foot of the mountain is the Sea of Suffering (*kuhai* 苦海), a Buddhist term for the state of all beings forced to drift un-enlightened in the mundane world. The image borrows it to designate the Ocean of *Qi* (*qihai* 氣海) in the alchemical body. The flow of *qi* originates here, at the mountain's foot. It then flows up through the Governing Vessel (*dumai* 督脈) along the back of the body (left in the image) and enters the energetic cycle at the Gate of Destiny (*mingmen* 命門) where it feeds the flow of essence. From there it goes through the Double Pass (*shuangguan* 雙關)⁸ to the peak of Mount Kunlun in the head, where it transforms.

---

⁷ The diagram is mentioned in Despeux and Kohn 2003, 185. For more on body charts and diagrams, see also Despeux 1994; 2000. On the ancient *Duren jing*, including partial translation, see Bokenkamp 1997. For its role under Huizong, see Strickmann 1978.

⁸ As described in the *Taiji liandan bijue* 太極煉丹秘訣 (Secret Instructions on the Non-Ultimate Elixir Cultivation, JH 19, ch. 3), the Double Pass is located "above the Tail Gate

After doing so, it descends along the Conception Vessel (*renmai* 壬脈) along the front of the body (right side in the image), moving from the Heavenly Pass (*tianguan* 天關)[9] past the throat—usually described as the Twelve-storied Tower (*shier cenglou* 十二層樓)—into the immortal womb at the center of the abdomen, above which the Jade Chamber (*yufang* 玉房) is located. In the womb, the cyclical sign *wuyi* 戊巳 represents the internal mating of cosmic water and fire, *qi* and spirit (Despeux and Kohn 2003, 185).[10] The clockwise, left-to-right passage of *qi* in the body, moreover, accords also with the directional movement of the Buddhist pilgrim at a stupa, mountain, or during an internal pilgrimage.

Similar patterns also apply in the tantric vision of the body as cosmic mandala and sacred mountain. The pilgrim's route is marked by a stream that proceeds from the bottom left up along the outer slopes of the mountain and down on the right. In each case visualizations not only work at mountain locations but are equally relevant within the pilgrim's body. Places of power widely spot the mandalized body/mountain/cosmos. The pilgrim thus circumambulates these places until he or she gains access to the internal altar of the deity, pictured at the very center. Unlike the Daoist adept, Tantrikas usually "become" the deity through intentional visualization and identification. However, the two practices hold commonalities: both the Daoist and the Tantrika understand the internal pilgrimage to simultaneously effect pilgrimage ritual and access to sacred sites and knowledge, and to 'effect alchemical transformation' of the physical and spiritual self (Kilty 2004, 1).[11]

Alchemical Patterns

The body vision unique to internal alchemy first appears in the Song dynasty (960-1260). Following the Yuan (1260-1368), it continues to transform in response to socio-political and religious pressures, including new forms of Bud-

---

[at the perineum] where are altogether eighteen joints [e.g., discs in the spine]; it forms their center. Above it are nine joints; below are nine joints."

[9] According to the *Dadan zhizhi* 大丹直指 (Direct Pointers to the Great Elixir, DZ 244), this is located behind the brain.

[10] See *Jindan xinfa* 金丹心法 (Heart Method for the Internal Refinement of the Golden Elixir) by Wu Chongxu, ed. Tao 1989. It says: "The *shen* within the heart is the *yi*-earth 巳土, and its icon is the hexagram Li. The *qi* within the kidneys is *wu*-earth 戊土, and its icon is the hexagram Kan. When Kan and Li interact, they meld to form the *wuyi*. When the *wuyi* melds, *shen* and *qi* unite and form a non-sage fetus, and the yin *shen* emits!"

[11] For general overview of Buddhist mandalization and embodied symbolism, see Stoddard 1999. Kilty 2004 and Wallace 2001 translate and provide overviews of the mandalization of the body as cosmos and as mountain in the Kalacakra tradition; Wallace 2004 provides a table of correspondances. For images of a Buddhist pilgrimage mountain as mandalized cosmic, social, and individual body, see Huber 2004, 17-37; Snellgrove 1987, 1:277-349.

dhist tantra transmitted from Mongolia and Tibet (Neswald 2007), the development of new political dynamics across the western and northwestern frontiers (Wang 1995), and the transmutation of gender concepts (Furth 1999). Changes in these various areas intersect during the Ming dynasty (1368-1644) to create new interest in gendered practice. Some of them have been noted by scholars of the Confucian tradition (see Rowe 1998; Bray 1997); they are also essential in the rise of female alchemy (*nüdan* 女丹) (see Valussi 2003). Overall, the tradition was very lively and interacted with multiple cultural influences, so that different schools and masters imagined the body in different ways. Given this complexity, I can only provide a rough outline of some generally shared concepts and focus on certain specific terms and notions.

To begin, it is quite obvious that internal alchemy in its various forms retained the numerical values inscribed in early body visions. Groupings of three, five, eight, and so on continue to play an important role as foundations for the attainment of ultimate "oneness," complete in the tripartite body just as the cosmos is complete in the triad of Heaven, Earth, and Humanity (see Robinet 1994; 1995a; 1995b).

Another pattern that remains is the power of sacred charts and images (see Despeux 2000). Late imperial *neidan* authors accordingly leaned towards graphic imaginings of the body. In representations of the Wu-Liu school (see Fig. 3),[12] *qi* accordingly moves in a circle through the Governing and Conception Vessels, beginning at the genitals and flowing up the back of the lower and then upper torso. In the perfected being, the Governing Vessel meets the Conception Vessel in the palace at the top of the head, and conducts the *qi* back down the front of the body. Similarly the Western School describes the circulation of *qi* along channels that form a perfect circle in keeping with the ideal of sealing the body and creating a complete union of channels and circuits. This in turn matches the concept of creating and maintaining a sacred circle within and of the body, which coincides with concerns to "seal" it so that no essences can seep away or noxious substances intrude to break sacred purity and wholeness.

Central Channels
The internal cycle of purified energy, known as the Microcosmic Orbit (*xiao zhoutian* 小周天), works with four extraordinary vessels, considered to be the prime fields of life as the embryo grows in the womb. They are the Governing, Conception, Penetrating (*chongmai* 沖脈), and Belt Vessels (*daimai* 帶脈). As Zhao Bichen 趙壁塵 in his *Xingming fajue mingzhi* 性命法訣明指 (Clear Instruc-

---

[12] For more on the Wu-Liu School and other trends of internal alchemy in the Qing, see Esposito 1997; 2000. The figure is called *Wenyang lingdan tu* 溫養靈丹圖 (Chart of Warming and Nourishing the Numinous Elixir). It appears in the *Xingming guizhi* 性命圭旨 (Imperative Doctrines on Inner nature and Destiny, JH 5, ZW 314; dat. 1615).

tions to the Prescripts for Inner Nature and Destiny, ZW 26, dat. 1800s; trl. Despeux 1979; Lu 1970) says:

> In front it passes through the Conception Vessel, in the back through the Governing Vessel. Horizontally it moves along the Belt Vessel and in the center it passes up and down the Penetrating Vessel. Below it goes through the Yang Pass; above it reaches through the heart. Above and forward, it penetrates the navel; below and behind, it passes the kidneys. This is the Microcosmic Orbit.

As shown here (Fig. 3), the first two flow from the perineum along the back and the front of the body to the head; the third and fourth, the Penetrating and Belt Vessels, create a vertical and horizontal line in the center, running between the head and pelvic floor and between the navel and the kidneys, respectively. The dotted lines between the cranium and forehead at top and the coccyx and sexual organs at bottom represent bridges, established through internal practice. They create a rounded, heavenly body complete unto itself.

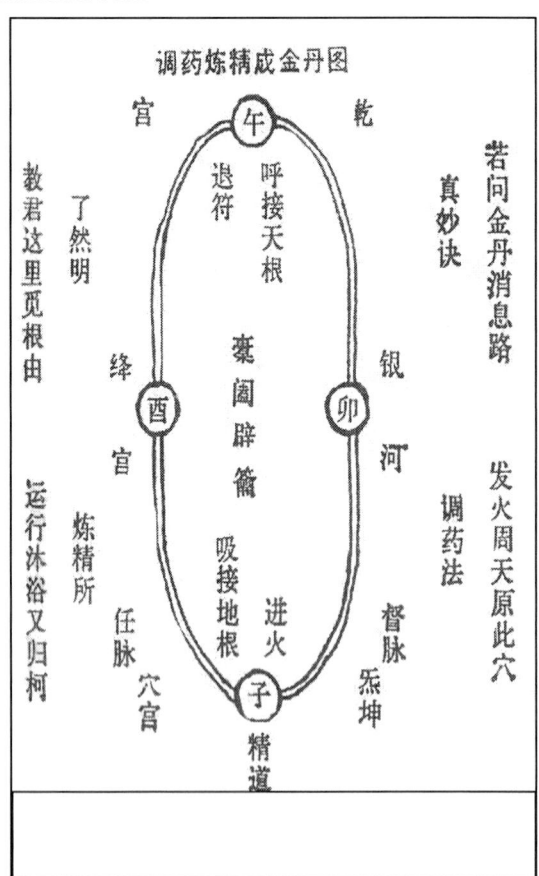

The creation of such a body implies that it is a unity, sealed like a mantic circle. The *neidan* body is thus an integrated, cosmic unity replete with all the various elements and processes of the greater universe, including those that transform the state before creation into existence and that signify the potential "return" to a pre-existence way of being. These states, moreover, are represented as the hexagrams, heavenly stems, or earthly stems. The latter commonly mark both space—the eight directions on the mariner's compass—and time—the twelve two-hour time periods of the Chinese day. They are clearly present in Fig. 3, where they are placed along the various channels to show cosmic time and nodes of transformation.[13]

By localizing time and space inside the body, these cosmic dimensions and thus creation itself may be seized and manipulated. "Once the human body exactly replicates and includes the whole of the cosmos – while still being an element itself – cosmogenesis merges with embryogenesis" (Lévi 1989, 106). By replicating and inverting the process of cosmic generation in the individual's self, he or she can reverse the polluting circumstances of birth and ordinary human development. The essences of life—blood, pus, urine, saliva, sweat, tears, and other bodily effluvia—which are normally expelled are cleansed instead: they are retained in the body as sacred treasures and progressively etherealized until they come to form the sacred elements of immortality. The adept eventually creates a pure fetus. Gestating it within the body, he or she returns to a state of original purity. "In other words, the crudest physiological substance assumes a heraldic value because its secretions are integrated into a symbolic system in which they correspond to divine effigies" (Lévi 1989, 123) The key to success accordingly begins with being able to identify these substances and to activate the main areas of transformation.

Elixir Fields
The most important transformation points in internal alchemy are the three cinnabar or elixir fields. Each houses the Three Treasures: essence, *qi*, and spirit; each resides in one of the three major parts of the body: head, chest, and abdomen. Known as the Niwan Palace, the Purple Palace (*zigong* 紫宮), and the Ocean of *Qi*, they match three Buddhist fields of transformation of the main aspects of the self: body, speech, and mind).[14]

The upper elixir field in the head is consistently identified in its specific location, but can also be linked with the Gate of Heaven the place from where celestial energies are accessed or, alternatively, through which the spirit embryo passes to ascend to the otherworld.[15] The central field is sometimes also called the Scarlet Palace (*jianggong* 絳宮) and placed in the solar plexus; texts variously

---

[13] Fig. 3 shows the earthly stems punctuating the sacred circle. Beginning at *zi* at the lower dotted pathway and rising up the back, the *qi* passes to *chou, yin, mao, chen*, and *si*. From *wu* at the upper dotted line near the forehead, it descends through *wei, shen, you* , and *xu*, to end at *hai*. At the cente, the crossroads between the Belt and Penetrating Vessels, moreover, is the character *zhong* 中 (center). Above and below are the words for the trigrams Li and Kan, symbolizing cosmic fire and water.

[14] Miller 2003, 393. Whereas the Buddhist notion may indeed be the origin of the term Niwan Palace, it also adopts distinctive features not seen in Buddhist thought or the tantras; meanwhile, the heart assumes features of the Buddhist "body" *cakra* in the body-speech-mind triad of *cakras*. The lower elixir field is also identified with the Sea of Suffering.

[15] See *Dadan zhizhi* on the Gate of Heaven as Niwan; *Huangting jing* as a point between the eyebrows. The *Nüjindan koujue* 女金丹口訣 sees it as an exit point (2.33a).

identify it as the heart or as a place near the navel, with the early *Laozi zhongjing* locating it at the eyes.[16]

The *Xingming guizhi* of the 17th century identifies it as the Yellow Court (*huangting* 黃庭) and provides a method on how men can recognize and activate it. Sitting with the legs folded in front, adepts have their left leg facing out and right leg facing in to represent yang encompassing yin. Their left thumb makes a circle with the middle finger, surrounding the right thumb placed inside the left hand to represent yin encompassing yang. Placing the hands at the lower elixir field, adepts regulate their breath to attain a state of internal absorption. As they concentrate on the space between the eyes, a benevolent light appears, while a luminous *qi* forms to create a cavity between the heart and the kidneys. A positive, non-empty void, this forms the lodge of spirit and *qi*, which in turn opens up the Yellow Court.

Another way of speaking about the elixir fields is in terms of interior palaces, most importantly the Heaven Palace (*qangong* 乾宮), the Scarlet Palace, and the Earth Palace (*kungong* 坤宮). These mark three energetic directions or bodily levels and are placed on the outside of an energy circuit that in turn is punctuated by four of the twelve earthly stems: they designate the cardinal directions and main seasons in cosmic time and space.

At the very bottom of the illustration, the Earth Palace is shown below the *Qi* Cavity, straddling the stem *zi*. Rising up the Governing Vessel along the spine to the right of the picture, the energy flows along the Silver River or Milky Way (*yinhe* 銀河) and reaches the stem *mao*. Associated with the star-crossed lovers, Weaving Maid and Cowherd Boy, this celestial body marks the point where the adept mixes yin and yang. At the top of the cycle, the energy flow reaches the forehead, the Heaven Palace which surrounds the stem *wu*, marking the moment in time-space for the circulated elixir to rise to the Niwan Palace. From there it descends along the front of the body to reach the stem *you* (on the left in the illustration), where it enters the Scarlet Palace of the heart, a location that can also be reached through the Belt Vessel via the Yu and Luo Gates.

In women, the three elixir fields are called "destinies." They are described in the *Nü jindan* 女金丹 (Women's Golden Elixir, in *Nüdan hebian* 4, dat. 1892): "The upper one is the Yang Cavity; the middle one is the Yellow Chamber; the lower one is the Elixir Field." In general location these match the Niwan Palace, the Yellow Court, and the Ocean of *Qi* in men, but they are distinct energy centers unique for women that emerged in the late imperial period. Again the *Nü jindan*:

---

[16] Texts that make these idenfications include *Jinting wuwei miaojing* 金庭無爲妙經 (Marvelous Scripture of the Golden Courtyard of Nonaction, DZ 1399, ch. 3), *Suling jing* 素靈經 (Scripture of Great Simplicity, DZ 1314), and Zhao Bichen's work.

> Women have three destiny centers: they are purple, white, and yellow. Yellow radiance signifies the elixir field; this is the place where the elixir is generated. White radiance is the fetal prime; this is the place where the fetus is congealed. Purple radiance is the blood; this the sea where blood is generated. The one above is the Yang Cavity: that at center is the Yellow Chamber; the one below is the Elixir Field. (Poem 5, comm.)

In girls, essence concentrates in the Yang Cavity in the head; it does not descend to form the menses and retains a pure, white color. In mature women, essence collects in the Yellow Chamber and forms breasts, emerging on occasion as breast milk. Every month, it descends into the Elixir Field, where it is transformed and expelled as menses. A central feature of the alchemical enterprise is to make it return upward and revert to a purer state.

Another dimension of the elixir fields appears in an energy center known as the *Qi* Cavity *(qixue* 氣穴*)* that holds *qi* for dispersal in the body either through ordinary activity or for immortality cultivation. In later traditions of internal alchemy, its location is gender-dependent: in men, it is in the central elixir field, 1.3 inches below the navel; in women, it is between the breasts and known as the breast chamber. As the *Nü jindan* describes it:

> The lower *Qi* Cavity is the bloody prime or breast chamber. It is between [the breasts], 1.3 inches from either. It is not the same as the two breasts! Men's center of destiny is the elixir field; therefore they take the lower elixir field as their *Qi* Cavity. Women's center of destiny is in the breast chamber; therefore they take the breast chamber as their *Qi* Cavity. [In ordinary people,] when yang reaches its zenith, it transforms into yin and rushers from the Cave, transforming into yin blood to flow out of the body.... If one takes the *Qi* Cavity as being always 1.3 inches below the navel (as indicated for men), this is an error. (Poem 9, comm)

The Gate of Destiny

The Gate of Destiny is a major energy center in the lower abdomen, generally associated with the sexual organs. Opening it is often the first step of alchemical initiation, so that its location and identification are crucial for the practitioner. Unfortunately, texts are rarely consistent with identification. As shown in Fig. 4a (from the *Xingming guizhi*), the Gate of Destiny is located just below the navel, with the Gate of Mystery just below the kidneys. The heart, seat of the spirit, lets *qi* pour out like a spout; it feeds and receives energies from the liver, throat, and kidneys—connected to the generation and distribution of essence. Fig. 4b, on the other hand, locates it twice: along the spine, in the fourth vertebra above the kidneys, and also in the right kidney.

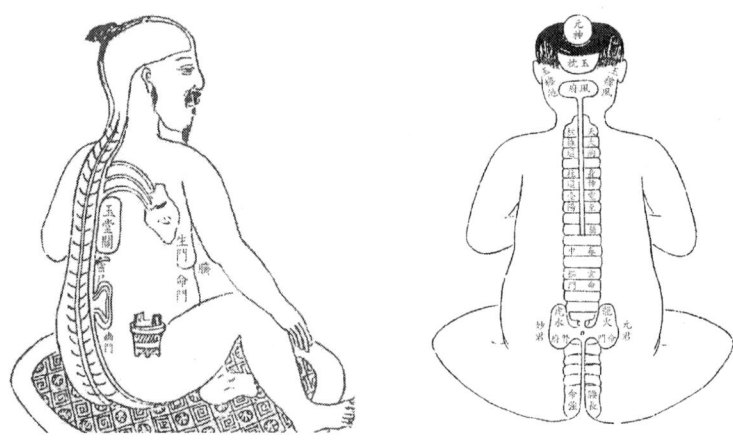

Fig. 4a,4b

An earlier source, the *Daoshu* 道樞 (Pivot of Dao, DZ 1017, dat. 1151) places it below the navel and identifies it with the genitals (ch. 8); in another section, consistent with the *Xingming guizhi*, the text agrees with the vision of Chinese medicine and locates it in the right kidney (ch. 3). The *Jinxian zhenglun tushuo* 金仙證論圖說 (Illustrated Discussions of Evidentiary Discourses of the Golden Immortals, ZW 132; dat. 1799, sect. 10), identifies this gate with the Yang Pass: "Below the Dark Prime is the Yang Pass. It is also called the Gate of Destiny. This is the point in men and women where they secrete essence." [17]

Regardless of the exact placement of the Gate of Destiny, its function is always related to the secretion of essence. Within the Microcosmic Orbit, it lies at a point where essence passes into a self-refining circuit that eventually leads to immortal life; alternatively it may be where essence leaves the body entirely, leading to the gradual degradation of life and eventual death. It is therefore a gate leading to potentialities: the trajectory *qi* takes from here determines life and death.

---

[17] In Chinese medicine, the Gate of Destiny a also pressure point along the Governing Vessel. Some texts link it with the lower elixir field in men; others, with the spleen. In a completely different vision, the *Huangting jing* identifies it with the nose, the navel, or a point behind the Yellow Court, i.e., between the kidneys.

Loci of Transformation

Alchemical transformation depends on the use of a crucible and furnace (*dinglü* 鼎爐). An illustration from the *Weisheng shilue* 衛生史略 (Brief History of Health and Sanitation; dat. 1936), represents them as a vessel sitting atop a tripod burner, located in the lower abdomen, spreading heat to the five inner organs that are depicted in mandala-like fashion.

Adepts must be able to properly locate and prepare them for the great work, then they must add various appropriate ingredients. Once all is ready, they can light the furnace and continue to tend its fires so they become hotter and cooler in accordance with the proper "firing times" (*huohou* 火候; see Robinet 1989, 316-17; 1995) As in external alchemy, location and function of both crucible and furnace are subject to a great deal of concern and even heated debate. Sexual alchemists read the sexual organs as the crucible, while Complete Perfection masters understand it as a region located below the navel (*Xiuzhen biannan* 2.13). Both traditions, moreover, acknowledge an internal and an external crucible, commonly identified as the elixir field (external) plus the *qi* inside it.

From Ming times onward, the texts speak of a greater and a lesser furnace. On the lesser furnace, the *Xingming guizhi* says:

> For the cultivation of the Elixir and the Golden Fluid, one must first secure the furnace and erect the crucible. The crucible acts as an implement, although of neither gold nor iron. The furnace acts as a tool, although of neither jade nor stone. The Yellow Court [central elixir field] acts as the crucible; the *Qi* Cavity [in the chest area] acts as the furnace. The Yellow Court is just above the *Qi* Cavity; they are intimately linked at the place in the body where the hundred meridians converge [e.g., the Hundred Meeting point at the top of the head] . . .

The text then emphasizes the necessity to "erect and secure" the furnace and crucible. The *Qi* Cavity is "secured" rather than "erected," as it is understood to be continuously present in the body. To secure it, adepts calm and control the movement of interior waves and winds that may be generated through indigestion or irregular breath as well as through serious disease or excessive emotions. The crucible, on the other hand, is a mandalic transformation of internal elements; it must be erected through focused concentration.

The greater crucible and furnace, which correspond to the trigrams for Heaven (Qian 乾) and Earth (Kun 坤), serve to "congeal destiny" and "mate interior yin and yang," defined as the "root of inner nature." Their importance derives less from their physical location than from their position along the energetic circuit that adepts create when they join the upper and lower bridges between the major vessels. At the level of smelting internal yin and yang to obtain the higher medicine, the organization of the body has become less identified with physical locations and structure than with transformational processes; it remains significant mainly as a vessel holding celestial transformations. Location changes of energetic centers in this transformational process are the logical result of a movement away from biological function toward higher levels of refinement. As elements and processes no longer encounter blockages inherent in the biological system, the bio-transformative functions of the body—digestion, respiration, pulse, and so on—become etherealized along with their crude elements and a displacement of processes occurs.

The River Cart and the Three Passes
In order to move the body's essences from one energy center to another, the adept employs a series of "carts." The River Cart (*heche* 河車) is one of several vehicles, such as the Ram, Deer, or Ox Carts. In Song *neidan*, the term River Cart appears first in Liu Haichan's 劉海蟬 (fl. 1031) *Chuandao ji* 傳道集 (Transmissions of Dao, DZ 263, chs. 14-16): "The circulation of unified *qi* is called River Cart." This indicates that it is not so much a vehicle as a route of *qi* transit, i.e., the path the *qi* takes as it circulates around the torso and head.

The *Yangsheng bilu* 養生秘錄 (Secret Record of Nourishing Life, DZ 579) supports this when it identifies it as the correct *qi* that flows down the Conception Vessel along the front of the body. In the Zhong-Lü tradition, the *Baiwen pian* 百問篇 (Hundred Questions, ed. *Daoshu* 5) says: "The gastric cavity is the River Cart. This is the heavenly river, the *qi* of the True Unity of the Water Bureau. From the heavens it comes to penetrate through the nose and mouth. Therefore it is called the River Cart." It is thus safe to conclude that the River Cart is an expression for the dynamic movement of the internal *qi* circuit, signifying energy as it flows through the 'northern' or frontal regions of the body, associated with the Water Bureau or uro-genital system. Rather than a localized manifestation, it signifies a specific aspect of body phenomena and interior processes.

Later sources connect the River Cart with conscious intention and the progression of essence along the Microcosmic Orbit. More plain spoken in their expression, they coined the term Path of the River Cart (*heche lu* 河車路) to create more precision and specified the point between the shoulder blades as a key factor. As there are both fire and water in the body, so there are fast and slow movements along the circuit. These are denoted by the Deer and Ox Carts, respectively. The divine inner nature is further described as the Great Ox Cart., while warming *qi* is the Ram Cart. Adepts make use of the different carts, engaging appropriate imagery at various specific moments matching the movement of *qi* as it transits through the body.

As adepts consciously move *qi* up through the Governing Vessel along the spine, they need to open the Three Passes, major gates which permit the passage of essences in alchemical transformation. They are: Tail Gate (*weilü* 尾

閭) at the coccyx; Narrow Strait (*jiaji* 夾脊) in the mid-back; and Jade Pillow (*yuzhen* 玉枕) at the back of the skull.

Wang Chongyang 王重陽 (1112-1170), founder of the school of Complete Perfection, provides an apt description in his *Jinguan yusuo jue* 金關玉鎖訣 (Explanations of Jade Lock and Golden Pass, DZ 1156; see Eskildsen 2004; Komjathy 2007). According to him, the *qi* departing from the Tail Gate is imagined as three carts departing from Mt. Keng. They rise up the back and move through the Double Pass between the kidneys, then enter a verdant creek and pass between the shoulder blades, where they separate to continue in two directions toward the Peak of the Heavenly Terrace located in the head. Through concentrated practice the landscape opens up, and adepts are able to move with their *qi* through the Gate of Heaven at the top of the head to ecstatically roam about the heavens above.

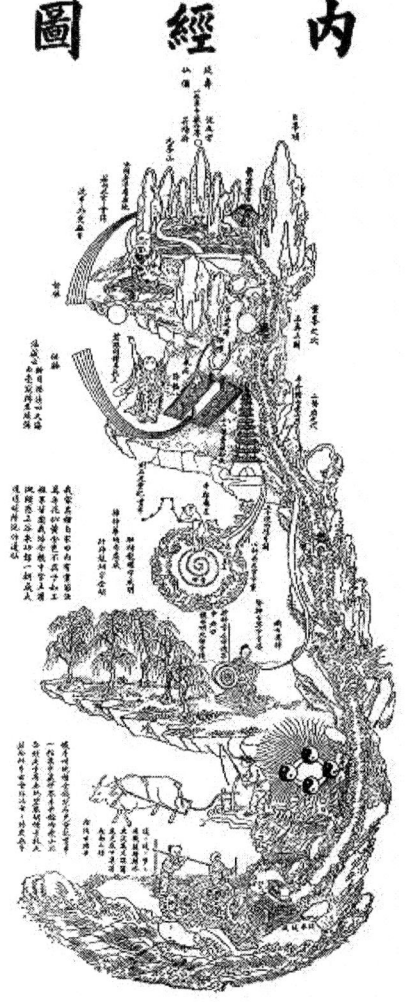

The landscape Wang Chongyang envisioned may be similar to that depicted in the magnificent image *Neijing tu* 內經圖 (Chart of Internal Passageways, dat. 1898; see Russelle 1933; Komjathy 2008) as shown here (Fig. 5). Here the Tail Gate is an architectural structure at the bottom of the image, behind two children who are working a water wheel to send *qi* up along the spine. Narrow Strait appears as a gate-like building halfway up the spine and about level with the stars of the Dipper, wielded by a lad standing on a spiral. The Jade Pillow is not shown, but would be located along the upper spine, below eye-level, from where the path leads into the verdant plains at the foot of Mount Kunlun.

The Tail Gate is an important center in the trajectory of *qi*-circulation. The name also appears in the ancient geographical text *Shanhai jing* 山海經 (Classic of Mountains and Seas), where it is a jade mountain "east of the Fusang tree" that also serves as one of eight cosmic pillars. The Han poet Sima Guang 司馬光 placed it in the region of the Kuroshio current (see Needham 1976), while a Song text identifies it as the place where the waters of the oceans pour into the Nine Underworlds (Major 1993, 165), making it an entry point into the hells. In the human body, the Tail Gate is poised right above the place where ordinary men and women lose their essence. As their essence seeps away in the form of semen or menstrual blood, they slip closer to death. Reversing the process at the Tail Gate, on the other hand, adepts of internal alchemy initiate their progress toward immortality.

The Narrow Strait is the point along the passageway where the Deer carries the load. The adept gingerly passes *qi* through this point of potential obstruction and disaster. Hu notes that "when the great medicine is carried through the Narrow Strait, if the progression is blocked and [the cart] cannot move, [the cart] cannot be pulled by the will. One must wait until it suddenly once again move of its own accord." (Hu and Lu 2004, 599) It must not be forced. The *qi* cannot pass through the narrow passage until it is properly warmed. Heated, the *qi* is more viscous and flows easily through the aperture.

Also known as the Iron Rampart (*tiebi* 鐵壁) or the Wind Pond (*fengchi* 風池), Jade Pillow is an important point in human physiognomy because of its strategic location for the passage and refinement of *qi* in the body. The shape and nature of the Jade Pillow indicate the capacity for *qi* passage, blockage, and refinement; accordingly, Chinese physiognomy finds in the Jade Pillow markers of an individual's longevity and health potential. Kohn notes this point is also listed as one of the divine features of Laozi in *Youlong zhuan* 猶龍傳 (Like unto a Dragon, DZ 774, 3.9a-10a) and *Hunyuan shengji* 昏元聖記 (Sage Record of Mystery Prime, dat. 1191, DZ 770, 2.36ab) (1996b, 207-9).

In Chinese medicine and alchemy, this point marks a special point in the human body, where internal and external meridians meet, allowing communication with external stimulate and potential loss of *qi*. Moreover, the passage of *qi* narrows dramatically at the Jade Pillow, and is easily obstructed (*Huanyuan pian* 還原篇).[18] Not surprisingly, modern TCM identifies it as a common blockage point resulting in hypertension and headache. Its stimulation dispels wind and dampness and restores blood and *qi*. The alchemist, challenged to conserve *qi*, must break through the Iron Rampart and allow the refined *qi* to enter the brain region and upper palaces of the body. In *neidan*, opening of the Jade Pillow thus permits access to the heavenly realms of transformation in the head.

---

[18] TCM finds the Jade Pillow (called Wind Pond) an essential point for acupuncture to treat hypertension, headache, and other ailments resulting from *qi* blockage to the head.

Energy Centers

Besides the Jade Pillow and the Gate of Heaven, the head also houses three major centers: the Ancestral Cavity (*zuxiao* 祖竅), the Valley Spirit (*gushen* 谷神), and the Mysterious Pass (*xuanguan* 玄關).

The first is located between the eyes and sometimes identified with the Niwan Palace. Zhao Bichen associates it with immortals' respiration which the adept seeks to emulate. The adepts' initial goal is thus to secure the Ancestral Cavity, located between the eyes, behind the Mysterious Pass, and in front of the Valley Spirit.

> Although both breathe through mouth and nose, ordinary people employ the larynx while their breath moves in and out through mouth and nose. Therefore it cannot enter the Ancestral Cavity and return to the root. The perfected being's respiration circulates internally and is measured in the "four comings and goings." It does not employ inhalation and exhalation through nose and mouth. Thus each respiration returns to the root. (*Xingming fajue mingzhi*)

Similarly, the *Nü jindan* identifies the use of the Ancestral Cavity with embryonic breathing and emphasizes the goal of "returning each breath to the root." It says:

> The Buddha says: The first meditation stills all thoughts: the mind no longer generates or disperses them. The second meditation stills respiration: the breath no longer goes in or comes out. When the breath no longer comes in or goes out, it is retained and *qi* obtains nourishment. A form of breathing is reached that no longer employs exhalation and inhalation through nose and mouth. It is like before a person is born; his or her breathing follows the respiration of the mother. It is like creating a fetus, nourishing it, then letting it go.
>
> This respiration is centered in the Ancestral Cavity. Although breathing through nose and mouth, ordinary people cannot reach the Ancestral Cavity and return to the root. In perfected beings, on the other hand, every respiration returns to the root. Therefore Zhuangzi says, "Ordinary beings' respiration employs the larynx; perfected beings' respiration employs the heels."
>
> If you desire to seek the respiration of perfected beings, you must regulate the respiration of the postnatal *qi* and make the perfected respiration return to the root in the ancestral cavity. This *qi* is hidden in the Ancestral Cavity. (2.18a-b)

The *Kunjue* 坤訣 (Instructions for Female Daoists, dat. 19th c.) further identifies the Ancestral Cavity as the pivotal mechanism. It says: "The pivotal mechanism is between the eyes. Above it is the Heavenly Valley [Spirit Valley], below is the Spring Cavern. You must correctly identify these two without errors" (3a).

The Valley Spirit, next, a term first found in *Daode jing* 6, is associated with the upper elixir field or Niwan Palace. The *Daofa huiyuan* 道法會元 (A Corpus of Taoist Ritual, DZ 1220; dat. 14th c.; Boltz 1987, 30, 47; Loon 1979) identifies it as the "Heavenly Valley of the Niwan" in the head and notes that it is the home of the conserving spirit (ch. 76). The spirit residing in this area further transits through a pass that allows adepts access to the grand mystery of Dao. This is the Mysterious Pass. Its name picks up on a phrase in *Daode jing* 1, where the "mystery of mysteries" is described as "the gate of all subtleties."

The Mysterious Pass is not at a fixed location; rather, it opens at the moment when cultivation practices cause the first emergence of true yang. In technical illustrations, it appears as floating above the head and manifesting at the right transformative moment. The adept is pictured with legs folded in the lotus position, left hand grasping a finger of the right. Above the head, three circles indicate the processes occurring within. On the left and right are two Taiji circles: in one the white is to the left; in the other, to the right. The Taiji circle on the left is the Jade Rabbit; the one on the right, the Golden Bird. In the center is a white circle bounded by a dark line, indicating pure yang. Three lines of text running top to bottom, right to left, read: Portal of the Mysterious Female; Ancestral Cavity of the Dark Pass; Root of Exhalation and Inhalation. While Zhao Bichen already locates the Ancestral Cavity in the head, the Portal, Pass, and Root are all experiential phenomena rather than concrete, identifiable loci. The adept cannot access these until practice leads to their experience.

At the far end of the body, a key point is the center of the soles of the feet, known in Chinese medicine as the first point of the kidney meridian and commonly called Bubbling Spring (*yongquan* 湧泉). Before engaging in advanced practice, adepts must open all body junctures so the *qi* can flow freely from head to foot and cross the finger tips of each hand. The medical classic *Huangdi neijing lingshu* 黃帝內經靈樞 (Yellow Emperor's Inner Classic, Numinous Pivot, trl. Wu 1993) notes that the spirit emerges from Bubbling Spring, while the *Kunjue* links it with the Spring Cavern: "If the Heavenly Valley is not hot, the *qi* will not ascend; if the Bubbling Spring is not hot, the *qi* will not descend."

Bubbling Spring is accessed after adepts are well versed in the Microcosmic Orbit and can expand the energy flow to the extremities. Zhao Bichen describes this as the last of five steps for "Cultivating the Microcosmic Orbit: Transforming Essence into *Qi*." He says:

> First, on inhalation, essential *qi* passes from the Gate of Destiny along the Governing Vessel to the top of the head. Second, on exhalation, it moves down the Conception Vessel and returns to the Gate.
>
> On the next inhalation, it passes to the Belt Vessel, where it separates and moves to the back along the two sides of the waist, rises up between the shoulder blades [like the bladder meridian in Chinese medicine], and stops. On the following exhalation, it moves in two streams from the shoulder blades along the outer arms. Known as the yang cir-

cuit [along the outer arms], it has the *qi* moving from the middle finger to the palms, where it stops. On the next inhalation, it goes from the palms along the yin circuit [along the inner arms] to return to the breasts, where it stops again.

Upon exhalation, the *qi* next moves from the front of the breasts in two currents to the Belt Vessel and from there returns as one to the Gate of Destiny. On inhalation, it rises up again to a point about two inches below the heart and stops there. This point is part of the Penetrating Vessel. On the following exhalation, it descends back to the Gate of Destiny.

From here it flows in two streams along the outer legs to Bubbling Spring, then—still in two streams—it returns along the inside of the legs, riding the fifth inhalation. On the final exhalation of the practice, the *qi* moves back to the Gate of Destiny and rests there. (*Xingming fajue mingzhi*)

Bubbling Spring may be understood as the furthest point on the Microcosmic Orbit, where the individual's exterior frame meets earth through the soles of the feet and provides a direct connection to the innermost parts of the adept's body: as the first point on the kidney meridian, it is where water meets metal. In *neidan*, it serves to transition the alchemical transformation of *qi* from metal to water. The extracted *qi* rises from Bubbling Spring to the center of the torso, moving along the inner thighs to the Gate of Destiny on the Belt Vessel.

Conclusion

When discussing the alchemical body, we have a tendency to dissect and objectify its parts rather than see the body as intended: a unified and complete cosmic individual. We must constantly try to overcome the tendency to see points and passages as concrete objects. Rather, they are transitional moments in an experiencing self. Each major point is a place of individual agency and action, where the adept, guided by his or her own sensory experiences, integrates ritual learning with individual practice to create the experience of self-transformation. Each locus along the body is an integral part of the embodied self which includes emotion, feeling, energy, blood, tissue, sinews and bones. Both the nonmaterial emotions or feelings and the tactile aspects of the body (blood, tissue, etc.) are integral parts of the embodied self.

The *neidan* and qigong body is not simply an object but an integrated and living, embodied self. Thomas Ots (1995) emphasizes this distinction of the Chinese ritual body as active and agentive. He suggests the Chinese body is best understood as a lived-body (*Leib*) rather than an object-body (*Körper*). That embodied self is itself the seat of immortality seeking; the self and the body are taken as one. The living body cannot be denied or objectified; each locus is discovered by the individual adept who, under the guidance of a master, *experiences* these loci. The adept works these loci and creates herself in the image of the immortal Laozi—the body of the cosmos, walking on the cusp of creation. By understanding the holistic structure of the microcosmic body, the adept seizes the capacity to transform herself into a perfected embodied self, free of the hazards of age, disease and pain.

This feature of the alchemical body has several implications: most importantly it contains multiples of ones, or a "multiplex unity" (Lévi 1989). The complexities of the five organs collapse into the unity of the five phases. The complexities of the meridians collapse into the unity of yin and yang. The complexities of alchemical transformation collapse into the unity of the cosmos; these further collapse into the unity of emptiness and Dao. The unity of the microcosmic body forms to basis for alchemical potential. Through unity with Dao and emptiness, the adept embodies the potential for all forms of becoming.

Another essential feature is that the multiplex unity of the body must be understood to be an experiencing, dynamic, and lived body, not simply an object to view, review, or study. Then again, while the body landscape is mapped out as a general guide to embodied experience, individual bodies are unique and their landscape cannot be accurately mapped nor can it be reliably fixed to the biological realities of an anatomical body. The alchemical body described here is thus a rough approximation which may only suggest what the adept may encounter and help to guide the individual in his or her journey toward immortality. Therefore, *neidan* literature repeatedly emphasizes the crucial need for a master to help guide the adept through this experiential process.

Each body transformation is unique to individual blockages of *qi*-flow acquired through negative and positive habits, past injuries, exercise patterns, and other lived experiences. The divine body of Laozi may indeed be the goal of the adept, but each individual embodiment of Dao has peculiar manifestations and measures of experience. Individuals' exterior appearance is largely ignored in *neidan* descriptions: the essential lies in the flow of essences within the body. Exterior appearance is only described in terms relevant to *qi*-flow. Thus, for example, the description of the Jade Pillow in the *Youlong zhuan* is meaningful because it indicates Laozi's superior ability to radiate *qi* through a crucial and narrow point along the Microcosmic Orbit.

External features and even gender are only significant in so far as they implicate the flow of *qi* in the individual body. Whereas distinct practices are developed for men, women, old, and young, variation in practice is driven solely from the imperative to adhere to the cosmic structure and phase of the individual adept's body, and the consequent variation in *qi* flow. Male and female bodies are understood to imbricate yin and yang in distinctive manners: this creates the basis for gender-based difference in body structures. Likewise, young and old bodies are situated as different phases in the aging process, each with different microcosmic structures. Given the difference in bodies, variations in practice must persist. It is up to the adept to discover his or her own underlying unity with Dao through practice and experience.

Bibliography

Bokenkamp, Stephen. 1997. *Early Daoist Scriptures*. Honolulu: University of Hawai'i Press.

Boltz, Judith M. 1987. *A Survey of Taoist Literature: Tenth to Seventeenth Centuries*. Berkeley: University of California, China Research Monograph 32.

Bray, Francesca. 1997. *Technology and Gender: Fabrics of Power in Late Imperial China*. Berkeley: University of California Press.

Chan, Wing-tsit. 1957. "Transformation of Buddhism in China." *Philosophy East and West* 7.3-4 :107-16.

_____. 1963. *A Source Book in Chinese Philosophy*. Princeton: Princeton University Press.

Despeux, Catherine. 1979. *Zhao Bichen: Traité d'alchimie et de physiologie taoïste*. Paris: Guy Trédaniel.

_____. 1994. *Taoïsme et corps humain: Le Xiuzhen tu*. Paris: Guy Tredaniel.

_____. 2000. "Talismans and Sacred Diagrams." In *Daoism Handbook*, edited by Livia Kohn, 498-540. Leiden: E. Brill.

_____, and Livia Kohn. 2003. *Women in Daoism*. Cambridge, Mass: Three Pines Press.

Eskildsen, Stephen. 2004. *The Teachings and Practices of the Early Quanzhen Taoist Masters*. Albany: State University of New York Press.

Esposito, Monica. 1997. *L'alchimia del soffio: La pratica della visione interiore nell'alchimia taoista*. Rome: Ubaldini Editore.

_____. 2000. "Daoism in the Qing (1644-1911)." In *Daoism Handbook*, edited by Livia Kohn, 623-58. Leiden: E. Brill.

Furth, Charlotte. 1999. *A Flourishing Yin: Gender in China's Medical History, 960-1665*. Berkeley: University of California Press.

Gyaltso, Khedrup Norsang. 2000. *Ornament of Stainless Light: An Exposition on the Kālacakra Tantra*. Translated by Gavin Kilty. Boston: Wisdom Publications.

Hahn, Thomas H. 1988. "The Standard Taoist Mountain and Related Features of Religious Geography." *Cahiers d'Extrême-Asie* 4: 145-56.

_____. 2000. "Daoist Sacred Sites." In *Daoism Handbook*, edited by Livia Kohn, 683-707. Leiden: E. Brill.

Hu Fuchen 胡孚琛, and Lu Xichen 呂希沉. 2004. *Daoxue tonglun* 道學通論. Shehui kexue wenxian.

Huber, Toni. 2004. *Cult of Pure Crystal Mountain: Popular Pilgrimmage and Visionary Landscape in Southeast Tibet*. New York: Oxford University Press.

Kalinowski, Marc. 1985. "La transmission du dispositif des neuf palais sous les six-dynasties." In *Tantric and Taoist Studies*, edited by Michel Strickmann, 2: 773-811. Brussels: Institut Belge des Hautes Etudes Chinoises.

Kilty, Gavin. 2004. "Introduction." In *Ornament of Stainless Light: An Exposition on the Kālacakra tantra*, edited by Norsang Gyaltso, Khedrup, 1-18. Boston, Mass.: Wisdom Publications.

Kohn, Livia. 1991. "Taoist Visions of the Body." *Journal of Chinese Philosophy* 18:227-52.

_____. 1995. *Laughing at the Dao: Debates among Buddhists and Taoists in Medieval China*. Princeton: Princeton University Press.

_____. 1996a. "New Perspectives on Taoist Culture." *Journal of Chinese Religions* 24: 159-67.

_____. 1996b. "The Looks of Laozi." *Asian Folklore Studies* 55: 193-236.

_____. 1998. *God of the Dao: Lord Lao in History and Myth*. Ann Arbor: University of Michigan, Center for Chinese Studies.

Komjathy, Louis. 2002. *Title Index to Daoist Collections*. Cambridge, Mass.: Three Pines Press.

_____. 2007. *Cultivating Perfection: Mysticism and Self-Transformation in Quanzhen Daoism*. Leiden: E. Brill.

_____. 2008. "Mapping the Daoist Body: The *Neijing tu* in History." *Journal of Daoist Studies* 1:67-92.

Lévi, Jean Francois. 1989. "The Body, the Daoists' Coat of Arms." In *Fragments for a History of the Human Body*, edited by Michael Feher. New York: Zone Books.

Lincoln, Bruce. 1975. "The Indo-European Myth of Creation." *History of Religions* 15: 121-45.

Loon, Piet van der. 1979. "A Taoist Collection of the Fourteenth Century." In *Studia Sino-Mongolica: Festschrift for Herbert Franke*, edited by Wolfgang Bauer, 401-5. Wiesbaden: Franz Steiner: Münchener Ostasiatische Studien.

Lu, Kuan-yü. 1970. *Taoist Yoga — Alchemy and Immortality*. London: Rider.

Major, John S. 1993. *Heaven and Earth in Early Han Thought: Chapters Three, Four and Five of the Huainanzi*. Albany: State University of New York Press.

Miller, James. 2003. "Daoism and Nature." Pp. 393-410. In *Nature Across Cultures: Views of Nature and the Environment in Non-Western Cultures*, edited by Helaine Selin et al., 393-410. Dordrecht, Boston, London: Kluwer Academic Publishers.

Needham, Joseph. 1976 [1962]. *Science and Civilization in Ancient China*. 5. III. Cambridge: Cambridge University Press.

Neswald, Sara. 2007. "Rhetorical Voices in the *Neidan* Tradition: An Interdisciplinary Analysis of the *Nüdan hebian*." Ph.D. diss., McGill University, Montreal.

Ots, Thomas. 1994. "The Silenced Body—the Expressive *Leib*: On the Dialectic of Mind and Life in Chinese Cathartic Healing." In *Embodiment and Experience:*, edited by Thomas J. Csordas, 116-38. Cambridge: Cambridge University Press.

Pregadio, Fabrizio. 2006. *Great Clarity: Daoism and Alchemy in Early Medieval China*. Stanford: Stanford University Press.

Robinet, Isabelle. 1989. "Original Contributions of *Neidan* to Taoism and Chinese Thought." In *Taoist Meditation and Longevity Techniques*, edited by Livia Kohn, 297-330. Ann Arbor: University of Michigan, Center for Chinese Studies Publications.

_____. 1994. "Le rôle et le sens des nombres dans la cosmologie et l'alchimie taoïstes." *Extrême-Orient, Extrême-Occident* 16: 93-120.

_____. 1995a. *Introduction a l'alchimie interieure taoïste: De l'unité et de la multiplicité*. Paris: Editions Cerf.

_____. 1995b. "Un, deux, trois—les differentes modalites de l'un et sa dynamique." *Cahiers d'Extrême-Asie* 8:175-220.

Roth, Harold D. 1999. *Original Tao: Inward Training and the Foundations of Taoist Mysticism*. New York: Columbia University Press.

Rowe, William T. 1998. "Ancestral Rites and Political Authority in Late Imperial China: Chen Hongmou in Jiangxi." *Modern China* 24.4:378-407.

Rousselle, Erwin. 1933. "*Nei Ging Tu*: Die Tafel des inneren Gewebes: Ein taoistisches Meditationsbild mit Beschriftung." *Sinica* 8:207-216.

Schipper, Kristofer M. 1994. *The Taoist Body*. Translated by Karen C. Duval. Berkeley: University of California Press.

_____, and Franciscus Verellen. 2004. *The Taoist Canon: A Historical Companion to the Daozang*. Chicago: University of Chicago Press.

_____., and Wang Hsiu-huei 1986. "Progressive and Regressive TimeCycles in Taoist Ritual." In *Time, Science and Society in China and the West*, edited by J. T. Fraser, 185-205. Amherst: University of Massachusetts Press.

Seidel, Anna. 1969. *La divinisation de Lao-tseu dans le taoïsme des Han*. Paris: Ecole Française d'Extrême-Orient.

Sivin, Nathan. 1987. *Traditional Medicine in Contemporary China*. Ann Arbor: University of Michigan, Center for Chinese Studies.

Snellgrove, David. 1987. *Indo-Tibetan Buddhism and their Tibetan Successors*, vol. 1. Boston, MA: Shambala.

Stoddard, Heather. 1999. "Dynamic Structures in Buddhist Mandalas: Apradaksina and Mystic Heat in the Mother Tantra Section of the Annutarayoga Tantras." *Artibus Asiae*: 169-213.

Strickmann, Michel. 1978. "The Longest Taoist Scripture." *History of Religions* 17: 331-54.

Valussi, Elena. 2003. "Beheading the Red Dragon: A History of Female Internal Alchemy in China." Ph. D. Diss., School of Oriental and African Studies, University of London, London.

Wallace, Vesna. 2001. *The Inner Kālacakra: A Buddhist Tantric View of the Individual.* New York, NY: Oxford University Press.

_____. 2004. *The Kālacakra: the Chapter on the Individual together with the Vimalaprabhā.* New York, NY: American Institute of Buddhist Studies at Columbia University, Columbia University Press.

Wang Xiangyun. 1995. "Tibetan Buddhism at the Court of Qing: the Life and Work of lCang-skya Rol-pa'i rdo-rje [Rolpay Dorje] (1717-1786)." Ph.D. diss, , Harvard University, Cambridge, Mass.

Wu, Jing-Nuan. 1993. *Ling Shu or The Spiritual Pivot*. Washington, D.C.: The Taoist Center.

Yates, Robin D.S. 1994. "Body, Space, Time and Bureaucracy: Boundary Creation and Control Mechanisms in Early China." In *Boundaries in China*, edited by John Hay, 56-80. London: Reaktion Books.

History and Early Lineages

Guangbao Zhang[1]

Chinese society underwent a thorough transformation from the late Tang to the Northern Song dynasties (9th-10th c.). The time saw the end of ancient and medieval structures and the beginning of modern society, involving massive change in class and social structure, notably the decline of the high aristocracy and accompanying rise of the middle class as represented by the merchants (Shiba 1970). Scholars describe the Tang-Song transition in various terms (Ebrey and Gregory 1993), but the indisputable fact remains: there was a complete change in the overall political and social system, such as the civil service examinations, which allowed middle and even lower class people to move up to higher social status (see Haeger 1975; Hymes and Shirokauer 1993; Kracke 1968). A major contributing factor, aside from various economic and infrastructure developments, was the discovery and spread of printing technology, which facilitated wide communication and made classical books available to the common people so that they could be educated and take the civil service examination (see Bol 1992).

As the result of these changes, many private educational institutions or academies were established. There were also two important historical events that had a strong effect on social change. One is the Uprising of Huang Chao 黃巢 in 881, a war of the common people against the higher classes (Miyakawa 1974); the other is the Reform of Wang Anshi 王安石 (10221-1086), an internal political power struggle among the ruling class (Liu 1959; McKnight 1992). Both events put a strong pressure on the power structure of the upper classes and aided the ongoing reconstruction of the social system. The political and economic transformation under the Song also manifested itself on the social and ideological levels.

The time was one of rare freedom of thought: the three teachings (Confucianism, Daoism, and Buddhism) were competing freely and pluralistic values contested with each other. As the Song adopted the Tang's cultural policy of intellectual diversification and the equal treatment of the three teachings, it brought about a major phase of intellectual freedom and creativity, quite like

---

[1] Translated and edited by Robin R. Wang.

that in the earlier Spring and Autumn period (771-479 B.C.E.). It is thus rightly called the "second axis period' of Chinese intellectual history. In terms of Daoism, moreover, it was its second heyday or golden age after its flourishing and political influence under the Tang, a time that bought forth the main feature of new Daoist schools and various forms of popular veneration and practice. Internal alchemy, too, arose in this period; it has been the central Daoist method of cultivation ever since (see Fukui et al. 1990; Hu 1999).

Internal alchemy as much as its external counterpart is a major method of Daoist cultivation; it has played an important role in various Daoist schools from the late Tang dynasty onward. The term *neidan* 內丹 implies two sets of meaning: broad and general as well as narrow and specific. In the broad and general sense, it refers to all kinds of cultivation methods aimed at the realization of the ultimate Dao. In the narrow and specific sense, it defines techniques specific to the process of internal alchemy.

Studying the history and development of internal alchemy, one must pay attention to four important questions:

1) Where did the term *neidan* originate and how did it develop?

2) How has *neidan* diverged from traditional Daoist cultivation? How does it effect the leap from mere techniques to oneness with Dao?

3) How has internal alchemy started and developed as a religious school? Into what schools did it grow? And how do they relate to and differ from each other?

4) What is the relation between *neidan* and traditional Daoist cultivation methods, such as concentration, guiding *qi*, external alchemy, and sexual practices? What are the main differences between them?

We can use four terms to capture these issues: internal alchemy, Dao of internal alchemy, Daoist religious alchemy, and Daoist inner cultivation. We can also rephrase them in the affirmative by stating that:

1) Internal alchemy is a specific Daoist expression and does not occur elsewhere in Chinese culture.

2) The Dao of internal alchemy means Daoist techniques that afford realization of Dao through internal cultivation.

3) Daoist religious alchemy involves different schools or branches that each developed specific versions of practice.

4) Daoist inner cultivation is closely related yet also substantially different from the way of internal alchemy (see Zhang 2001)

All these four aspects of internal alchemy are closely interrelated and sometimes even interchangeable. Our focus in the following is on Daoist religious alchemy and its various schools as they were formally established after the mid-Tang dynasty. However, it is also important to remember that it relied on a vivid tradition of inner cultivation that can be traced back to before the Qin and Han dynasties, as apparent in *Daode jing*, *Guanzi*, *Zhuangzi*, and various medical manuscripts. Yet in these early sources the techniques typically served the preservation and enhancement of physical health and some of them were not associated with the realization of Dao. In other words, they did not contain a vision of oneness between techniques and Dao.

This only arose in the Eastern Han dynasty, when the *Taiping jing* 太平經 (Scripture of Great Peace) emerged. The text documents a leap from health techniques to realization of Dao. Presenting many cultivation techniques, such as concentration, guarding the One, breathing exercises, and sexual practices, it yet elevates them to the level of Daoist attainment. Rather than merely for physical benefits, it applies these methods toward a deeper contemplation of Dao and uses them to break through the limits of life in favor of a transcendent existence.

The *Taiping jing* is thus in many ways the earliest source for what became typical in *neidan*. It demonstrates the Daoist transformation of techniques from health exercises toward manifestations of Dao. It also shows how Daoist thinkers linked the heavenly with the human Dao (see Zhang 1998). Building on this and expanding these ideas, internal alchemy began to grow in the mid-Tang and from there evolved its earliest representatives of the Zhong-Lü school.

Medieval Forerunners

Internal alchemy can be traced back to the middle of the Tang dynasty, when Daoist masters systematized various traditional methods—meditation, *qi*-guiding, healing exercises, embryo respiration, diets, and sexual techniques—and connected them with a creative interpretation of external alchemy (see Li 2000; Zhang YM 1987). The latter had fallen into disrepute because several emperors had died from elixir poisoning and a more internal mode of transformation became advisable. Prior to this, though, the transmutation of internal energies and the activation of infant-like deities in the body had already played a key role in the methods of Highest Clarity (Shangqing 上清) Daoism, which arose in the fourth century C.E. and became dominant under the Tang (see Pregadio 2006; Zhang 1993). Internal alchemy can therefore be seen as the result of three distinct strands of Daoist practice that combined creatively and fruitfully from the mid-Tang onwards: energetic transmutation, a systematization of integrated practices, and the interiorization of operative alchemy.

New and unusual at the time was the tendency to search for the path of internal cultivation while yet working with external alchemy. Various insightful Daoist monks began to dislike external alchemy and instead turned to traditional techniques of breathing and concentration. They developed a new and creative interpretation of these methods in alchemical terms and thereby opened a completely new path toward Dao. Key figures of the Tang were:

Ye Fashan 葉法善 (Daoyuan 道元, 616-720), the son of a famous Daoist family who lived for 104 years. Described as the Celestial Master of Guangbian in Zeng Zao's 曾慥 *Daoshu* 道樞 (Pivot of Dao, DZ 1017; dat. 1151), he was also the author of the *Zhen longhu jiuxian jing* 真龍虎九仙經 (Perfect Scripture of the Nine Immortals Dragons and Tigers, DZ 227).

Luo Gongyuan 羅公遠 (Siyuan 思遠, n.d.), a well-known resident of Mt. Qingcheng in Sichuan, described as the Perfected of Yongyuan 永元真人 in *Daoshu*. He studied Daoist techniques from a young age and wrote a commentary to Ye Fashan's book as well as a poetry collection known as the *Sanfeng ge* 三峰歌 (Songs of Three Mountains).

The Buddhist monk Zeng Yixing 僧一行 was well-versed in the classics and had an extraordinary memory. Known as the National Master of the Six Pervasions 六通國師 in *Daoshu*, he was a famous astronomer and *Yijing* cosmologist.

All three claimed that the basic cultivation materials could be found in the body and that the difference between internal and external alchemy lay in their essential ingredients. External alchemy took its materials from nature, using lead and mercury, four yellows,[2] eight minerals, as well as gold and silver—depending on the school. Internal alchemy, on the contrary, sought its raw materials within the human body. For example, Ye Fashan divided them according to water and fire, both available here: heart being fire and kidneys being water.

He then rephrased traditional inner cultivation to understand it as a way of creating the Golden Elixir—a term he mentions variously while yet not using the term *neidan*. In addition to the claim that the raw materials could be found in the human body, Ye also argued that the Golden Elixir could only be successfully formed though the interaction of internal fire and water. He thus formulated a fundamental principle of Dao of internal alchemy.

External and internal alchemy differ in their interpretation of "fire." In external practice, of course, it is quite easy: fire is nothing more than regular, real fire as produced through the burning of bamboo, plants, animal waste, and so on. However, the fire in internal alchemy is metaphorical. There are two popular views: one says it is the intention (thought); the other says it is found in quietude. In fact, these two are the same since the potent intention of cultivation can only be properly activated in meditative stillness. They are imitations of the catalyzing fire of external alchemy activated through the mind.[3]

In addition, the Tang masters considered the human body as the stove for brewing the elixir and called it the "body stove" (*shending* 身鼎). They saw the body as an image of the stove in external alchemy, even advising practitioners

---

[2] Four yellows (*sihuang*): realgar, orpiment, sulphur, and arsenic, all of which include the word "yellow" (*huang*) in their Chinese names.

[3] The later thinker Zhen Yixing even differentiated four kinds of fire: burning body fire, fighting yin fire, spiritual tortoise fire, and capturing ghost fire.

to imitate the shape of a stove in their posture by crossing the left leg over the right and using the hands for support. They were also the first to coin the term "divine embryo" (*shentai* 神胎), applying it mainly to the work of mental concentration, an imagination of physiological change. Their various concepts soon led to the formation of the first school of internal alchemy proper (see Yang 1998).

The Zhong-Lü School

Going beyond the creative Tang thinkers' understanding of Daoist cultivation, the first formal school of internal alchemy arose as the result of the massive failures of external practice in the late Tang, whose poisonous elixirs caused the demise of several emperors. Both court officials and Daoist practitioners became very critical of the practice and favored a more internal approach. Thus while followers did not eschew external practice completely, they accepted the criticism and came to value internal cultivation higher, thereby finding greater success with less fatalities.

Founding Immortals
The first formal school to represent this new trend is called Zhong-Lü 鍾呂派, combining the surnames of its two founding immortals Zhongli Quan 鍾離權 and Lü Dongbin 呂洞賓. Both figures are members of a group known as the Eight Immortals (*baxian* 八仙), a group of seven men and one woman said to have inspired each other in the attainment of transcendence, who have continued to serve humanity by appearing in séances and inspirations. As a group, they were presented first in theater plays of the thirteenth century, portrayed as an eccentric and happy lot who respond to pleas in emergencies and grant favors and protection. They remain highly popular today, as symbols of long life and happiness, shown on congratulation cards for various happy occasions as well as in shops and restaurants as signs of good luck and enjoyment. They play an active part in Chinese folk culture and have been featured time and again in comic books and popular movies (see Lai 1972).

Zhongli Quan, also known as Han Zhongli, is the most senior of the group and the main agent of conversion for the others. The story goes that he was originally a general under the Han dynasty whose troops were completely vanquished in Central Asia. Desperate, he fled to a remote village where he encountered a Daoist immortal and learned to ascend to Heaven, helping others from his new position despite his failure in his official duties. He is usually depicted as a large, stately man with a round pot-belly (see Yang 1958). There is little firm historical information about him, and he may well be a late-Tang or early-Song literary creation.

Lü Dongbin (Chunyang 純陽) is the most popular immortal of the group. He appears frequently in spirit-writing sessions and serves as the patriarch of many Daoist groups and techniques. Depicted as a Confucian gentleman with aristocratic features and a sword, Lü is best known for the story of the "Yellow Millet Dream":

> Lü dreamt that he went to the capital as a candidate of the imperial examination and passed it at the top of the list. Starting his career as a junior secretary to one of the Boards, he rapidly rose in rank to positions at the Censorate and the Hanlin Academy. Eventually he became a Privy Councilor, after he had occupied, in the course of his unbroken success, all the most sought-after and important official posts.
>
> Twice he was married, he further dreamt, and both wives belonged to families of wealth and position. Children were born to him. His sons soon took themselves wives, and his daughters left the paternal roof for their husbands' homes. All these events happened before he even reached the age of forty.
>
> Next he found himself Prime Minister for a period of ten years, wielding immense power. This corrupted him. Then suddenly, without warning, he was accused of a grave crime. His home and all his possessions were confiscated, his wife and children separated. He himself, a solitary outcast, was wandering toward his place of banishment beyond the mountains. He found his horse brought to a standstill in snowstorm and was no longer able to continue the journey.

Then Lü wakes up, finding that while he went through an entire official career and family life, his millet has not even cooked yet. He realizes that life is but a fleeting dream and decides to leave the world to become an immortal, following Zhongli Quan for his training. The latter then puts him through ten trials, in which his selfless nature and sincere dedication to Dao are examined. For example, once he comes home to find his family dead: without great wailing and sorrow, he proceeds to arrange the burial, understanding that life is unstable and death but another transformation. Another time, he encounters a hungry tiger ready to pounce on a flock of sheep: disregarding his personal safety he throws himself in the tiger's path. Passing all ten trials, he is eventually accepted as Zhongli's disciple and becomes a leading immortal, not only among the eight but for the faithful in general, who find him supportive and ever ready to provide oracles and supernatural advice (see Yetts 1916).

Lü Dongbin appears first in the late Song dynasty, where he is mentioned in Daoist texts, popular novels, literary essays, and various inscriptions (see Baldrian-Hussein 1986; Katz 2000), such as Weng Baoguang's 翁葆光 *Wuzhen pian zhu* 悟真篇注 (Commentary on "Awakening to Perfection"). The Daoist canon contains a number of documents, including an inscription from the Jin dynasty known as the *Tang Lü Chunyang zhenren sitang ji* 唐純陽呂真人祠堂記 (Record at the Shrine of the Tang Perfected Lü Chunyang). The common claim here is that Lü was born in 798 in Henan and became a successful scholar and poet yet, due to one reason or another, took up Daoist path and studied avidly with Zhongli Quan and various other learned masters.

Main Texts

The texts of the Zhong-Lü school claim to be records of his Daoist training, written either in dialogue format or as lyrics. Many are only known by their titles and the occasional citation,[4] but a few have survived in the Daoist canon. They include:

—the *Zhong-Lü chuandao ji* 鍾呂傳道集 (Zhongli's Transmission of Dao to Lü: A Collection; in *Xiuzhen shishu* 14-16 [DZ 263], see Baldrian Hussein in Schipper and Verellen 2004, 801);

—the *Lingbao bifa* 靈寶畢法 (Complete Methods of Numinous Treasure, DZ 1191; see Baldrian-Hussein 1984), the most complete outline of alchemical stages as envisioned by the school;

—the *Huncheng ji* 渾成集 (Anthology of Complete Accord, DZ 1055), a collection of poems by Lü Dongbin compiled by He Zhiyuan 何志淵 around the year 1251 (Baldrian-Hussein in Schipper and Verellen 2004, 936);

—the *Qinyuan chun danci zhujie* 沁園春丹詞註解 (Explication of the Alchemical Lyric "Spring in the Garden by the Qin [River]," DZ 136), an interpretation of a poem ascribe to Lü by Yu Yan 俞琰 (1258-1314) (see Baldrian-Hussein in Schipper and Verellen 2004, 845);

—and the *Pomi zhengdao ge* 破迷正道歌 (Song for Dispelling Doubts Concerning the Correct Path, DZ 270), a poem attributed to Zhongli Quan, first mentioned around 1250 (see Baldrian-Hussein in Schipper and Verellen 2004, 831-32).

Beyond these works, Zeng Zao's *Daoshu* contains numerous citations of Zhong-Lü materials, and there are various treatises on cosmological and alchemical diagrams, biographic works, and later discussions that explicate the tradition (see Schipper and Verellen 2004, 802-12; Loon 1984).

The first two of these extant works, the *Chuandao ji* and the *Lingbao bifa* (both consisting of three chapters), are core works not only of the Zhong-Lü school but of internal alchemy in general, highly valued by all different lineages and traditions. Written as dialogues between Zhongli Quan and Lü Dongbin, they describe the principles, processes, and methods of the practice. Clearly cited in *Daoshu*, they were available and even popular by the end of the Northern Song. Later alchemical masters make frequent reference to them and they appear in important bibliographies and reference works.

---

[4] Lost texts include the *Jiuzhen yushu* 九真玉書 (Jade Book of Ninefold Perfection), *Chunyang zhenen jindan jue* 純陽真人金丹訣 (Perfected Chunyang's Formulas for the Golden Elixir), *Chuanjian ji* 傳劍集 (Collection of Sword Transmissions), *Zhenchang ji* 真常集 (Collection of Perfect Permanence), and the *Danjue yanzheng lun* 丹訣演正論 (Broad and Proper Discussion of Elixir Formulas).

Leading Masters

As far as we can tell from the records, the main historical protagonists of the Zhong-Lü school—aside from its legendary immortal founders—were Shi Jianwu, Cui Xifan, Liu Haichan, and Chen Pu.

Shi Jianwu 施肩吾 (Xisheng 希聖; fl. 820) lived on Daoist mountains in Jiangxi and claims to have received Dao from Lü Dongbin. His main book is the *Xishan qunxian hui zhenji* 西山群仙會真記 (Record of the Host of Immortals and Assembled Perfected in the Western Mountains, DZ 246), a collection of the lives and deeds of famous Jiangxi immortals. Compiled by his tenth-century disciple Li Song 李竦, it is a classic of internal alchemy that establishes Zhongli Quan and Lü Dongbin as fathers of the tradition and sets the standard for model lives to come (see Baldrian-Hussein in Schipper and Verellen 2004, 804-05). Without it, there would be no Zhong-Lü's text system in Daoist history.

Cui Xifan 崔希范 (fl. 880-940) is best known as the author of the *Cuigong ruyao jing* 崔公入藥鏡 (Master Cui's Mirror on the [Admixture of] Materials, in *Danfang xuzhi* [DZ 900]), a *neidan* poem that bore a great influence during the Song and appears variously in the canon (see Baldrian-Hussein in Schipper and Verellen 2004, 843-45). In addition to being an early representative of the Zhong-Lü school, he was also a primary master of internal alchemy.

Liu Haichan 劉海蟾 (fl. 1031) served as a leading government official in the state of Yan before becoming a student of Zhongli Quan's lineage and compiling his main work, the *Huanjin pian* 還金篇 (Reverting [Metals] to Gold; lost). A prominent figure in the popular culture and literary circles of the Northern Song, he was also a vital player in the development of internal alchemy—being credited with giving guidance to masters of a variety of schools.

Chen Pu 陳朴 (Chongyong 冲用; fl. 1078) lived during the Five Dynasties and early Song. Fleeing to Sichuan to escape the political upheaval, he met Zhongli and Lü in the Qingcheng range and became their disciple. In 1078, already over a hundred years old, he supposedly met a senior statesman in Nanjing and advised him on issues of government. His main work is the *Chen xiansheng neidan jue* 陳先生內丹訣 (Master Chen's Formulas for the Internal Elixir, DZ 1096); it became popular in the twelfth century and cemented basic teachings and lineage traditions of internal alchemy.

These major masters transformed the rudiments of late-Tang internal alchemy and took it to a more mature stage. They created a new level of Daoist cultivation by grounding the system in a metaphysical heavenly Dao and emphasizing the principle of "as above so below." They also integrated the various early practices to replace the fragmented patterns of the middle ages with a coherent system and step-by-step arrangement. In addition, they separated internal alchemy from all sorts of extraneous and alien practices, creating a new and systematic form of internal cultivation.

Later Schools

According to common understanding, the Zhong-Lü school divided into two major branches: the Southern School (Nanzong 南宗) and the Northern School (Beizong 北宗), each led by a group of senior masters, the Five Patriarchs in the south and Seven Perfected in the north.

Southern Patriarchs

The first leader and founder of the Southern School was Zhang Boduan 張伯端 (Pingshu 平叔, Ziyang 紫陽; 987-1082). He studied the classics at a young age and grew up to occupy a minor government position, then was drafted into military service. In 1069, he met Liu Haichan in Chengdu (Sichuan) and began his studies of internal alchemy. His best known work is the *Wuzhen pian* 悟真篇 (Awakening to Perfection, in *Xiuzhen shishu* 30 [DZ 263]), a series of verses on the concoction of the inner elixir (trl. Cleary 1987). In addition, he also wrote the *Jindan sibai zi* 金丹四百字 (Four Hundred Words on the Golden Elixir, DZ 1081; trl. Cleary 1986) and the *Jinbao neilian danjue* 金寶內練丹訣 (Alchemical Formula for the Inner Refinement of the Golden Treasure, DZ 240).[5]

Zhang Boduan's contributions to the history of *neidan* are twofold. First, he is credited with establishing the Southern School which paved the way for internal alchemy to gain major acceptance among Song society and being adopted by various devotional Daoist schools. Second, his main work, the *Wuzhen pian*, emerged as a central text of the entire tradition and became widely popular. Numerous Daoist and other literati wrote commentaries to it—nine alone being collected in the Daoist canon.

Following him was Shi Tai 石泰 (1022-1158), who too served as a minor government official, then retired to study with Zhang, extending his life to 138 years. His work is the *Huanyuan pian* 還源篇 (Returning to the Source, DZ 1091).

Xue Zixian 薛紫賢 (Daoguang 道光; 1078-1191) left home to become a Buddhist monk. In 1106, he met Shi Tai who became his teacher and emerged as the third patriarch. His main works are the *Huandan fuming pian* 還丹復命篇 (On Reverting the Elixir to Recover Life, DZ 1088) and a commentary on the *Wuzhen pian*.

Chen Nan 陳楠 (Nanmu 南木 or Cuixu 翠虛; fl. 1213) originally made a living by repairing wooden buckets. Besides learning internal alchemy from Xue Zixian, he was also a serious student of Thunder Rites. He lived in the southern province of Hunan, where he established a religious community. His

---

[5] For more, see Pregadio 2000; Schipper and Verellen 2004, 816-17 and 828-29.

writings are collected in a volume called *Cuixu pian* 翠虛篇 (Collected Works of [Master] Green Vacuity, DZ 1090).

The last major master of the Southern School is Bai Yuchan 白玉蟾 (Ge Changge 葛長庚; fl. 1194-1229). He had many Daoist names, e.g., Haiqiongzi 海瓊子, Wuyi sanren 武夷散人, Qiongshan daoren 瓊山道人, and Shenxiao sanli 神霄散吏. Having killed another human being in his youth, he strove for moral and personal excellence throughout his life. A highly talented Daoist who studied not internal alchemy but also Thunder Rites and forms of Buddhist meditation, he was a very productive writer and community organizer. He formed large Daoist communities and had a great influence in society.

Bai Yuchan integrated many aspects of Buddhist cultivation into his vision of internal alchemy and greatly enriched the Southern School. He also constructed the school's genealogy and promoted its overall development. His main writings include the *Haiqiong Bai zhenren yulu* 海瓊白真人語錄 (Recorded Sayings of Perfected Bai Haiqiong, DZ 1307), the *Haiqiong wendao ji* 海瓊問道集 (Haiqiong's Enquiry of Dao, DZ 1308); and the *Haiqiong chuandao ji* 海瓊傳道集 (Haiqiong's Transmission of Dao; DZ 1309) (Schipper and Verellen 2004, 927-30). He was by far the most prolific of the various masters.

The Northern School

The Northern School is essentially the same as the school of Complete Perfection (Quanzhen 全真) as headed by the founder Wang Chongyang 王重陽 (1113-1170) and his main disciples, the Seven Perfected.

Wang Chongyang set out as a student of Confucianism and failed the civil examinations several times. He then obtained employment as a low-level county official. In 1159, he met two extraordinary men who initiated him into Daoist secrets and began an exploration of Daoist cultivation. While identifying the two immortals as Zhongli Quan and Lü Dongbin, he also followed the teachings of Liu Haichan and certain Buddhist teachings. On this basis, he developed his own brand of internal alchemy. Although his main training took place in Shaanxi, near modern Xi'an, his main community building took place in Shandong, where he met and trained his main disciples who spread his teachings throughout the country (see Yao 2000; Zhang 1995).

His writings are collected in the *Chongyang quanzhen ji* 重陽全真集 (Complete Perfection according to Chongyang, DZ 1153), the *Chongyang jiaohua ji* 重陽教化集 (Instruction and Conversion according to Chongyang, DZ 1154), and the *Chongyang zhenren shou Danyang ershisi jue* 重陽真人授丹陽二十四訣 (24 Instructions of Perfected Chongyang to [Ma] Danyang, DZ 1158) (Schipper and Verellen 2004, 1158-60).

His main disciples, the Seven Perfected are Ma Yu 馬鈺 (Danyang 丹陽; 1123-1183), Tan Chuduan 谭處端 (Changzhen 長真; 1123-1185), Wang Chuyi 王處一 (Yuyang 玉陽; 1142-1217), Liu Chuxuan 劉處玄 (Changsheng 長生;

1147-1203), Qiu Chuji 邱處機 (Changchun 長春; 1148-1227), He Datong 郝大通 (Taigu 太古; 1140-1212), and the woman Sun Buer 孫不二 (Qingjing sanren 清靜散人; 1119-1182).[6] Some of them were born in the upper classes and owned land in Shandong, while others had some previous Daoist exposure or family connection. They all found themselves attracted to Wang's teachings and became his followers. When he died, after having trained them for several years, they joined together to accompany his coffin back to his hometown, then dispersed to teach the new methods all over the country, establishing separate lineages and creating a new dimension of Daoism.

The single most important of Wang's successors was Qiu Chuji. Having lost his parents at a young age, he became a Complete Perfection follower at age 19, completing his training under the master, he set out to develop his own community, creating the still-dominant Longmen 龍門 (Dragon Gate) lineage and ascending to the patriarchy upon the death of Liu Chuxuan in 1203. His main call to fame came in 1219, when Chinggis Khan—on the verge of conquering China—summoned him to his traveling court in Central Asia and empowered him as leader of all Chinese religions. In one stroke, Complete Perfection thus became the leading religious organization of the empire: it flourished greatly and established the position of central power it still holds today.

Lineage Structures

The Five Patriarchs of the Southern School and the Seven Perfected of Complete Perfection formed the core of internal alchemy as an organized institution; they were highly respected in many Daoist temples and communities. Although both lines focused on the cultivation of internal alchemy with the goal of oneness with the Dao, they also had important differences. The Five Patriarchs practiced mostly among ordinary people; they were neither formally recognized as Daoist monks nor did they have their own monasteries. They might be called popular masters or training guides for the common folk rather than Daoist leaders.

The Northern School, too, was originally a popular movement, Wang Chongyang never having been ordained or undergone formal training. Only after he established various centers and required celibacy and the adherence to monastic rules from his increasingly numerous followers did Complete Perfection become a formal institution. Similarly it was Chinggis Khan's appointment of Patriarch Qiu as leader of all Chinese religions that catapulted the organization to the political stage and caused its rise to national importance (see Yao 2000; Goossaert and Katz 2001). The transition from a folk cultivation group to a Daoist religious school was thus not complete until the mid-thirteenth cen-

---

[6] For sources on their lives and works, see Schipper and Verellen 2004, 1134-67. Other studies of Complete Perfection include Tsui 1991; Yao 2000; Komjathy 2007.

tury. Since then, the Northern School has continued to spread its influence and increasingly integrated the methods and teachings of the Southern School. In fact, the distinction between the two really only arose at the time of integration with the goal of making a difference among the early lineages. Before then, the terms Southern or Northern School simply did not exist.

The Southern School, moreover, only nominated the Five Patriarchs as its leaders *ex post facto*, when Bai Yuchan and his disciples in the Southern Song rose to success and constructed the lineage. Among *neidan* practitioners Bai Yuchan was known best for his wide range of knowledge and his extraordinary Daoist arts. He played an important role in promoting Daoism in society and encouraged its spread among the people. His unique contribution to internal alchemy was directly related to his effort at proliferating Daoist teachings. Connecting his ideas to the works of Zhang Boduan, he also instituted a relationship with the methods of Complete Perfection that were influenced by Zhong-Lü teachings. This resulted in the transition of internal alchemy from a loose oral tradition to an integrated, organized system. In addition, his lineage formation caused the distinction into Southern and Northern Schools and simplified the complex history of internal alchemy by reducing it to two main streams. The downside was that he did not include many other influential Daoists that had a major impact on internal alchemy, such as Shi Jianwu, Chen Tuan, and Liu Xiyu.

Zhong-Lü Teachings

The foundation of all later versions of internal alchemy lies in the teachings of the Zhong-Lü school, whose texts provide a systematic account of the principles, processes, and proposed results of the practice. To understand the variations that occur in later centuries and the modifications different schools imposed on the system, it is important to get a good grasp of the basic teachings. They can be summarized in three key concepts:

1) Human beings, in structure and rhythm, match Heaven and Earth while the human body is a microcosmic replica of the greater universe;

2) all cosmic and human patterns are governed by the continuous rise and fall of yin and yang;

3) at the root of creation, as well as of human gestation and growth, there is the power of pure yang, a potent, semi-material force that is completely primordial (of Before Heaven) yet pervades human and natural unfolding (see Yang 2001; 2004).

Heaven and Earth
The natural universe has a steady rhythm of rise and fall, a pattern of cycles and a system of internal organization that are pervasive and can be easily observed. The system is present not only in the natural world but also determines the internal patterns of the human body and life.

Expressing this system in terms of yin and yang, texts of the Zhong-Lü school typically set the beginning of the cycle in winter, when yin reaches its extreme and proceeds to generate yang. It reaches its pinnacle in the summer, when yang has risen to its utmost and begins to arise again. This in turn continues to grow until it reaches its zenith in winter and produces a new sprouting of yang. One complete cycle makes a full year and each month and day follows this cycle. It is thus due to the continuous, systematic interplay of yin and yang that the myriad beings are born, flourish, and decline.

In this context it is important to understand that, although the texts talk about yin and yang in separate terms and as different entities, they are really only aspects of one underlying cosmic *qi* that pervades all and is one with Dao. Rather than being independent agents, yin and yang just describe positions and energetic movements of the one *qi*.

Now, human beings as the most intelligent creatures among the myriad beings are much like Heaven and Earth and the human body is their microcosmic replica. Thus the biological rhythms of the human body closely match the cyclical movements of Heaven and Earth, and the macrocosmic transformations of the universe can elucidate microcosmic changes in the body. Just as yin and yang wax and wane in the course of a year, so the *qi* and blood circulate in the human body in the course of a day. Zhong-Lü materials in the *Daoshu* explains:

> At midnight (the *zi* hour), kidney *qi* begins to rise. In the early morning (*mao*), it moves to the liver, which is the storehouse of yang-*qi* and thus marks the rising of yang. As the *qi* arrives here, it matches the position of the spring equinox..
>
> At noon (*wu*), the *qi* arrives at the heart, where it accumulates and begins to generate fluids. This matches the summer solstice. Yang ascends to its utmost and gives rise of yin as the heart produces fluids. This matches the beginning of fall. This fluid next moves into the lungs, which are the storehouse of yin-*qi*. As the fluids reach their height, they begin to descend to a yin position. This matches the fall equinox.
>
> Finally, in the evening (*zi*), the fluids move to the kidneys and accumulation to generate yin-*qi*. This matches the time of the winter solstice. At this point, yin descends fully to Earth and begins to give rise to yang.
>
> The circulation of yin and yang is constant; it occurs daily. Maintaining this process smoothly one can reach long life.

The initial movement of *qi* in the kidneys, the generation of fluids in the heart, and the cyclic changes in the body are defining principles of microcosmic time in this system. Paying close attention to the four nodes in the day—midnight, morning, noon, and evening—Zhong-Lü masters matched them with the high points of the four seasons and created an integrated bodily rhythm that closely matches the natural cycle.

The goal of internal alchemy, then, is to make all body parts, and especially the inner organs, *qi*, blood, and fluids interact as smoothly as possible to create a continuous and undying pattern of energetic exchange. However, if the human body is already a complete system that functions as smoothly as Heaven and Earth, why do we need to practice? The explanation is that people cannot live forever because the *qi* of yin and yang in the biological system degenerates over time. It also has to do with the inherent nature of the inner organs which exchange *qi* according to the productive or controlling cycles, thus creating the potential for irregularities as well as damage or exhaustion over time. Thus human existence is not infinite, but suffers from limits of time and form.

Internal alchemy accordingly serves to promote the smooth circulation of yin and yang in the human body, thereby to prevent degeneration and entropy. As yin and yang interact smoothly and are refined to subtler and more primordial levels, moreover, they come to form the immortal embryo in the body. The texts call this "giving birth to a body within the body" and note that the creation of the immortal embryo provides the means of full attainment of Dao.

Yin and Yang

To reach this goal, practitioners consciously isolate and refine yin and yang energies within their bodies. They find them in the five inner organs, which they associate with directional, mythic animals and divine figures. Thus the liver is linked with the green dragon of the east and inhabited by the Pure Lad; the heart is related to the red bird of the south and the residence of the Young Lady; the lungs match the white tiger of the west and form the home of the Gold Immortal; the kidneys are related to the intertwined turtle and snake of the north and house the Divine Infant; and the spleen connects to the yellow dragon of the centerwhile providing the residence of the Yellow Dame.

In addition, the various body fluids have their own nomenclature, which changes depending on the degree of refinement. Thus there are the Golden Fluid, Jade Liquor, and Divine Water used for the saliva and various refined internal energies, as well as the flowery pond which is the poetic name of the mouth. Beyond that the Golden Bird and the Jade Rabbit designate the pure *qi* of heart water and kidney fire.

The latter are of particular importance, as the heart and kidneys are the seat of original fire and water. According to the understanding of traditional Chinese medicine, the heart is yang and the fire while the kidneys are yin and water. However, in Zhong-Lü internal alchemy, pure yin resides in the yang-*qi* of the heart and is called the dragon or the Golden Bird; similarly there is pure yang in the yin-*qi* of the kidneys, which is called the tiger or the Jade Rabbit. Practitioners extricate the pure yin and yang from their other elements to attain the raw materials of the process. Their intermingling and copulation, then, makes up the path of alchemical refinement. Zhongli Quan says:

> As practitioners focus their mind in concentration, they move the trigram Li [fire], which they extricate from their kidney-*qi*, to the heart. Breathing slowly through the nose and swallowing a full mouth of saliva, they allow the unification of the *qi* of the kidneys and the heart. This process generates the fluids. Next they move the trigram Kan [water], which they extricate from the fluids in the heart, to the kidneys and allow it to connect with the kidney-*qi*. As a result, there is pure fire in the fluids and pure water in the *qi*. They intertwine and intermingle. This is the copulation of dragon and tiger. With proper care and cultivation, they form a pure embryo in about three hundred days.

Blending the *qi* of the heart and kidneys is thus central to Zhong-Lü internal alchemy. Only by doing so can the immortal embryo be created and eventually evolve into a refined version of the adept's body: the body residing in the body, *qi* generating *qi*. Mixing the different forms of pure *qi* is thus the material basis of transcendence in Zhong-Lü internal alchemy

From here the system proceeds in a total of twelve stages. Adepts begin by consciously matching yin and yang, condensing and dispersing water and fire, and letting dragon and tiger intermingle. Next, they gather the elixir materials and sublimate them into vapid gold. From here, they enter more advanced levels. These involve reverting Jade Liquor into the elixir and circulating it around to refine the physical body. Following this, adepts harvest the Golden Fluid from their internal energies and merge it with the growing elixir, then circulate this for further refinement of body and mind. The last three steps are bowing to the primordial powers while cultivating *qi*, practicing inner observation for productive exchange, and—finally—shedding the physical form to ascend into Heaven. The system accommodates the key factors of picking the materials, fixing them in the body, adjusting the fire, creating a refined version of body and mind, and attaining oneness with Dao—all present throughout the later tradition, which adds more philosophical details and exact procedures as to how practitioners in their spirit form exit the physical body, attain Dao, and attain transcendence.

Pure Yang

Masters of the Zhong-Lü school, in their focus on water and fire in the heart and kidneys, also emphasize the concept of pure yang. They insist that, although pure yang and pure yin are valuable materials for internal cultivation, the final product of the immortal elixir is not a mere mixture of pure yin and pure yang, but pure yang. This seems to be not quite reasonable. How can an elixir created from pure yin and pure yang go beyond the field of yin and yang and reach into a state of pure yang?

The Zhong-Lü texts do not provide a clear explanation, but emphasize that pure yang manifests in three aspects. First, it is the domain of immortals, while pure yin is the realm of ghosts and yin-yang is the home of human beings. That is, human beings have a special position in the greater universe that sets them apart from celestials and the underworld and is not defined by any specific energy but allows communication with and transformation into others. Second, pure yang is the original seed material of the immortal elixir and thus forms the ultimate source of all internal cultivation. And third, pure yang is spirit, the indefinite power of mental and cosmic cohesion that allows practitioners to transcend the limitations of the physical human world and enter into the realm of no-form and ultimate being.

The concept of pure yang already played a role in Tang Daoist teachings. For example, the Daoist visionary and poet Wu Yun 吴筠 (d. 778) notes that the common people tend to destroy their inherent yang through their yin actions while Daoists refine their yin nature through yang cultivation and thus enjoy longevity and become immortals (see DeMeyer 2006). Before that, the notion was not common: the *Daode jing* gave priority to yin and emphasized the harmony between yin and yang. It was only under the influence of the *Yijing*, where three yang lines make up the trigram for Heaven (Qian) that the notion of pure yang entered into Daoist discourse.

In actual practice, pure yang is generated through the interaction of the internal organs in the body, especially the heart and kidneys, which are less biological organs than energetic constellations that hold the raw materials of the internal elixir. Zhong-Lü texts show the kidneys as being in charge of *qi* yet also containing pure water, i.e., the tiger. Similarly, they present the heart as being in charge of the body fluids yet also housing pure fire, i.e., the dragon. As pure dragon and tiger, these *qi* form the vital ingredients of internal refinement—sometimes also called, in imitation of external alchemy, the body's lead and mercury. The crucial task for practitioners is to move the pure dragon and tiger into the Yellow Court in the center of the abdomen and make them interact and penetrate each other until they produced the seed of the immortal embryo.

How, then, do these two energies come about? The pure *qi* in the fluids as generated in the heart comes originally from the liver, which receives it from the *qi* of the kidneys. Once the *qi* has reached the heart, it becomes manifest in the fluids, which in turn surround the pure *qi*, which is the dragon. According to this understanding, all original raw materials of internal cultivation go ultimately back to the kidneys. Masters of the Zhong-Lü school call them "the *qi* of the primordial elixir" and understand their generation as parallel to the fetal development during pregnancy. The fetus's growth in the womb begins with the kidneys, from which all the other organs grow: spleen, liver, lungs, heart, small intestine, large intestine, stomach, and gall bladder, leading on to the other parts of the body. The key organs are all *qi*-storing and yin in nature, thus the texts say that after the kidneys, the central "four organs in human beings all belong to yin."

The primordial pure yang-*qi* of the kidneys is present in everyone from birth. While it gives rise to the various other organs and bodily parts during embryonic gestation, in internal alchemy it transforms into divine fluids after having passed through the liver and the heart—transforming from original yin energies into powers of pure yang. The fluids then return to the kidneys via the lungs, thereby completing a full cycle of *qi* circulation.

The pure yang at the root of alchemical transformation, moreover, also matches the refined primordial *qi* at the root of creation in the greater universe, allowing practitioners to imitate cosmic movements of creation in their internal practice. Just as the pure yang circulates harmoniously in the body, so Heaven and Earth participate in an integrated cyclical system that never ends and never lessens. In other words, each entity that exists in the world, as much as the world as a whole, consists of a self-containing cycle of energetic vibration and circulation. All cycles match each other and move along in perfect alignment, both internally and externally. Internal alchemy thus works by coordinating practitioners' efforts with the patterns of the greater universe and realizing the magnitude of the whole within the confines of the human body. Both, moreover, rely ultimately on primordial *qi*, the pure yang power at the root of all being, which is not so much an identifiable, physical substance as a spiritual, generative power, the potent mover behind all. Utilizing this to the utmost, adepts can thus open the transcendent path toward ultimate Dao.

How, then, can we best understand this primordial, pre-creation *qi*? If it is something beyond our world, it is beyond time and space and part of the completely other, the "that." We call it "that" because we cannot find a better term to describe it. However if this *qi* is part of the "that," then it cannot really be the seed of internal alchemy. It is too far beyond the world to be subjected to empirical processes such as firing, increasing, refining, and so on. Yet, if primordial *qi* indicates a power that is of a manifest nature yet just happens to be prior to the empirical world, internal alchemy is finite, however much it strives to be completely transcendent and however much cosmology suggests its infinity. We are left to speculate on these issues: Zhong-Lü texts do not provide a detailed discussion of these philosophical issues.

Conclusion

Internal alchemy began with a group of thinkers and practitioners in the mid-Tang dynasty and reached its first formal expression in the teachings of the Zhong-Lü school in the early Song, which became foundational to all later schools. Masters of the school consciously separated their teachings from traditional forms of internal cultivation and developed their unique vision, methods, and terminology. They adopted many concepts and terms from external, operative alchemy as well as from the *Daode jing* and *Yijing*.

In terms of practice, they integrated internal cultivation methods common in the middle ages, yet made sure to set the school apart by criticizing thirty-one techniques as "lesser, heterodox methods." They insisted that only the specific set of Zhong-Lü practices and their systematic twelve-step path allowed practitioners to reach immortality and attain oneness with Dao. Beyond this, they also systematized the various methods they supported, classifying them into greater, medium, and lesser, and organized the otherworldly realm by dividing the immortals into five types: ghost, human, earth, spirit, and celestial, each with a unique position in the system. Most of all, the Zhong-Lü protagonists actively engaged in promoting an innovative cultivation system, which sets them clearly apart from the masters of previous dynasties.

Following in the wake of the Zhong-Lü school, internal alchemy divided into a Southern and a Northern strand, among which the Northern, the school of Complete Perfection, has remained dominant to the present day, integrating the various early schools as well as teachings created in later dynasties and adopting them organizationally in the form of sub sects and lineages. While there is, therefore, no clearly defined Zhong-Lü school or practice in today's system of internal alchemy, its influence has been pervasive and its teachings have remained present as an essential substratum of all the different forms.

Bibliography

Baldrian-Hussein, Farzeen. 1984. *Procédés secrets du joyau magique*. Paris: Les Deux Océans.

_____. 1986. "Lü Tung-pin in Northern Sung Literature." *Cahiers d'Extrême-Asie* 2: 133-70.

Bol, Peter K. 1992. *"This Culture of Ours": Intellectual Transitions in T'ang and Sung China*. Stanford: Stanford University Press.

Cleary, Thomas. 1986. *The Inner Teachings of Taoism*. Boston: Shambhala.

_____. 1987. *Understanding Reality: A Taoist Alchemical Classic by Chang Po-tuan*. Honolulu: University of Hawaii Press.

DeMeyer, Jan. 2006. *Wu Yun's Way: Life and Works of an Eighth-Century Daoist Master*. Leiden: E. Brill.

Ebrey, Patricia B., and Peter N. Gregory, eds. 1993. *Religion and Society in T'ang and Sung China*. Honolulu: University of Hawaii Press.

Fa Guolong 戈国龙. 2001. *Daojiao niedan xue tanwei* 道教内丹学探微.Chengdu: Bashu shushe.

_____. 2004. *Daojiao neidan xue shuoyuan* 道教内丹学溯源. Beijing: Zongjiao wenhua.

Fukui Kōjun 福井康順 et al., eds. 1990. *Daojiao* 道教. Translated by ZhuYueli 朱越利译 Shanghai: Shanghai guji.

Goossaert, Vincent, and Paul Katz. 2001. "New Perspectives on Quanzhen Taoism: The Formation of a Religious Identity." *Journal of Chinese Religions* 29: 91-94.

Haeger, John W, ed. 1975. *Crisis and Prosperity in Sung China*. Tucson: University of Arizona Press.

Hu Fuchen 胡孚琛. 1999. *Daoxue tonglun* 道学通论. Beijing: Shehui kexue wenxian.

Hymes, Robert P., and Conrad Shirokauer, eds. 1993. *Ordering the World: Approaches to State and Society in Sung Dynasty China*. Berkeley: University of California Press.

Katz, Paul R. 2000. *Images of the Immortal: The Cult of Lü Dongbin at the Palace of Eternal Joy*. Honolulu: University of Hawaii Press.

Komjathy, Louis. 2007. *Cultivating Perfection: Mysticism and Self-Transformation in Quanzhen Daoism*. Leiden: E. Brill.

Kracke, E.A. 1968. *Civil Service in Early Sung China*. Chicago: University of Chicago Press.

Lai, T. C. 1972. *The Eight Immortals*. Hong Kong: Swinden Book Co.

Li Ling 李零. 2000. *Zhongguo fangshu kaoxiu dingpan* 中国方术考修订版. Beijing: Dongfang.

Liu, James T.C. 1959. *Reform in Sung China: Wang An-shih (1021-1086) and His New Policies*. Cambridge, Mass: Harvard University Press.

Loon, Piet van der. 1984. *Taoist Books in the Libraries of the Sung Period*. London: Oxford Oriental Institute.

McKnight, Brian E. 1992. *Law and Order in Sung China*. Cambridge: Cambridge University Press.

Miyakawa, Hisayuki. 1974. "Legate Kao P'ien and a Taoist Magician, Lu Ying-chih, in the Time of Huang Ch'ao's Rebellion." *Acta Asiatica* 27: 75-99.

Pregadio, Fabrizio. 2000. "Elixirs and Alchemy." In *Daoism Handbook*, edited by ivia Kohn, 165-95. Leiden: E. Brill.

_____. 2006. *Great Clarity: Daoism and Alchemy in Early Medieval China*. Stanford: Stanford University Press.

Schipper, Kristofer, and Franciscus Verellen, eds. 2004. *The Taoist Canon: A Historical Companion to Daozang*. 3 vols. Chicago: University of Chicago Press.

Shiba, Yoshinobu. 1970. *Commerce and Society in Sung China*. Translated by Mark Elvin. Ann Arbor: University of Michigan, Center for Chinese Studies.

Tsui, Bartholomew P. M. 1991. *Taoist Tradition and Change. The Story of the Complete Perfection Sect in Hong Kong*. Hong Kong: Christian Study Centre.

Yang Lihua 杨立华. 1998. "Liang Song neidan daojiao ji qi yuanyuan yanjiu" 两宋内丹道教及其渊源研究. Ph. D. Diss., Beijing University, Beijing.

Yang, F. S. 1958. "A Study of the Origin of the Legend of the Eight Immortals." *Oriens Extremus* 5: 1-20.

Yao, Ted. 2000. "Quanzhen—Complete Perfection." In *Daoism Handbook*, edited by Livia Kohn, 567-93. Leiden: E. Brill.

Yetts, Percifal. 1916. "The Eight Immortals." *Journal of the Royal Asiatic Society* 1916, 773-807.

Zhang Guangbao 张广保. 1993 *Zhongguo fangshu xingqi daoyin quan* 中国方术行气导引卷. Beijing: Renmin Zhongguo.

_____. 1995. *Jin Yuan Quanzhen jiao neidan xinxing xue* 金元全真教内丹心性学. Beijing: Sanlian shushe.

_____. 1998. "Taiping jing: Neidandao de chengli" 太平经—内丹道的成立. In *Daojia wenhua yanjiu* 道家文化研究, edited by Chen Guying 陈鼓应, vol. 13. Beijing: Sanlian shushe.

_____. 2001. *Tang Song neidan daojiao* 唐宋内丹道教.Shanhai: Shanghai wenhua.

Zhang Yingming 张荣明. 1987. *Zhongguao gudai qigongyu xianqin zhexue* 中国古代气功与先秦哲学. Shangha: Shanghai renmin.

The Southern School

Cultivating Mind and Inner Nature

Xichen Lu[1]

The Song and Yuan dynasties saw important developments in internal alchemy, which grew into two key schools. One is the Southern School (Nanzong), also known as the school of the Golden Elixir (Jindan pai 金丹派); the other is the Northern School, also known as the Complete Perfection (Quanzhen 全真) (see Ren and Chen 1989; Skar 2000; Skar and Pregadio 2000; Sun 1968).

The alleged founder of the Southern school was Zhang Boduan 張伯端 (987-1082), a Sichuan aristocrat well versed in Confucianism, Buddhism, and Daoism as well as in astronomy, geography, medicine, and military strategy. After attempting to pass the civil service examination several times, he met the Daoist master Liu Haichan 劉海蟾 (fl. 1031) and studied with him (see Baldrian-Hussein 1976; Fa 1991). The tradition has him continue the methods of Zhongli Quan 鍾離權, Lü Dongbin 呂洞賓, and Chen Tuan 陳搏, and focus most strongly on the *Daode jing* 道德經 (Book of Dao and Its Virtue), *Yinfu jing* 音符經 (Scripture of Hidden Talismans), and *Zhouyi cantongqi* 周易慘同契 (Tally to the Book of Changes) in his internal alchemy theories.

Zhang specifically combines conceptual theory with practical exercise and divides the cultivation process into four stages: building the foundation; refining essence (*jing*) into vital energy (*qi*); cultivating *qi* into spirit (*shen*); and refining spirit to merge with or return to the void. He further integrates certain Buddhist principles, speaking of the illumination of the heart-and-mind (*xin* 心) and the opening of inner nature (*xing* 性) as part of the Daoist path. Doing so, he says, the adept can return to original nature (see Chen 1985).

---

[1] Translated and edited by Robin R. Wang.

Zhang's main work is a collection of poems known as the *Wuzhen pian* 悟真篇 (Awakening to Perfection; in *Xiuzhen shishu* [DZ 263]). Of central importance in internal alchemy, it has reached almost iconic status over the centuries and is still essential for practitioners.[2] Zhang Boduan's teachings were transmitted to Shi Tai 石泰 (d. 1158); from him, they passed on to Xue Zixian 薛紫賢 (d. 1191), Chen Nan 陳楠 (d. 1213), and Bai Yuchan 白玉蟾 (1194-1229). Together they form the Five Patriarchs of the Southern School (*nanzong wuzhu* 南宗五主). Among them, Bai Yuchan was most influential,[3] his philosophy of the heart-and-mind and inner nature represents the key teachings of the school.

Mind Cultivation

For Zhang Boduan, the cultivation of mind and inner nature is the foundation of internal alchemy. In this he differs significantly from the Zhong-Lü school, associated with the legendary figures Zhongli Quan and Lü Dongbin, which flourished in the late Tang and early Song dynasties. Zhong-Lü methods focused mainly on the cultivation of essence and *qi*, but left out the mind-and-heart, which in their system refers merely to the function of one of the five inner organs. According to them, the kidneys match water and manifest in the will, the heart matches fire and manifests in the mind/spirit, the liver matches wood and manifests in the spirit soul, the lungs match metal and manifest in the material soul, and the spleen matches earth and manifests in the intention.

Unlike this, in Zhang Boduan the concept of mind-and-heart has gained a new level of conceptual importance. He makes a distinction between "the mind of the Golden Elixir" and "the mind of daily life." Taking action and dealing with everyday affairs means to employ the mind of daily life; nonaction, on the other hand, signifies the mind of the Golden Elixir as it appears in advanced practitioners. Using the mind of the Golden Elixir to deal with events, one can manifest "true nature" or "original spirit." However, most people have lost the connection to their original state of being, having been polluted by postnatal constraints and the social environment. People are unable to manifest the mind of the Golden Elixir or deal with beings using an attitude of nonaction. Therefore there is a great need to diligently cultivate the mind and improve the ability to adjust it. *Neidan* cultivation will allow it to attain a pure and quiet state and manifest true and original nature. The emphasis placed in Zhang's system on

---

[2] Translations and discussions include Cleary 1987; Fukui 1987; Imai 1962; Ren 1990.

[3] For more on this lineage, its construction, and the works involved, see Boltz 1987, 173-79. Bai Yuchan was a Confucian but he killed someone due to a conflict. He retired to Mount Wuyi and studied with the Daoist master Chen Nan. A detailed study of his life and work appears in Wang 2004. An examination of his thought is found in Liang 1993.

mental and meditative cultivation thus marks an important distinction from previous practices which focused more on breathing and longevity exercises.

Zhang's system follows the basic *neidan* stages of transforming essence into *qi* (energy), *qi* into spirit, and spirit into Dao, but he places the cultivation of mind and inner nature first, paying only secondary attention to the concept of destiny, the more physical dimension of the practice. His idea of inner nature is truly comprehensive, complete with ontological and epistemological elements. He identifies it in three ways: as the power behind the spirit which governs essence and *qi* and thus the ability to adjust consciousness in an appropriate way; as the root of the living person, everyone's primordial human nature; and as the source of ethical and psychological patterns, an inherent level of moral discipline and personal identity.

For Zhang, the mind too is an essential substance full of ontological meaning. On the one hand, it is a universal principle that guides the myriad beings; on the other hand, it is the carrier of inner nature. As he says: "Mind is the house of inner nature." Inner nature is implicit in the mind and comes from it. This shows that mind connects destiny or biological life with inner nature or the person's spiritual identity; it serves as a bridge between inner nature and destiny. In other words, he claims that inner nature and destiny cannot be directly controlled by human voluntary consciousness.

In modern psychological terms, this means that there is a level within human beings, the "primordial inner nature," that is hidden deeply in the subconscious and not easily accessible to conscious manipulations. However, there is a way in which one can limit or even eliminate the worldly mind of daily usage and instead allow the mind of the Golden Elixir to shine forth and take over, even in the management of ordinary events. To do so, one must maintain a tranquil and deeply peaceful state of mind. In other words, through the cultivation of mind one can enter the level of the subconscious and find oneness with Dao. Doing so, the primordial spirit will appear. The mind being completely empty and at peace, moreover, it comes to regulate the movement of essence and *qi*, thus affecting the health of body. Arguing in this manner, Zhang claims that the mind has the function of "mastering all beings" and can adjust the relationship of inner nature and destiny.

Chen Nan, Zhang Boduan's disciple and Bai Yuchan' teacher, places an even greater emphasis on the role of the mind in internal alchemy. This is made clear in a discussion with Bai Yuchan. According to the *Xiuxian bianhuo lun* 修仙辯惑論 (To Discriminate Errors in Immortal Cultivation, in *Xiuzhen shishu* 修真十書 [DZ 263]), he divides the methods of internal alchemy into three levels: upper, middle, and lower, then says:

> The upper method utilizes the spirit, the spirit soul, the material soul, and the will as key medicinal ingredients; it applies practice while walking, staying, sitting, and reclining as adjustable fire, thereby allowing a natural movement and unfolding of the elixir.

> The middle method makes use of the liver, heart, spleen, and lungs as key medicinal ingredients; it applies years, months, days, and hours as adjustable fire, thereby leading to a state of embracing emptiness and guarding the One.
>
> The lower method uses essence, blood, marrow, and *qi* as key medicinal ingredients; it applies closing, swallowing, touching, and massaging as adjustable fire, thus involving the practice of visualization in descending and ascending motion.

The cultivation of inner nature through spirit, the souls, and the will as raw medicinal ingredients of the divine elixir is thus the highest way. As Zhang Boduan already points out in his *Qinghua biwen* 青華秘文 (Secret Texts of Qinghua, DZ 240), most important in this context is deep absorptive meditation, which he describes as "concentration and quiet sitting." This is a state of thinking without thinking, a complete oneness within the meditation itself that results in a state of calm day after day, like a hen sitting on her eggs waiting for them to hatch. "When the spirit returns and the *qi* circulates, one will naturally witness the opening of the ultimate gate. It is so great, there is nothing beyond it; it is so small, there is nothing within it. From this position, one then picks the primordial *qi*, the mother of the Golden Elixir. Then one diligently cultivates it until one reaches the level of the immortals," Bai Yuchan notes in his *Liangzhu zhixuan pian* 梁著指玄篇 (Liang's Pointers to the Mystery, ed. *Xiuzhen shishu*).

Like Chen Nan, Ban Yuchan also underlines the importance of mind cultivation in internal alchemy. In this same work, he clearly recognizes the relationship between inner nature (as representing the physical form or body) and spirit (the force in the person that connects to the heavenly realm). He claims that:

> In inner nature, the spirit is master; the spirit is the core of inner nature. In the spirit, inner nature is highest; inner nature is the core of the spirit. Uniting the spirit as manifest in the body with the inner nature of the spirit is called returning to the root and extending life. This creates clear Dao and a pure heart.

Spirit is thus the leader in the relationship of body and mind; it endows the body with life and vigor. Cultivation of mind is the highest mental activity in the relationship between spirit and mind. It activates the individual's potential and gives a new meaning to the person's mental activities. If through cultivation of mind one can penetrate all mental activities, one will be able to awaken to the Dao.

In his *Haiqiong Bai zhenren yulu* 海瓊白真人語錄 (Recorded Sayings of the Perfected Bai Haiqiong, DZ 1307), Bai Yuchan further discusses the importance of mental cultivation in internal alchemy. He says:

> All the various methods are really only methods of the mind. Methods are the minister of the mind; the mind is the ruler of all methods. The mind is the master of inner nature [the body]. The mind is the house of the spirit. A tranquil and peaceful mind brings about an efficient spirit. If the mind is distracted, spirit will go away or fall into a rage.
>
> An empty mind, on the other hand, brings about the concentration of positive *qi*. A simple and pure mind leads to the harmony of yang. Blood and *qi* are not obstructed and can flow smoothly. If will and intention can be in a state of nonaction, all desires come to rest. There are no distracted thoughts in the mind and the intention is not distracted into outside affairs. Then the mind constantly returns to oneness and flows naturally.

Mental cultivation is thus most important. Practitioners must keep the mind empty and quiet at all times while using the body as the furnace to refine essence, *qi*, and spirit to eventually attain the Golden Elixir and oneness with Dao.

The cultivation of the mind as understood in the Southern School also involves aspects of psychological training and moral discipline. It treasures human life and is concerned with the creation of values and personal meaning. In this, it shifts away from earlier tendencies that focused dominantly on caring for the body and one's biological life. Rather, it is serious about the exploration of spiritual life and mental attainment in practitioners. In this, it not only gives new direction to internal alchemy but also broadens it to new dimensions. It develops Tang tendencies by providing deeper and more profound discussions of the key elements of essence, *qi*, and spirit.

Oneness with Dao

Awakening to Dao and attaining oneness with it are key goals of all Daoists; they form the ultimate purpose of Daoist cultivation. However, the precise ways in which adepts are to attain these goals differ from school to school.

Texts of the Zhong-Lü school tend to remain rather vague with regard to defining internal alchemy and its outlines are often inconsistent. For example, the *Zhong-Lü chuandao ji* 鐘呂傳道集 (Zhongli's Transmission of Dao to Lü: A Collection; in *Xiuzhen shishu* 14-16) says that "refining essence generates perfect *qi*, cultivating *qi* leads to oneness with spirit, and cultivating spirit leads to oneness with the Great Dao." On the other hand, it also says that one should "use complete destiny to unite with Dao" and that human beings are "most precious among the myriad beings. Only human beings can exhaust the principles of all beings, understand true nature, protect destiny, and guard life to attain oneness with Dao." This latter statement sounds very much as if one should find oneness with Dao from the level of destiny or physical cultivation and shows that the masters of the Zhong-Lü school had not reached full clarity about the relationship of cultivation and awakening to Dao.

"Using complete destiny to unite with Dao" is also rather unclear. Destiny usually refers to the physical energies of essence, *qi*, and other material substances in the body. "Complete destiny" thus seems to mean that one should best cultivate oneself on the biological level. In fact, through this cultivation adepts can only enhance their material frame but will not be able to realize oneness with Dao. This is because Dao penetrates all yet transcends their material levels. It is impossible to be with Dao merely by having an attitude of complete destiny or by being dedicated to guarding life.

In other words, in the Zhong-Lü tradition, Dao that is attained by realizing complete destiny is not the constant or ineffable Dao at the center of creation. This Dao manifests itself in all forms of existence and transcends all beings; one can only become one with it through the spirit and thus through the cultivation of the mind-and-heart. This cultivation can bring about enlightenment to the Great Dao and allow practitioners to enter the realm of "cultivating essence to generate perfect *qi*, cultivating *qi* to unite with the yang spirit, and cultivating the spirit to attain oneness with Dao."

Zhang Boduan recognized this problem and clarified the intrinsic relationship between Dao and the specific forms of cultivation in internal alchemy. In his *Wuzhen pian*, he says: "Dao comes from the ultimate void and generates the one *qi*; the one *qi* generates yin and yang; yin and yang merge in harmony and form a triad. The triad then brings forth all life, and the myriad beings flourish" (ch. 12) This outline matches the model of cosmic evolution as already formulated in the *Daode jing*. "Dao brings forth the One, the One generates the Two, the Two produce the Three, and the Three create the myriad beings" (ch. 41). Just as Dao brings forth the one *qi*, from which first yin and yang and then the multiplicity of life evolve, so individual Daoists are to cultivate their *qi* and transform it to produce the Golden Elixir through the interaction of yin and yang. The system matches the cosmic pattern of creation, reversing the way in which the myriad beings generate, transform, and form a triad with Heaven and Earth.

Now, the basic feature of the transformative Dao is the notion of the flowing transformations (*zaohua* 造化). Zhang suggests that practitioners should know and experience the flowing transformations, yet in their cultivation focus on its reversal: returning to the root and going back to original Dao. He explains that as yin and yang return to the One, the elixir will naturally mature and spread throughout the body. By placing the *Daode jing*'s teaching of returning to the root into the framework of alchemical practice, Zhang elucidates the core of reversal cultivation: "The myriad beings all return to their roots. Returning to the root is the constancy of existence." Cultivation thus enables adepts to go against the natural order of progress and unfolding; it redirects the processes of aging, sickness, and death, and allows practitioners to preserve eternal youth. Zhang also notes that this method of reversal is very difficult to grasp for ordinary people. The goal of his work is to help people learn about this cultivation. At the same time, to prevent improper people from adapting and possibly abusing it, he employs highly obscure language and uses many images and analogies.

Bai Yuchan continues Zhang's theory of the close connection and even unity of mind and Dao. In his *Liangzhu zhixuan pian*, he claims that "the mind is the Dao" and explicates the position of Dao in more detail. For him, Dao is the ultimate being beyond all restrictions and limitations. He says:

> Dao exists everywhere in the universe and is not affected by beings. It manifests first in primordial *qi* prior to all existence and ultimately is nothing but emptiness and nothingness. It is mysterious and cannot be measured in any way. It is so large that there is nothing beyond it; so small that there is nothing inside it. It is so great that it contains all of Heaven and Earth; so tiny that it can enter even a feather. Sages rely on their mind to connect with it. This is what we call Dao.

Dao for Bai is thus not only the resource of all life. Oneness with Dao is also a necessary prerequisite for longevity. As he notes in his *Haiqiong wendao ji* 海瓊問道集 (Haiqiong's Enquiry of the Dao, DZ 1308):

> Everyone receives life because of the primordial *qi* of Dao. At first the person is joined in *qi* with the mother inside the womb, then he or she is born in the world and has the umbilical cord cut off. From this point onward, the primordial *qi* rests in the elixir field.
>
> This perfect *qi* continues a direct link to the Gate of Heaven and thus connects the person to Heaven. It rises up to enter the Niwan Palace in the head; it moves down to enter the elixir field in the abdomen. Thus a passageway of perfect *qi* is opened.
>
> Rid yourself of desires and perfect *qi* will begin to unfold. Then the body flows into a state of no-form and becomes one with Dao. As such it can will live for eternity. So we think: If Dao is already in the body, why not respect it?

Bai Yuchan's internal alchemy integrates the Buddhist concept of mind and he often refers to his personal experiences of Buddhist meditation. The mind is thus an important factor in his understanding of internal alchemy. "If there are no distractive thoughts, the will will not go out and the mind will be constantly at one. If then the will moves naturally, the mind will be enlightened." Bai uses Buddhist conceptions of mind and inner nature to elucidate a deeper understanding of the link between mind and Dao. According to him, Dao is nonsubstantial existence while the mind can reach the stage of pure emptiness. An utterly calm mind can be alight with Dao and get close to it. Again, the *Haiqiong wendao ji*:

> Dao does not desire emptiness, but emptiness returns to it naturally. Similarly, if human beings empty their minds, Dao will return to them naturally. Dao is originally nameless: it cannot be reached nearby; it

> cannot be lost in the distance. It is neither square nor circular, neither inside nor outside. Only the sage can intuit it in a state where the three poisons have no root and the six desires have no seeds. This is true enlightenment: a state that is part of emptiness and nonbeing.

This shows how important it is to cultivate Dao. The early part of the passage clearly reflects ancient Daoist thought, developing concepts of "flowing with Dao and joining emptiness." But the last sentence has a strong Buddhist flavor, emphasizing enlightenment and emptiness. Thus Bai brings Buddhist teaching into Daoism.

In the same work, Bai also emphasizes the intrinsic connection and even unity between mind and Dao. He sates: "To attain Dao, one relies on the mind; the mind is Dao;" and: "If the mind is empty, it will be at one with Dao. As long as the mind is not empty, it is contrary to the Dao." Dao, superior and noble, exists in everyone's mind; there is no need to seek it outside of oneself. Following the instructions of the great masters and diligently engaging in cultivation, one can come to grasp Dao. However, Dao cannot be known through the senses, such as ears, eyes, mouth, and nose. Nor can one reach it through the normal channels of conscious, intellectual knowing. The only way to attain it is though an enlightened mind-and-heart. One should thus use the pure mind to unite with Dao and apply Dao to join the mind. Then subject and object can become one. As Bai says in the *Liangzhu zhixuan pian*:

> Use the pure mind to become one with Dao: this is Dao. Understand Dao to meet the mind: this is mind. Dao is satiated in mind and mind is satiated in Dao. There is no other Dao outside of the mind and there is no other thing outside of Dao.

This line of thinking is very similar to the Buddhist view that "mind is principle." But Bai's view on the relationship between mind and Dao is deeper and more concrete. The mind of the practitioner and the ontological Dao at the root of existence become one, and all sensory distinctions disappear. One has a mystical experience. Dao and mind extend to their greatest dimension, opening a state that cannot be described in words. Continuing his explication in the *Liangzhu zhixhuan pian*, Bai says: "The greatness of Dao cannot be described; if you can describe it, it is not Dao. The ultimate Dao is void and mysterious. The vastness of mind cannot be compared; if it is comparable, it is not the perfect mind. The perfect mind is clear and acute." Through the cultivation of mind and inner nature, practitioners can thus attain a high level of spiritual attainment and psychological skills in their experience of oneness with Dao.

The Practice of Inner Nature

The Southern School did not just enhance the theoretical dimension of internal alchemy; it also focused on practical procedures. After the Tang dynasty, the discussion on how to control the fire in *neidan* cultivation had moved increasingly from the abstract and general to the concrete—a pattern that reflects the overall development of internal alchemy. The Southern School's procedures on how to cultivate inner nature and destiny thus offer a meaningful resource on actual practice.

Zhang Boduan contends that the best way to create the inner elixir is to begin with the cultivation of destiny, then move on to the cultivation of inner nature. In other words, one should start with clear action and end with nonaction. The cultivation of destiny is action, that is, following concrete, physical methods to cultivate longevity. The cultivation of inner nature, on the other hand, is nonaction; it reflects a stage of the complete integration of essence, *qi*, and spirit with no more need for specific methods. At this level, adepts only need to maintain their cultivation in a state of nonaction. Why, then, does Zhang emphasize that one should first cultivate physical nature or destiny and only then move on to refine the heart-and mind or inner nature?

To begin, we can say that destiny is the carrier of inner nature. One must have a good destiny: one needs a healthy and well-functioning body as the foundation for seeking inner nature. Without that, how can inner nature be? Zhang recognizes that most people know the importance of nonaction but do not understand that in order to practice nonaction, one must have physical action as a basis. Liu Yiming 劉一明 (1733—1821),[4] the Qing Daoist master and scholar explains this in his *Wuzhen zhizhi* 悟真直指 (Direct Pointers to Awakening to Perfection, ZW 253):

> In the way of the Golden Elixir, one must develop action to return to the primordial and cultivate the treasure of destiny. Once one obtains the treasure of destiny and has stabilized it to the point where it no longer changes, one can guard the One and merge with the way of nonaction. In this manner one attains true nature and reaches highest Dao.

This shows that the cultivation of destiny comes first; inner nature is established later, on a higher level. Nonaction in the cultivation of inner nature, moreover, is the highest stage; it must be founded on action, which means concrete physical cultivation. Without this foundation, one cannot attain highest Dao.

---

[4] For more on Liu Yiming, his life and work, see Esposito 2000, 631-32. A translation of his *Yijing* commentary is found in Cleary 1986.

The methods of destiny are comparatively easy to understand and follow. In contrast, Zhang Boduan in his *Wuzhen pian* claims that the way of inner nature is more mystical and much harder to grasp. It is, therefore easier to begin the transformative process with the cultivation of destiny. As he has it:

> The "empty mind" [as reached through the cultivation of inner nature] and the "full stomach" [representative of the cultivation of destiny] both have profound meanings. The empty mind requires the clear recognition of the heart-and-mind; it might be better to begin by cultivating mercury [i.e., operative alchemy and the cultivation of bodily essence and *qi*] to attain the full stomach. (ch. 19)

The Qing Daoist Dong Dening 董德寧, in his commentary to the *Wuzhen pian* (ZW 397), similarly explains that the empty mind is based the recognition of the mind and the proper seeing of inner nature. He compares it to moon-light reflected in water: it is hard to get. Instead of trying to reach out for the impossible, it is thus better to begin by working toward the full stomach, that is, to cultivate essence and *qi*. Overall, there seems to be a strong agreement that adepts should first cultivate essence and *qi* to stabilize the elixir in the body, then turn to the cultivation of mind and realize their true, original nature.

However, the cultivation of destiny and that of inner nature are intrinsically related and cannot be separated. The way of destiny is the foundation, while the way of inner nature is the goal. Yet both also go closely together, and the cultivation of destiny on the practical and physical level depends on the cultivation of inner nature on the spiritual level. That is to say, one can only succeed in cultivating destiny if one disregards social status and profit, restricts desires, and practices moral goodness in cooperation with others. All these lead to the fundamentally necessary state of calm mind and harmonious internal *qi*. It will further lead to a state of complete internal, biological harmony which is essential for the formation of the elixir. It thus becomes clear that mental concentration, the active cessation of all thoughts and ideas and establishment of a deeply calm state of mind, is a key method for the cultivation of inner nature as much as the foundation of the cultivation of destiny.

In accordance with this notion, Zhang Boduan points out that an elementary practice of quiet sitting or meditation must begin with breath control and lead to the attainment of a completely "unmoving mind," a state of deep inner calm. Only when the mind is tranquil can true inner nature be attained. Along the same lines, in the cultivation of destiny, one must control internal fire through the spirit and the will—the foundation of mental power and its active function, respectively. Adjusting the movements of essence and *qi* thus requires a great deal of mental stability and control over inner nature. This means that the condition of internal fire depends on the profound "ability of endurance"—an ability developed through controlling mind and enhancing inner nature. This ability is a power of psychological control and depends closely on moral cultivation. Practitioners must purify the mind, eliminate desires, and take control of their thoughts. In this way they can adjust the firing times and avoid its excess or depletion.

Zhang also places a great deal of emphasis on moral discipline for successfully overcoming various obstacles in the cultivation of destiny. In the *Wuzhen pian*, he claims: "There is an easy or a hard way in cultivation. It depends on me as well as on Heaven. If one does not accumulate virtue, there will be ghosts that bring about numerous obstacles" (ch. 56). "Depends on me" refers to the practitioner's self-motivation and moral behavior; "depends on Heaven" indicates one's internal genetic conditions and the luck one encounters in the world. Both these come about naturally and cannot be sought out. Thus, "depends on me" means that one consciously makes an effort to accumulate virtue and behave morally. If one does not accumulate goodness, cultivation will be interrupted by ghosts and demons—which can only be held at bay through moral cultivation. Although Zhang thus places the cultivation of destiny first, he still brings the moral cultivation of inner nature into the process of destiny refinement.

According to Zhang, the cultivation of destiny is therefore a technical working procedure, which yet relies on a fundamental psychological aptitude and the accumulation of virtue and goodness as necessary conditions. After the cultivation of destiny one uses it to nourish inner nature and cultivate spirit to ultimately return to emptiness. Eventually one reaches a stage beyond life and death, good and evil:. This is the world of ultimate moral freedom. In his *Wuzhen pian*, he makes the case for cultivating destiny but his main point throughout remains the importance of cultivating inner nature and moral discipline.

Bai Yuchan's Vision

Bai Yuchan continues Zhang Boduan's vision of dual cultivation: he similarly places destiny first and inner nature second. However, he also emphasizes the importance of "concentrating spirit" while on the level of bodily cultivation. He says: "The mystic advantage of physical cultivation is rooted in concentrating the spirit. As the spirit is concentrated, *qi* is collected; as *qi* is collected, the inner elixir approaches completion" (*Haiqiiong wendao ji*). This indicates that although the cultivation of destiny is the first step in the process of internal alchemy, completing the elixir still rests on concentrating the spirit. Similarly, a successful cultivation of destiny assists the empowerment and good condition of the mind and inner nature. "When the elixir is complete, the physical form will be stabilized; once the physical body is stabilized, the spirit will be complete," he says.

Compared to Zhang Boduan, Bai Yuchan incorporates more Buddhist cultivation methods and places a greater emphasis on the role of inner nature in relation to destiny. He notes that spirit is the subject while essence and *qi* are objects that serve mainly as carriers of the spirit. If essence and *qi* are not strong and properly stored, the spirit has no place to stay. This position further elevates inner nature in the process. In addition, he also offers a more concrete interpretation of inner nature and destiny: "Spirit is inner nature," he says; "it belongs to the trigram Li (fire). *Qi* is destiny; it belongs to the trigram Kan (water)" (*Liangzhu zhixuan pian*). Inner nature thus refers to human consciousness, the force that controls all mental functions, while destiny indicates essence and *qi*, the material and biological elements of the person. Cultivating the former accordingly has a more significant place in Bai's teaching.

Refining one's disposition and transforming *qi* open the gate to Daoist cultivation. At the same time, empting the mind and calming the spirit form the foundation of elixir cultivation. Bai also tries to correct the common tendency to focus on the way of destiny (action) while disregarding the way of inner nature (nonaction). He notes that cultivation is not primarily about circulating or transforming bodily essence and *qi*. Rather, the cultivation of mind and inner nature is most essential. It means to cultivate no-mind and attain a state of utmost emptiness and inner clarity. Practices relating to inner nature are thus most vital in his teaching, however much he may laud the dual cultivation of inner nature and destiny.

Beyond integrating Buddhist notions into the vision of the Southern School, Bai also adopts Confucian teachings of limiting desires and nourishing the flood-like *qi*, which are originally methods of moral cultivation and psychological adjustment. He reinterprets them to have a direct impact on the cultivation of destiny, just as the person's level of internal cultivation. Again, his vision clearly focuses on the essential importance of the cultivation of mind and inner nature.

Bai's unique approach is most obvious when he talks about the "seven returns and nine reversions" (*qifan jiuhuan* 七反九還). Usually, these refer to a series of cultivation stages, in the course of which the Three Treasures (essence, *qi*, and spirit) become one and return to the primordial state. In contrast to most writers who praise these stages as highly mysterious and complex, Bai claims that they are not mysterious at all. Rather, they simply refer to a return to original meaning and are nothing but an expression of the method of "no mind as and no ideas as ideas." Thus he says in his *Liangzhu zhixuan pian*:

> Seven and nine are yang numbers. If one realizes no-mind as mind, no ideas as ideas, and reaches the summit of clarity, one attain the stage of purest yang. At this moment, the body disappears . . . and there is a body outside of the body. It is an extraordinary event. Emptiness is broken, and the whole body appears.

Altogether, the Southern School thus combines Laozi's theory of nonaction and no-mind with various cultivation methods of internal alchemy, Buddhist views of cosmic principle and enlightenment, and Confucian moral discipline. It shifts the cultivation focus from the outer body to the inner self and continues the tradition of the dual cultivation of destiny and inner nature, with a strong tendency to emphasize mind and inner nature over body and destiny. At the same time, it develops the meditative techniques that strengthen inner nature, both to help in the cultivation of destiny and to attain ultimate oneness with Dao. The school thus enhances the intrinsic link between the cultivation of the biological and spiritual life and creates a new level of philosophical and technical maturity in internal alchemy.

Bibliography

Baldrian-Hussein, Farzeen. 1976. "Chang Po-tuan." In *Sung Biographies*, edited by Herbert Franke, 1: 26-29. Wiesbaden: Franz Steiner.

_____. 1984. *Procédés secrets du joyau magique*. Paris: Les Deux Océans.

Boltz, Judith M. 1987. *A Survey of Taoist Literature: Tenth to Seventeenth Centuries*. Berkeley: University of California, China Research Monograph 32.

Chen Bing 陳兵. 1985. "Jindan pai Nanzong qiantan" 金丹派與南宗淺談. *Shijie zongjiao yanjiu* 世界宗教研究 1985/4: 35-49.

Cleary, Thomas. 1986. *The Taoist I Ching*. Boston: Shambhala.

_____. 1987. *Understanding Reality: A Taoist Alchemical Classic by Chang Po-tuan*. Honolulu: University of Hawaii Press.

Esposito, Monica. 2000. "Daoism in the Qing (1644-1911)." In *Daoism Handbook*, edited by Livia Kohn, 623-58. Leiden: E. Brill.

Fan Guangchun 犯廣春. 1991. "Zhang Boduan shengping kaobian" 張伯端生平考辨. *Zhongguo daojiao* 宗教道教 1991/4: 12-16.

Fukui Fumimasa 福井文雅. 1987. "Goshin hen no kōsei ni tsuite" 悟真篇の形成について. *Tōhōshūkyō* 東方宗教 70: 22-37.

Imai Usaburō 今井宇三郎. 1962. "Goshinhen no seishō to shisō" 悟真篇の形程と思想. *Tōhōshūkyō* 東方宗教 19: 1-19.

Komjathy, Louis. 2002. *Title Index to Daoist Collections*. Cambridge, Mass.: Three Pines Press.

Li Yuanguo 李遠國. 1988. *Qigong jinghua ji* 氣功精華集. Chengdu: Ba-Shu shushe.

Liang Dapeng 梁大朋. 1993. "Bai Yuchan de daoxing yu xueshu" 白玉蟾的道性與學術. In *Hainan wenhua lunwen ji* 海南文化論文記, 27-47. Taipei: Hanhua wenwu.

Ren Linhao 任林豪. 1990. "Zhang Boduan yu *Wuzhen pian* ji nanzong de chuancheng" 張伯端與悟真篇紀南宗的傳承. *Dongnan wenhua* 東南文化 1990/6: 65-75.

_____, and Chen Xiaoji 陳肖技. 1989. "Daojiao nanzong kaolue" 道教南宗考略. *Zhongguo daojiao* 中國道教 1989/1: 23-33.

Robinet, Isabelle. 1995. *Introduction à l'alchimie intérieure taoïste: De l'unité et de la multiplicité*. Paris: Editions Cerf.

Skar, Lowell. "Ritual Movements, Deity Cults, and the Transformation of Daoism in Song and Yuan Times." In *Daoism Handbook*, edited by Livia Kohn, 413-63. Leiden: E. Brill.

_____, and Fabrizio Pregadio. 2000. "Inner Alchemy (*Neidan*)." In *Daoism Handbook*, edited by Livia Kohn, 464-97. Leiden: E. Brill.

Sun Kekuan 孫克寬. 1968. *Yuandai daojiao zhi fazhan* 元代道教之發展. Taichung: Donghai daxue.

Wang, Li. 2004. "A Daoist Way of Transcendence: Bai Yuchan's Inner Alchemical Thought and Practice." Ph. D. Diss., University of Iowa, Des Moines.

Neidan Methods for Opening the Gate of Heaven

Stephen Eskildsen

Zhang Yuanhua 張元化, was the cleric in charge of the Beiji guan 北極觀 (North Culmen Temple) in Rufen 汝墳 (Henan). He flourished during the Taiping Xingguo reign (976-984) and was a highly acclaimed master of Daoist rituals and healing techniques, i.e., talismans and medicines. On numerous occasions he displayed clairvoyance and extraordinary prowess at detecting and vanquishing demons. He also secretly engaged in self-cultivation, although nobody knew what methods he practiced.

One evening Zhang appeared in the dreams of people throughout the prefecture, bidding them farewell. The same night, he suddenly died in his sleep. During his burial, his coffin was extremely heavy; it was as though it was loaded with stones and iron objects. After a libation and prayer were administered, the coffin became lighter. Just before lowering the coffin into the ground, the mourners opened the lid to look inside. On top of his head they discovered a hole large enough to put an arm into. "People who knew" (*shizhe* 識者) remarked, "this is [what is called] the cicada shedding its shell" (*chanshui* 蟬蛻).

One day not long thereafter, Zhang appeared before a pomegranate hawker. He introduced himself, handed him a letter, purchased some pomegranates and told him to deliver these to the Beiji guan. When his disciples there saw the letter they indeed recognized their master's writing. They took the hawker into the Portrait Hall (*yingtang* 影堂) to view the master's portrait; he confirmed that this was indeed the man he had encountered. The narrative ends by stating that locals "up to the present" like to make portraits of him and worship him. It also mentions that he composed a "Recycled Elixir Lesson" and some short poems in order to transmit the way of self-cultivation to the world.

The above narrative is found in the *Lishi zhenxian tidao tongjian* 歷世真仙體道通鑑 (Comprehensive Mirror through the Ages of Perfected Immortals and Those Who Embody the Dao, DZ 296; 48.2a-4a), the massive compendium of Daoist hagiography compiled by the Yuan period cleric, Zhao Daoyi 趙道一 (fl. 1294-1307). The story apparently claims that the renowned wonder-working cleric Zhang Yuanhua attained immortality by liberating his spirit from his body through a hole in the head. When the corpse was put in the coffin, Zhang's spirit had still not left—which seems to be why the coffin was heavy—but it did leave once some sort of prayer and libation was administered. The coffin became light, and a gaping hole was discovered in the head of the corpse. The ensuing portion of the narrative then sets out to demonstrate that Zhang's liberated spirit was indeed alive and could readily appear before the living—not as some sort of hazy ghost but in a solid body no different from that of a living person: it could even purchase fruit and wield a brush. Also, Zhang appeared in people's dreams shortly before undergoing physical death. This may indicate that he was able to project his spirit in and out of his body even before his final, dramatic liberation.

The story may well imply that Zhang's secret method of self-cultivation was internal alchemy. Although the specific soteriological claims of *neidan* texts vary, they typically claim that alchemical masters can create within themselves an immortal spirit—known as the yang spirit—that survives eternally regardless of whether or not the ordinary physical body does. The yang spirit can, if it so chooses, assume corporeal properties (form, solidity, speech, eating, etc.) and appear before mortals and interact with them. Should it lack this ability, or is limited in its powers and freedom, this is said to be because it is still immature and of yin quality. Texts also commonly claim that adepts can project this yang spirit in and out of the body even before physical death. When it exits the body, moreover, it usually leaves from the top of the head.

Of course, the most unique and startling part of Zhang Yuanhua's story is that a gaping hole, large enough to insert one's arm, was discovered in the head of his corpse. His mastery of internal alchemy, here complemented by posthumous libation and prayer, seems to have physically altered his skull. This, then, leads to certain questions:

How common among Daoists and internal alchemists was the belief that adepts of the highest attainment opened holes in their skulls? How was the hole supposed to be opened? Was the hole to be large and visible the way it is in Zhang Yuanhua's story? Was the opening of a hole in the head absolutely imperative? What was the range of benefits thought to be attainable through opening such a hole? Are similar notions and practices to be found in other traditions and cultures? How do their methods and motives resemble or differ from those of the Daoists?

Certainly not all *neidan* treatises recommend opening a hole in the head. Most notably, perhaps, such a procedure is not endorsed in highly influential *neidan* texts such as the *Zhong-Lü chuandao ji* 鍾呂傳道集 (Zhongli's Transmission of Dao to Lü: A Collection; in *Xiuzhen shishu* 14-16 [DZ 263]), the *Lingbao bifa* 靈寶畢法 (Complete Methods of Numinous Treasure; DZ 1191), and the *Xishan qunxian huizhen ji* 西山群仙會真記 (West Mountain Record of the Host of Immortals and Assembled Perfected, DZ 246)— in what may called the "principal Zhong-Lü texts" that date to around the 11th century (see Baldrian-Hussein 1984). Although these texts speak in lively detail of the method for sending the spirit out through the head, along with accompanying visions, sensations and other unusual phenomena, they do not say that one must open a hole during this process.[1] Perhaps the author(s) thought a hole was unnecessary since the yang spirit can pass through solid surfaces anyway. Although the *Zhong-Lü chuandao ji* does in one passage mention the "opening of the summit" (*kaiding* 開頂) (*Chuandao ji* 14.71), it enumerates it along with many other techniques and training methods that are to be deemed as "minor methods of side schools" (*pangmen xiaofa* 傍門小法)—methods constituting something less than the Great Dao, which are at best limited in the results that they can bring.

In the following, we shall examine methods for opening the head that appear in three *neidan* texts of different periods, showing varying methods and a range of perceived benefits. First is the *Chen xiansheng neidan jue* 陳先生內丹訣 (Master Chen's Internal Alchemical Lesson, DZ 1096),[2] which most likely dates from the Northern Song, around the year 1078. Next is the *Danjing jilun* 丹經極論 (Ultimate Discourse on the Elixir Scriptures, DZ 235) from the classical period of *neidan* (i.e., Southern Song and Yuan). And third is the *Dacheng jieyao* 大成捷要 (Expedient Essentials on the Great Accomplishment),[3] an anonymous compilation from the modern period.

---

[1] Adepts are to enter trance and embark on a visionary journey through their inner physiological landscape. They see themselves mounted on clouds, dragons, cranes, phoenixes, or tigers (formed from the *qi* generated from the liver, heart, spleen, lungs and kidneys), and ascending up to a seven-storied tower at the Heaven Palace, which is in fact the top of their head (while in this trance, adepts also feels as though the body is floating in midair). The splendors of the inner landscape are likely to create attachment and longing in the hearts of adepts, who nonetheless must strengthen their resolve for liberation, ascend the tower, and jump off. Then suddenly, as though waking from a dream, one will have a "body outside the body" bearing the countenance and lustrous complexion of an infant. See *Lingbao bifa* 3.9b-11a; *Chuandao ji* 16.27a-30b; *Huizhen ji* 5.8b-10a.

[2] An alternate version, called *Cuixu pian* ("Green Vacuity"), appears in *Xiuzhen shishu* 17 (DZ 263).

[3] My citations of this text will be from the 1988 edition published in Taiyuan (Shanxi Province) by the Shanxi Renmin Chubanshe (Shanxi People's Press). This edition bears three different prefaces, the first of which bears no date, the second of which bears the date of 1929 (Minguo [Republic] 18), and the third of which bears the date of 1933 (Minguo 22). The first and second prefaces tell seemingly conflicting stories concerning where (Songshan 嵩山 vs. Laoshan 嶗山), by whom (Wang Qianyi 王乾一 vs. Zhu Wenbin 朱文彬) and how the text was found and brought into circulation. The text itself makes numerous quotes from and references to major Qing-dynasty *neidan* masters, particularly Liu Huayang 柳華陽 (fl.

Master Chen's Method

The *Chen xiansheng neidan jue* can be tentatively dated to around 1078, based on statements in its preface. The text notes that Chen Pu 陳朴 transmitted his "lessons on the inner elixir" to the "old rube of Huainan" (*Huainan yesou* 淮南野叟) after having arrived in Nandu 南都 (modern Nanyang near Luoyang) in the *wuwu* 戊午 year of the Yuanfeng reign (1078). The same preface also states that Chen Pu had been taught by Zhongli Quan, and thus had the same teacher as Lü Dongbin. However, the theories and methods of the text are different from those of the principal Zhong-Lü texts, or any other extant *neidan* text, for that matter (see Eskildsen 2001).

Master Chen's method by which the hole in the head is to be opened is described toward the latter part of the text, as follows:

> When the elixir reaches the seventh cycle, you must remove yourself from the commotion of the market places and enter deep into the mountains. Calmly sit amidst the rocky crags, holding your breath and concentrating your spirit. Cut off the breath that comes and goes through the mouth and nose. Make the true yin and yang converge inside your belly. Seize the creative power of Heaven and Earth and make it adhere to your four extremities. After a thousand days, your five organs will change completely and the embryonic *qi* will transform into immortal bowels.
>
> Then you will feel a hole open up in the gate of the summit, which will emit a red and black vapor. This is the embryonic *qi* dispersing. After a thousand days, the hole in the Summit Gate will seal shut. The embryonic *qi* is expelled completely, the merit of seven cycles is complete. From this point onward, the five viscera will bear fruit, and you will not take in food of the kind cooked in smoke and fire (22b).

This asserts that an actual, physical hole forms on the top of the head, which closes again after about three years. This hole, however, does not function as an exit point for the spirit. The hole opens up merely so that the last remnants of womb-*qi* can be expelled, as a part of the final stage in the transformation and immortalization of the inner anatomy. An additional effect of this transformation is, it seems, that the adept no longer needs to eat, since he now grows his own food inside himself.

This not to say that the *Chen xiansheng neidan jue* is silent regarding matters of spirit-excursions and out-of-body experiences. The early part of the text tells adepts how to cultivate a trance—through inner concentration and breath-holding—in which the spirit grows and expands beyond the borders of the body, to the point where it contains the entire universe. This trance culminates

---

1790). It also quotes much earlier (some even ancient) figures in a seemingly loose and creative manner suggestive of revelation by planchette.

with a vision of a bright ball of light coming down ("the descending of the elixir"), and leaves adepts with numbness in their limbs, which may linger on for quite a while even after coming out of trance (4ab).

In subsequent exercises, adepts nurture in themselves a holy fetus (*shengtai* 聖胎), which will be able to exit the body and travel greater distances as it matures (7b-16b).[4] Curiously, however, the text says nothing about making an opening on the top of the head—rather, the spirit just seems to suddenly appear outside the body, face to face with the adept.

When the spirit reaches its full maturity, it can travel limitless distances. Adepts at this point gain psychic powers, such as the abilities to see things in remote locations, to know the future, and to read minds (11b, 12b). They no longer dream in their sleep, and no longer fall into bad rebirths (14ab). Yet, they are far from reaching the highest attainment, which is physical immortality and heavenly ascension in the physical body. Adepts must proceed to transform their bodies physically to the point where they are pure yang, and hence do not cast a shadow (16b-19a). Even their inner anatomy must be completely transformed—and this is where the hole in the head comes in handy.

Thus, the opening of the hole in the head is not associated with the exiting of the spirit and seems to bear a whole different connotation. The latter parts of the text outline a transformation in the adept's body that can be described as a trans-gendering and a reversion to the fetal state. The penis shrinks away, leaving a hole in its place; an umbilical cord grows from the navel (20b-25b). In light of this, the opening of the hole in the head may bear a connotation of reversion to infancy, since the skulls of babies have soft, membrane-covered points—called fontanels—where the sutures have not yet ossified and sealed shut. The fact that internal alchemists were well aware of this will be very apparent in our next text, the *Danjing jilun*.

The *Danjing jilun*

The *Danjing jilun* dates to the 12th century or later. It was written by an anonymous author WELL versed in Zhang Boduan's 張伯端 *Wuzhen pian* 悟真篇 (Awakening to Perfection) and its exegetical tradition.[5] This text seems to represent the viewpoint of somebody connected to the influential Southern School (Nanzong 南宗) that regards Zhang Boduan as its patriarch and the *Wuzhen pian* as a foundational work. Nonetheless, its discussion on the sending out of the spirit is rather unique; it raises the question of whether it represents a new

---

[4] Interestingly, in this text, the spirit-body is said to gradually replicate the adept's person not only in its outer countenance but also in its inner anatomy, i.e., it comes to have its own five organs, and its psychic make up, such as the spirit and material souls.

[5] Baldrian-Hussein points out that it can be no earlier than the 12th century, since it cites and uses Weng Baoguang's *Wuzhen pian* commentary (Schipper and Verellen 2004, 834).

development in the tradition or whether it is simply describing phenomena that were experienced all along but had not been explicitly described in the other writings. It says:

> Since ancient times there has been no other method for divine immortals than to send out the spirit. The spirit is the original spirit of my body. When the *qi* is sufficient, the spirit is numinous. When the spirit is numinous, it will emerge by itself. This is not to be compared to methods of visualization.
>
> The exiting of the yang spirit cannot be seen by demons and spirits, nor can it be known by them. What demons and spirits can know and see is a yin spirit, not a yang spirit. When, after three years or a thousand days of practice, the preserving and nurturing is complete, the *qi* will be sufficient and the spirit full; it will exit and enter freely.
>
> The body outside the body is none other than the dharma body. When gathered it takes on form; when dispersed it becomes *qi*. It cannot be pondered upon in terms of forms and traces. A yin spirit has neither form nor trace, nor can it divide its body and change its form. A yang spirit can have one body or as many as hundreds and tens of bodies. Each can drink and eat, and each can communicate. Combine them, and they again become one. This is what is meant when it is said: "That which is holy but yet cannot be known is called divine."
>
> In its appearing and hiding, it cannot be fathomed. Its transformations are without limit. Whether one thousand or ten thousand *li* away, it can get there in an instant. Things of the past and of the future, it all knows. Only then can it be called a yang spirit.
>
> The exiting and entering of the yang spirit is all from the Gate of Heaven. When the Gate of Heaven first opens, it is as though a large axe is cutting into the brain. Do not be surprised. The [crown of the head] will move like the fontanel of a baby. Guard it as sacred in the secret room; do not casually let it out.
>
> When it first emerges, it will circle about on your right and left, staring back at the divine chamber and the hut. When the spirit has become experienced at exiting, you will see everything whether your eyes are open or shut. After this make it go and come amid space. First, it should go ten steps, then a hundred, and then a thousand. Gradually let it out further. As soon as you let it out, gather it back in. After a long while, you can make it go as far away as you like.
>
> When the spirit exits, leave one deity to watch, attend, and protect the dwelling [body]. Admonish the deity to protect it. This god is the golden-armored god in the brain. Upon exiting, entrust it with stabilizing the Summit Gate, lest there might be [a malicious spirit] that assumes a false name and form to try and enter into my spirit's dwelling. [Tell the golden-armored god], "Do not allow it inside. When you [see] me return, call out my surname, then I will become one [with my body]. If one does not carry out the regimen that takes three years and [a further] nine years, how can one reach this [level of attainment]? (9a-10a)

This passage begins by explaining how and why a yang spirit is superior to a yin spirit—a favorite, recurring theme in *neidan* literature. Significantly, it states unequivocally: "The exiting and entering of the yang spirit is all from the Gate of Heaven." It thus seems that if the spirit were to exit from any other part of the body, it would be something less than fully yang.

Most interesting here is how adepts are said to feel intense pain when the Summit Gate is first opened. They will feel a quivering movement on the crown of the head, similar to that commonly witnessed on the crania of newborn babies. Thus, while this discourse does not quite go as far as to say that an actual hole forms in the head, it does say that adepts feel a very vivid sensation of excruciating pain, and suggests that an actual physical change occurs in the skull directly under the skin. The physical alteration makes the adept's body resemble that of a baby. This is considered auspicious, since it bears connotations of rejuvenation and reversion to infantile simplicity of the sort idealized in the *Chen xiansheng neidan jue* (as well as the *Daode jing*).

Also noteworthy is how adepts undertake a special precautionary measure against the threat of usurpation by an imposter. Deeply in disembodied trance, they are in a highly vulnerable state, flirting with death in that they replicate the basic phenomena thought to occur at death, defined as the separation of spirit from body. It appears that the sensation of having the head cut open with an ax was also understood within *neidan* circles—by at least the 14th century, but perhaps earlier—to replicate what naturally occurs at death.

Evidence of this is also found in the *Lingbao guikong jue* 靈寶歸空訣 (Instructions on Returning to the Void, DZ 568), compiled by Zhao Yizhen 趙宜真 (d. 1382).[6] This text is a fairly vivid and detailed Daoist manual on dying—how to predict how soon one will die, what to expect at the time of death, and how to comport oneself at death and during what immediately ensues thereafter, so as attain a favorable outcome (see Eskildsen 2006). Coincidentally, it dates from roughly the same period as its more famous Buddhist counterpart, the *Tibetan Book of the Dead*, "rediscovered" by the *Ter-tön* Kar-ma Ling-pa.[7] The *Lingbao guikong jue* has:

---

[6] Zhao Yizhen was one of the leading Daoists of the late Yuan and early Ming periods. He is regarded as one of the patriarchs of the Qingwei 輕微 (Pure Tenuity) School, one of the most important lineages of the Thunder Rites. In his postscript he states that his work is in part based on an older text that had been in circulation for some time and which was purported to be the work of the semi-legendary Chan Patriarch Bodhidharma (fl. 500), but expresses strong skepticism regarding Bodhidharma's putative authorship. See Schipper and Verellen 2004, 1095-96, 1290; Schipper 1987.

[7] Tibetan Buddhism has the idea that tantric masters of extraordinary attainment sometimes hide texts and images in secret locations and guard them with spells that keep them hidden until conditions are right for them to be discovered. Such treasures are called *terma*, and those who discover and reveal them are called *tertön*. The main difference between the two works is that instructions of the *Lingbao guikong jue* are directed at meditation practitioners facing their own death whereas those of the *Tibetan Book of the Dead* are meant to be

> Various sights of people and things will come, drawing you toward the paths of karma to receive transmigration. Firmly hold your mind-seal without craving or becoming attached. When the axe splits [your head], do not be scared or resent it. (4a)
>
> At the moment the energy is cut off, you may feel the sensation of being split apart with an ax; do not be scared. As it becomes dark do not flee or hide; it is essential to hold firmly to the mind-seal without wavering. After a while, you will become stable. (4b-5a)

During the process of dying one sees many visions, luring one into various types of undesirable reincarnation if one becomes attracted, horrified, or distracted by them. One needs to maintain composure and concentration at all times, facilitated by "holding to the mind-seal" (*xinyin* 心印). The exact meaning of "seal" is unclear. It could mean that one mentally or verbally recites a prescribed incantation, chants the *Xinyin miaojing* 心印妙經 (Wondrous Scripture of the Mind-Seal, DZ 13), or forms a sacred hand gesture.[8]

Of course, more obvious and striking is that people feel a sensation of being split open with an ax at the moment "the *qi* is cut off" at death, that is, when vital energy departs fully from the body. The *Danjing jilun* makes the same claim regarding the moment when the Gate of Heaven is first opened in meditation.

Modern Practice

Modern alchemical exit practice is documented vividly in the *Dacheng jieyao*, written probably in the late 19th or early 20th centuries and published perhaps for the first time in 1929, after having been kept for some time in the Chongfu gong 崇福宮 (Palace of Venerating Happiness) on Mt. Song 嵩山.[9] The author

---

whispered by a monk into the ear of a dying person, who may or may not be a tantric adept. See Evans-Wentz 1960; Freemantle and Trungpa 1976; Mullin 1986.

[8] The *Xinyin miaojing* is a standard text recited in daily liturgies at Daoist monasteries. It dates no earlier than the late Song, but was around in Zhao Yizhen's time. For more on "seals" as hand gestures, see Mitamura 2002.

[9] The text has several editions: *Dacheng jieyao* (Jinzhou 錦州, Liaoning: Sanyou 三友, undated); *Dacheng jieyao xingming shuangxiu xinyin koujue tianji miwen* 大成捷要性命雙脩心印口訣天機秘文 (mimeographed hand copy: property of Cornell University Library, undated); *Tianji miwen* 天機秘文 (Taipei: Zhenshanmei 真善美 , 1966); *Dacheng jieyao* (Taiyuan 太原 : Shanxi Renmin 山西人民, 1988); and Yang Qingli 楊青黎, *Dacheng jiejing* 大成捷徑 (Taipei: Zhenshanmei, 1964). Some prefaces bear dates, the earliest being 1929. If not indicated otherwise, I use the Taiyuan 1988 version.

appears to have been an anonymous disciple of a certain Jingjuezi 靜覺子,[10] and may have been somehow connected to or influenced by a lay sectarian society such as the Xiantian dao 先天道 or the Tongshan she 同善社.[11] Spirit writing (*fuji* 扶乩) or some other sort of psychic inspiration may have been involved in producing the text, since it is made up of a series of discourses attributed—often anachronistically or implausibly—to a wide variety of *neidan* masters, legendary immortals, deities, and other luminaries.

Its "Oral Lesson on Opening the Gate of Heaven" (*Kai tianmen koujue* 開天門口訣) reads as follows:

> Wei Boyang said, "The yang spirit moves to the Summit Gate. At this time, amid stillness, gaze inward. In the crown of your head there will be the Genuine Fire of Samadhi. Amid stillness look outward. Above your head there will be the Divine Fire of the Great Yang [the sun].
>
> Use your genuine will, keeping it serene, luminous, concentrated, and collected. Make the upper fire shine downward, and the lower fire burn upward. Attack [the crown of the head] by sandwiching it between the inside and outside, thus boiling and refining. [The two fires] meet a hundred times to dry out the head. Like a whole pond of silver waves, the head is filled with golden fluid as the two fires converge and attack.
>
> With the rumbling of thunder, the inner building of the Purple Capital bursts open. In a sudden moment you are aware that a red brightness has pervaded the realm and purple flames have filled the sky. With the rumbling of swift thunder and lightning, the Summit Gate is open. As though you have given birth to a small child, it breathes and moves
>
> The fontanel is unsealed. It is the size of a coin, and as thin as cotton fabric (emphasis added). The skull will seem caved in [because the] bone of the scalp has burned away. When the Summit Gate first opens, it is as though a large axe were splitting apart the brain; the pain is hard

---

[10] In a section entitled "Daojiao yuanliu pu" 道教源流譜 (which in some editions of the text is placed within the front matter as a preface), one finds the phrase, "I obtained from the Patriarch Master Jingjue the limitless Great Dao, transmitted from the Most High" (Taiyuan 1988, 15). In the Cornell Library edition, the text's main exposition is preceded by the general heading "Mind Seal Oral Lesson of Jingjuezi" 靜覺子心印口訣.

[11] Two prefaces found in the Taiyuan 1988 edition (that bear the date of 1933) tell of how the text was acquired by Zhu Wenbin, a member of the Tongshan she. The section entitled "Daojiao yuanliu pu" contains references to deities such as the Golden Mother (Jinmu 金母; the supreme goddess revered in various sectarian societies) and Tianfei 天妃 (Mazu 媽祖), and refers to the "Great Way of the Prior Heaven" (*xiantian dadao* 先天大道). On the two organizations, see DeKorne 1941; Topley 1963; Lin 1984; Jordan and Overmyer 1986; Wang 1995; Goossaert 2007, 313-14;

to bear. However, you must not be afraid. After three days, the pain will naturally be completely relieved. (*Dacheng jieyao*, 95 [Taiyuan, 1988])

The ascription of this discourse to Wei Boyang 魏伯陽, 2nd century alchemist and immortal, known as the putative author of the alchemical classic, the *Zhouyi cantongqi* 周易參同契 (Tally to the Book of Changes) is almost certainly spurious, which means the text was composed later, either by conscious compilation or through spirit-writing revelation. Whatever the case, this passage relates a unique method for opening the crown of the head and provides a vivid description of its concrete, physical effects.

Here, the hole is supposed to be "burned" open by means of the intense visualization of two types of "fire" that are generated from the inside and the outside. The heat, it appears, not only burns open a hole, but also makes the Golden Fluid gurgle and spurt. The next portion of the text is problematic; it seems to offer two possible interpretations. It may describe the appearance and size of the spirit that emerges when the Gate of Heaven opens. Or it may say that the adept's fontanel has become unsealed, creating an opening the size of a coin, covered by a skin or membrane as thin as cotton cloth and quivering like the crown of an infant's head. This latter interpretation (which I have chosen in my translation) tends to be supported by what follows immediately in the text, where it says that the "burning" did in fact burn away actual bone, thus altering the structure of the skull. Perhaps not surprising, then, is the statement that the phenomenon causes horrendous pain, which goes away only after three days.

The two subsequent discourses, "Oral Lesson on the Heavenly Pivot on the Body Outside the Body and the Gathering in of the Golden Light" (*Shenwai youshen shou jinguang tianji koujue* 身外有身收金光天机口訣) and "Oral Lesson on the Heavenly Principles on Controlling the Exiting and Entering of the Yang Spirit" (*Tiao yangshen churu tianji koujue* 調陽神出入天機口訣) are devoted to the exiting, manifestation and returning of the yang spirit.

The first text, attributed to Cihang Daoren 慈航道人 (Daoist of the Merciful Voyage); i.e., the Bodhisattva Avalokitesvara (Guanyin 觀音), tells adepts to concentrate their spirits, visualize the dharma body (i.e., yang spirit), close their eyes, and imagine themselves leaping out from the Gate of Heaven. After doing so, they will feel as though they have awakened from a dream, and will have the "body outside the body", which will hover at a distance of three or four feet from the ordinary physical body (*Dacheng jieyao*, 95-96).

Apparently the vantage point and locus of consciousness are now in the externalized yang spirit, and adepts perceive their ordinary physical body from the outside. At this point they experience visions of family, ancestors, relatives, immortals, buddhas, and the like, all of which they must take care not to pay attention to. After a while they will see a large, circular light of golden or white color emerge from the physical body. Adepts must use their concentration and visualization to move the dharma body into this light and concentrate the mind on the light. The light will shrink down to the form of a one-inch long golden thread, and at this point adepts should imagine themselves sucking in this golden thread. This will cause the dharma body to return back into the physical body.

The second work, attributed to Chen Xiyi 陳希夷 or Chen Tuan 陳搏, discusses the danger that the spirit may—contrarily to one's intentions—depart permanently and cause death. It first explains that this by and large occurs because adepts are lax in their self-refinement. After briefly endorsing the above-described method of concentrating on the golden light, it warns that the yang spirit must not be sent in and out in a careless manner, since the prevailing tendency of the yang spirit is to disdain the physical body as though it were a clod of manure or dirt, and to not want to return to it (*Dacheng jieyao*, 97-98).

Thus, the author(s) or compiler(s) of the *Dacheng jieyao* understood the "opening the Gate of Heaven" and the emergence of the "body outside the body" as procedures that can inadvertently lead to death if performed wrongly or carelessly.

Comparing the Practices

So far, we have examined three different methods for opening the crown of the head that appear in texts representative of the early, classical, and modern periods of *neidan* history. While the opening of the crown was apparently a widespread concern of *neidan* practitioners of different periods and schools or lineages, there is some variation in the specific techniques used to open the crown, the perceived benefit anticipated, and the extent to which the structure of the skull was thought to be altered. Two of the three texts (with the possible exception of the *Chen xiansheng neidan jue*), see the opening of the crown of the head—and especially the subsequent spirit excursions—as perilous and potentially even fatal, and thus describe measures for avoiding or overcoming such dangers.

The method for opening the crown in the *Chen xiansheng neidan jue* calls for the holding of breath and mental concentration, but apparently no active imagination. This is said to eventually cause the convergence of yin and yang in the belly, the transformation of the five viscera into "immortal bowels", and the opening of hole in the crown of the head through which red and black vapor ("embryonic" *qi*) is expelled. After a thousand days, the opening is said to seal shut again. The *Danjing jilun* similarly does not seem to provide a specific visualization or mechanical procedure for opening the head. Rather, the spirit, when it has become sufficiently yang, seems to burst through the skull on its own, causing extreme pain and making the fontanel quiver like that of a baby.

The *Dacheng jieyao*, on the other hand, has adepts visualize fires from inside and outside the body converging on the scalp and burning through it, causing intense pain, thunderous rumbling, and the gurgling of the Golden Fluid in the head. The text also states that the "fires" burn through actual bone (but perhaps not skin), causing the skull to have a caved in appearance, and leaving a thin layer of skin or membrane covering a fontanel opening the approximate diameter of a coin.

Thus, all three texts claim that the crown of the head is opened through yogic procedures of contemplation and breath control, which may or may not entail active imagination, and none speaks of a hole bored manually or surgically. One would guess that the narrator of Zhang Yuanhua's story meant to imply that he had mastered such yogic procedures. Of course, in his story it is also implied that his spirit left through the head only after libations and prayers were administered before his coffin. The texts—since they are, after all, meditation texts—make no mention of such ritual procedures being necessary for opening of the head and the liberation of the spirit.

None of the texts speak of anything quite so dramatic as a hole opening in the head that is big enough to insert one's arm into; however each text seems to indicate that the skull is actually opened or structurally altered to some extent. In the *Chen xiansheng neidan jue* an actual hole does open, which however closes again after about three years. The size of the hole is unspecified, but it is at least large enough allow vapors to pass through. The *Danjing jilun* does not exactly say that a hole is opened in the scalp; however, since we are told that the adept feels extreme pain, and that the fontanel begins to quiver, the strong implication is that the skull's structure—at least under the surface of the scalp—has been radically altered. What seems to be implied in the *Danjing jilun* is stated explicitly in the *Dacheng jieyao*, which also seems to say that the hole in the skull is about the diameter of a coin.

In two of the three texts, the main purpose for opening the crown of the head is to allow the spirit to exit. The exception here is again the *Chen xiansheng neidan jue*, where the hole opens well after the spirit—which seems to need no hole in order to exit—has already become mature and well-traveled. The hole serves instead as a route for expelling "womb *qi*" in the process of refining the inner anatomy. In the view of this text, the highest goal is *not* the immortality of the spirit alone; thus the maturation and excursions of the spirit are but a juncture located roughly midway through the immortality regimen as a whole.

The view of the mainstream traditions of the Song and Yuan periods (Zhong-Lü, Quanzhen, Nanzong) is that the immortality of the yang spirit that casts aside the fleshly body is indeed the most praiseworthy, lofty soteriological attainment—this is, predictably, the view of the *Danjing jilun*. However, some of the most influential Song *neidan* texts (such as the principal Zhong-Lü works) make no specific mention of opening the crown of the head, leaving the impression that such a procedure or phenomenon was unknown or considered unessential. The *Danjing jilun* seems to suggest—albeit far from conclusively—that in fact the opening of the crown was an integral part of Zhong-Lü and Southern School *neidan*. In the modern text, the *Dacheng jieyao*, the sending out of the spirit certainly constitutes a lofty level of attainment. The opening of the crown is certainly integral to this.

However, according to the *Dacheng jieyao*, the best adepts never entirely cast aside the flesh. Rather they continue to train, "facing a wall" for nine more years, after which the fleshly body becomes fully refined, and one day pulverizes and disappears into thin air (*Dacheng jieyao*, 100-01). All the texts agree that when the mature yang spirit becomes able to exit and travel great distances, adepts gain tremendous psychic powers, such as those of seeing and knowing of things at great distances and in the future, or of reading other people's minds.

Symbolically and functionally, the opening of the crown of the head seems to be related to both birth or infancy and death. The parallel between the opened fontanel of the *neidan* adept and that of an infant is drawn explicitly in the *Danjing jilun* and *Dacheng jieyao*, and also seems to be implied in the *Chen xiansheng neidan jue*. The further implication seems to be that adepts whose crowns have been opened have been physically rejuvenated, and have psychologically regained something of the purity, innocence, simplicity and spontaneity of childhood.

As noted earlier, Daoists—or at least some of them by the time this particular text was compiled (14th c.)—envisioned the natural process of dying as entailing some of the same phenomena (the sensation of being cut open with an ax, followed by tempting visions) thought to occur when opening the crown and sending out the spirit in *neidan* meditation. Furthermore, the opening of the crown and the sending out of the spirit were thought to be highly perilous undertakings that amounted to a flirtation with death—thus various precautionary or protective measures are described, such as entrusting a golden-armored brain god to guard the opening (*Danjing jilun*) or visualizing and sucking in a golden light (*Dacheng jieyao*).

These measures, in basic principle and purpose, resemble what is recommended for dying adepts in *Lingbao guikong jue*, since they require adepts to remain calm and focused, and serve to prevent one from being lured into an evil rebirth. While the three texts do not explicitly state as much, their methods could in a sense be viewed as "death rehearsals" that will enable adepts to cope with death in the best possible manner if, alas, death itself (in the mundane sense) cannot be entirely avoided. If one is to read deeper into the symbolic and psychological significance of this *neidan*-death parallel, perhaps the implication is that the opening of the skull and liberation of the spirit restores one's consciousness to the omniscient, unfettered state, at one with the universal Dao, that it enjoys as long as it is not trapped and degraded in a fleshly body and an individual ego.

A Cross-Cultural Perspective

Not limited to China and the methods of internal alchemy, the opening of the crown of the head also occurs in Tibetan Buddhism and in certain mystic circles of Europe and North America.

The French Buddhist devotee, Alexandra David-Neel, in her 1932 account of her experiences in Tibet and surrounding regions, describes a time in Sikkim when she spied on two Tibetan monks in the forest, who were sitting in a meditation posture and taking turns—in between long intervals of silence—shrieking out "*hik*!", in what she describes as a "peculiar abnormal shrill note." The shrieks seemed to require great effort, and indeed, one of the monks at one point put his hand on his throat and spat out a stream of blood. Also, as David-Neel noticed, the monk had a long piece of straw standing straight up out of his head.

Later, her interpreter Dawasamdup, who also produced an early translation of the *Book of the Dead* (see Evans-Wentz 1960), explained that they were rehearsing the ritualistic cry meant to open a hole in the head of a dying person, through which the "spirit" can escape. Rehearsal and mastery of the cry has an effect on the monk himself—that of causing a hole to form in his own head large enough to insert a piece of straw. Indeed, the monk must be careful, when merely rehearsing, not to combine the syllable *hik* with the syllable *phat*, since the latter syllable is designed to separate the spirit from the body, which would cause death (David-Neel 1971, 13-14).

Actually, strenuous and perilous though it may be, the repeated rehearsal of shrieking *hik!* is indeed thought to confer soteriological benefits. In Tibetan Buddhism, death, if properly prepared for and rehearsed, is a great opportunity for the immediate attainment of buddhahood, or, less ambitiously, rebirth in a Pure Land. The shrieking of *hik* is carried out within the Yoga of Consciousness Transference, meant to enable adepts to gain rebirth in the Tusita Heaven, the Pure Land of the Bodhisattva Maitreya.

The method involves first visualizing Tusita and invoking Maitreya to come and take his position up above the self. The adept visualizes her body in a form clear as crystal, with the central channel running up its center, from a space three finger-widths under the navel, up to the crown of the head. In the energy center along this channel at the heart, she sees the "mystic drop" of a white color tinged with red. Maitreya, seated right above the adept, is seen to have his own central energy channel, which meets with that of the adept, at the crown of her head. With shrieks of *hik* the adept makes the mystic drop, which embodies his vital energy and consciousness, leap up, first to the throat, then to the crown of the head. However, the adept is told not to project the mystic drop out of the head—even temporarily—since this is said to diminish life expectancy. With repeated practice, a blister may begin to form at the top of the head.¹² According another testimony, the blister formed in such a manner may also emit pus or blood (Mullin 1986, 77, 173-91).¹³

The Yoga of Consciousness Transference is thus carried out as a rehearsal for the moment of death (as is the case with various other tantric meditations).¹⁴ At the time of death it is hoped that the adept's mystic drop (his vitality or consciousness) leaves the body through the hole in the top of the head, which in turn results in rebirth in Maitreya's Pure Land. Whether one uses this specific method or not, the assumption in Tibetan Buddhism is that liberation from the crown of the head will lead to a favorable rebirth—if not in the Tusita Heaven, perhaps as a *deva* in some other heaven—or better, immediate buddhahood. Liberation through other places in the body, such as an eye, nostril, armpit, genitals or feet, will lead to lesser rebirths (human, *asura*, beast, hungry ghost, hell) (Powers 1995, 292-93). This is why care is taken—whether for oneself, or for a fellow dying human—to open a hole in the skull from which the vitality or consciousness can escape.

In Europe and North America some people advocate trepanation—surgically boring a hole in the head—for the purpose of enhancing psychic power and spiritual well-being. The main underlying logic is that trepanation modifies inter-cranial pressure to increase brain blood-volume, thus enhancing the power and vitality of the brain. Advocates also claim that children—whose fontanels have not sealed shut—have a higher state of consciousness, less rigid and self-conscious, more imaginative and creative and spontaneous, and that this higher state can be reclaimed by surgically reopening the skull.¹⁵

---

¹² See The description of this method comes from an 18th century treatise by Tse-chok-ling Ye-she Gyal-tsen.

¹³ This testimony comes from Glenn Mullin' mentor, Ge-she Nga-wang Dar-gye. He also mentions that the syllable *phat* is used to bring the consciousness back into the body—which certainly differs from the explanation given by Dawasamdup to Alexandra David-Neel. He also speaks of projecting the consciousness outside the body while still alive, without, however warning of any detrimental physical effects that such practice would bring. Thus his view also differs somewhat from that conveyed in Tse-chok-ling Ye-she Gyal-tsen's description of the Yoga of Consciousness Transference.

¹⁴ In the Highest Yoga Tantra of Indo-Tibetan Buddhism, the advanced yogic procedures (during which the "winds" are directed into the body's central channel and made to dissolve in the "indestructible drop" in the heart) are thought to parallel the psycho-physical phenomena that occur naturally at the time of death. See Powers 1995, 245-51, 293-97.

¹⁵ The most conspicuous advocacy group for voluntary trepanation is ITAG (International Trepanation Advocacy Group), founded and led by the American Peter Halvorson. ITAG's official website (trepan.com) presents extensive discussion (with many pictures!) concerning trepanation and its perceived benefits. One of the pioneering figures in the voluntary trepanation movement was a Dutch physician Bart Huges, who in 1962 wrote a short treatise entitled, "The Mechanism of Brain Volume" (this can be downloaded from ITAG's website) and a monograph entitled *Homo Sapiens Correctus*. See article from Wikipedia, the free encyclopedia. See http://en.wikipedia.org/wiki/trepanation.

Both Tibetan Buddhism and modern Western trepanation show similarities as well as differences from what is said in Daoist *neidan* texts. Of course, in the case of Tibetan Buddhism one needs to keep in mind the possibility of interaction or influence on Daoism that may have gone in either direction or both ways—whether it was the variety introduced during the Tang, or the Tibetan form heavily patronized by the Mongol and Manchu rulers of China.

In the Daoist and Tibetan cases, the hole is produced entirely by non-surgical means. However, in the Tibetan case, the loud shrieking of specific syllables is employed. In Daoism, there is no shrieking or any other sort of vocalization. In both the Daoist and Tibetan cases, the procedures for opening the crown and sending out the spirit are thought to parallel what naturally occurs at death. Thus, one could conjecture that in both Daoism and Tibetan Buddhism the procedures serve to some extent as "death rehearsals;" such indeed is their *primary* purpose in the Tibetan case.

Also, in both Daoism and Tibetan Buddhism it is feared that the "rehearsals," if carried out wrongly or carelessly, can lead to premature, inadvertent death. Furthermore, in both traditions there is the idea that the spirit must exit from the top of the head in order to bring about the best soteriological outcomes, and that an exit from anywhere else on the body will lead to lesser or even grievous results. The greatest difference between the two traditions is that the Daoist texts claim that the spirit should be sent out of the body repeatedly during meditation, in spite of the great dangers, since the repeated excursions bring about great psychic powers and can ultimately be conducive to refining and immortalizing the body as well as the spirit. In the Tibetan case such audacious claims of physical longevity or immortality are not made, and the projection of the consciousness outside the body while "rehearsing" is discouraged, since it is thought to merely deplete the body of its vitality.

Modern practitioners of trepanation, who surgically open their skulls, are obviously very different from Daoist internal alchemists. However, they do echo the Daoists' claim that the opening of the head elevates consciousness and enhances psychic powers. They also resemble the Daoists in how they romanticize and aspire toward the infantile condition.

So, what are we to make of the fact that people of diverse traditions put forth similar claims about opening the crown of the head and the benefits to be found therein? Can the fontanel really be opened through meditation, without recourse to manual boring or surgery? Does opening a hole in the head—whether through meditation or surgery— actually confer any of the benefits claimed? These questions can only be properly addressed through a more extensive, scientific, experimental inquiry. If there is a universal concern lying behind the various methods and theories for opening the head, perhaps it is the yearning to expand the consciousness beyond the limitations and tribulations that seem to be imposed by physicality and ego-hood.

Bibliography

Baldrian-Hussein, Farzeen. 1984. *Procédés secrets du joyau magique*. Paris: Les Deux Océans.

David-Neel, Alexandra. 1971 [1932]. *Magic and Mystery and Tibet*. New York: Dover.

DeKorne, John C. 1941. *The Fellowship of Goodness: A Study in Contemporary Chinese Religion*. Grand Rapids.: John C. DeKorne.

Eskildsen, Stephen. 2001. "Neidan Master Chen Pu's Nine Stages of Transformation." *Monumenta Serica* 49: 1-31.

_____. 2006. "Emergency Death Meditations for Internal Alchemists." *T'oung Pao* 92: 373-409.

Evans-Wentz, W. Y. 1960. *The Tibetan Book of the Dead*. New York: Oxford University Press.

Freemantle, Francisca, and Chögyam Trungpa. 1974. *The Tibetan Book of the Dead*. Berkeley: Shambhala.

Goossaert, Vincent. 2007. *The Taoists of Peking, 1800-1949: A Social History of Urban Clerics*. Cambridge, Mass.: Harvard University. Press

Jordan, David K., and Daniel Overmyer. 1986. *The Flying Phoenix: Aspects of Chinese Sectarianism in Taiwan*. Princeton: Princeton University Press.

Lin Wanchuan 林萬傳. 1984. *Xiantian dadao xitong yanjiu* 先天大道系統研究. Tainan: Tianju shuju.

Mitamura, Keiko. 2002. "Daoist Hand Signs and Buddhist Mudras." In *Daoist Identity: History, Lineage, and Ritual*, edited by Livia Kohn and Harold D. Roth, 235-55. Honolulu: University of Hawaii Press.

Mullin, Glenn H. 1986. *Death and Dying: The Tibetan Tradition*. New York: Arkana.

Powers, John. 1995. *Introduction to Tibetan Buddhism*. Ithaca: Snow Lion Publications.

Schipper, Kristofer M. 1987. "Master Chao I-chen (?-1382) and the Ch'ing-wei School of Taoism." In *Dōkyō to shūkyō bunka* 道教と宗教文化, edited by Akizuki Kan'ei 秋月觀英, 715-34. Tokyo: Hirakawa.

_____, and Franciscus Verellen, eds. 2004. *The Taoist Canon: A Historical Companion to the Daozang*. 3 vols. Chicago: University of Chicago Press.

Topley, Marjorie. 1963. "The Great Way of the Former Heaven." *Bulletin of the School of Oriental and African* Studies 26.2: 362-92.

Wang Jianchuan 王見川. 1995. "Tongshan she zaoqi lishi (1912-1945) chutan" 同善社早期歷史初探. *Minjian zongjiao* 民間宗教 1/1995:57-82.

Summoning the Thunder Generals

Internal Alchemy in the Thunder Rites[*]

Shin-yi Chao

The Thunder Rites (*leifa* 雷法) entered the Daoist ritual repertoire relatively late in Chinese history. Daoists of the early eighth century C.E. recorded the existence of rituals (*fa* 法) that deployed thunder deities to combat ostensibly heretical spirits.[1] An account of a conversation in mid-ninth century Sichuan, recorded by the scholar-official Sun Guangxin 孫光憲 (ca. 900-968), mentions a certain Register of the Thunder Lord (*leigong lu* 雷公籙) which was accepted as legitimate by some Daoist priests but rejected by others—including the Heavenly Masters school —for lack of canonic authenticity (Sun 1959, 179-80). In the story, thunder deities possessed official duties and positions (*zhi* 職), suggesting that the process of incorporating them into the Daoist divine bureaucracy had begun at the time.

It was probably no coincidence that Sun Guangxian paid attention to the story; at the time, a popular Daoist exorcistic order was known for practicing the Thunder Rites. Those who were initiated into the order would receive, among other ritual texts, a one chapter manuscript called *Beidi leigong fa* 北帝雷公法 (Ritual of the Thunder Lords of the Northern Emperor), according to the *Sandong xiudao yi* 三洞修道儀 (Protocol for the Practice of the Way of the

---

[*] I would like to thank Drs. Daniel Overmyer, Livia Kohn, Xun Liu, Julius Tsai, Kevin Clark, and the anonymous readers who patiently read, commented, and corrected this paper. All remaining mistakes are mine.

[1] See Lagerwey's entry on the *Yuqing jing* 玉清經 (Scripture of Jade Purity) in Schipper and Verellen 2004, 525.

Three Caverns; DZ 1237, 1.9; ZHDZ 42.259c),[2] a one-chapter book on the ranks and protocols of Daoists (*daoshi* 道士 and *nüguan* 女官).[3] Nevertheless, the *Sandong xiudao yi* also informs us that the order in question was outside the seven established ranks of ordained Daoists.

One region with a particularly rich Daoist and popular tradition was the Ba-Shu 巴蜀 area, stretching from the Chengdu plain of Sichuan to western Hubei. The Register of the Thunder Lord mentioned by Sun Guangxian was here particularly associated with the so-called Purgation of Heavenly Fairness (*tiangong zhai* 天公齋) as described in the *Tiangong xiaomo huguo jing* 天公消魔護國經 (Scripture on Heaven's Fairness Dissolving Disasters and Protecting the Country, DZ 654). The recipients of this register, moreover, were located in Xinfan (near Chengdu) and Jiangling (Hubei). Beyond this, the areas traditionally ascribed to the birth to the Thunder Rites include Jiangxi (Mt. Huagai), the lower Yangzi reaches, and Guangdong.

Song Thunder

In the early tenth century, the use of thunder deities in Daoist rituals was still controversial and limited to a select number of initiates. By the twelfth century, the ritual landscape had changed considerably. In the final decades of the Northern Song dynasty, Thunder Rites took a central position on the imperial religious stage and rose to great significance. Lin Lingsu 林靈素 (d. 1119), the powerful Daoist adviser of Huizong (r. 1100-1126) and propagator of the Divine Empyrean (Shenxiao 神霄) school, was renowned for performing the Five Thunders rituals.[4] The Heavenly Masters, too, embraced the practice. Thus Zhang Jixian 張繼先 (1092-1126), the thirtieth Heavenly Master, designed several Thunder Rites (Skar 2000, 433; Ren 1999, 738). Plus, there were various twelfth-century ritual compendia marked by the prevalence of Thunder Ritual.

Thunder Rites serve to summon rain (or clear weather) and to exorcise harmful spirits. Since ghosts and demons were thought to cause illness in Dao-

---

[2] "DZ" indicates the numbers of Daoist texts in Schipper and Verellen 2004. "ZHDZ" stands for *Zhonghua Daozang*, the punctuated version of the Daoist canon (Beijing: Huaxia chubanshe, 2004). Numbers and letters indicate volume, page, and column.

[3] Although the *Xiudao yi* was written in 1003 (Schipper and Verellen 2004, 973-74), it contains information from the early tenth century; its source was the Daoist master Liu Ruozhou 劉若拙 who was already eminent during the Kaibao reign (968-975) of Emperor Taizu; see *Lishi zhenxian tidao tongjian* 歷世真仙體道通鑑 (Comprehensive Mirror of Successive Generations of Perfected Immortals and Those Who Embody the Dao; DZ 296) 47.16 (ZHDZ 47.531a).

[4] Even the *Songshi* (History of the Song), which denounces Lin Lingsu as a fraud, has to admit his capability in performing the Five Thunder Rites (462.13529).

ist pathology, the ritual was also a therapeutic remedy.[5] Cases in which thunder ritual masters successfully treated demonic possessions (read: psychotic disorders) or blew up temples of rival deities with thunderous burst of flames appear in various non-Daoist sources. Modern scholars have offered scientific explanations of such miraculous ritual powers, including the effects that "ritual theater" could produce on patients' psychological condition (Davis 2001, 107-14) and Daoist masters' expertise in the use of gunpowder (Boltz 1993, 285-86). However, to the codifiers of the Thunder Rites, the true efficacy of their performance derived from the fact that they were carried by the thunder deities under the commend of initiated ritual masters.

Interpretations of the exact nature of the thunder deities vary (Skar 1997, 178; 1995, 226), but the bottom line is that they are forces of thunder and lightning that carry out the demands of the ritual masters. Summoning the thunder deities in order to command them forms the core of the Thunder Rites. Their many schools are thus different systems of methods and theories designed to control the deities in question. Each new set of methods claimed to be more efficacious than the old, and new schools grew around them to glorify the masters and the teachings.

On the other hand, the various new schools also shared a common trend: that is, the emphasis on the internal exercises. Thunder Rites as an external application of internal cultivation are well described by the influential Daoist master Wang Wenqing 王文卿 (1093-1153):

> The Five Thunders Ritual of Beheading and Investigating the Demons has the Dao as its core and ritual as its application. Cultivating [the ritual] inwardly, one can eradicate the Three Corpses [that harm people], . . . leave behind the shackles [of the body], transform the spirit, and become a transcendent (*xian* 仙) of the higher realm. Applying it outwardly, one can eliminate demonic spirits, summon thunderclaps by talismans, breathe the essence of the "five *qi*," and unite the generals of the Five Thunders.[6] (*Daofa huiyuan* 61.1; ZHDZ 36.367c)

---

[5] Haunting ghosts are not necessarily demonic; they could be vengeful entities trying to obtain justice. See Bokenkamp 2007. Ghosts acting from justifiable revenge were a valid concern of ritual masters performing exorcism during Song times, as reflected in contemporaneous anecdotes, see, for example, the story in Davis 2001, 88-89.

[6] "Summon thunderclaps by talismans" is a rather liberal translation of *kanhe leiting* 勘合雷霆. The term *kanhe* (lit. "investigate" and "match") alludes to the action of inspecting records or documents to make sure they match each other. A ritual master dispatches talismans, which serve as symbols of authenticity and authority, in order to deploy the force of thunder. The thunder force obeys the ritual master only if the talismans match their counterparts kept in the celestial realm. See Despeux 2000, 501; Campany 2002, 61-67; Bokenkamp's entry on "fu" (符) in Pregadio 2005, 35-38.

Thus, controlling the thunder force constituted only half of the benefits produced by the Thunder Rites. The meditation involved in the rituals also transformed the adept into an immortal.[7] As this paper will show, the meditative techniques that allowed the ritual master to "summon and unite with [thunder generals]" (*zhaohe* 召合), followed the same principles of internal alchemy or other exercises that promise to transform the practitioner into a deity during the ritual.

Scholars have noted the principle of employing internal alchemy in the meditation techniques of the Thunder Rites (Skar 1995; Davis 2001, 26). However, discussion on the operational level is scarce. The liturgical manuals of the Thunder Rites, unlike theoretical treatises, offer demonstrative examples of exactly how *neidan* imagery and language operated in a key Thunder Rites liturgy, namely Summoning the Generals (*zhaojiang* 召將). It should be made clear that internal alchemy did not necessarily lead to forming the meditative techniques used to summon the thunder generals. What I argue is that the Daoists' application of *neidan* concepts and terminology "naturalized" the Thunder Rites meditative exercise that subjected the priests' own identity to the domination of the divinities. The Daoist masters reinterpreted the phenomena of identity alteration in their traditional theology through the principles of internal alchemy and thus managed to maintain a theological coherence after embracing the Thunder Rites movement.

Internal Practices of Thunder Masters

Daoist clerics in general are "gentlemen [or gentlewomen] of the Dao." They are men and women ordained into the celestial hierarchy who possess the authority to command lesser deities. Their religious authority is confirmed through the admittance ceremony, an imperially inspired protocol, together with initiatory knowledge contained in scriptures, oral transmissions, and the ceremonially bequeathed ritual register (*falu* 法籙). Whenever in the course of history new gods developed, the creation of new rituals became necessary. In theory, the thunder deities were perceived as more violent than others and controlling them required an innovative approach. In executing Thunder Rites, clerics accordingly found that they had to form a union with the gods to get them to do what they wanted. To achieve this, the masters were advised to refine their *qi* 炁 (breath, vital energy), and harmonized it with that of the deities.

As scholars have pointed out variously, *qi* plays an important role in writings on Thunder Rites (Skar 1997, 177-78; Liu 2001; Ren 1999, 750). In Daoist

---

[7] The principle of "the Way as the core, the ritual as the application" in Thunder Rites, as Liu Zhongyu argues, can be traced back to *Huashu* 化書 by Tan Qiao 譚峭 of the early 10th century; see his "On Correct Ritual of the Five Thunders," esp. 16-18.

theories, the thunder deities, like all other phenomena in the cosmos, are manifestations of *qi*. They appear actively in the ritual masters' meditative visions and respond to their summons because their well-cultivated *qi* creates a kind of telepathic correspondence (*ganying* 感應) between them and the gods. Wang Wenqing explains that the initiates should summon the thunder deities with their "spirit of primordial life" (*yuanming zhi shen* 元命之神) and join the deities' *qi* with their own.[8] Bai Yuchan 白玉蟾 (1194–1229), another prominent Daoist adept, warned initiates that if their *qi* was imperfect, the deities would not respond however plentiful the sacrificial offerings of food and wine (*Daofa huiyuan* 70.10; ZHDZ 36.440a).

How, then, should a ritual master cultivate the *qi* in order to efficaciously summon and join the thunder deities? An excellent example appears in the liturgical manual *Leimen zuoyou famo shi Gou Bi er Yuanshuai fa* 雷門左右伐魔使苟畢二元帥法 (The Left and Right Demon-Conquering Agents of the Portal of Thunder, the Two Marshals Gou and Bi), contained in the *Fahai yizhu* 法海遺珠 (Pearls Retrieved from a Sea of Rituals; DZ 1166).[9]

The text opens with the "Oral Transmission of the Five Thunders" (*Wulei koujue* 五雷口訣) which places it in the Five Thunders ritual repertoire. Next comes a description of the meditation used to summon two exorcist deities, the Generals Gou 苟 and Bi 畢 named in the title. They exist in two realms simultaneously, the cosmos and the body. The practitioner first invokes their cosmic version: riding on radiant *qi*, they emerge from the thresholds of the Gate of Heaven and Door of Earth at the altar. As soon as they arrive, the practitioner summons their internal manifestation from within the body. This requires a specific form of internal practice, *neigong* 內功: "internal efforts" or "internal achievement." It begins with sitting in stillness and quietude, then engaging in active visualization:

> First visualize a golden radiance and see it turning into a bright moon rising between your kidneys. It penetrates all the way to the head where it transforms into a lofty perfected.
>
> Next, visualize the Heavenly Pass and the Earthly Axle commingling in the clear water below the navel. The turtle [Heavenly Pass] faces north and the snake [Earthly Axle] faces south; they exhale two breaths: one bluish-green, the other white, which emerge from the navel. The two breaths meet. Inhale and swallow [the breaths] as they descend to the pre-creation [Before Heaven] Cavity and enter the kidneys separately.

---

[8] *Daofa huiyuan* (Daoist Methods, United in Principle; DZ 1220) 61.1 (ZHDZ 36.367c).

[9] *Fahai yizhu* 34.7-15 (ZHDZ 41. 562a-64c). The *Fahai yizhu* is a collection of the ritual manuals of the mid-fourteenth century. It contains materials that date back to the twelfth century. See Boltz 1987, 51; Schipper and Verellen 2004, 1090.

Now let the blue-green breath on the left and the white breath on the right combine with the yellow breath in the center and join in the Yellow Court at the navel. Then transmit the heart fire downwards to refine this mixture of *qi* into an awesome and frightening radiance: this is the Purple Golden Elixir.

Move this elixir so that it ascends to the Narrow Strait [upper spine] through the Twelve-storied Tower [trachea]. As it is about to arrive in the head, inhale pure *qi* through the nose. Let it go directly through the back of the nose, soaring upwards.

Now visualize two deities riding on the two *qi* in black and red coming out from the left and right. Together with the two generals who are emerging from the Gate of Heaven and Door of Earth they stand in the golden radiance. All of a sudden, they merge with the internal elixir. Once this is done, send [the elixir] to the Primordial Cavity, and enter into great stillness.[10]

When then you write the talismans, blink your eyes seven times, recite the Golden Radiance Incantation once, visualize the lofty perfected, and blink your eyes again to bring forth [the internal version of] the two generals. Visualize the external generals descend to form a union. Then, carry out [the writing of the talismans].

The main part of this visualization practice is the generation of the Purple Golden Elixir (*zijindan* 紫金丹) within the body. Two streams of internal *qi* of blue-green and white coloring mingle with two external *qi* that are probably those of the two generals outside of the body. The mixture then returns to the body and moves to the kidneys. Both blue-green and white streams then emerge from the kidneys and join the yellow *qi* in the central part of the body. Next, the concoction is refined (*lian* 煉) by the heart fire at the Yellow Court in the center, the region of the middle cinnabar or elixir field (*dantian* 丹田). The colors of the three *qi* match those of wood, metal, and earth in accordance with the five phases. Together with the fire of the heart and the kidneys, which are associated with both water and fire, they complete the set of the five phases in meditative practice. Through repeated integration and refinement, moreover, different streams of *qi* fuse, intensify, and purify. The resulting product is the Purple Golden Elixir.

The process clearly contains some unmistakable traits of internal alchemy, which center on maneuvering *qi* within the practitioner's body under the cosmological patterns of yin and yang, the five phases, and the Eight Trigrams of the *Yijing* 易經 (Book of Changes), commonly expressed in the vocabulary of operative or external alchemy. On top of these, the process aims at producing

---

[10] The Primordial Cavity (Yuanxue 元穴) might be an abbreviation of Primordial Pass Cavity (Guanyuan xue 關元穴), the pressure point located between the kidneys. The Primordial Pass, in the tradition of the Highest Clarity visualization manual *Huangting jing* (Yellow Court Scripture), is located three inches below the navel, where the lower cinnabar or elixir field is found. See Robinet 1993, 81.

the elixir within one's body. *Neidan* practitioners use their bodies as a cauldron for concocting the elixir by carrying out psycho-physiological exercises. They see the human body as a microcosm and find "illumination by returning to the fundamental order of the cosmos" (Robinet 1989, 300).

Once the Purple Golden Elixir has taken shape, the practitioner meditatively guides it upward from the Narrow Strait (*jiaji* 夾脊) to the head. The Narrow Strait, located on the spinal column between the shoulder blades at the twenty-four vertebra, is the middle of the Three Passes (*sanguan* 三關) in the *qi*-circulation of internal alchemy. It is also the locus where the *qi* is refined into spirit (*shen*). As the *Neijing tu* 內經圖 (Diagram of Internal Pathways; see Komjathy 2008) indicates: "From the Double Pass of the Narrow Strait all the way through the head, this is the root of the paths of cultivation."[11]

When it reaches the head, the Purple Golden Elixir goes through yet another phase of refinement. It encounters the pure *qi* inhaled through the nose. As expressed in a *neidan* text, "the *qi* of Heaven and Earth enters from the nose and connects with the ancestral *qi* of the kidneys: they mingle together."[12] Thus two streams of *qi*, blue-green and white, the same as those that produce the Purple Golden Elixir, emerge from the kidneys. To activate the thunder deities, masters of the Five Thunders thus adapt the principles of internal alchemy to their particular form of internal cultivation and make active use of *neidan* practices in a ritual context. The meditative method is reminiscent of Highest Clarity (Shangqing 上清) style meditation, one of the sources of internal alchemy. Yet, the ritual manual explicitly uses words like Purple Golden Elixir and the "inner elixir" to characterize the results at various stages of the meditative process. It is through the lexicon of internal alchemy that the codifiers understood and expressed the required "internal efforts" or *neigong* of their ritual.

Eventually the two internal deities exit the practitioner's body to meet their cosmic manifestations. Their two versions fuse and become what the text calls the "internal elixir" (*neidan*), which the practitioner stores in his body. This completes the practice. As the gods, in the form of the internal elixir, return into the practitioner's body, his "internal achievement" presumably progresses one more step. He can then proceed to write potent and empowering talismans to control the thunder gods.

All talisman writing should be undertaken in conjunction with the active visualization of the divine generals as they emerge from the body and unite with their cosmic manifestation. Another text on Thunder Rites similarly states:

---

[11] The *Neijing tu* was probably produced no earlier than Qing times. Yet, it bears concepts of early origin. The defining characteristic principles of internal alchemy are not specific to certain stages of the tradition's development.

[12] *Dadan zhizhi* 大丹直指 ((Direct Pointers to the Great Elixir), edited by Chen Yingning 陳攖寧 (1880-1969) and collected in Hu and Wu 2006, 389-96; see esp., 392, *Lun heche* 論河車. This version of *Dadan zhizhi* is different from the canonic text in DZ 244.

"Use my spirit to merge with theirs [the thunder generals'] spirits; use my *qi* to unite with their *qi*. Spirit and *qi* are formless, but they form into talismans" (*Daofa huiyuan* 4.12; ZHDZ 36.27c). No thunder deity had the power to resist a talisman produced in such a manner.

Initiates internalized the *qi* of the thunder deities on a regular basis as they cultivated their internal version. In other words, ritual masters generated thunder deities within their bodies. As Pregadio points out, the innate body gods prominent in medieval Daoist meditation were discarded in internal alchemy and survived only in ritual performances based on the Numinous Treasure (Lingbao 靈寶) school (2006b, 150). Seen from the above descriptions of meditation in the Thunder Rites, furthermore, it appears that *neidan* practitioners discarded the medieval, pre-Tang concept of body gods in favor of a new one. The adepts now were told to generate an essence through meditation that would take the shape of the proper deities as the ritual demanded.

Deity Transformation

The visual exercises of thunder masters represents a cumulative achievement that requires regular practice over quite some time. It is difficult for the newly initiated who have not practiced their internal efforts for very long to merge with thunder deities. This is made clear by Deng Yougong 鄧有功, a twelfth-century codifier of liturgical compendia of the Heavenly Heart (Tianxin 天心) ritual lineage (see Hymes 2002, 271-77). According to the *Shangqing Tianxin zhengfa* 上清天心正法 (Correct Ritual of the Heavenly Heart of Highest Clarity; DZ 566, 2.1-2; ZHDZ 30.248bc), he proposed a procedure that "would not go wrong even once in 10,000 times." He called this method "the way of deity transformation through internal refinement" (*bianshen neilian* 變神內鍊) and claims that it resulted in the incarnation of a deity authoritative enough to command multiple subordinate entities.

In the section devoted to methods of defeating mountain demons (*shanxiao* 山魈), Deng instructs initiates on meditative techniques to prepare for battle:

> Whenever you want to control mountain demons, ... when you set out on your quest, first cleanse yourself and attend an audience with the Highest Emperor in silent [meditation] to respectfully make your case [for performing the exorcism].
>
> Visualize the Northern Emperor leaving his stellar palace, ascending to the [audience] hall, and taking his seat. The emperor next summons the Perfect Warrior along with other [deities] and orders them to take control of the source of wickedness in the Three Worlds.
>
> Next, envision the Perfect Warrior coming directly to the front of the [altar] table with the proper decree. Stand up! [Perform the ritual sequence of] deity transformation and become the grand general, the Per-

> fect Warrior, himself – with loosened hair and bare feet, holding the fire sword of samādhi in the right hand and forming a mudra with the left hand, while standing on the turtle and snake.
>
> After concluding this deity transformation, walk the stellar net of the Three Terraces and the Dipper. Once all that is complete, invoke the officials and generals of all the many bureaus of the Southern Court, visualizing them one by one. (5.1; ZHDZ 30.267a)

The ritual master thus acquires divine authorization from the Northern Emperor through an audience at the heavenly court.[13] After listening to (and presumably approving) the case, the Northern Emperor orders the Perfect Warrior (Zhenwu 真武) to descend into the human realm to pacify the wicked. The god's descent takes the form of moving directly to the front of the altar table, i.e., the very spot where the ritual master is lying prostrate. Once he has arrived, the ritual master begins the next step of meditation to become (*wei* 為) the god. Only after completing the transformation through internal refinement can the master begin the ritual choreography that summons divine officers and generals (*guanjiang* 官將).

How, then, is deity transformation by internal refinement conducted? Again, it is a meditative exercise. Practitioners first visualize (*cun* 存) their body as a withered tree (*kushu* 枯樹) being burned by heart fire (yang, Li 離 trigram) and washed away by kidney water (yin, Kan 坎 trigram). What remains is pure *qi* as a shining pearl. Next they recite the deity transformation invocation and visualize themselves mutating into an infant (*ying'er* 嬰兒). The infant, in a bubble of red radiance, grows larger. After further hand gestures and invocations, they see the radiant bubble burst and the infant transform at will into either the Heavenly Master, the Perfect Warrior, or the martial deity Tianpeng 天蓬.[14] Having obtained the identity of these high authorities, the ritual master then calls on divine generals and officials to perform the task.

Generating and cultivating an infant in one's internal body is a concept only too familiar to students of internal alchemy. *Neidan* texts, besides applying terms like "the perfected" (*zhenren* 真人) and "mysterious pearl" (*xuanzhu* 玄珠), often call the elixir an embryo (*tai'er* 胎兒) or holy fetus (*shengtai* 聖胎) and show it in the form of a baby (Pregadio 2006a, 205). Of course, they did not invent the idea of an embryo dwelling in the microcosm of the body as the essence of the self; rather, it can be traced back as far as the later Han dynasty in the second century C.E., when the *Laozi Xianger zhu* 老子想爾注 (*Xiang'er*

---

[13] For a historical analysis of the Northern Emperor and his connection to medieval forms of exorcism, see Mollier 1997.

[14] "Heavenly Master" undoubtedly refers to Zhang Daoling. Tianpeng is one of the oldest divine commanding generals in Daoist ritual. His invocation appears in the *Zhen'gao* 真誥 (Declarations of the Perfected; DZ 1016) by Tao Hongjing 陶弘景 (456-536).

Commentary to the *Daode jing*) was composed (see Bokenkamp 1997). The *Laozi zhongjing* 老子中經 (Central Scripture of Laozi; DZ 1168), also from the early medieval period, includes references of nourishing the "perfected self" (*zhenwu* 真吾) which resides in the stomach in the form of an infant (*chizi* 赤子). However, in these early texts, the infant is innate, unlike in internal alchemy of the Song where it must be generated by the practitioner (Pregadio 2006b, 138). In this sense, the infant in Deng's method is consistent with the liturgy of internal alchemy but not with that of earlier traditions.

Still, even then fusion of the ritual master's *qi* and that of the deity is still necessary. A liturgical manual of Five Thunders Ritual called *Zouchuan hunlian fashi* 奏傳混鍊法式 (Model Rites for Submission, Dispatch, Mixing, and Refinement) appears in the *Fahai yizhu*. It says:

> Form both your hands into the mudra of deity transformation, then place them next to your waist. First visualize yourself as a withered log of wood. Join your thumbs to the tips of the middle fingers, inhale the *qi* of the south, and merge it with that of the heart to form the perfect fire (*zhenhuo* 真火). Next, flick your thumbs from the tip of your middle fingers to set the log afire. Immediately, the flame rises up. Now put your thumbs on the tips of your index fingers to generate the wind of the Xun 巽 trigram to blow away the ashes. Leave no traces.
>
> Following this, visualize an infant growing larger in your cinnabar field. See him with loose hair and barefoot, clad in a black robe and golden armor, looking like the Perfect Warrior. Beneath his feet, there is a green turtle exhaling *qi* that merges with that of the kidneys; there is also a red snake exhaling *qi* that merges with that of the heart. (2.1-2; ZHDZ 41.454c-455a)

The mudra mentioned at the beginning of the citation indicates that the purpose of the practice is to transform oneself into the divinity. The first step is to visualize oneself as a "withered log of wood." Next one reduces the material body through ritual burning to a state of non-existence–not only burning it to ashes but raising a wind to blow the ashes away. Wood and wind are two key cosmological phenomena represented by the Eight Trigrams. After thus symbolically destroying the old body, adepts next generate a new body in the form of an infant that represents the new, perfected self (see Pregadio 2006a, 211). The new body then grows into the Perfect Warrior, with whom adepts merge with the help of the god's emblematic animals, turtle and snake. The turtle represents the trigram Kan (water), while the snake stands for the trigram Li (fire). Both exhale *qi* that mixes with that of the practitioner's kidneys and heart—again associated with water and fire. Once both the divine and human *qi* have merged completely, the ritual master completes the procedure of deity transformation and becomes the god. He is thereby empowered to deploy divine troops to vanquish demons.

Despite the claim of being foolproof, Deng's method of deity transformation by internal refinement still requires cultivating the bond between the submissive ritual master and the patron-like deities. Several manuals offer more specific instructions in this regard. For example, the *Xuantian jizou lingwen* 玄天急奏靈文 (Efficacious Writing for Quick Submission to the Dark Heaven) teaches practitioners to have a daily audience with the Perfect Warrior in the following manner:

> Everyday in the very early morning or in the quiet of night, sit straight, click your teeth, and swallow the saliva twenty-four times. Visualize a bright spot between the kidneys, seeing light shoot up along the spine to the back of head and entering the Niwan Palace [upper elixir field].
>
> Silently recite the Incantation of the Golden Radiance and chant the full title of the "Transformation of the Heavenly Worthy of the Golden Gate [Perfect Warrior] three times. See how, after a few moments, the radiance spreads and shines in all ten directions. Next see the Dark Emperor [i.e., Perfect Warrior] sitting upright on the Mountain of Jade Capital, which [internally] is the Niwan Palace.
>
> Sit as still as a mountain. Next, meditate on the four agents on duty: the agent of the heart emerging from the left eye, the agent of the liver emerging the right eye, plus the two agents of the lungs and kidneys emerging from the ears. They stand completely still in the clouds and pay obeisance by kneeling and bowing their heads.
>
> Next, see yourself—in the form of a perfected with a writing-tablet in his hands—come out from the Yellow Court. Kneel upright and bow in audience [to the god]. After finishing your report [*qishi* 啓事], meditate on the golden radiance as it emerges from the four directions as before. Following this, return to the Scarlet Palace to look down on the spot between the kidneys, where you see brightness. Sit completely still. At this point the process (*shi* 事) is finished.
>
> If this audience is for the capture of malicious spirits, meditate on the Dark Emperor with loosened hair, bare feet, and ferocious expression; see divine soldiers guarding him carefully on each side. If the situation is more ordinary, meditate on the god's cheerful face. Should it be to rescue someone from misfortune, meditate on his compassionate countenance. (*Fahai yizhu*, 20.8; ZHDZ 41.489c)

In this daily veneration, the god—in this case the Perfect Warrior—is like a powerful supervisor who listens patiently to the ritual master's report and reacts accordingly. The relationship between the two parties is direct and interactive. The bureaucratic model commonly used to characterize Daoist rituals of petitioning heavenly authorities does not capture the dynamics between the ritual master and the divinity. It is better captured by the honorific address "ancestral master" (*zushi* 祖師), which is often used to refer to the founding saint of a ritual lineage in Thunder Rites manuals. The title denotes more accurately the role the deity plays in this type of meditative practice. And, of course, the

Perfect Warrior has, among many other honorific appellations, also the title "ancestral master."

The Ancestral Master

The divine supervisor and meditative partner so important to the masters of Thunder Rites appears in Daoist ritual as early as the Heavenly Masters of the Later Han. The concept is prominent already in the *Chisong zi zhangli* 赤松子章曆 (Master Redpine's Petition Almanac; DZ 615), an important collection of rituals concerning the presentation of petitions to the heavenly court developed by generations of Heavenly Masters (see Nickerson 1997, 238; Verellen 2004). The text says:

> Prostrate yourself in front of the [altar] table. Visualize red *qi* coming out from your heart and ascending to Heaven.[15] . . .
>
> Soon you see the eighteen-foot Gate of Heaven. Your numerous guards all have to stay here. Only General Zhou, the functionaries on duty, and the petition-submitting jade lad who carries the actual petition in his hand go on though the gate. Turn west and pay your respects to the ritual master of Orthodox Unity of the Three Heavens whose name is Zhang Daoling. After bowing to him, relate the circumstances and reasons for your petition and memorial.
>
> As the Heavenly Master approves, bow on your knees nine times,[16] then go on to the Phoenix Pavilion and enter through the door. In a moment, a divine lad clad in vermilion robes and black cap emerges to receive the petition from the petition-submitting jade lad. He enters [the Phoenix Pavilion], then after a short while comes out again and leads [you] to see the Most High [Lord Lao]. . . as well as the Great One. . . .
>
> Submit the petition to the Most High and see him read through it. Next, the Great One makes a note on the petition recording the wishes of the Most High. He assigns it to the [office] Jade Platform of Great Purity, telling the administrators to write "comply" on it. . . .
>
> To conclude bow on your knees twice, bid farewell to the Most High, and take your leave. Bow on your knees twice again to bid farewell to the Heavenly Master. (*Chisong zi zhangli*, 2.26-7; ZHDZ 8.638bc)

Zhang Daoling, the ancestral master who founded the Heavenly Masters school, plays a pivotal role in this petition-presenting ritual. He is the first authority that the ritual master meets in the heavenly court. He pre-approves the petition, and the rest is mere formality since the Most High is expected to

---

[15] Although the text here seems to suggest that the red *qi* ascends to the sky, the following clearly indicates that the priest takes the journey.

[16] The original phrase is *tianshi jiubai* 天師九拜 which reads: "The Heavenly Master bows on his knees nine times." This does not make sense. I changed the text according to a similar version in the *Shangqing Tianxin zhengfa* 6.8 (ZHDZ 30.274c).

comply with the request. Zhang leads the ritual master in audience with the Most High and helps him obtain final approval. He is of central importance.

In the Thunder Rites of the Song, the ancestral master's role became even more significant. A manual entitled *Jinque xiansheng jiashu biwen* 金闕先生家書秘文 (Secret Text of Letters Home by the Master of the Golden Gate; *Fahai yizhu* 27; ZHDZ 41.523a-527b) contains descriptions of rituals to "capture haunting spirits and demolish their temples" as well as to pray for rain or clear weather (41.524b). These are typical functions of a Thunder Rite. The "letter home" in the title refers to a request submitted to the Perfect Warrior—in the text is addressed by his more exalted title Supreme Emperor of the Dark Heaven (Xuantian shangdi 玄天上帝)—for authorization of a ritual performance.[17] To dispatch the letter, the ritual master "burns incense, transforms into the divinity, walks the net of the Dipper, forms the "jade mudra" with his right hand and "sword mudra" with his left, and strikes the command-tablet (*ling* 令) three times." All these are specific preliminary exercises that form the basic program of Daoist ritual. After this, a rite called Summoning the Generals involves chanting the names of the Four Functionaries of Dark Heaven (*sizhi gongcao* 四值功曹) as well as of the "numerous marshals and generals of the Thunder Bureau."

After the chant, the ritual master begins the meditative journey to his audience with the Perfect Warrior, called the "visualization and meditation for presenting the letter home" (*bai jiashu cunyun* 拜家書存運). During his formal audience, he then submits the letter (petition) to the heavenly court. He sets out by visualizing a ray of red radiance coming out of the heart. After this, the text instructs:

> Look directly at the Gate of Heaven located in the north. Visualize the red radiance from the altar reaching directly to the Gate of Heaven, moving off for tens of thousands of miles with no end [in sight]. Four envoys on duty are standing in front to lead the way. One of them respectfully holds the letter in his hand, while the generals and officers listed in the [priest's] ritual register [and thus at his beck and call] follow behind.
>
> Ride the red radiance and off you go. After a while, see a long bridge, illuminated with flickering lights. After crossing the bridge, again stride on the red radiance and keep going.
>
> Soon you see a golden tower of twelve stories. Climb to its top, then once again get on the red radiance and move further. See a red bridge coming into sight. Cross it to see the Jade Gate of Central Heaven covered by colorful clouds. Enter the gate. The generals and officers listed in your registers have to remain here; only yourself and the four envoys on duty enter.

---

[17] A similar version of this petition-dispatching meditation appears in *Xuantian jizou lingwen*, contained in *Fahai yizhu* 20.6 (ZHDZ 41.488a).

> Once through the gate, turn right and go into the Yousheng yuan 佑聖院 (Courtyard of the Aiding Sage) which is heavily guarded by generals and thunder deities. Enter its gate. The four envoys respectfully hold the letter and pass it to the perfected official in charge of petitions. The perfected official receives the letter and, with a cheerful smile, respectfully presents the petition. He then leads the practitioner directly to the hall. Bow down on your knees nine times, get up. . . . make a report point by point as you wish. (*Fahai yizhu* 27; ZHDZ 41.524bc)

After the audience, the ritual master returns from the heavenly court via the same route. Once again clicking his teeth and swallowing saliva, he concludes the ritual of submitting the letter home. Following this is the rite of "dispatching the letter to the generals on commission" (*fa jiashu qianjiang* 發家書遣將). It serves to send the various divine generals and soldiers to carry out the ritual master's commands.

In this rite, the Perfect Warrior acts as the ancestral master, paralleling the role of Zhang Daoling in the earlier text. Although he is addressed with the exalted title Supreme Emperor, the location of his office, in a side compound of the heavenly palace not unlike that of Zhang Daoling's, betrays the true protocol. As a matter of fact, the letter home is typically used for submitting petitions to ancestral masters in Thunder Rites. It is thus noteworthy that approval from a mere ancestral master, even if he was as exalted as the Perfect Warrior, was all the ritual master needed to command the thunder generals. As the ancestral master rose in prominence, traditional authority figures such as the Most High were accordingly less central in the Thunder Rituals. This transition, moreover, was the end result of a process that involved practitioners' daily visualization of and contact with ancestor masters. Their rise, it seems, reflects the close association between practitioners and masters in the formation of Thunder Rite lineages.

Conclusion

The key to an efficacious Thunder Rites performance is the ritual master's success in summoning the thunder generals. Two methods of summoning are dominant: in one the master commands the deities by a telepathic-like correspondence made possible through his regular practice of internalizing the *qi* of the deities in question; in the other the master assumes the identity of a high authority in the Daoist pantheon. They developed from two distinct but complementary Daoist interpretations of the thunder deities.

Daoist masters, such as Bai Yuchan and Wang Wenqing, emphasized that thunder gods were fundamentally materializations of *qi*. In light of such an understanding of the nature of thunder deities, their life stories and miracles hold little importance in the rituals (Skar 1997, 178). What is important is that the ritual masters have cultivated their own *qi* sufficiently. By the twelfth century, internal alchemy had been so well developed that it could offer the proper theory and techniques for the ritual masters to cultivate their *qi* for the purpose of visualizing thunder generals.

However, hagiographies of the thunder deities still take a prominent position in many ritual manuals found in the Daoist canon. The deities appear as apotheosized saints or rectified demons who had been granted titles and offices in the lower ranks of the celestial hierarchy. This indicates that the thunder deities were not always regarded as pure *qi* even within the canonic tradition, yet their material aspect made it possible for them to receive positions in the divine bureaucracy. In accepting the thunder deities as individual beings and granting them titles, Daoists institutionalized the subordination of the newly assimilated spirits. For centuries, this had been the traditional method for absorbing local cults without endangering the status of established masters and veteran deities.

Nevertheless, something new emerged when thunder masters who had taken over the role of traditional Daoist dignitaries emerged as high-ranking officials with the authority to command lower functionaries, such as the thunder generals. Deng Yougong's method of deity transformation thus enabled ritual masters to assemble a thunder army to demolish various demons, not by obtaining the authority of an office but by becoming identical with a high authority. As Judith Boltz points out, ritual movements since the tenth century were not content simply to invoke the deities. Rather, they developed the innovation of ritual masters becoming the deity, so they could be "perceived not merely as a manipulator of divine forces but as the agent through whom they took charge" (1987, 25).

Ordained Daoists then and now consciously distinguish themselves from neighborhood shamans, passively awaiting divine possession like puppets; rather, they aspire to be puppeteers in charge of the action. Thus, when they speak and act in the manner of a deity, divine possession is not an acceptable explanation for their identity transformation. As Schipper points out, Daoists classify techniques of possession as "vulgar rites" and replace them with "the inner ritual of meditation" in their liturgy (1985, 34).

Yet, how could one "become" a deity through meditation? What kind of meditative techniques are there in the Daoist tradition that could provide a theoretical basis for a human being to morph into a god? The answer is *neidan*. The master's temporary apotheosis is the result of transforming his internal body or true-self into the deity. Just as this transformation reflects the great efforts Daoist masters took to separate themselves from the agents of popular religion, the contribution of internal alchemy to Daoism went far beyond meditation. The cultivation of the immortal embryo not only led to the personal immortality of the practitioner but his transformation into a deity became the central aspect of powerful rituals of petition, exorcism, and cosmic control, especially manifest in the rites associated with newly prominent martial deities and officials of the Bureau of Thunder.

Bibliography

Bokenkamp, Stephen R. 1997. *Early Daoist Scriptures*. With a contribution by Peter Nickerson. Berkeley: University of California Press.

_____. 2007. *Ancestors and Anxiety: Daoism and the Birth of Rebirth in China*. Berkeley: University of California Press.

Boltz, Judith M. 1987. *A Survey of Taoist Literature: Tenth to Seventeenth Centuries*. Berkeley: University of California, China Research Monograph 32.

_____. 1993. "Not by the Seal of Office Alone: New Weapons in Battles with the Supernatural." In *Religion and Society in T'ang and Sung China*, 241-306, edited by P. Ebrey and P. N. Gregory. Honolulu: University of Hawaii Press.

Campany, Robert Ford. 2002. *To Live As Long As Heaven and Earth: A Translation and Study of Ge Hong's Traditions of Divine Transcendent*. Berkeley: University of California Press.

Davis, Edward L. 2001. *Society and the Supernatural in Sung China*. Honolulu: University of Hawai'i Press.

Despeux, Catherine. 2000. "Talismans and Sacred Diagrams." In *Daoism Handbook*, edited by Livia Kohn, 498-540. Leiden: E. Brill.

Hu Haiya 胡海牙 and Wu Guozhong 武国中 eds. 2006. *Zhonghua xianxue yangsheng quanshu: Chen Yingning xiansheng dui jiankang changshou xueshuo zuchu de dute gongxian* 中华仙学养生全书: 陈撄宁先生对健康长寿学説作出的独特贡献. Beijing: Huaxia chubanshe.

Hymes, Robert. 2002. *Way and Byway: Taoism, Local Religion, and Models of Divinity in Sung and Modern China*. Berkeley: University of California Press.

Komjathy, Louis. 2008. "Mapping the Daoist Body (1): The *Neijing tu* in History." *Journal of Daoist Studies* 1:67-92.

Liu Zhongyu 刘仲宇. 2001. "Wulei zhengfa kaolun" 五雷正法考论. *Zongjiao xue yanjiu* 宗教学研究 52:14-21.

Mollier, Christine. 1997. "La méthode de l'empereur du nord du mont Fengdu: une tradition exorciste du taoïsme médiévale." *T'oung Pao* 83:329-85.

Nickerson, Peter. 1997. "The Great Petition for Sepulchral Plaints." In *Early Daoist Scriptures*, by Stephen Bokenkamp, 230-74. Berkeley: University of California Press.

Pregadio, Fabrizio, ed. 2005. *The Encyclopedia of Taoism*. London: Curzon Press.

_____. 2006a. *Great Clarity: Daoism and Alchemy in Early Medieval China*. Stanford: Stanford University Press.

_____. 2006b. "Early Daoist Meditation and the Origins of Internal Alchemy." In *Daoism in History: Essays in Honour of Liu Ts'un-yan*, edited by Benjamin Penny, 121-58. London: Routledge.

Ren Jiyu 任繼愈, ed. 1999. *Zhongguo daojiao shi* 中國道教史. Beijing: Zhongguo shehui kexue chubanshe.

Robinet, Isabelle. 1989. "Original Contributions of *Neidan* to Taoism and Chinese Thought." In *Taoist Meditation and Longevity Techniques*, edited by Livia Kohn, 297-330. Ann Arbor: University of Michigan, Center for Chinese Studies Publications.

_____. 1993. *Taoist Meditation*. Translated by Norman Girardot and Julian Pas. Albany: State University of New York Press.

Schipper, Kristofer. 1994. *Taoist Body*. Translated by Karen C. Duval. Berkeley: University of California Press.

_____. 1985. "Vernacular and Classical Ritual in Taoism." *Journal of Asian Studies* 65: 21-51.

Schipper, Kristofer, and Franciscus Verellen, eds. 2004. *The Taoist Canon: A Historical Companion to the Daozang*. 3 vols. Chicago: University of Chicago Press.

Skar, Lowell. 1995. "Ethical Aspects of Daoist Healing: The Case of Song and Yuan Thunder Rites." In *East Asian Science: Tradition and Beyond*, edited by Keizō Hashimoto, Catherine Jami, and Lowell Skar, 221-29. Osaka: Kansai University Press.

_____. 1997. "Administering Thunder: A Thirteenth-Century Memorial Deliberating the Thunder Rites." *Cahiers d'Extrême-Asie* 9: 159-202.

_____. 2000. "Ritual Movements, Deity Cults, and the Transformation of Daoism in Song and Yuan Times." In *Daoism Handbook*, edited by Livia Kohn, 413-63. Leiden: E. Brill.

Sun Guangxian 孫光憲. 1959 [10th c.]. *Beimeng suoyan* 北夢瑣言. Shanghai: Zhonghua shuju Shanghai bianji suo.

Verellen, Franciscus. 2004. "The Heavenly Master Liturgical Agenda According to Chisong Zi's Petition Almanac." *Cahiers d'Extrême-Asie* 14:291-343.

Numinous Father and Holy Mother
Late-Ming Duo-Cultivation Practice*

Xun Liu

> As for the practice of the 'other,' it is to borrow what the 'other' possesses to refine for what 'I' does not have. It is the key to perfecting Dao, and the wondrous secret for the ultimate transformation. It is not to be confused with what the world calls the deviant ways of the bedchamber arts. All the immortals and buddhas who ascended to Heaven have done so without exception by this means. Aside from it, is there another way to perfection? . . .
>
> At the moment of gathering the drug, the two *qi* commingle, surging forth like tides. So the word "battle" is employed as a metaphor to inspire awe and restraint in the practitioner. But there are those dumb wits who do not understand this. Upon seeing such terms as "seeking battles, dispatching the General, slighting the Enemy and disturbing the Essence," they revile them as theories of the "Gathering Battles at the Triple Mounds."[1]

Cao Heng 曹珩, a Daoist master of internal alchemy and medical writer from Xin'an county (Anhui) composed this impassioned defense in the summer of 1631. At this time, duo-cultivation practice was known by terms such as "the other" (*bijia* 彼家) and had been reviled as immoral and deviant in the public eye. As Cao observed, there were many similarities in the symbolism and language employed in both duo-cultivation practice and bedchamber arts which contributed to public perception. At a deeper level, however, the public's proclivity toward condemnation of duo practices came from an anxiety about the way duo-cultivation allegedly operated: an exploitative "borrowing" to obtain

---

* Earlier versions of the chapter were presented first at the Conference on Daoist Cultivation, held in April, 2000 on Vashon Island near Seattle and at the 2003 AAS annual meeting in New York. I thank the participants who commented on the earlier versions at these venues. I also thank Charlotte Furth, Livia Kohn, and the anonymous readers for their useful comments which helped improve the chapter.

[1] Cao Heng, *Daoyuan yiqi* 道元一氣 (The Unitary Qi of the Way's Origin; dat. 1634), reprint Beijing: Beijing Normal University Press, 1990, 1:28, 58.

what the 'other' had in her body to refine and replenish what "I" did not possess. Despite euphemistic terms, such "borrowing" involved a delicate and potentially volatile exchange of valuable, vital bodily energies between man and woman. For many, such "borrowing" did not differ from the known deviant techniques of the bedchamber arts and the Triple Mound Gathering.[2]

It was precisely this tendency to conflate or confuse the duo-practice with other sexual techniques that provoked such an eloquent and impassioned defense from Cao Heng. While the public's reaction was predictable, Cao's insistence on differentiating the practice from the rest of the "deviant techniques" requires a more elaborate and nuanced analysis.

Unfortunately our knowledge about duo-cultivation remains limited. What we know tends to be either ideologically biased or unbalanced. As a result, duo-cultivation has been routinely condemned as a socially subversive and morally corrupting sexual deviation. Even in some of the most recent, open-minded Western scholarship, the secluded duo-practices of the late imperial period have been classified with the sexual gathering or plucking practices, with the bedchamber arts and cultivation of long life.

But is such perception and appraisal based on historical fact? Has sufficient consideration been given to all textual evidence on the subject? Is a more contextualized and alternative interpretation of the practice possible? Let us begin our inquiry by looking at the sources.

Sources

My study uses mainly four texts, often identified with duo or yin-yang cultivation of the late Ming. While scholars may reasonably differ on their specific date, I have accepted them as products of that period.

First is the *Xuanwei xinyin* 玄微心印 (Heart-to-Heart Transmission of the Mysterious and the Delicate), written by a group of four practitioners.[3] It has been attributed to the so-called Eastern School of the yin-yang cultivation tradition, pioneered and represented by the Ming internal alchemist Lu Xixing 陸西星 (1520-1606; see Liu 1976, 175-225).[4] My research has led me to believe that

---

[2] We still lack a truly perceptive study of the sexual inner alchemical techniques. For introductory surveys of the literature of the sexual and erotic techniques of self-cultivation, see Van Gulik 1961; Needham 1983; Wile 1992.

[3] The text has several editions, besides the one in ZW 379. ("ZW" stands for *Zangwai daoshu*, numbers refer to Komjathy 2002.) Sun Dianqi mentions an 1827 two-volume one by Fu Jinquan 傅金銓 (1999, 201), possibly an off-print of Fu's collection, the *Zhengdao bishu* 証道秘書 (Esoteric Books in Confirmation of the Way; ZW 395; dat. before 1827).

[4] Chinese scholars like Li Yuanguo have based the ascription to the Eastern School primarily on an impressionistic similarity between techniques described in the text and methods advocated by Eastern School representatives like Lu Xixing. See Li 1991, 1870.

while no precise dating can be ascertained, the text's content seems consistent with other Ming duo-cultivation works.

The second work is the *Sanfeng danjue* 三豐丹訣 (Master Sanfeng's Alchemical Instructions, ZW 380), a compendium of three texts. The first is a hagiography of the legendary Ming alchemist Zhang Sanfeng and a collection of alchemical poems attributed to him. The second is called *Jindan jieyao* 金丹節要 (Essential Excerpts of the Golden Elixir); it provides a detailed explanation of the steps and timing involved in secluded duo-cultivation. The third text is the *Caizhen jiyao* 探真輯要 (Secrets of Gathering the True *Qi*), a collection of rhymed instructions further explaining various practice stages, methods, and processes. It must be pointed out that both the *Xuanwei xinyin* and *Sanfeng danjue* still lack reliable dating and authentication.

The remaining two works have more reliable dating. The *Jindan zhenchuan* 金丹真傳 (True Transmission of the Golden Elixir, ZW 398) was originally published by the alchemist Sun Ruzhong 孫如忠 in 1615. Like the previous two texts, it was preserved in its present form due to the collection efforts of Fu Jinquan 傅金銓 during the Jiaqing and Daoguan reigns (1796-1850).

Finally, the *Daoyuan yiqi* 道元一氣 (Unitary *Qi* of the Original Dao; ed. Tao 1990, 37-123) was written by the physician and alchemist Cao Heng (Yuanbai 元白, fl.1630s), over a period of five years and first published in 1636. These books provide a rich textual environment wherein we can examine the doctrine, spiritual and ethical dimensions, and technical aspects of duo-cultivation from the perspective of advocates and practitioners.

Critiques and Dissents

The legitimacy of sexual cultivation practices was called into question early on. Criticism intensified noticeably during and after the Song dynasty. In his famous ballad on internal alchemy entitled *Luofu cuixu yin* 羅浮翠虛吟 (Cuixu's Musings on Mt. Luofu), Chen Nan 陳楠 (Cuixu 翠虛, ?-1213) of the Southern Song delivers a scathing attack on a host of what he considered "side-door" practices, including plucking and gathering, the bedchamber arts, the yin elixir, and the manipulation of women (*Cuixu pian*, DZ 1090). But the most comprehensive critical taxonomy of sexual cultivation practices was delivered by Li Daochun 李道純 in his *Zhonghe ji* 中和集 (Compendium of Central Harmony, DZ 249, dat. 1306). He classifies sexual and deviant practices into three classes of three ranks each, condemning the lower three in particular. He further rates each as "deviant ways," "ways outside the Way," and "side-doors" according to their relative degrees of moral deviance.

Others, like Gu Jianqing, tend to relegate it uncritically to the so-called "Muddy Water alchemical techniques," following the standard Confucian condemnation (Hu 1994, 1336).

While early opponents of sexual cultivation were quick and vehement in their condemnation, they showed little interest in understanding subtle differences among the varied practices. Yet their censure proved both compelling and lasting. Indeed, the righteousness of the early censure was so much beyond reproach or refutation that it became established as a rhetorical convention as well as a moral tradition in the writings of internal alchemy that had to be reckoned with by all later alchemists, be they for or against duo-practice.

But even amidst the clamor for moral rectitude and spiritual orthodoxy, a few irreverent voices of discord could still be heard. Among both opponents and proponents, the effort to distinguish proper from "deviant" practices persisted. Even a vocal critic of sexual cultivation practices in internal alchemy made an attempt at such distinction. In his compendium *Daoshu* 道樞 (Pivot of Dao, DZ 1017), Zeng Zao 曾慥 renders a severe attack on a range of sexual techniques under the category of "manipulation of women." He denounces them as nothing more than the deviant "way of the yellow and red" of the early Heavenly Masters in the late Han, as pursuits that would lead to death rather than life. As such they must be attacked by beating the drums of the punitive Lords of Heaven, Earth, and Water. However, citing the immortal Lady Ziwei of the fifth century, even Zeng notes that the Perfected One's practice of "the visions of the duo" was to be distinguished from the "sexual intercourse of man and wife." Zeng's inadvertent defense and distinction not only allows for the existence of duo-cultivation, but also suggests that its practice differs from mundane sexual union in that the perfected seemed to have only "dwelled on the vision of the duo" without engaging in the "acts of the husband and wife" (ZHDZ 20:618-19).

For proponents of the practice, the difference was not only obvious but meaningful. Indeed, an early prescription for duo-cultivation appears in the *Yangxing yanming lu* 養性延命錄 (On Nourishing Inner Nature and Extending Life, DZ 838), probably compiled by the disciples of Sun Simiao 孫思邈 in the seventh century. It describes "a way for attaining immortality for both men and women." The goal of this practice thus differed significantly from other bedchamber arts which tended to center exclusively on lengthening the life of the male practitioner. It was also different in that it required meditative visualization and breath control in the female as well as the male partners and made no mention of multiple females needed for the practice.

A similar distinction also appears in the late Song text *Zituan danjing* 紫團丹經 (Zituan's Alchemical Scripture, DZ 878).[5] It differentiates "the coition that goes along with" the natural reproductive process from "the coition that goes against" it, the former resulting in the "mundane" whereas the latter cul-

---

[5] The text is of uncertain authorship but cites pre- and early Song authors of internal alchemy. For more details, see Schipper and Verellen 2004, 841-42.

minates in the "sacred." In addition, a host of regimens were devised for achieving "the sacred coition."

Thus two trends existed in the writings of internal alchemy before the Ming. The dominant trend either ignored or confused any real or perceived differences between sexual techniques and duo-cultivation. It had gained ascendance since the Song, establishing the moral censure of sexual cultivation as a rhetorical convention that was later adopted by both proponents and opponents of duo-cultivation.

Yet parallel to this dominant trend, a strand of dissent strained to affirm the distinction of duo-cultivation from other sexual practices. As consumer culture rose and the merchant's libertine lifestyle gained currency among the literati class, interest in erotic arts, literature, sexual techniques, and practices widened throughout late-Ming society (see Brook 1998). Shen Defu 沈德符, the observant chronicler of social, political, and cultural changes, commented that from the early fifteenth to the late sixteenth centuries, many court officials and literati actively engaged in sexual techniques and love potions for political as well as lascivious purposes.[6] As such techniques proliferated among ambitious literati and enterprising Daoists, the already opaque differences claimed by earlier writers between duo-cultivation and other erotic and life-nourishing techniques blurred further. This blurred boundary in due course elicited impassioned apologies from defenders of duo-cultivation.

Late-Ming Understanding

The differences Cao Heng saw between duo-cultivation and other, rampantly erotic and sexual practices appear in several areas: the normative conceptualization of self and body; the self-discipline and goals of the practice; and the technological, economic, and material dimensions associated with the practice. These are differences and distinctions of quality, not of degree; they represent a alternative construction of sexuality and the body based on Daoist-informed ascetics, self-discipline, and the spiritual desire for transcendence and immortality as opposed to prevalent libertine pursuits centered on erotic pleasures and emotional attachments by merchants and literati alike.

Duo-cultivation proponents like Cao Heng sought to legitimize the practice by linking the union of man and woman to the cosmogony of the universe. In so doing, they consecrated the practitioners' bodies in the halo of the orthodox cosmology of the society at the time. Yu Taizhen 諭太真, one of the four transmitters of the *Xuanwei xinyin*, says:

---

[6] See his *Wanli yehuo pian* 萬曆野獲篇 (A Compilation of Gatherings From the Wild of the Wanli Reign, ed. 1959), ZHDZ 21:541-50. Shen describes a trend among late Ming literati to participate in and promote the use of such practices as bedchamber arts, red potions, autumn stone, and other aphrodisiacs.

> One is the Dao. What carries Dao? Dao is carried in the duo. "Duo" is the name for yin and yang. . . . Heaven without Earth is not Heaven; Earth without Heaven is not Earth. From where else does the sage derive his principle?
>
> The sun without the moon will not be as radiant; the moon without the sun will not be as luminous. On what else does the multitude of beings depend for nurture? Viewed as such, Heaven, Earth and the sage evolve from the One into the Two. Then they reunite from the Two back into the One. (ZW 379:302)

Yu's categories go beyond traditional cosmological concepts. Aside from being complementary ontological principles and forming the primordial, generative *qi* of the universe, the duo and yin-yang also have specific, concrete meanings: they refer to the bodies of the man and woman united in cultivation practice. By equating duo-cultivation with the cosmic process of creation, proponents consecrated the practice as the sacred process of cosmic genesis. Duo-practitioners therefore were the sacred embodiment of creation.

Such efforts at self-consecration stem from a profound anxiety and trepidation which duo-cultivators felt about the tremendous risk and rigor involved in their enterprise. Internal alchemy fundamentally serves to reverse the process of human life which nature has dictated: conception, birth, growth, aging, illness, and death. It seeks to engender a kind of life that can be sustained for eternity. Thus it defies the constraints of nature by uncovering, manipulating, and even "going against" or "reversing" its principles and movements.

Adepts of internal alchemy thus often perceive their practice as an enterprise aiming at either outsmarting or wresting control over natural transformations away from Heaven and Earth. Any misstep in such an enterprise is fatal. But the lure of success also looms large. The *Sanfeng danjue* describes what a successful practitioner can expect in this grand gamble:

> The Great Dao stems from before the time of multiple phenomena. It weaves and interlaces together Heaven and Earth after the genesis from the original One. If one can treasure the Dao by entering it in sincerity, holding onto it in quietude, applying it with gentleness, and practicing it with diligence, one will revive from death and return to the undifferentiated origin, transcending the mundane and entering sagehood. One will overtake the double brilliance of the sun and the moon. (ZW 380:336-37)

The text then goes on to cite the Yellow Emperor's ascension to the empyrean as a model for the practitioner. Being involved in an enterprise that aimed at being coeval with Heaven and Earth, participants in duo-cultivation practice could be expected to be nothing less than divine. It thus comes as no surprise that many late-Ming texts of duo-cultivation reveal a self-perception that describes its adepts as sages or deities and the very union of the male and female practitioners as an experience that relives the wonders of cosmic creation. The sense of primordial creation is vividly captured in the following illustration from the *Daoyuan yiqi* which shows the intertwining and resonating bodies of a male and a female practitioners afloat in a micro universe:

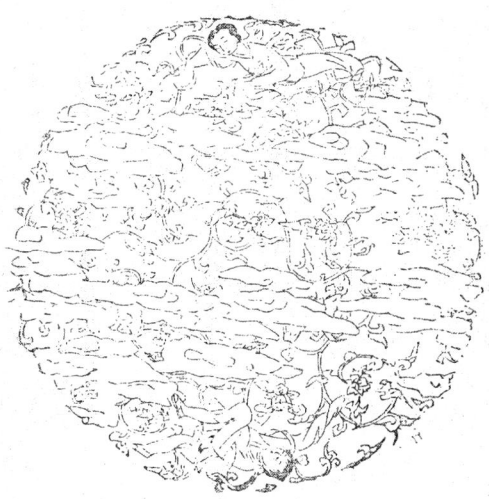

Fig.1: The Correspondence of Mount and Marsh.

To proponents of duo-cultivation like Yu Taizhen, the bodies of the engaged man and woman were divine. He likens them to the "phenomenon of Heaven and Earth and the image of the sun and the moon in the sky" (*Xuanwei xinyin*, ZW 379:302). Similarly, citing Zhang Boduan's 張伯端 (984-1082) *Wuzhen pian* 悟真篇 (Awakening to Perfection), Sun Ruzhong argues that male and female cultivators, often referred to as "vessels and crucibles," were the Numinous Father and Holy Mother (*lingfu shengmu* 靈父聖母). Through their consecrated union, they would engender and gestate an immortal fetus. With further practice of warm incubation, this fetus would ultimately grow into a celestial immortal (*Jindan zhenchuan*, ZW 399:873).

Ethics and Discipline

To achieve immortality, proponents felt they could not leave anything to chance when it came to a practice that involved men and women. Too much was at stake. To ensure success, they paid particular attention to training the practitioners' minds before dispatching them to the chamber. They accordingly taught normative values of reciprocity, detachment, discipline, and made threats of horrible punishments to ensure proper conduct before and during practice.

Underlying the divine self-perception of duo-cultivators was the concept of conjugal matrimony. The texts attempt to set forth normative values to govern practitioners' minds. They emphasize conjugal harmony and emotional reciprocity between male and female participants in order to secure success. The *Xuanwei xinyin* urges the male cultivator to be benevolent towards his female partner. He must submit to her feelings and appeal to her heart, taking great care that she be provided with the best food, clothing, and other necessities. He must cultivate a genuine rapport with the female partner, without which "the Phoenix does not chirp and the Turtle will not rise." Citing the Song adept Chen Nan, the text notes that if there is no common language between the two, they cannot become true husband and wife. If the rapport is not there, there can be no successful cultivation (ZW 379:310). Thus emotional harmony and reciprocity were clear preconditions for engendering the rising of the vital and generative fluids within the female body and for ensuring the successful give-and-take during the practice.

The texts further attempted to instill the proper mindset into the male cultivator toward both practice and his female partners. The *Sanfeng danjue* cautions the practitioner that he must maintain the utmost sincerity throughout the practice. Success depended on his inner rectitude and sincerity (ZW 380:344-51). The *Jindan zhenchuan* similarly specifies that a proper attitude toward the female partners is vital to the successful outcome. The male practitioner has to "revere the female participants as deities, love them as his own parents, care for them with probity and integrity, and requite them with benevolence." He must be free of impure thoughts in his heart and without any lust in his mind, remaining fully sincere, upright, and earnest in his approach to the practice (ZW 398:865).

Failure to comply and the engendering of any impure thought or behavior during the practice would bring on disaster. The *Xuanwei xinyin* thus admonishes the male cultivator to be free from passionate attachments while with his female partner. During coitus for drug gathering and transfer, his mind must remain focused on the practice of Dao. To ensure such a mental focus, the cultivator should visualize the presence of Officer Wang, the celestial protector who administers the transmission of alchemical secrets, standing menacingly with a whip in his hand and overseeing the delicate practice. Even a single lascivious thought could cause the practitioner to become a candidate for hell and fall into the lower rebirth realms of hell dwellers, hungry ghosts, or animals. His body would be destroyed and dispersed (ZW 379:318)

The *Jindan zhenchuan* further warns that any transgression in the chamber was fatal to male adepts. They provoked the wrath of various deities such as the Thunder Lord, and even the mere mention of the deviant sexual practice known as the "Plucking of the Triple Peaks" sufficed to cause nine generations of the practitioners' descendants to fall beyond rescue (ZW 398:873)

The concern for individual transgressions in practice and their obvious social and moral ramifications also led many internal alchemists to attack what they perceived as deviant and unorthodox practices. Following the earlier tradition set forth by adepts like Li Daochun, Cao Heng in his *Daoyuan yiqi* painstakingly enumerates nine deviant and ten heterodox practices among duo-cultivation techniques. He laments that people do not understand the subtle yet vital differences between the mundane and the transcendent, between the practice of "going against" and that of "going along with" the creative force of prenatal *qi*. They engage in all kinds of deviant practices and indulge in sexual abandonment and excess. He attacks such malpractices as blocking the spread of the correct way of duo-cultivation and specifically censures the employment of pre-pubescent girls and the use of young children for their coital fluids. He vigorously condemns these practices as killing oneself and destroying Dao (Tao 1990, 190-98).

Coition of Spirits

Beyond cosmology and ethics, late-Ming duo-cultivators went to great efforts to mark the boundaries of their practice in the realm of actual techniques. One difference appears in the postures used and assumptions underlying them.

In contrast to the vast repertoire of coital body positions in the bedchamber arts, the male practitioner in duo-cultivation was constantly reminded that he was to maintain a calm and quiet body posture. He was not to engage in the regulated puffs of breaths, the dazzling array of varied positions, and the combinations of shallow and deep thrusts characteristic of the bedchamber arts. Duo-cultivators thought of these as crude and eschewed them, foregoing physical exertion and varied postural changes among partners. They also did not match other sexual techniques in their elaborate systems of manual, oral, genital, and other manipulations to elicit or liberate vital *qi* from the female body, nor did they subscribe to their sophisticated systems for detecting the germination and activation of *qi*.

Rather, duo-cultivation texts emphasize quietude and stillness for both partners and insist on arousing the female *qi* through emotional and intuitive relations. This suggests a different way of thinking about the vital energies at work in the human body: more ethereal, primordial, and even transcendent.

Less susceptible to the physical thrusts or manipulation as found in the bedchamber arts, such *qi* seems to respond more to the inner, personal matching of the partners' hearts.

While in the bedchamber arts and other sexual techniques, the aroused *qi* manifested through various physical symptoms such as gasps, moans, bodily twists, or languid limbs, in duo-cultivation it only revealed itself as a fleeting, ethereal flash of light between the eyebrows of the female partner and was experienced by the male as the omnipotent, transforming elixir. This is perhaps the reason why duo-cultivators like Cao Heng disdainfully referred to the bedchamber arts as the "alchemical methods of mud and water." For him, such encounters involved exchange of bodily fluids rather than the ethereal and transformative energies of cosmic *qi*.

Although late-Ming texts offer varied descriptions of the steps and procedures for duo-cultivation, they concur in their conceptualization of the alchemical body. According to them, at birth the human body is endowed with a heavenly energy known as true *qi* or the *qi* of Before Heaven. The very energy that creates, multiplies, and sustains life in both males and females, it manifests in different postnatal forms: blood in females and semen in males. It increases each year as the body grows into puberty, reaching its pinnacle at age sixteen in males and at age fourteen in females. After that, it begins to drain and deplete, a process further hastened by illness and sexual indulgence. In internal alchemy, this course toward decay and death is known as "going along with" nature.

But this is not the ultimate Dao. Rather, the goal of the practice is to reverse the natural course of entropic decay by harnessing the potent energy of *qi* and returning it to the pristine state of eternal perfection known as undifferentiated chaos. Such was the way of "going against" that differentiates the sacred from the mundane.

Consistent with these perceived differences, duo-cultivators devised techniques to maximize the rejuvenation of *qi* during practice which differed significantly from other sexual practices. The texts accordingly prescribe a set of unique coital ways, some of which unequivocally proscribe against any genital contacts. Thus, the *Jindan zhenchuan* says:

> [When the Numinous Father and the Holy Mother] are at work, their spirits are in union, but not their bodies. Their *qi*-energies are in coition, but not their forms. The male must not loosen his garb and the female must retain her robe. They mutually respect each other like divine deities; love each other like father and mother. They keep still without moving until they feel moved by each other, and only then become interconnected. (ZW 398:863).

While duo-cultivators therefore promote the coition of spirit over body, they yet leave nothing to chance and also apply close physical contact. Indeed, the authors of the *Xuanwei xinyin* describe a special device for the male practitioner. Evocatively termed the Zither Bed (*qinchuang* 琴床), Fire Stoking Raft (*bohuo fazi* 撥火筏子), or Heaven-ascending Ladder (*shangtian tizi* 上天梯子), the contraption is made of cypress wood. Wide around the top and narrow at the end, it is tailored to the size of the human body. It had a certain ritual purpose as well as a practical function of contraception (ZW 379:312, 316, 319).

Fig.2: The Zither Bed

The *Daoyuan yiqi*, too, shows several devices it calls the Bellows (*tuoyue* 橐籥), whose practical function is yet unclear.[7]

While, therefore applying practical means to ensure success, late-Ming duo-cultivators remained adamant in their emphasis on the moral, spiritual, and bodily preparations they demanded before practitioners could enter the practice chamber. Augmenting the cosmic *qi* in the bodies both in psychological and physiological ways they hoped to ensure the attainment of immortality and transcendence.

---

[7] Cao Heng also discusses the Zither Bed in his treatise on the use of duo-cultivation for healing and introduced three other different devises used for duo-cultivation known as "Bellows." See *Daoyuan yiqi*; Tao 1990, 36-39. Based on Cao's discussion of the "bellows," I suspect these devices are employed by duo cultivators at the nostrils (right), genitalia (left), and navel (not shown) for gathering and exchanging vital *qi*.

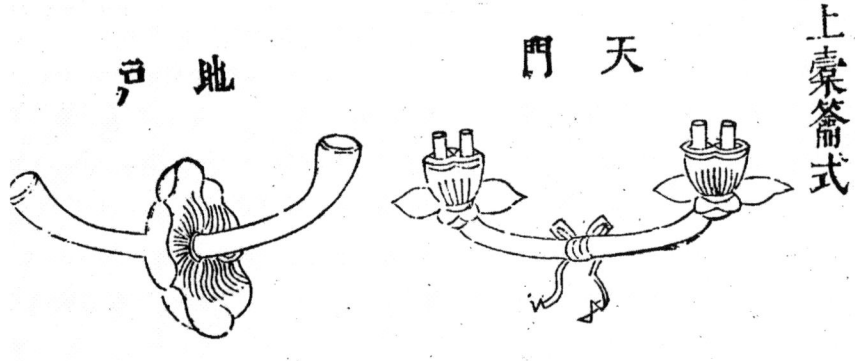

Fig. 3: The Bellows.

A Spiritual Quest

Many Ming texts represent duo-cultivation as a long and arduous journey in search of alchemical secrets, teachers, partners, companions, and material resources. A clear account appears in the *Jindan zhenchuan*, where Sun Ruzhong tells the story of his father's lifelong yearning for transcendence and long life, detailing his years of tenacious seeking of a transmitting adept and alchemical knowledge, and outlining his dogged efforts to form fellowships, secure funds, and obtain supplies for the success of the practice.

According to Sun, his father Sun Jiaoluan 孫教鸞 was born in the 17th year of the Hongzhi reign (1504) in the age-old family in Denghuang 登黃 (Shandong). Jiaoluan developed an interest in Daoism early in his youth, then traveled to various mountains and practiced regulating *qi* for several years. At the age of 20, in 1524, he met his first teacher, Master Qin Yehe 秦野鶴, from whom he learned the method of keeping to the center to gather drugs for embryonic gestation and divine rebirth. Next, Master Wang Yungu 王雲谷 taught him the essential teachings of embryonic breathing through the Mysterious Pass and embracing the One to attain nonaction.

In addition, Jiaoluan formed a close fellowship with the enthusiast Li Ruohai 李若海. Having acquired various methods, the two went into the circular chamber and practiced sitting for over a year. After completing this secluded practice, he allegedly felt some inner effulgence and was able to foretell future events. Although his fellow practitioner thought this extraordinary power was a clear sign of attainment, Jiaoluan was still unsatisfied with the result. He did not consider his newfound power as the same as the immortals' way of flight and ascendance.

He duly went on another search which lasted six years. On this tour, he met the adept Shiguzi 石谷子 who taught him the secret formula known as the Golden Vessel and Fire Talisman Jade Fluid for Refining the Self, as well as that of the Golden Fluid for Refining the Physical Form. After he returned to his friend Li Ruohai with these new instructions, he reconstructed the practice chamber and devoted all his resources to the practice, but still failed to achieve the desired ascendance. He often bemoaned that he had not acquired the full secret of the chamber practice and that a single variation in oral transmission could mean a world of difference in practice.

It was not until a certain Master An 安老師 called upon him unexpectedly that he finally met his true teacher. Master An pointed out that his chamber practice had been based on a misunderstanding of cosmic genesis:

> Without the union of yin and yang things will not germinate; just as the chicks cannot be hatched out of self-ovulated eggs. The 'I' or the male himself is truly yin inside and yang outside. Without acquiring the true lead of the other to return to the mercury, how can any one expect to gestate a holy fetus for a new of a buddha or immortal? (*Jindan zhenchuan*, ZW 398:860)

He specifically stressed that the desired elixir was not the same as the drugs gathered in the bedchamber arts. Though Master An's words ran genuinely true to the ears of Jiaoluan and Ruohai, they were not enlightened.

Then one day Jiaoluan recalled an encounter he had with a Daoist divination master while visiting Mt. Hua. He had asked the diviner for the name of the adept who destined to transmit the alchemical truth to him. The diviner replied enigmatically: "*An wei ru shi*" 安爲如師 (Who/An will be your master?). Jiaoluan repeated the question twice more, only to receive the same answer. When he later recollected this, it gave him a measure of revelation. Master An's unexpected call not only corroborated the divination he had received from the Daoist, but also confirmed the strong traditional belief that it is harder for a disciple to find a master than for a knowing master to seek out a worthy disciple.

Finally convinced of the authenticity of Master An's identity and the veracity of his teachings, Jiaoluan and Ruohai pleaded in earnest for Master An to stay and accept them as disciples and teach them the secrets of chamber practice. Master An replied that if Jiaoluan and Ruohai would assist him in his endeavor of transcending life and death, he would divulge to them all the practice secrets.

They agreed, and Master An proceeded to describe the nine stages of chamber practice. Jiaoluan and Ruohai were greatly enlightened and performed disciple rituals to Master An. They cross-checked his procedures with the alchemical classics, found them accurate, and gave up their doubts and hesitations. Soon they secured a special house for the master and began to procure the "vessels and crucibles, tigers and dragons, zither and sword" and other materials needed. Concerned that their combined financial resources were insufficient, Ruohai also secured the financial backing of another enthusiast by the name of Chen Daoxuan 陳道軒. The three of them supported Master An in his secluded chamber practice for more than three years. He duly accomplished all stages of the practice and departed.

Jiaoluan's own practice remained secondary. He was already in his eighties when he finally secured the financial support of his two sons and their fellow cultivators and was able conduct the practice. In so doing, Jiaoluan had to break a long-held Daoist taboo against transmitting the alchemical secrets to one's own heirs. Despite this and despite his advanced years, he was apparently successful in his chamber practice. He passed away sitting a chair in 1610 at the age of 106. His son Ruzhong reports that as he passed on, a luxuriant white *qi* hovered over the his head and an exotic fragrance spread around the room. Amazed at the phenomena, commoners and literati from the village came to pay him tribute.

After Jiaoluan passed away, Ruzhong carried on. He wrote that he stayed in seclusion for about three years. Claiming that he did not want to privatize his father's teachings, he came out of seclusion and took to the road in search of fellow cultivators and enthusiasts. In 1612, he arrived in Kaifeng. Interested in a book sold at a local bookstore, he came to a fortuitous meeting with the author and another enthusiast of secluded chamber practice. Officials serving at the provincial *yamen*, both were well-versed in duo-cultivation. At the behest of his new friends, Ruzhong wrote down his father's secret teachings, to which they added a detailed commentary on each of the nine steps. It was completed in 1615 (*Jindan zhenchuan*, ZW 398:860-61).

Like Sun Jiaoluan, many practitioners saw duo-cultivation as a spiritual quest for knowledge and truth. Cao Heng's quest is another case in point. As a young man he had already learned the notorious sexual gathering technique known as the Art of the Triple Mounds. Dissatisfied with the approach, he became interested in other practices, such as purist solo practice and Buddhist meditation. He traveled around for many years to seek out teachings numerous adepts of various persuasions. Yet despite his wide exposure to both the school of "the other" (sexual techniques) and the "pure and quiet" approach (meditation), Cao remained unconvinced of their veracity and efficacy. For years he vacillated between sexual and meditative practices while entertaining doubts and skepticism about both. It was only in 1626 when touring an ancient sacred site near Wuchang in Hubei that he ran into his true master who convinced him of the veracity of the duo-cultivation method and became its devoted adept (*Daoyuan yiqi*, Tao 1990, 37-123)

Travels such as those undertaken by Sun and Cao formed an integral part of the practice. They served several functions, most fundamentally offering a convenient way for novices and masters to find each other. More importantly, they offered a steady framework or channel for the flow of unorthodox knowledge. Given the constraints of the moral and social conventions at the time, adepts' travels created a relatively unrestricted space for the easy exchange and open discussion of otherwise morally suspect subjects.

Constructing the Sacred Space

Another essential aspect of the practice, also prominent in Sun's narrative, is the construction of the practice chamber. It is often called the circular chamber (*huanshi* 圜室) with the word "*huan*" denoting the round shape of the celestial body and thus referring to Heaven. According to a legend recorded in the *Shiyi ji* 拾遺記 (A Record of Lost Stories) by Wang Jia 王嘉 (d. 390), people of the Kingdom of Filial Cultivation used these to raise captured sea-dragons (Schafer 1980, 13-53). A space for the captivity and cultivation of protean creatures, the place implies separation from the world, celestial connections, seclusion, and a special environment for transformation and metamorphosis.

These implications were not lost on late-Ming alchemists—both solo and duo practitioners—as they organized their practice space. It usually took several steps to prepare and build the chamber. First, one had to select a proper site, such as a holy mountain or blessed place (*fudi* 福地). For example, Wu Shouyang 伍守陽, in his *Tianxian zhengli qianshuo* 天仙正理淺說 (A Brief Exposition of the Celestial Immortal's Orthodox Principles) on solo alchemical refinement, cautions that small and low mountains were to be avoided when selecting the site because they were infested by mineral and wood spirits that sapped the practitioner's *qi* and blood. There were no orthodox deities in these mountains and they were not proper for refining the golden fluid or divine elixir. Citing the *Baopuzi* 抱朴子 (Book of the Master who Embraces Simplicity, DZ 1185), he then provides a list of mountains where cultivators are well protected (ZW 127:859-50)

For Wu, the blessed places must be secure from wars, free of encroachment by local potentates, and far away from communication and transportation arteries. Again referring back to the *Baopuzi*, he insists that they had to be separated from the world: Daoist seekers travel differently from ordinary people and they reside in places other than those inhabited by common folk. Neither in speech nor body should they intermingle with the latter (ZW 127:850). The spatial isolation of the mountains is thus an outward expression of the practitioners' interior seclusion.

The second step in chamber construction concerns its overall layout with regard to safety, privacy, peace, and convenience. Wu Shouyang suggests that while the site should be located away from major arteries, it could well be located near a city or town to allow easy access to resources and necessities. However, he cautions against building a fanciful or ornate structure which might attract the attention of thieves and burglars. It should be also be placed away from the woods where there might be disruptive noises of wind and birds.

Wu then goes on to prescribe the dimensions of the chamber. It was not to exceed one *zhang* (10 feet) in height, width, and length, allowing three to five cultivators to live comfortably and discouraging brigands from seizing it for a hide-out. In addition, the chamber was to be built with double-layered walls to shield cultivators from wild animals and poisonous insects. Its interior should support a proper balance of dimness and light to ensure its occupants' physical health and mental well-being (ZW 127:850).

Beyond these basics, the *Sanfeng danjue* offers specific information on site selection, chamber construction, and interior arrangements for duo-cultivators. It shares the concerns for security and sanitation, as well as about potential interference by evil spirits, hungry ghosts, and marauding bandits with the *Tianxian zhengli qianshuo*,[8] but then moves on to address the special needs of duo-cultivators. As the practice shifted away from secluded mountains and into towns, and because it invariably involved the participation of young females, it tended to invite close social and moral scrutiny. Distrust, misunderstanding, censure, and even persecution were likely. Social harmony, neighborly peace, and access to local political and financial resources thus formed important criteria for site selection and chamber construction. As the text says:

> If one has to live in a city or town, rely on a family with both wealth and power. If one relies on a family with power but without wealth, then it is difficult to secure provisions for the practice. If one relies on a family with only wealth but no power, one will have no means of suppression when incurring external complications. . . . It [the site] must have kind-hearted neighbors. (ZW 380:339)

In the section entitled "Constructing the Alchemical Platform," it further offers a detailed diagram description. The multi-tiered structural division of the house and the surrounding high walls bespeak the practitioner's concern for public prying and detection. He says:

> The alchemical house consists of three tiers of rooms. In front of the anterior hall is an open courtyard. The front hall is flanked by gate chambers on the left and right.
>
> The second or middle tier of the house consists of a center chamber plus left and right chambers, each divided into three subchambers. The subchamber on the left is the kitchen; that on the right is the storage room where the treasures for the practice are kept. The center room

---

[8] The *Sanfeng danjue* cautions: "When living in the countryside, he is to select a site composed of either red or yellow mud. The site must not contain any old tombs or graves. It must have a sweet water spring and kind-hearted neighbors. It is best located away from livestock barns and cesspools. Any clear and quiet mountain or valley is a blessed place for the practice. All other places are not suitable" (ZW 380: 339).

of the kitchen holds the tablet for the Celestial General in charge of food preparation. [The center of] the three rooms of the central chamber holds the divine tablets of the lineage master, the Five Patriarchs, the Seven Perfected, and the Sixteen Celestial Generals.

On their table place pure water, fragrant candles, flower vases, antiques, and the self-chiming clock. Set the clock right on time. Also place a whole set of classics there. Perform rituals of homage in the morning and at night.

The right and left rooms of the center chamber are the bedrooms of the practice guardians. They are completely separate, leaving only an opening of about one foot in diameter to allow food to be passed through.

The rear tier is composed of three further chambers. Those on the right and left each contain three subchambers. The center hall, too, divides into three subchambers, with the Blue Dragon Chamber in the east and the White Tiger Chamber in the west. The central subchamber holds the tablet of the lineage master, placed for worship in the due *zhi* and *wu* orientations. To its left is the Alchemical Chamber; to its right, the Divine Chamber.

All windows are to be kept bright and the tables wiped clean. A tall wall is built all around the practice house to keep intruders from peeping and spying. The garden terrace and alcove are quiet and hidden, where flowers and plants are grown and cranes and deer are raised. It is a place where the quiet maids can relax. (*Sanfeng danjue*, ZW 380:340) [9]

Though the chamber described here may seem more elaborate than others,[10] its structural layout and interior arrangement reflect the same concerns for security and seclusion while its spatial organization and interior partitioning work with the effect of geomantic, cosmological, and divine forces on the transformative process. This is most obvious in the placement of the tablets of deities, immortals, lineage patriarchs, and transmitting master. It is also apparent in the designation of the male practitioners' chamber as Blue Dragon and that of the female participant as White Tiger as well as in their separate orientation to the east and west. All this unmistakably reveals the duo-cultivators' effort at recapturing the transformative process and cosmic creative energy.

In addition, the presence of deities' and patriarchs' tablets shows the desire to create the chamber as spiritual sanctuary or sacred space, as much as practitioners' worship invokes a comparison with Confucian ancestral rites in ordinary households. Just as the man of the Confucian household tried to ensure his virility and fertility through ritual offerings to his ancestors, the duo-cultivators sought to enhance their chance of immortality by appealing to the powers and protection of celestial deities and lineage patriarchs. Just as ances-

---

[9] The *Xuanwei xinyin* provides a similar list of deities to be worshiped; it also includes the Thunder God and the practitioner's transmission and initiation masters (ZW 379).

[10] The chamber in the *Xuanwei xinyin* is more spartan and matches that prescribed by Wu Shouyang (ZW 379:312).

tral rites reminded the householders that the climactic joy of the conjugal bed served the larger purpose of family procreation and prosperity, so the worship of deities and patriarchs cautioned duo-cultivators that they must strive for the ultimate goal of elixir concoction in the quiet serenity of the practice chamber while staying vigilant against such transgressions as lustful urges and loss of seminal control. As Confucian ancestral rites and the goal of procreation and prosperity shaped the conjugal bedchamber in ordinary households, so alchemical rituals and the goal of transcendence and immortality informed, inspired, and ruled the sacred space of the alchemical chamber.

Alchemical Fellowships

Proper use of the chamber, beyond all care and worship, also involved the right kind of alchemical fellowship. As shown in Sun's account, this constituted another important aspect of the practice, involving cooperation for land purchase, chamber construction, payment of female participants, as well as the provisioning of food, clothes, and necessities for up to several years. All this required large sums of cash and a steady source of revenue. No one practitioner would have sufficient resources for the task, so a community was necessary.

Beyond the personal means of individual followers, resources also included the oral secrets of the practice, precious information that could lead to immortality. Alchemical secrets formed a dearly prized capital that adepts often used in exchange for financial support. Not only morally suspect, but also personally extravagant, duo-cultivation suffered frequent attacks from both Confucians and solo practitioners, being denounced as causing financial ruin and wrecking homes. Yet it was precisely due to the huge cost that the practice necessitated economic fellowships among practitioners—such as the joint venture of Sun Jiaoluan, Li Ruohai, and Chen Daoxuan or the one among Sun Ruzhong and his friends.

Beyond sheer economic necessity, practitioners also valued fellowships for other purposes, such as providing mutual assistance and support for the long and arduous practice. Throughout, the main practitioner depended on the assistance of his alchemical fellows for food, clothes, and protection from interruptions, whether human or natural. In addition, he needed support in preparing and instructing both the male cultivator and his female participants, in determining the timing of propitious moments of drug sprouting and gathering, and most importantly in sustaining his life during the post-gathering stage which led to a semi-intoxicated coma that could last up to seven days while the newly acquired drug settled (*Xuanwei xinyin*, *Sanfeng danjue*; ZW380:339-40).

Cao Heng, in his *Daoyuan yiqi*, places particular emphasis on the role of the fellow cultivators, describing the fellowship as "Ring of the Three" (*sanhuan*) and thus highlighting the mutual dependence and interconnection between the main practitioner and his fellow cultivators. He also uses the term "Ring of

Avowed Death" to describe the main adept who vows to sacrifice his life to achieve the desired perfection through chamber practice. Since he depends for food, clothes, and security on his fellow cultivators, they are called the "Circle Rings." More than that, since they also provide ethical support, one fellow cultivator is called the "Ring of Life"—a partner charged with the responsibility of regulating and enlightening the others and ensuring the safety of the main cultivator. Cao defines their responsibilities as provisioning and protecting the practice, sharing and joining in all activities, as well as providing advice, admonition, and instructions (*Daoyuan yiqi*; Tao 1990, 107-09).

In practice, the fellows served as both monitors regulating the conduct of the main adept and as consultants advising and instructing on practice details. Being entrusted with powers over life and death, they had to fulfill strict ethical criteria. The *Jindan jieyao* notes that practitioners must seek out fellows of the same heart and friends who will stick with them through life and death. They must be pure and harmonious in temperament, loyal, filial, and brotherly as well as industrious in the upkeep and protection of the chamber practice (see *Sanfeng danjue*, ZW 380:339; also *Daoyuan yiqi*; Tao 1990, 108). The anguish of many practitioners in their search for the right practice partners is vibrantly evident in Cao Heng's words of 1631:

> It is truly more difficult to find a practice companion than an adept! Alas, I have traveled all over the realm, but have not been able to find any comrades who can join me in exploring the mystery of the chamber practice. I shall keep my eyes peeled in search for them. (*Daoyuan yiqi*; Tao 1990, 109)

With oral secrets, practice chambers, female participants, necessary supplies, and the alchemical fellowship all secured, the adept is finally ready to enter the chamber for practice. To do so, he is advised to first select a propitious day to pay homage to the celestial deities and his lineage patriarchs, during which he submits a written appeal asking for help and protection. Only after the ritual has been properly completed, can the practitioner enter the chamber to begin the Great Work in cooperation with his practice partners and female participants (see *Xuanwei xiyin*, ZW 379:312; *Sanfeng danjue*, ZW 380:342).

Conclusion

Duo-cultivation in the late Ming is a unique phenomenon that deserves to be understood in its own right rather than on the basis of appearances and prejudices. It is different from other forms of sexual practice as often associated with the libertine lifestyle of literati and merchants. It is also quite distinct from the sexual gathering techniques and erotic pursuits presented to Westerns audiences in the writings of Van Gulik (1961), Needham (1983), and Wile (1992). Given its social and cultural milieu, the practice could not entirely escape the strictures of the late-Ming patriarchic order. Although morally conscientious proponents like Cao Heng advocated for "gratitude and compassion toward the cauldrons" and "riddance of evil practices," duo-cultivators never seemed to have gone completely beyond predominantly male-centric preoccupations and goals. However, the absence of gender equality in the practice should not make us oblivious to the defining boundaries that separated it from other sexual practices. Modern values cannot do justice to a spiritual body practice that formed an important part of internal alchemy and has to be honored through proper historical understanding.

Bibliography

Brook, Timothy. 1998. *The Confusion of Pleasure: Commerce and Culture in Ming China.* Berkeley: University of California Press.

Hu Fuchen 胡孚琛, ed. 1994. *Zhonghua daojiao da cidian* 中華道教大辭典. Beijing: Shehui kexue chubanshe.

Komjathy, Louis. 2002. *Title Index to Daoist Collections.* Cambridge, Mass.: Three Pines Press.

Li Yuanguo 李遠國. 1991. *Zhongguo daojiao qigong yangsheng daquan* 中國道教氣功養生大全. Chengdu: Sichuan cishu chubanshe.

Liu, Ts'un-yan. 1976. *Selected Papers from the Hall of Harmonious Wind.* Leiden: E. Brill.

Needham, Joseph, et al. 1983. *Science and Civilisation in China,* vol. V.5: Spagyrical Discovery and Invention—Physiological Alchemy. Cambridge: Cambridge University Press.

Schafer, Edward H., 1980. *The Divine Woman: Dragon Ladies and Rain Maidens in T'ang Literature.* San Francisco: North Point Press.

Schipper, Kristofer, and Franciscus Verellen, eds. 2004. *The Daoist Canon: A Historical Companion to the Daozang* Chicago: University of Chicago Press.

Sun Dianqi 孫殿起. 1999 [1936]. *Fanshu ouji* 販書偶記. Shanghai: Guji.

Tao Bingfu 陶秉福, ed. 1990. *Daoyuan yiqi* 道元一氣. Beijing: Beijing shifang daxue chubanshe.

Van Gulik, Robert H. 1961. *Sexual Life in Ancient China.* Leiden: E. Brill.

Wile, Douglas. 1992. *Art of the Bedchamber: The Chinese Sexual Yoga Classics Including Women's Solo Meditation Texts.* Albany: State University of New York Press.

Female Alchemy

An Introduction

Elena Valussi

Female alchemy (*nüdan* 女丹) developed within the milieu of internal alchemy (*neidan* 內丹), with which it shares technical terminology and practical processes. However, compared to the historical development of *neidan*, *nüdan* is a rather late tradition, as the first individual texts appear in the late Ming and the first full-fledged manuals are from the late eighteenth century. *Neidan* and *nüdan* not only share similar language and contents, but they are also produced within the same network of Qing authors and practitioners as *neidan*.

While the intellectual milieu within which *nüdan* arises and its language are similar to those of *neidan*, the *raison-d'être* of *nüdan* has different origins from that of *neidan*, partly because of the different historical period in which it emerges, and partly because of the gender specificity of this tradition. Thus *nüdan* has a historical origin firmly based within the milieu of the Qing period. Its emergence is closely linked to contemporaneous social and cultural developments, especially as it pertains to the role of women. A society increasingly interested in restricting female social behavior is behind the very emergence of an alchemical tradition for women, previously felt unnecessary, which proposes a practice to conduct safely at home. This social and historical pressure is also evident in the large amount of space devoted to moral injunctions for women in *nüdan* texts.

Nüdan authors and editors insist in their prefaces on the importance of this tradition because of the intrinsic physiological difference of women as well as because of their different, and much reduced, access to teachers and written materials. However, women had been practicing alchemy, albeit in numbers less numerous than men, from the beginning of *neidan*; physiological differences between male and female practitioners had always been present, and occasionally a different practice for women was discussed in Daoist texts from the Song dynasty onwards. However, it is only in the Qing period that physiological differences and, I will argue, renewed focus on morals, coupled with the widespread diffusion of internal alchemical knowledge, combine to produce a full-fledged tradition separate from *neidan*, which is then categorised as a practice for males. Anxiety about the public religious activities of elite women also concurs to the development of a safer practice to conduct at home.

The texts insist on the different physiological structure of men and women, with specific attention to the female reproductive system, and especially to the role of the breasts, of the uterus, and of blood, in its many guises as energetic base, menstrual flow and breast-milk. Based on this physiological difference, while in the standard *neidan* practice three-stage sequence *jing* is refined into *qi* and *qi* refined into *shen*, in female alchemy the first step is different: the practice starts from refining blood (*xue*) into *qi*. The first step is described as being much more complicated that of male practice since in females blood is a powerful element capable of major physiological disruptions and often responsible for serious illnesses. Both the breasts and the uterus are important elements of the initial refinement of blood into *qi*, which happens through a series of breast massages, abdominal massages, breathing exercises and internal visualizations.

Historical and Social Background

Nüdan emerged in the seventeenth century and developed into a full-fledged tradition by the eighteenth and nineteenth century. However, the first texts to mention gender-specific practices for women are earlier, and are found in the *Daozang*. These texts, though, only peripherally point to separate practices for women and there is no evidence, dating from this time, of an alchemical literature just for the use of women.[1]

---

[1] The *Lishi zhenxian tidao tongjian* 歷世真仙體道通鑑 (A Comprehensive Mirror on Successive Generations of Perfected Transcendents Who Embody the Dao; DZ 296) by Zhao Daoyi 趙道一 (fl. 1294-1307), contains hagiographic accounts of Daoist women, mostly from the Song dynasty; *Lishi zhenxian tidao tongjian juan* 55:2a. In the *Chongyang zhenren jinguan yusuo jue* 重陽真人金關玉鎖訣 (Formulas of the Golden Pass and Jade Lock of the Perfected Chongyang; DZ 1156), by Wang Chongyang 王重陽 (1112-1170) there are several mentions to female practice, e.g., . 10b, 16a, 20a. The *Daoshu* 道樞 (The Pivot of the Dao; DZ 1017), a twelfth century anthology of earlier texts of internal alchemy, also includes a mention of female practice (*Chongzhen pian* 1a). The *Chunyang dijun shenhua miaotong ji* 純陽帝君神化妙通紀 (Annals of the Wondrous Communications and Divine Transformations of the Sovereign Lord Chunyang; DZ 305), is a collection of legends on Lü Dongbin 呂洞賓. Episode 106 tells of a 16-year old girl who, to escape her parents plan to marry her, hides away on a mountain. Here she meets an old man who tells her: "I will slay your Red Dragon." Another important example is a Song commentary to the *Wuzhen pian* 悟真篇 (Awakening to Perfection) by Xue Shi 薛式 (d. 1191) (in DZ 142), which mentions breast

More extensive practices are described in two texts from the late Ming, written by the medical authors Cao Heng 曹珩 (fl. 1632) and Fu Shan 傅山 (1607-1684). Cao Heng, in 1632, wrote the *Nügong quebing* 女功卻病 (Women's Practices for Repelling Illness). This is a section in the *Baosheng biyao* 保生祕要 (Essential Secrets for Conserving Life), the second part of the longer treatise *Daoyuan yiqi* 道原一氣 (Unitary *Qi* of the Dao's Origin, ed. 1636), a work that brings together medicine and internal alchemy. Fu Shan, on the other hand, received the *Duan honglong* 斷紅龍 (Beheading the Red Dragon) as an appendix to a collection of texts transmitted by the immortal Lü Dongbin. The collection is called *Shangcheng xiudao bishu sizhong* 上乘修道秘書四種 (Four Secret Volumes on the Unsurpassable Refining of the Dao; *Daozang jinghua* 12.2). Both larger works by these medical authors combine medical treatments and alchemical techniques for men and women. In the two short *nüdan* texts, descriptions of the important loci in the female alchemical body as well as of specific practices for women are given, even though many details of the process are not clarified. The *Duan honglong* says:

> The perfected man [Lü] said:
> All those who practice refinement for female perfection, must first . . . sit until the *qi* in the body circulates freely. One day before the menstruation, at the hours of *zi* and *wu* [midnight and noon], start the practice. At midnight, put on your robe and sit with legs crossed, hands holding firmly to the sides of the ribs.
>
> After [the *qi*] has ascended and descended within the body a few times, press the left heel against the vagina and the rectum, clench the teeth, close the eyes, shrug the shoulders, and lift up with great strength. Imagine the *qi* in two red channels rising from the womb, passing through the Three Passes, and ascending to the Niwan.[2] From here it descends to the root of the tongue and pours into the breasts.
>
> Practice like this continuously until the body is warm, then stop. Use a white silk kerchief and insert it into the vagina to compare the quantity [of blood] to last month's and to see if there is any. Again, like before, [use] the circulation [of *qi*] to scatter blood and *qi* in order to avoid illnesses. In less than a hundred days [the flow] will cease. (2b)

---

massages and bodily refinement. For a discussion, see Valussi 2003, 70-76.

[2] The Three Passses are the Tail Gate (*weilü*) at the coccyx, Narrow Strait (*jiaji*) at the upper spine, and Jade Pillow (*yuzhen*) at the base of the skull. They are gateways for the circulation of *qi* during the small circulation or Microcosmic Orbit (*xiao zhoutian* 小周天). Once the *qi* has ascended through the Passes, it reaches the Niwan, the upper cinnabar or elixir field. From there, it descends through the front of the body, reaches the coccyx and rises through the spine again. This circulation process is repeated several times and its aim is the refinement of the *qi*. In this passage, the difference from standard *neidan* and qigong circulation practices is the definition of the womb and of the breasts as loci of refinement.

This passage is the first written evidence of a coherent approach to female alchemical practice.

In the Qing, several important alchemical authors mention *nüdan* practices in their *neidan* texts and collections. In the eighteenth century, we have examples in Liu Yiming's and Min Yide's works, both Longmen patriarchs, and in Fu Jinquan's work, a Daoist practitioner and local religious leader in Sichuan.

Liu Yiming 劉一明, a Gansu Longmen patriarch of the eleventh generation, was active in the northwest, throughout Shanxi, Gansu, and Ningxia.[3] One of his most famous works, the *Xiuzhen biannan* 修真辯難 (Discriminating Difficult Points in the Cultivation of Perfection) was published in 1798. It purports to record a conversation between Liu and a disciple that took place in 1782, recorded in question and answer format.[4] It includes a section of five questions that discuss female alchemy in simple, direct terms. The main questions seem to revolve around "difference." How are the male and female body differentiated and why? How does this difference affect the practice and the final result? Is this difference contingent or of a higher nature?

The answers are clear and direct. Male and female bodies have physiological differences, therefore it is natural that the practice should follow a different path at first. Soon, though, their bodies are more and more similar and their practice also becomes the same. Liu stresses that, from the perspective of the Dao, males and females have no difference:

> 93. It was asked: Dao does not differentiate between men and women. Why do they have differences [in practice]?
>
> He responded: As for their Dao, it is the same; as for their use, it is different. Then, they are not the same in their inherent nature, and their body and structure have differences. Therefore, they share the way of inner nature and destiny, but in the use of the practice are greatly dissimilar. (34b-36a)

Liu also mentions female alchemy in another of his writings, the *Huixin ji* 會心集 (Collection of Meetings of Minds; dat. 1801), which contains the long poem *Nüdan fa* 女丹法 (Methods for Female Alchemy), written in sixty 7-character verses (*Waiji* 2.6a-7a; ZW 8:691-92). This poem, too, describes the *nüdan* practice clearly and with authority.

Min Yide 閔一得, a Jiangnan Longmen patriarch of the 11th generation, is the author of the *Gushu yinlou cangshu* 古書隱摟藏書 (Texts Stored in the Hid-

---

[3] Information on his life appears in various sources, but according to the *Jinxian zhi* 金縣志 (Gazetteer for Jin County, ch. 13) he was born in Shanxi, in the town of Quwo 曲沃. His other names were Wuyuanzi 悟元子, Supuzi 素朴子, and Beihe sanren 被褐散人.

[4] In *Daoshu shier zhong* 道書十二种 (Twelve Books on the Dao), by Liu Yiming, 1819: *ji* 7. Reprinted in 1990 from an 1880 edition (Beijing: Zhongguo zhongyi yao chubanshe). Also in *Zangwai daoshu* 8:467-92 (abbreviated ZW).

den Pavilion of Ancient Books; dat. 1834) in 28 *juan* (ed. Wuxing: Jingai Chunyang gong). It contains the *Niwan Li zushi nüzong shuangxiu baofa* 泥丸李祖師女宗雙修寶筏 (Precious Raft on Paired Cultivation of Women by Master Li Niwan) and the *Xiwangmu nüxiu zhengtu shize* 西王母女正途十則 (Xiwangmu's Ten Precepts on the Proper Female Path), which were transmitted to Min in 1799 by Xiwang mu 西王母, the Queen Mother of the West. Unlike those in Liu Yiming's collections, these texts are received through spirit-writing and include sections on female proper behavior.

They all tend to describe female practice in matter-of-fact terms, discussing the differences and similarities between male and female bodies and practices and applying a terminology reminiscent of late-Ming medical texts. Their presence in larger *neidan* collections by well respected Daoist authors attests to the fact that *nüdan* had been incorporated as a part of the mainstream alchemical discourse and that it was a well-established tradition by this time.

The first full-fledged collection of *nüdan* materials is the *Nü jindan fayao* 女金丹法要 (Essential Methods for the Female Golden Elixir; ZW 11:512-41), collated in 1813 by the Daoist author and local religious leader Fu Jinquan 傅金銓. Born in Jinxi 金谿 (Jiangxi), he traveled extensively through south China before settling down in Baxian 巴縣 (Sichuan) in 1817, where he "opened an altar for transmission and to receive texts through spirit-writing." The *Nü jindan fayao*, as other materials in his collected works—the *Jiyizi zhengdao bishu shiqi zhong* 濟一子證道秘書十七種 (Jiyizi's Seventeen Secret Books on the Verification of the Dao)—was received in this manner. Fu starts its preface by justifying his work as necessary for all women seriously interested in internal alchemy. He says:

> Since early times perfected women have been many, but their methods of refinement have not been recorded in books. In this era few have heard of them. Women practice for three years, while men need nine years [to reach perfection]. Even though as a daily practice it is quite easy, finding a master is very difficult. Men can go and seek a fortune [and a master with affinity] for a thousand *li*, but for women, leaving the inner chamber by just half a step is very difficult. There are thousands of chapters of alchemical treatises, but they do not list or include female practice. So I have put together this book. (1a)

Fu thus links the need for writing this book to women's difficulty of finding proper manuals and guidance, since they cannot leave the inner quarters and seek masters as easily as men. This statement is repeated in different ways in many other prefaces to *nüdan* works; it is a proof of the growing unease with female religious activities outside the home. However, the lack of specific instructions for women is not the only reason for printing collections: almost half of the text is devoted to moral and behavioral instructions, to be implemented before the beginning of the alchemical practice.

Another important collection from the very end of the Qing dynasty is the *Nüdan hebian* 女丹合編 (Combined Collection on Female Alchemy), collated by the Daoist intellectual He Longxiang 賀龍驤 in 1906 at the Erxian an 二仙庵 (Hermitage of the Two Immortals) in Chengdu. This collection is the culmination of the *nüdan* tradition in the Qing; it is the largest, most organized, most comprehensive, and clearest of all (see Valussi 2008).

From the first texts in the late Ming to the *Nüdan hebian* in the late Qing, we thus see a tremendous development of the *nüdan* tradition. In the course of 300 years, *nüdan* discourse went from a short mention in a medical or alchemical text through larger sections in alchemical works to full fledged manuals.

Why, then, was there such a production of alchemical manuals for women in the Qing? The emergence of *nüdan* is linked to several different and parallel developments. One is the widespread diffusion of Longmen Daoist teachings, of which alchemy is a part, to all levels of society. Another is the growth of the printing industry, which allowed this knowledge to spread more widely. This diffusion of knowledge often happened within the realm of spirit-writing cults, and almost all *nüdan* materials have their origin in spirit writing séances. A third development is the increased focus on morality, joined by the diffusion of morality books and ledgers of merit and demerit.

Daoist Resurgence

At the beginning of the Qing, the resurgence of Daoist practice was closely linked to the spreading of the Longmen school (see Mori 2004; Esposito 2000; 2001; 2002). The active proselytising of Wang Changyue 王常月 (d. 1680), seventh Longmen patriarch and abbot of the Baiyun guan 白雲觀 (White Cloud Temple) in Beijing, opened the gates of the temples and offered initiation to almost anyone willing to enter. The Longmen community found their center of influence and conversion in the southeastern provinces of Jiangsu and Zhejiang. Many of Wang's disciples established ordination platforms and settled their temples on mountains in this area, and Longmen branches began to sprout. By the Qianlong (1736-1796) and Jiaqing (1796-1821) eras, Longmen schools had branched out not only in the southeast, but also other areas of China. As a result, knowledge that had been closely guarded in Daoist lineages, and which included *neidan* teachings, became more widely available. One of the areas where this is evident is vernacular literature, a literary genre that developed in this period. Many scholars of literature have noted the appearance of Daoist and alchemical elements in late Ming and Qing novels (e.g., Liu 1962; 1970);[5]

---

[5] Examples of Daoist elements in novels include characters and features in the *Jinping mei* 金瓶梅 (The Plum in the Golden Vase; Roy 2001, 505n.20) and *Xiyou ji* 西游記 (Journey to the West; Liu 1985; Despeux 1985; Yu 1987). Recently Wang Guogang (1990), Wang

this is a testimony of the spreading of these ideas, if not actually practices, to the wider public.

Printing
The spread of printing as well as an increased differentiation of published materials led to an increased access to writings by a wide range of people. In the case of religious materials, this meant that alchemical treatises could be diffused widely among the population; that this indeed happened is evident from the mention of alchemical methods in numerous literary sources (Dean 1998, 55). The cheap printing and wide local distribution of religious materials, moreover, contributed to the localization of religious knowledge. Small printing houses as well as local religious organizations flourished.

This development could not have been so successful without another one: the increasing number of alchemical writers active in the Qing. Often people who had failed the examination or low-level bureaucrats, they did not fit into the government machine and devoted themselves to the development of local religious traditions.[6] The parallel development of local religious groups and the emergence of small printing houses fostered the production and diffusion of religious knowledge at the local level. A good example of this development was Fu Jinquan, a local religious leader who received spirit-written materials from immortals like Lü Dongbin at an altar. Part of a family of publishers, he issued the works through his company, the Shancheng tang 善成堂 (Hall of Achieving Goodness), originally founded by his older relative Fu Jinduo 傅金鐸 near Chengdu. Besides forming a religious community, Fu spent the last part of his life printing the texts he received, edited, and authored, including alchemical treatises and *nüdan* texts.

Morality
Due to increased social mobility, the inability of the examination system to absorb all literati into official employment, and the social dislocation and turmoil connected with the Ming-Qing transition, there was an increasing focus on morality. This is obvious not only from the increased publication of morality books, but also from the transformation of the ledgers of merit and demerit into more sanctioning books (see Brokaw 1991; Theiss 2004).

The increased focus on morality is evident especially in *nüdan* collections from the mid-Qing. These manuals not only describe female practice as different from male, as was the case in late-Ming texts, but they also encompass large

---

Gang (1995), and Jennifer Oldstone-Moore (1998) have shown how the entire novel can be seen as the journey of an adept through alchemical practice.

[6] On the Qing bureaucratic crisis, see Dean 1998: 51: "The examination system was unable to absorb increasing numbers of candidates into the civil service. A growing population of literate men and women had to look elsewhere for employment, entertainment, and enlightenment." See also Dean 1998, 20, 54.

sections that describe the correct moral behavior of women. This characteristic appears to a different degree in all female alchemical texts from the mid to late Qing. The *Nüdan shize* 女丹十則 (Ten Rules on Female Alchemy) includes a section on female behavior which stresses the need to be filial, respect the in-laws, and maintain purity, chastity and modesty in private and public venues. Some of the precepts address specific issues of meditation and alchemical practice, but even in these cases the suggestions are of modesty and purity as well as silence, seriousness, cleanliness, and determination:

> You have to have a firm determination in collecting your heart-mind. In general, when you enter the way of refinement, you need to embrace it with your whole body, even [be prepared to] devote several lifetimes to it. You ought not to lose your strong heart-mind and firm will. If there are mistakes, assess them in advance. (12ab)

Some ideas expressed here reflect those found in morality books for women, such as, for example, the *Neixun* 內訓 (Instructions for the Inner Chambers), a work by Empress Mingren written in the early Ming (1404) which enjoyed great distribution in the Qing, because it was included in Wang Xiang's *Nü sishu* 女四書 (Four Books for Women). Another book whose ideas are reflected in female alchemical treatises is Lü Kun's 呂坤 (1536-1618) *Guifan* 閨範 (Standards of the Women's Quarters).

In the Qing, the activities of women outside the home were monitored closely, and their religious practices increasingly criticised (see Dudbridge 1991; 1992; Prazniak 1986). The growing desire of women to seek instruction in religious practice produced anxieties which fostered the emergence and swift development of the *nüdan* tradition. In the prefaces, the editors justified the compilation of *nüdan* texts as a response to the specific needs of women in relation to their spiritual journeys. These needs, though, had to be pursued from within the inner chambers and with practices that did not endanger their morality and social standing. Several prefaces to *nüdan* collections described the threats that unsafe religious practices posed to women, and to the *status quo* in general. He Longxiang, in the preface to the *Nüdan hebian*, says:

> There are those women who, even though their mouths are pure, their hearts are like wolves and tigers; they look at their parents in law and sisters in law like rivals and enemies.
> There are those who mistakenly take part in heterodox sects and do not know the correct way. . . . others are lured into lewd chambers.
> There are those who secretly attract good girls to serve as human cauldrons, as they serve as the Yellow Dame [*huangpo* 黃婆][7], and as a result lose their name and integrity.

---

[7] In partner practice, this term refers to a woman who, during essential phases of the alchemical process, helps the practitioners unite or procures female adepts for male adepts.

> Then there are those good women who do what palace ladies like to do: they enjoy serving as cauldrons [*ding* 鼎][8] in order to seek the achievement of immortality, [but they just] continue to lose their good name and integrity.
>
> And there are those who go on pilgrimages, enter temples and throw themselves in a disorderly manner at Buddhist and Daoist monks; others again plant the seed of passion into male teachers of good schools. And, of course, there are those who merely use the Dao to collect riches (pref. 2b-3a).

Why was there the need for such a tradition after centuries of non-gendered alchemical treatises (and probably non-gendered practice)? Even though most if not all of those who could afford alchemical practice had always been men, *neidan* texts did not, until the emergence of *nüdan* in the Qing, clearly differentiate practitioners according to gender. By stating this difference, and acknowledging that what had been written before that time was therefore mainly directed to men, writers of female alchemy formed and at the same time satisfied the need for a tradition of female alchemy. Non-gendered in principle, in practice internal alchemy had been, since its full development in the Song, primarily a male domain. By the late eighteenth century, women had begun to be mentioned, but mostly as "cauldrons" in male practices, or as colleagues in duo cultivation (see Liu 1997).

With the increasing availability of written texts in most households, the spread of literacy to women of higher classes, and women's increasingly active involvement in religious activities, there was certainly a more fertile ground for the creation and diffusion of religious literature for women. This tradition was thus not only a response to women's needs and demands or an assertion of their presence in the religious arena, but also a reaction to the worries that these demands produced within the established elite. The prefaces to the various *nüdan* collections, written by the men who collected them, show that their aim was to set the basis for a safe, controllable, and manageable female practice. This would not take women away from home or expose them to improper influences, a growing concern especially in Qing China's reactionary attitudes towards women.

The women targeted by this literature were mainly of the elite. They had at least rudimentary reading skills, leisure time and space to practice, alone or together with other women. Their status would have been tainted by intermingling with male teachers or fellow practitioners as well as by travelling outside

---

[8] In sexual practice, this term is an euphemism for the body of a young girl, used as the cauldron for the transformation of the essences that the male deposits there and, later, plucks from it for his own refinement.

the home.⁹ In terms of age, while this practice was open to adult women of all ages, the practice of menopausal women plays a strong role, which indicates that they often started practicing after completing their familial duties. However, many texts also mention that one should start the practice at the onset of the first menstruation. This would have produced tension and the need for intense mediation inside the family. At this point, there is no historical evidence that this was a practice used within nunneries or communities of marriage resistance which did exist in south China.¹⁰ More research is required.

A Rhetoric of Difference

The perceived structural and social differences between men and women led to a new practice for women, complete with indications of correct social behavior and moral injunctions. The authors of these texts prescribed a theory for a "different" female practice and then proceeded to create texts to describe it. Directed to one gender, *nüdan* relates the theory and practice of alchemy closely to the structure of that gender and thereby defines, for the first time in such an overt manner, practices used in a gendered context. The theoretical and cosmological difference between male and female structures formed the base of the creation of a gender-specific tradition, which allows for a different practice. Once one structure was selected over another theoretically, the need "naturally" arose to create a complete textual tradition. In this way, *neidan* became suddenly a dual tradition, including *nandan* 男丹 and *nüdan*. The term *nandan* only appears in texts of *nüdan*, as a way to assert this tradition against its opposite, the other "pole" in the sudden polarization of *neidan*. Here is how one alchemical author describes the gender difference:

> The great Dao does not ask about men and women. Both of them can obtain accomplishment [of the practice]. Therefore, the way of the men is to become a Perfected Man, the way of the woman is to become a Primordial Princess [*yuanjun* 元君].
>
> From time immemorial, alchemical treatises discussing the work of male refinement have been numerous. But they do not discuss the female way of refinement. If there are those who discuss it, they do not go beyond an approximate exposition. They do not cover women. They stretch their meaning by saying that if people have the same inner nature and life-force, they then will follow the same practice. They speak of male practice but they do not go into trouble explaining female practice. They do not know that the man is yang outside and yin inside and

---

⁹ This can be inferred by reading the prefaces to *nüdan* collections, and by the very little information gathered about actual practitioners. He Longxiang, in the preface to his *Nüdan hebian*, mentions his female relatives as his primary inspirators for its collation (6ab).

¹⁰ These communities made large use of precious scroll (*baojuan*) literature, but not, as far as I know, of *nüdan* literature. See Prazniak 1986; Sankar 1978; Topley 1954; Wolf 1975.

the woman is yin outside and yang inside. Their inner nature is different, their structure and form are not the same. Even though they have the same inner nature and destiny, the way they practice is greatly different.

The *Xiuzhen biannan* says: "As for men starting the practice, refining their *qi* is fundamental; as for women starting the practice, refining the form is fundamental."

Xuzu says: "When men have completed the practice, they will not leak *jing*. When women have completed the practice, they will not leak menses [blood]." The way they return to the first pass [the first step of the practice] is very different for them. When it comes to refining the self, obtaining the pill, returning to the cinnabar, warming and nurturing, forming the embryo, letting the spirit go out and the like, even if [female practice] is the same as male, there are still slight differences in the order. (*Nü jindan fayao*, preface)

Social Differences

One justification for the emergence of *nüdan* literature stems not from structural but social differences. Closely echoed by the preface to the *Nü jindan fayao*, the preface to the *Nüdan hebian* notes:

> There are Heaven and Earth and then there are men and women. Of men, many attain immortality; of women, few attain immortality. Why? Because men can wander and look for the Dao, whereas for women it is difficult to leave home and find a master. Alchemical books for men are very numerous, but alchemical books for women are few and far between, and are not transmitted. Seven or eight men out of ten can read and understand a written text, but only one or two out of a hundred women can. (1a)

Both prefaces show a revealing insistence on the same set of themes: texts for women are lacking, and thus only few women who want to practice can do so. Being always confined in the inner quarters, they cannot meet teachers and have no discernment between good and bad teachers, right and wrong practices. In this situation, the writers say, what could be better than a practice with which, without leaving home, the young girl can transform her *qi*, the old lady can ward off illnesses, and the widow can maintain her chastity (*Kunyuan jing*, 2nd pref., 4a).

Because of their different social standing, it is difficult for women to act in the same way as men when seeking the Dao. Their education is not comparable to that of men, therefore it is difficult for them to read alchemical treatises. If that were not enough of an obstacle, leaving home to seek a master is unthinkable for a woman of good social standing. Therefore, it is said, this newly created literature will be welcome in the inner quarters, because it is written in a simple language. It will satisfy the spiritual needs of women without exposing them to the threats of the outside world. This justification is clearly linked to the anxiety perceived by the elite about women's religious activities.

Structural Differences

The issue of structural differences is prominent in He Longxiang's preface to the *Nüdan hebian*. It includes the most complete description of cosmological, physiological, and practical differences between men and women within the *nüdan* tradition. The differences are divided according to three categories: innate nature (*bingxing* 秉性), structure (*xingti* 形體), and practice (*gongfa* 功法).

The categories are telling. Innate nature includes distinctions at the cosmic and fundamental level: yin and yang, yielding and unyielding, stillness and motion, the trigrams Kan and Li, the moon and the sun, impurity and purity. Structure means distinguishing bodily features, sexual attributes, fluids like blood and semen, different kinds of energy. Practice involves differences in training that result from the cosmic and structural differences. While being all-encompassing, this description is not as detailed as some of the passages within the manual itself, especially when discussing the practice.

As regards differences in innate nature, He says:

> Just as the man is yang, and yang is clear, so the woman is yin, and yin is turbid. Male nature is hard, female nature is soft. A man's feelings are excitable, a woman's feelings are tranquil; male thoughts are mixed, female thoughts are plain.
>
> The man is fundamentally in movement, and movement facilitates the loss of *qi*; the woman is fundamentally quiet, and quietude facilitates the accumulation of *qi*. The man is associated with the trigram Li and, like the sun, he can complete a whole circuit of the heavens in one year. The woman is associated with the trigram Kan and, like the moon, she can complete a whole circuit of the heavens in one month. For a man, *qi* is difficult to subdue; for a woman, *qi* is easy to subdue. These are the differences concerning innate nature. (4ab)

Women are physiologically turbid and impure, but by nature they are also soft, tranquil, quiet, and of plain thought. Men are physiologically pure, but also hard, excitable, with mixed thoughts, and in constant movement. These differences influence the way in which they practice and the results of the practice. While a woman has to be more conscious of her turbid nature, her quietness helps her in the accumulation of *qi*. A man starts with a pure nature, but his constant movement means easy loss of *qi*. Men and women derive their innate characteristics from two different areas of the cosmos: male is Qian (Heaven) and female is Kun (Earth). This concept is not new. We find it already in the *Yijing* 易經 (Book of Changes), from which *nüdan* borrows heavily.

One step further, the male structure is likened to that of the trigram Li (fire), yang outside and yin inside, while the female structure matches that of the trigram Kan (water), yin outside and yang inside. This cosmic difference, in turn, causes differences in terms of the shape and form of male and female bodies (*xingti* 形體), their fluids and energies. Consequently, men and women follow different paths.

Kan is a powerful image: the yin outside, transposed onto the female body, is what needs to be refined, drained of its coldness and dampness, made to turn to yang. The yang inside, on the other hand, facilitates the females last stage, when the yang spirit, emerging from her interior, will not be obstructed on its way out. The cosmic differences between yin and yang, Kan and Li, Qian and Kun, are not just parallel to the description of men and women, but affect their bodily shapes and their practice. Because of their constitution women have to work intensely on their outer structure, cosmologically symbolized by the external yin lines of Kan and physiologically materialized in menstrual blood. In a parallel way, the male structure, outwardly yang, is not difficult to transform.

He's preface next discusses structural differences:

> The man has a knot inside the windpipe [Adams apple], the woman does not. The male breasts do not produce liquids and are small; the female breasts produce liquids and are big. A man's foundation is convex [tu 凸]; a woman's foundation is concave [ao 凹]. In the man [the convex organ] is called the Essence Chamber [jingshi 精室]; in the woman [the concave organ] is called the Infant's Palace [zigong 子宮]. In men the vital force is located in the Ocean of Qi; in women the vital force is located between the breasts.
>
> In the man, generative power [lit. "kidneys"] is located in the pelvis; in the woman, generative power originates from the blood. In the man [the generative power] is the essence, its color is white and its name is White Tiger [baihu 白虎]; in the woman it is the blood, its color is red and its name is Red Dragon [chilong 赤龍]. As for male essence, it is yin within yang; as for female blood, it is yang within yin. The power of male essence is more than sufficient; the power of female blood is insufficient. These are differences concerning form and structure. (4b-5a)

This section discusses both general physiological structure and specific differences. It mentions the breasts almost at the beginning: a fundamental element of female practice, they are the means through which the blood is refined and have no part in male practice. The author describes the female and male defining the fundamental organs very literally as convex and concave and emphasizing the Essence Chamber in males and the infant's palace in females. The essence chamber is where the male stores his seminal essence, it is located in the lower elixir field and its outward manifestation is the penis. The Infant's Palace is where the blood is stored in women, its outward manifestation is the vagina and in physiological terms it corresponds to the uterus. The female *qi* center is located between the breasts, where the blood gathers once it is produced by the heart and then flows down to the uterus and out of the body as menstrual blood. It ought to return here in the backwards trajectory of alchemical practice. While in men the seminal essence to be sublimated is called the White Tiger, in women the blood to be sublimated is called the Red Dragon. The reference to yin within yang for male essence and yang within yin for female blood is the physiological application of the trigrams Li and Kan described above.

Moving along, the following section presents differences in actual practice. They involve not only different loci where the practice takes place, but also different perspectives and processes:

> A man first refines the founding origin [*benyuan* 本元], and only subsequently the form [*xingzhi* 形質]; a woman, instead, needs to refine her form first and only then the founding origin. The male yang leaks downward, whereas the female yang moves upward. When a man has completed the practice, and the seminal essence does not drip away any more, this is called "subduing the White Tiger." When a woman has completed the practice and the menstrual flow does not drip away anymore, this is called "beheading the Red Dragon."
>
> In the man, seminal essence moves against the current and he becomes immortal; in the woman, blood moves upwards, ascending towards the heart cavity. The masculine practice is called "refining the *qi* of the supreme yang", the feminine practice is called "refining the blood of the supreme yin."[11] For the man we speak of "embryo" [*tai* 胎]; for the woman, on the other hand, we speak of "breathing" [*xi* 息].[12]
>
> When the man has subdued the White Tiger, the stem [penis] will retract and become similar to that of a young boy; when the woman has beheaded the Red Dragon, the breasts will retract and become similar to those of a male body. The man progresses slowly at the moment of the manifestation of the spirit, and he is slow in achieving the Dao; the woman progresses fast at the moment of the manifestation of the spirit, and she is also fast in attaining the Dao. A man can ascend [to Heaven] on his own; a woman, instead, needs to await salvation. Men must meditate facing the wall;[13] women who succeed in going back to emptiness are very few. The man will become a Perfected, the woman will become a Primordial Princess. These are the differences concerning the methods of practice. (5ab)

As in general *neidan*, the goal of female practice is to refine one's constitution, reclaiming the energies one received at birth and slowing their loss, thus delaying or eliminating death. But while the standard course of alchemical re-

---

[11] A detailed description of this method, which involves breathing exercises, regular breast massages, visualizing lights throughout the body, forming the immortal embryo, and the final manifestation of the spirit is given in several texts in the *Nüdan hebian*: see *Qiaoyang jing nügong xiulian* 1a, *Nü jindan* 2.23a, *Nüdan cuoyao* 2b. The three versions are almost identical. This preface uses information from all of these texts and streamlines them.

[12] A man must focus on visualizing an embryo forming inside his body, while a woman must concentrate on her breathing, since it will not be hard for her to visualize the embryo forming inside her body.

[13] The practice of "meditating facing a wall" refers to the legend of Bodhidharma, said to have spent nine years at the Shaolin Temple (Henan) meditating facing a wall, after cutting his own eyelids to avoid falling asleep.

finement proceeds from *jing* to *qi*, from *qi* to *shen*, and from *shen* to emptiness, women need to refine their blood, not their essence, into *qi*. The physical starting point for female practice is accordingly the *Qi* Cavity [*qixue* 氣穴], a point between the breasts. Through breast massages and visualizations, the blood that has previously descended from the *Qi* Cavity to the Infant's Palace is sent upward in a backwards motion. The Infant's Palace, moreover, is also called the Sea of Blood (*xuehai* 血海) and located three and a half inches below the navel. It is not to be confused with the lower elixir field, where male practice begins.

Unlike a man, a woman needs first and foremost to refine her exterior form, meaning her bloody and turbid constitution and her sexual characteristics (i.e., breasts). This attention to her exterior form directly relates to the structure of the female cosmological and physiological body that is yin and impure in nature. Through breast massages the blood that would flow down from the heart to the womb is thus sent upwards, back to the *Qi* Cavity between the breasts. Practitioners repeat this process many times, thus achieving the thinning and eventual disappearance of the menstrual flow, a process called beheading the Red Dragon. When this happens, other sexual characteristics change: the breasts shrink and the body becomes more androgynous. At this point the woman has completed the first stage of the practice.

For the next stage, that of transforming *qi* into *shen*, she can progress faster than a man because she is now concentrating not on her exterior form but on her internal embryo, and her internal structure is pure yang (like the trigram Kan). At the very last stage, however, that of ascension to Heaven, even though she has transformed all her external sexual characteristics as well as refined an internal immortal embryo, some of her nature still weighs her down and, unlike a man who can ascend directly, she needs to be called up by the immortals. Then she becomes a Primordial Princess.

The Female Body

The representation of the female body found in these texts borrows from brief depictions in Song Daoist materials and in the two Ming texts described earlier. It also relies on medical texts of the time which describe the female constitution as consisting of blood and therefore weaker, damper, more turbid, and harder to cure (Furth 1986; 1994). This notion is transferred to female alchemy in terms of the difficulty for women to complete the first step of the practice. Women have to struggle more than men in the first stage, and their attention must be focused on draining their structure of their excess liquid and dampness. Thus, for a woman, her outer structure is the first thing to focus upon, whereas men can immediately direct their attention to the core of their being, the *benyuan*, foundation and origin of their selves.

Blood is clearly the main element to be dealt with in the process of female refinement. It is related to several loci in the female body: produced by the heart-mind, it concentrates in the *Qi* Cavity at the breasts, then flows down to the Sea of Blood, and through practice reverts upward again to the *Qi* Cavity. Within the female body, blood is not just a fluid but a process. It changes shape and degree of purity, it transforms into milk, it is replenished and exhausted. The *Nüdan cuoyao* 女丹撮要 (Comprehensive Essentials of Women's Alchemy), contained in the *Nüdan hebian*, describes in detail the formation of the female body from the mingling of her parents' energies, the formation of blood and its exhaustion through menstruation.

> When a woman is not born yet, her father and mother join their essences. The [spermatic] essence of the father arrives first; the blood of the mother arrives second. Blood containing essence, this is the female form. (3b)

The passage goes on to describe how menstrual blood (called Heavenly Water) forms in the female body over the next fourteen years and how it is then squandered little by little every month until the woman reaches the age of 49. Alchemical practice serves to reverse this situation of depletion:

> If one wants to practice until the Qian body is complete, the movement goes upwards from the lower [elixir] field to the Yang Cavity. The spiritual fire will steam up like vapor and transform the flux into yellow, the yellow into white, and the white will change into nothingness. (*Nü jindan* 2.20ab)

The first aim of the practice is therefore to eliminate the menses. This should be accomplished not by stopping them and producing a menstrual blockage, identified in the texts as a disease to be cured, but by the gradual transformation and refinement of blood inside the woman's body in such a way that it does not any more appear in its usual forms outside the body (menstrual blood, milk). An erroneous process would jeopardize the adept's health.

In order to refine the blood, women have to implement a practice completely different from that of men at this stage, which is the massage of the breasts. Massaging the breasts helps revert the downward flow of blood from the *Qi* Cavity to the Sea of Blood. This massage is described in minute detail in several *nüdan* texts. For example:

> Intention is focused on the breasts, left and right it revolves thirty-six times in each direction. The lips [are sealed] above and below, the teeth clench firmly, the nostrils are closed tightly. Use internal breathing. With the palms of your hands, massage the breasts 72 times on each side, first softly and then more urgently, first lightly and then more strongly. In a hundred days the work will be completed, and they will acquire the form of walnuts. (*Nügong zhengfa*: 10ab)

Female Alchemy / 157

> With progressive practice, the breasts undergo physical changes, they become smaller and the nipples retract to look like those of a maiden or of a man: practice will result in your breasts becoming like those of a maiden, the form of those of a young girl, then the woman transforms into a male body. (*Xiwangmu nüxiu zhengtu shize* 9b)

The practitioner will have to practice this process several times, circling the energy according to the method of the Microcosmic (lesser celestial) Orbit. As the *Nügong lianji huandan tushuo* 女功煉已還丹圖說 (Illustrations and Sayings on the Female Practice of Refining the Self and Reverting the Elixir) says:

> Use the [methods of] the lesser celestial orbit and of the phases of fire.[14] Both also have oral instructions. Advance the yang fire and retreat the yin tally [*jin yanghuo tui yinfu* 進陽火退陰符].[15] Smelt and refine it. Both have timings and have regulations. When you have refined it for a month, the number of the small circulations is sufficient.
>
> As for the truth or falsity of the medicine, the coagulation, or the elixir, there is a self-verification: if the small elixir really has been coagulated, every time you enter the room and sit in quiet meditation, fire will exude throughout the body in the same way as vapor comes out of a steaming basket. You only ought to silently guard the Central Palace [*zhonggong* 中宮; i.e. the Sea of Blood]. Do not shout, but listen to its changes; in a moment you will see a pearl of fire, as a bean in size, shooting out of the Hall of Light [*mingtang* 明堂; at the top of the head], more than ten feet high, like a lightning-bolt. This then is the true proof of having set the basis and obtained the medicine. (3-4)

The texts often insist that at this delicate point one needs a teacher to be guided forward and avoid dangers:

> At this point there should also be oral instructions. You need to attend a master in order to avoid dangers. If you do not do this, I fear that the true fire will change into common fire; first guard against it burning the body, second guard against becoming mad.

Same Bodies?

Once women have managed to transform their bloody constitution and refine their blood into *qi*, they have achieved the first step of the practice. From then on, the differences between the sexes are minimal, and women can continue

---

[14] This indicates the track orbit along the two main lines, the Governing and Conception Vessels. The practitioner grasps the true yin and sends it in a circular motion along these, down the front and up the back of her body.

[15] This process, also called "phases of fire" (*huohou* 火候) or celestial orbit (*zhoutian* 周天), is common in *neidan* practices; it refines yin into yang energies through circulation.

their practice similarly to men. Therefore, the detailed description of women's differences in the first phase does not set the stage for a completely female practice, alternative to standard *neidan*. Instead, the beginning of the second phase brings about the deletion of this difference, where the penis retracts and the breasts shrink dramatically (*Nüdan hebian* 5a).

During alchemical practice, both men and women thus lose their secondary sexual characteristics. Does the author then imply that a woman, in order to complete the practice, has to become a man? The answer is that instead of women turning into men, both sexes aim to refine their bodies towards a more androgynous ideal. Cosmologically they strive towards integrating Kan and Li; physiologically they hope to refine those elements that keep them attached to a lower level of humanity, i.e., blood and raw essence. The shrinking of the penis and the loss of menses and disappearance of breasts are secondary effects of this path. The aim of the practice is to go beyond, to a stage where bodily differences do not matter any longer. The changes in the physical body are external indications of the changes happening at a more internal and subtle level. Liu Yiming notes:

> Someone asked: Once having attained the Golden Elixir, and after having ingested it, [it is said that] the woman turns into a man and the old into an adolescent. Is this true? [The Master] answered: In that case we are speaking of the principle, and not of the shape. The woman, having attained the Dao, has completely discarded the yin and her body turns into a complete yang body, the same as the body of a man who has achieved the Dao. For this reason it is said that "the woman turns into a man." . . . We are not speaking of a transformation of her illusory image [body]. (*Xiuzhen biannan* 1.10a)

On the other hand, even after this refinement, the female body somehow still retains traces of yin constitution that influence her ability to perform in the same way as the male.

Once the first step of the practice is concluded, once blood is transformed and dampness dried, the fundamental difference of the female body seems to disappear. Women can then practice following standard alchemical instructions, even more quickly than men. Why? Because once the coarser elements of the body (female and male) are refined, both genders are supposed to be at the same level and can proceed as equals.

> We can say that, as regards the laws of nature, there are no differences [between men and women]. I advice the female adepts to first find out points of contiguity where there are differences, and only then discover the differences hidden where there is similarity. In most cases, however, the contrasts are to be found before the beheading of the Red Dragon, whereas the major similarities emerge after the beheading of the Dragon. These are irrefutable and eternal arguments. (*Nüdan hebian*, pref. 5ab)

Two ideas seem to be very clear: female difference has a negative connotation and needs to be eliminated for a woman to attain complete refinement; and, once eliminated, nothing else will interfere with her attainment. Men's practice, on the contrary, does not start from a point of deficiency, but is simply a process of refinement from turbid to pure, leading directly to attainment.

There is, though, an obvious contradiction between what is described in the prefaces of female alchemical texts and what we read in the main texts. In fact, the main texts still mention differences in both structure and behavior even after the refinement of the female structure. Once they complete the practice, women still have to wait until the gods come to their rescue, while men can directly ascend to the skies. As the *Nüdan hebian* notes: "A man can ascend [to Heaven] on his own; a woman, instead, needs to await salvation" (5a).

In order to be accepted as "realized people," women have to perform more "good work" in society to cancel lingering structural imbalances. They have to "accumulate good." As the *Nüdan shize* says:

> Why is it that in order to complete the practice that leads to feminine perfection, it is necessary to "await salvation"? The reason lies in the [female] constitution, feeble and pervaded with blood. [The woman] who practices inner refinement and sublimation is able to complete a yang body. But even if the formation of the yang body is achieved, her yin and stagnant nature is not yet completely refined. . . .
>
> The situation is different for the male constitution. After a man has practiced until the accomplishment of an adamantine and indestructible body, he has completed the stage of return to vacuity and a spiritual light will pervade Heaven and Earth. Therefore a man does not need to await salvation: he will attain the Dao and complete perfection, he will ascend in person to the presence of the supreme divinities and wander to the quiet Penglai islands. For women, it is not like this. In order to complete the alchemical practice for women, it is necessary to widely cultivate merits and virtues. If the merits and virtues have been cultivated fully, then the sages from above will see it and take pity on them, and report it to the emperor. . . .
>
> Once the seeker of feminine perfection reaches this point, once she overcomes the stage of the manifestation of the spirit, she must wait for the salvation of the supreme sages who will lead her back to Authenticity. Only then the practice is completed. (16ab)

There are, thus, two distinct rhetorics at work. One says that once the first step is complete and the bodies refined, male and female practice proceed in the same way. This voice is countered by another that keeps repeating how the female is still different (and weaker).

Conclusion

To conclude, I find that texts of female alchemy reveal much about gender notions, the understanding of the female body, and the social tension between men and women at the time of their writing.

What is interesting about the texts is both how they were created and who they address. I argue that the emergence of female alchemy is a response to a growing need for a safe and morally acceptable practice for women. The elements for the creation of such a tradition were already there: women had been described as practicing differently from men in Daoist texts since the twelfth century while medicine had increasingly focused on the different physiology of males and females. Yet, for reasons described above, a literature just for women only began during the Qing dynasty.

Authors of these texts used already existing medical and alchemical notions about the female body, as well as pre-existing but newly flourishing ideas about the role of women in society, to build a different theory and practice in women's spiritual quest. The literature that ensued had two aims: assuaging fears arising from the heterodox practices that women were already following, and filling the needs of the increasing number of women with a desire to practice. The appearance of this literature, furthermore, made it imperative for women to follow a separate practice from men. It was no longer acceptable for women to follow the same practice as men, since now there was a new literature just for them, which clearly identified the differences.

Reading the prefaces and following the actual practices, though, it becomes clear that the differences highlighted, at the social and structural levels, are perceived as negative. Women are lacking in several ways, and this practice not only helps with their specificity but also restores the female body, rids it of its pollution, and replenishes it. Women's starting point is one of deficiency. This deficiency is overcome when the various differences on the bodily, spiritual, cosmological, and social levels are eliminated. This is not an easy task.

In sum, by reducing the female to a body that has to be cleansed from the turbidity of blood, the writers reveal their fear of pollution. By producing texts to be used in the inner chambers, they do the same thing on a different level, containing the dangers of women from spilling over into the male world. By expecting women to conform to the male practice once they are rid of their turbid constitutions, they invalidate their initial aim of creating a truly "female" alchemy, a practice that takes into account the female body and its specificities, seen as differences, not as deficiencies. By expecting women to perform "good works" at the last stage of the practice, in order to supplement their lacking structure, they reinforce the idea of difference that cannot easily be transcended. However, this literature should not be completely discounted as moralistic and paternalistic; it does afford women the opportunity to practice, and practice safely, away from criticism and perceived or actual dangers to themselves and the community.

Bibliography

Brokaw, Cynthia. 1991. *The Ledgers of Merit and Demerit: Social Change and Moral Order in Late Imperial China.* Berkeley: University of California Press.

Dean, Kenneth. 1998. *Lord of the Three in One: The Spread of a Cult in Southeast Asia.* Princeton: Princeton University Press.

Despeux, Catherine. 1985. "Les lectures alchimiques du *Hsi-yu-chi*." In *Religion und Philosophie in Ostasien: Festschrift für Hans Steininger*, edited by. G. Naundorf, K.H. Pohl, and H. H. Schmidt, 61-76. Würzburg: Königshausen and Neumann.

Dudbridge Glen. 1991 "A Pilgrimage in Seventeenth-century Fiction: T'ai Shan and the Hsing-shih yin-yüan chuan." *T'oung Pao* 7.

_____. 1992. "Women Pilgrims to T'ai Shan: Some Pages from a Seventeenth-century Novel." In *Pilgrims and Sacred Sites in China*, edited by Susan Naquin and Chün-fang Yu. Berkeley: University of California Press.

Esposito, Monica. 2000. "Daoism in the Qing (1644-1911)." In *Daoism Handbook*, edited by Livia Kohn, 623-58. Leiden: E. Brill.

_____. 2001. "Longmen Taoism in Qing China: Doctrinal Ideal and Local Reality." *Journal of Chinese Religions* 29:191-232.

_____. 2002 "The Longmen School and Its Controversial History during the Qing Dynasty." In *Religion and Chinese Society: The Transformation of a Field*, edited by John Lagerwey. Hong Kong: Chinese University of Hong Kong.

Furth, Charlotte. 1986 "Blood, Body and Gender. Medical Images of the Female condition in China 1600-1850." *Chinese Science* 7.

_____. 1994. "Ming-Qing Medicine and the Construction of Gender." *Jindai Zhongguo funüshi yanjiu* 2.

_____. 1999. *A Flourishing Yin: Gender in China's Medical History, 960-1665*. Berkeley: University of California Press.

Liu Ts'un-yan. 1985. "Quanzhen jiao he xiaoshuo Xiyouji" 全真教和小說西游記, in 5 parts. *Mingbao yuekan* 233:55-62; 234:59-64; 235:85-90; 236:85 90; 237:70-74

_____. 1962. *Buddhist and Taoist Influences on Chinese Novels*. Wiesbaden: Harrassowitz

Liu, Ts'un-yan. 1970. "Taoist Self-Cultivation in Ming Thought." In *Self and Society in Ming Thought*, edited by Wm.Th. DeBary, 291-331. New York: Columbia University Press.

Liu, Xun. 1997. "To Enter the Chamber: On Aspects of the Secluded Chamber Practice in Late Ming." Paper Presented at the 1997 Western Conference of the Association for Asian Studies, Boulder, Colorado

Mori, Yuria 森由利亞. 1994."Zennshinkyô Ryûmon-ha keifu kô" 全真教龍門派系譜考, in Dôkyô bunka e no tenbô 道教文化へU展望, ed. by Dôkyô bunka kenkyûkai 道教文化研究會, 180-211, Tokyo, Hirakawa

Naquin, Susan, and Chün-fang Yu, eds. 1992. *Pilgrims and Sacred Sites in China*. Berkeley: University of California Press.

Oldstone-Moore, Jennifer. 1998. "Alchemy and the *Journey to the West*: The Cart-Slow Kingdom Episode." *Journal of Chinese Religions* 26:51-66

Prazniak, Suzann. 1986. "Weavers and Sorceresses of Chuansha: The Social Origins of Political Activism among Rural Chinese Women." *Modern China* 12.2:202-29.

Roy, David. 2001. *The Plum in the Golden Vase or Chin P'ing Mei*. Princeton: Princeton University Press.

Sankar, Andrea. 1978. "The Evolution of the Sisterhood in Traditional Chinese Society: From Village Girls' Houses to Chai T'angs in Hong Kong." Ph.D. Diss., University of Michigan, Ann Arbor.

Theiss, Janet. 2004. *Disgraceful Matters: The Politics of Chastity in Eighteenth-Century China*. Berkeley: University of California Press.

Topley, Marjorie, 1954 "Chinese Women's Vegetarian Houses in Singapore." *Journal of the Malayan Branch of the Royal Asiatic Society* 27.1:.

_____. 1975. "Marriage Resistance in Rural Kwangtung." In *Women in Chinese Society*, edited by Margery Wolf and Roxane Witke. Stanford: Stanford University Press.

Valussi, Elena. 2003. "Beheading the Red Dragon: Female Inner Alchemy in Late Imperial China." Ph.D. Diss., University of London, London.

_____. 2008. "The *Nüdan hebian*, Its Editor and His Women." *Nannü: Men, Women and Gender in Early and Imperial China* 10.

Wang Gang 王崗. 1995. "Xiyouji - yige wanzheng de daojiao neidan xiulian guocheng" 西游記：一個完整的道教內丹修鍊過程. *Tsing Hua Journal of Chinese Studies* 25:51-86.

Wang Guogang 王國光. 1990. *Xiyouji bielun* 西游記別論. Shanghai: Xuelin.

Yu, Anthony. 1987. "Religion and Literature in China: The 'Obscure Way' of Journey to the West." In *Tradition and Creativity: Essays on East Asian Civilization*, edited by Ching-I Tu, 109-54, New Brunswick, N.J.: Transaction Books.

To Become a Female Daoist Master

Kundao in Training

Robin R. Wang

Daoism has always placed a great emphasis on the contributions made by women. In internal alchemy (*neidan*), too, women play important roles, held to have a "greater aptitude for transcendence and for communication with the divine and invisible world....Women's special abilities to intercede with the gods and to fulfill the vows of the faithful render them more efficacious and powerful practitioners than men" (Despeux 2000, 384). How, then, is internal alchemy practiced by women today? Is it still a valid practice among female Daoists? In this essay, I explore how female Daoists continue the traditional teachings in contemporary transformation, examining in particular the two-year training program for female temple leaders in China.

Internal alchemy tends to refer to three things: a coherent body of oral and written teachings which became a codified tradition in twelfth century; regimens of various practices; and an inner state realized through these practice (Skar and Pregadio 2000, 481). According to a Daoist masters, there are two routes internal alchemy as thus defined. One is the way of lower virtue (*xiade* 下德), to use a term from the *Daode jing*; the other is the way of higher virtue (*shangde* 上德). The former is based on self-conscious activity (*youwei* 有爲) and moves from the understanding of the cosmos to its source. "It requires discipline and uses cosmological and alchemical emblems as tools to guide the inner process of realization" (Skar and Pregadio 2000, 481).

The path of higher virtue, on the other hand, is based on spontaneous, unselfconscious and non-intervening way of being (*wuwei* 無爲). It begins with a deep awareness of the fundamental nature of reality and permits the immediate recognition of self and world. This path is only practiced by direct or oral transmission from master to disciples (*ibid.*). There is no question that there are still a few Daoists today who practice the way of higher virtue in their pursuit of internal alchemy. They tend to work in secret, living isolated in the depth of mountains and transmit the teachings by oral instruction. This form of the practice is hardly known and could only be studied if one spent a few years with the Daoists.

The way of lower virtue is comparatively much more accessible. Here practitioners make a conscious effort and engage in a wide range of cultivation methods, from reading classical texts to serving the community, learning—as a popular slogan has it—to "cultivate Dao in all things." [1]

From *Chujiaren* to Kundao

Female Daoists in China today are called *kundao* 坤道, a respectful and popular appellation for renunciants or those who have "left the family" (*chujiaren* 出家人). The latter term is a general expression to describe those who have left the householder's life and entered a religious order of either Daoists or Buddhists, male or female. Within this group, kundao specifically refers to female Daoist renunciants in a cherished and admiring way. The term combines two ancient concepts. Kun comes from the *Yijing* 易經 (Book of Changes) and refers to Earth as opposed to Qian 乾, Heaven. It is the highest expression of femininity and includes all things representing the feminine. Dao refers to the "way" with its many metaphysical and ontological implications.

There is no clear record of when the expression *kundao* was first coined. Among the Celestial Masters, female Daoists who were chosen to receive registers and talismans and who could participate in advanced practices were called female officers (*nüguan* 女官). In Highest Clarity, women practitioners were known as female Daoists (*nü daoshi* 女道士) or female hats (*nüguan* 女冠) due to their distinctive headdress (Despeux 2000, 384). In many literary texts, moreover, women Daoists were also described as female perfected (*nüzhen* 女真). The expression *kundao* is not recorded before the Qing dynasty and has only become popular in recent years.

Just as the origin of the name is unclear, so no one quite knows how many kundao there are. Wang Yier, chief editor of the *Journal of Chinese Daoism* at the White Cloud Temple in Beijing, says: "Half of the Daoists who are living in temples around China are kundao. There are over ten thousand of them. They are in many ways more sincere and committed to their faith than their male counterparts."[2] We can see just how important women Daoists are by

---

[1] This saying is heard frequently among Daoists today. It implies that everything they do in temple is a way of being Daoist and working toward the realization of Dao. A new interpretation of the practice, it also shows that one does not have to meditate to be a Daoist.

[2] Private interview, July 2006.

looking at their special training school on the Southern Marchmount (Nanyue 南岳) in Hunan.³

A two-year on-site program, this training institution forms part of the Chinese Daoist College (Zhongguo Daojiao Xueyuan 中國道教學院), which was originally founded by the Chinese Daoist Association in 1990. The first class of female students matriculated on September 12, 2005 and graduated on June 25, 2007. The class consisted of forty-eight female Daoists, selected from thirty-two temples in sixteen provinces. Its mission is summarized in the following slogan: *Honoring Dao, Respecting De; Learning and Cultivation Progressing Together* 尊道贵德, 学修并进.

The goal of the program is to train Daoist leaders who can manage and run temples all over the country and participate in the official administration of the religion. Upon graduation, the women return to their original temples and take on the responsibilities of managing them in a modern way. Usually aged between 21 and 35, this newly trained elite is set to become a vigorous force affecting the development of Daoism in the coming decades. For this reason, an examination of their training and vision helps us to understand the current vision of Daoist practice and the future prospects of the religion in China. Beyond this, since Daoism is one of the few religions that places no limitations on the roles of women, the school might offer a model for the place of women in religious institutions.

The kundao class takes place in the main temple (Damiao 大庙) at the bottom of the Southern Marchmount. Both are under the leadership of a well-known kundao master Huang Zhi'an, president of the Hunan Daoist Association, who also serves as the vice-president of the Chinese Daoist Association. She is the one of the most prominent female Daoists in China today, at least in terms of political and social involvement. A member of the People's Congress, she regularly attends sessions at the Great Hall of the People in Beijing. She is also the chief editor of the biannual journal *Hunan Daoism*, which contains ten sections that range from discussions of current events through presentations of classical texts and Daoist history to contemporary moral issues. Master Huang has the long-term vision and firm commitment to found a larger kundao academy in the next few years.⁴

For the moment, active students live and study in the temple facilities. Classrooms are located around a quiet courtyard; they contain new equipment

---

³ The Southern Marchmount is one of five central Daoist mountains, with a long history. According to legend, the Yellow Emperpor lived there and Zhang Daoling, the first Celestial Master, visited it. The matriarch Wei Huacun (252-334), one of the key revealing dieties of Highest Clarity, had a sanctuary there, and the *Huangting jing* (Yellow Court Scripture), a major meditative manual, is associated with the site. See Schafer 1977. Today, the mountain is home to thirteen temples with over forty female and thirty male Daoists.

⁴ The school recently acquired a large abandoned elementary school building which is now being renovated. The new building will be the future site of the academy.

and computing facilities. Learning and living conditions here are better than in many overcrowded Chinese colleges. Each dorm room is shared only by two students; a cafeteria provides three vegetarian meals a day. It even caters to the tastes of students from different regions, making saltier food for northerners and spicier food for southerners.

A wide and comprehensive curriculum has been designed for these students. The two years or four semesters of courses divide into three general categories: Basic Cultural Education (*wenhua ke* 文化课), Religious Studies (*zongjiao ke* 宗教课) and Daoist Practices (*daojiao xiuchi* 道教修持).

"Basic Cultural Education" comprises eight subjects: Chinese Language (4 semesters), Political Thought (4 semesters), Chinese History (4 semesters), Classical Architecture (4 semesters), English (3 semesters), Chinese Calligraphy (3 semesters), Computer Skills (2 semesters) and Basic Accounting (1 semester).

"Religious Studies" has fifteen subjects: History of Daoism (4 semesters), taiji quan (4 semesters), Classics (2 semesters), Daoist Rituals (2 semesters), Daoist Music (2 semesters), *Zhuangzi* (2 semesters), *Zhouyi* (2 semesters), *Heshang gong*'s *Commentary on the Daode jing* (1 semester), *Daode jing* (1 semester), Daoist Art (1 semester), Daoist Regulations (1 semester), Temple Management (1 semester), Daoist Ethics (1 semester), Daoist Cultivation (1 semester) and Daoist Immortals (1 semester).

"Daoist Practices" incorporates three aspects over two years: Cultivation of Character, Daoist Customs, and Morning and Evening Services.[5] All of these courses are required for every student; all students follow the same schedule. There is only one elective: learning to play a musical instrument. Every kundao must play at least one instrument, but each student can choose which one to learn.

The twenty-five classes are taught by a wide range of faculty. Some are Daoist practitioners from other temples in various regions. Others are experts or scholars of specific fields and work at nearby universities. For example, Professor Lu Xichen, a scholar of Daoist cultivation at Central Chinese Normal University, has taught the course on Daoist Ethics several times. Her lectures center on the Daoist value system and analyze its forms and changes through history. As she notes, the difference between the renunciants and her students in the city are two: Kundao are much more conscientious and hard working than college or even graduate students; however, their initial level of education is quite low.[6]

In addition, kundao students also practice calligraphy every day for the entire two years. At the end of program they publish a hand copied version of the *Daode jing* in Chinese brush work, each student contributing at least one

---

[5] The latter consists of a half-hour devotional service at the temple every morning and evening. It is required for all kundao. However according to regulations, a student can be excused for five days per month "due to special needs."

[6] Private interview, July 28, 2007.

chapter. It is usually a fine and artistic production. Beyond that, each student has to write a substantial graduation thesis. The first class's essays were published by the Chinese Daoist College in June, 2007.

A New Interpretation of Daoist Doctrine

How, then, do these young Daoist women relate to the ancient texts and to contemporary practice? As practitioners in modern China, how do they understand Daoism? Their graduation theses might shed some light on their faith and apperception of teaching and practice.

A total of forty-eight theses appears in the anthology *Huangting ji* 黄庭集 (Yellow Court Collection), grouped into five subjects: Realizing Dao (*Wudao pian* 悟道篇, 8 essays); Harmony (*Hexie pian* 和谐篇, 12 essays); Management (*Guanli pian* 管理篇, 11 essays); Cultivation (*Xiushen pian* 修身篇, 10 essays); and Nourishing Life (*Yangsheng pian* 养生篇, 7 essays). All essays are based on an interpretation and application of the *Daode jing*; they each contain quotations from the ancient classic as a major doctrinal resource and basis of justification.

Realizing Dao
This section consists of eight essays on topics that range from the virtues appropriate for a military general through the rhythm of music, policies for educational reform, ecological wisdom, and metaphysics to applied ethics. The discussions share the common presupposition that Dao is the root of Chinese culture and the highest notion of Laozi. Dao endows all conceptual understanding and practical implications with a rational justification.

In an explanation of what Dao is, Zeng Liyan argues against some scholarly views that attempt to classify Dao as either materialism or idealism or both. She claims that Dao is a unity between something (*you*) and nothingness (*wu*) that takes life as its basis. Dao is both the fundamental origin and the ground structure of the universe (CDC 2007, 44). Zeng explains why Dao is the origin of the myriad things: For one, concrete things with determined and fixed forms and natures must originate from something without determinate and fixed form; and for another, any concrete thing has temporal and spatial limits but the origin of the universe must itself be unlimited.

These two points show that there must be a limitless being without specific form at the root of the universe. Zeng concludes: "This stuff of no form, no image, no definition, and no limits is called Dao. As Laozi says: 'The Dao that can be talked about is not the constant Dao; the name that can be named is not the constant name.' Therefore Dao has a metaphysical transcendence which is beyond experience and language" (CDC 2007, 45). This, though, is only one aspect of Dao: it is its nothingness. But Dao has also something, which makes it the mother of the myriad things. This can be demonstrated in

Laozi's notion of Dao as the mother of world, which appears in many chapters of *Daode jing*."

This reading enables Zeng to maintain that Dao is a force of life which does not contain everything as pre-existing, but rather generates everything through change and transformation. In the discussion of the metaphysical and ontological characteristics of Dao, Zeng points out the difference between Daoist metaphysics and Western metaphysics. Daoist metaphysics (*xinger shang* 形而上) is not separate from physics or the empirical world (*xinger xia* 形而下), but sees the two as intrinsically connected. Metaphysical Dao manifests in the changes and transformations of the physical world in a relationship of structure (*ti* 体) and function (*yong* 用) (CDC 2007, 46). She cites *Daode jing* 39 on the power of attaining the one and says that Dao is the One.[7] The myriad things not only come from Dao but also develop their character through Dao.

According to Zeng, Western metaphysics tends to separate metaphysical reality from the empirical world so that the issue of how to know ultimate reality through the empirical world became a difficult problem. Zeng thinks that Martin Heidegger holds an "impressively similar view about metaphysics as Laozi" (CDC 2007, 47). She also explicates Daoist epistemology on how best to know Dao. Dao is the origin of the universe as well as the object of knowing. But how can this nothingness be known? The Daoist method of knowing is through quiet observation (*jingguan* 静观) and mystical exploration (*xuanlan* 玄览). These two methods are discernible in *Daode jing* 16, 50, and 10. Quiet observation is a state of mind when there is complete quietude and emptiness; it allows inward movement toward the root. Mystical exploration imparts a rational and intuitive reflection within this peaceful and empty mind. Once the mind attains solitary stillness and is like a clear mirror, everything in the world will appear in its and true knowing can take place. This is the method of Daoist knowing that forms a unity between the subjective "I" and the ultimate Dao.

This conceptual understanding of Dao also justifies several applications of Daoism to present events. Contrary to some popular views of Daoism as a disengaged doctrine far away from the human and social world, kundao actively participate in several on-going debates. For example, Liu Zhongzhen promotes a Daoist theory for China's education reform (CDC 2007, 15). She criticizes the formal education based on rote memorization directed toward the results of testing (using the Chinese expression "stuffing a duck" [*tianya* 填鸭]) and discusses the necessity of educational reform. However, such reform cannot be toward an aimless system which focuses only on self-expression or individual creativity. According to her, education reform should lead to "education returning," namely a return to the formation of the person or character (*renge* 人

---

[7] "Heaven attains the One to be clear; Earth attains the One to be peaceful; spirits attain the One to be magical; valleys attain the One to be full; the myriad things attain the One to live; kings and lords attain the One to control the world."

格). Daoist theory, and specifically the *Daode jing*, she notes, is full of astute observations regarding education. The ultimate purpose of education is to refine one's character and progress toward sagehood, not to get a good job or make money. Liu appeals to six passages in the *Daode jing* to exemplify the Daoist motivation, goals, and methods for education.

Another presenter, Xiao Zhitian, fashions a rational connection between a Daoist outlook and ecological insight. She cites *Daode jing* 25 to make the case that the myriad living things – including human beings – are generated through a natural movement of Dao. Human beings and everything in nature all come from the same origin, so they receive equal value. It is only within this broader dynamic equilibrium that living things can maintain their existence. Therefore human activities must align with the cyclical movement of nature. "Respecting the value of nature, sustaining the equilibrium between human beings and nature are important Daoist ecological thoughts. Human beings are unable to completely conquer or change nature; they can only adjust themselves to nature and share its blessings with the myriad beings. Following the nature of things without selfishness is the wisest choice for human beings" (CDC 2007, 29).

Xiao employs the story of Chaos (Emperor Hundun 混沌) in the *Zhuangzi* to emphasize how human beings can cause harm and disruption by imposing their own views and desires on nature. "Chaos" had none of the seven openings for the senses. His friends felt sorry for this and so bore openings into him. As a result, he died (ch. 6). Xiao deduces that the highest wisdom for human beings living in this universe is as follows: "The myriad things live together, their habitats are all interconnected; human beings reside with birds and beasts and are bound together with all beings" (CDC 2007, 29).

According to Xiao, there are two interrelated aspects in utilizing the above wisdom. First, human beings need to recognize the constancy (*chang* 常) of everything in the universe and in particular of the natural circle of life and death, growth and decay, going and returning. These patterns and regularities must be observed and followed by any rational mind. Second, the human mind needs to be content (*zhizu* 知足). *Zhizu* is knowing the limits (*du* 度) of desire and action. Natural resources are limited yet human desires are unlimited. Using limited resources to satisfy unlimited desires will necessarily cause conflict. "There is no greater disaster in the world than not knowing self-contentment; there is no greater sin than unlimited greed… Everything has its limit. Only knowing what contentment is can one find ultimate contentment" (CDC 2007, 31). Clearly these two elements are interdependent: one can only truly discern the patterns of nature if one has a quiet and peaceful mind; understanding of the patterns of nature in turn facilitates the restriction of unlimited desires. Xiao also attempts to solve the tension between environmental preservation and economic development by suggesting that economic advancement should grow from a sustainable natural balance not from plundering or looting nature.

Daoist Harmony

Harmony (*he* 和) has become a popular phrase in China through the promotion of the political slogan: "Constructing a harmonious society." There are twelve essays on this topic, the largest section in the collection. The discussions begin with the role and position of harmony in Laozi's thought. The basic claims are as follows:

—Harmony is the fundamental characteristic or property of Dao. The movement of Dao is a harmonious and cyclical movement. It is also a harmonious pattern of orderly transformation of yin-yang.

—Harmony is the constant virtue (*de*) of Dao. This is the reason why Dao is able to generate the myriad things. Harmony is what makes nature beautiful, the body healthy, society peaceful, and a state strong.

—Harmony is a manifestation of Dao. Dao must be known through harmonious relationships.

—Harmony is the core of Daoist faith and the guide for Daoist action. Daoist culture is a harmonious culture which is built on diversity and tolerance.

There are three types of harmony articulated in all these essays: harmony within one's self; harmony among people and society; and harmony between human beings and nature. Harmony within oneself communicates a balanced relationship between mind and body. The human body consists of spirit (*shen* 神) and energy (*qi* 气). "An unsettled mind will lead to the spirit being distracted; a weak heart will exhaust the *qi*. This is the cause of an unhealthy body. Physical sickness and disease result from the loss of bodily harmony. The yin and yang phases of *qi* are out of balance and the meridians are obstructed. To attain bodily health, one must have a harmonious mind which is at peace and free from strong emotions" (CDC 2007, 144).

This harmonious state also demands a proper attitude to and good relationship with material things. In the pursuit of material profits, one must stand on the ground of moderation and preserve a balanced psychological mindset. Material objects are not the only goal of human life. As things in modern society become more plentiful, many people feel their lives are more empty. This reveals the importance of the internal, of discovering and cultivating the self. So the true harmony between mind and body can only be fully realized in discovering the real self, a transcendent process of conquering the worldly self.

Harmony among people means the equality of all things and the existence of such harmony reflects the characters of the people involved. Human beings are equal because they all embody the same nature of Dao. This common possession of Dao nature grants a reason for no discrimination, no competition and no fighting. This Daoist stance upholds or preserves the center (*shouzhong* 守中) so that one is kind enough to respect others and open enough to accept others. This practice cultivates a water-like disposition and accomplishes a social harmony among people, a world harmony among states, and a religious harmony among faiths.

Harmony among human beings and nature celebrates two central Daoist beliefs: knowing and following the laws of nature (*shuncong ziran* 顺从自然) and respecting and treasuring all forms of life (*guisheng* 贵生). Nature is the home of all beings. Human beings should not only perceive nature from the point of "I" or "we" but rather also from the outlook of Dao itself. The Dao perspective witnesses the oneness of the myriad things, the interdependence all existence and the intrinsic value of all life. These convictions challenge anthropocentrism and oppose the position of treating nature as an object to be conquered and controlled. These beliefs and values are also observable in the practice of not taking life and in eating a vegetarian diet.[8]

Many theses point out that these three kinds of harmony can be carried out through three Daoist treasures. *Daode jing* 67 describes them: "I have three treasures which I maintain and protect: kindness or nurturing (*ci* 慈), frugality (*jian* 俭), and not daring to be first." Kindness is the foundation of these three treasures and the nature of Dao. In human beings it is the core of the other virtues. It is kindness toward other human beings and extending to all things. In nature it is the force of nurturing which facilitates the growth and flourishing of all things through four seasons. This ability for kindness can produce a harmonious relationship among all things.

Frugality as the second treasure of Laozi concentrates on nourishing life and pursuing longevity through a Daoist attitude toward life. Human life consists of essence (*jing* 精), *qi*, and spirit. The process of extending life is conceptualized through frugality as it applies to conserving these three basic elements of life: care for *qi*, honor spirit, and value essence. The principle of frugality also suggests a restriction and curbing of human desires to attain a stage of no desire, no competition and no forced action.

"Not daring to be the first" as the third treasure of Laozi puts forward "not contending" (*buzheng* 不争), which is an important principle for any true Daoist's actions. Softness and "not contending" are much cherished virtues in the *Daode jing*. Conflicts or struggles in the world usually result from desiring fame, profit, and power. The issue is whether these things are worth fighting for, given the shortness of life and the vastness of nature. Why not put one's energy into extending life itself rather than struggling for things that might endanger life? Human actions should be like water which is adaptive rather than competitive. These three treasures are all good lubricants for attaining all levels of harmony.

Nonaction and Management

For many centuries Daoist temples have been supported by local communities. Priests would perform rituals for locals; visitors would bring rice or other

---

[8] Kundao respect all things from nature. Why do Daoists have a long hair? Because they belief that human hair comes from nature and should be preserved.

goods; officials would give grants and support. In today China, with its increasingly free market economics and profit-driven tourism, mountain temples face many difficulties. They have to compete with local travel bureaus, which often charge large fees for entering the mountains, making worshippers less inclined to donate money to the temples. How to manage and sustain a temple is thus a serious challenge for Daoists. In order to survive in this reality, kundao leaders must learn the skills of contemporary management and apply them in a Daoist context. The collection of theses contains eleven essays trying to construct a Daoist theory and practice of management, to forge a link between religious faith and practical reality.

Liu Chengying starts with a question: what is a temple (*gongguan* 宫观)? According to her, the temple is a special religious community, a mystical and spiritual field, a divine place for Daoist cultivation (CDC 2007, 209). The temple is the soul of Daoism. Its flourishing and decline, the spread of its teachings, and the continuity of its traditions and rituals all depend on the temple. Thousands of years of Daoist history have revealed that the well-being of the religion and that of the temple are closely intertwined: the prosperity of Daoism rises and falls with temple conditions. "Now the temples are in the hands of our generation. Whether they soar or decline will depend on our will and commitment. Temples need our care as much as our families, our respect and honor as much as our mothers, protection and direction as much as our children . . . In our journey of becoming the Daoist master, the temple will grow along with us" (CDC 2007 209).

Liu also ponders the direction in which temples should move as they face current Chinese economic and cultural conditions. She evokes a Daoist principle of "adapting to changing times" and voices three possible paths (CDC 2007, 210). The first leads toward commercialization. She believes that economic development will be the primary force in the development of religious Daoism in the 21st century and that temples should maximize their resources and stimulate financial growth through multiple layers of business and commercial activities. For example, most of the temples in China today are also hotels that provide local cuisine and comfortable accommodations for tourists at reasonable prices. Many Daoists work in these businesses as cooks, waitresses, and entertainers. Popular fortune tellers charge large fees to clients for discussion of their present and future. Liu calls for the development of commercialized temples, but warns that this development should not be motivated by profit seeking alone. Rather, it must be based on faith and the will to spread Daoism with a focus on benefiting all life.

The second direction she points out leads toward corporative management. The commercialization of temples will inevitably bring about a corporate-like structure. Rather than the traditional relationship of one master and many disciples, the temple is best administered by a board of directors, leading to the formation of inner circles. Liu lists the advantages and disadvantages of this new structure. It is beneficial because it brings about stability that cements continuity of leadership. It can also encourage capable Daoists to stay rather than move on to other places. However, the structure might also instigate divisions and corruption, creating problems for anyone who has a different point of view.

The third path leads toward strengthening the Daoist faith. The fundamental reason for the decline of the religion and the poor condition of temples has been the secularization and weakening of the faith. Daoism today is not as sincere or pure as it was in the past. From a theological perspective, it has become a rational choice of faith, thus leading to an increase in secular perspectives. From the point of view of religious practice, many Daoists want a more modern and comfortable lifestyle which may lead to a weakening of faith. Liu contends that although a religious life can be open and subject to change, the religious spirit underlying the commitment should remain the same.

Liu moves from the importance of temples and the directions in which they might develop to the establishment of a management system. She articulates five Daoist structures or regulations for ensuring an internally well-ordered and socially well-functioning temple:

—Basic commands (*jiaoyi* 教义). Daoist commands, such as encouraging quietude and nonaction, guarding the One, respecting the Dao and honoring virtue form the foundation of the religion. They provide basic principles for thought and action. Every follower must adhere to them.

—Organizational rules (*jiaogui* 教规). Every temple must have its own system of rules and regulations to support and reinforce Daoist faith. These are a part of Daoist moral cultivation.

—Rituals and ceremony. This system consists of various forms of prayer, worship, and festival celebrations formed through tradition, history, and culture. All these activities have profound and lasting symbolic meaning; they serve to purify the mystical and divine aspects of spirit.

—Personal self-restraint. This obliges everyone living in the temple to impose certain disciplines upon themselves. This aspect has been weakened in modern times, where the only rules to obey are laws of state. The temple is bound to uphold a sense of religious obedience.

—Overall maintenance. This covers a broader area, such as accounting, supplies, buildings, safety, health, and diet. They must all be supervised by qualified staff.

Like Liu's, so other essays in this section apply Laozi's concept of nonaction to different aspects of modern organizations. The heart of the theory is the personal quality and character of the managers. Managers must embody Daoist teachings in order to develop certain dispositions, such as courage, charisma, and decisiveness. The highest virtue for managers is to be like water and exhibit the "seven qualities of goodness" (*qishan* 七善):⁹ broad vision, profound mind, generous giving, trustworthy speech, ability to order, acute insight, and timeliness.

This water-like management style operates on three levels. First, a manager has to distinguish between important issues and trivial things. Matters that have a long-term effect and bear on the whole of the community should be acted on with intentional action (*youwei*); things pertaining to daily routine should be let go (*wuwei*). This approach of balancing action and nonaction ideally enables a manager to maximize her energy and resources in order to secure successful leadership. Second, a manager has to know how to select the right people and designate proper responsibilities. This echoes Laozi's view of good skill in governing: "The ruler remains in nonaction while the minister acts with intention." The more leaders appoint talented workers and motivate them to perform tasks with excellence, the more effective their administration will be. Thus an appropriate relationship between centralized power and divided powers is established. Third, a manager has to coordinate and synchronize a diverse range of human relationships: among Daoists within the temple, between them and the worshipers of the community, and between the temple and the government. The key to maintaining harmony in these relationships is the ability to communicate on conceptual, emotional, and psychological levels. Managers must acquire the power of making people cohere around her.

Daoist Cultivation

Daoist cultivation in the essays tends to involve two major aspects: ethical refinement and nourishing of body and mind. Often authors work by elucidating the *Daode jing* and aim at fostering inherent Dao-nature (*daoxing* 道性).

Daoist cultivation as normative and ethical refinement is based on reasoning in the *Daode jing*. For example, the concept of softness and weakness (*rouruo* 柔弱) is lauded as a high Daoist ethical ideal as it represents the beginning and continuity of life (CDC 2007, 311). Not only can it be observed in all life forms in nature but can also be applied to human life and may well be the best means for success and self-protection.

According to the kundao Yang Xintai, softness and weakness represent a fundamental moral principle and serve as an essential precept for believers. She suggests five ways to live out this ethical code:

---

⁹ CDC2007, 223. The concept goes back to *Daode jing* 8: "In residing, the earth is good. In the heart, depth is good. In giving, benevolence is good. In speaking, sincerity is good. In governing, ordering is good. In affairs, ability is good. In movement, timing is good."

—Like water, being soft and weak allows the person to always give without expecting a reward. It places personal interests low and gives highest position to selflessness.

—An attitude of weakness and softness creates a high level of endurance and perseverance. When things are beyond one's control, there is only one way: be patient and allow life to test one's will, character, and endurance.

—Being weak and soft lets one embrace acceptance and tolerance. With an open mind and kind heart, one can face divergences and resolve conflicts.

—In a position of weakness and softness, one can compete without fighting and gently reach success. In a situation of competition, one should ask oneself questions like: Who is the competitor? Whom do I want to conquer? The center of attention should not be on winning or losing but on one's own mind and emotional state. Ultimately one realizes that the real competitor is oneself and one needs to conquer destructive thoughts and feelings.

—Being weak and soft, one comes to define success not as wealth, power, and status but as achievement in Dao. For Daoists, the final triumph is the perfect control of thoughts and a way of acting in proper timeliness.

Daoist cultivation also includes nurturing the body and mind. In this sense, the teaching can be a form of psychotherapy. Seven theses address how one should perceive, comprehend, and feel about the inner self, outside events, and overall surroundings. Most commonly authors emphasize the Daoist value of respecting life. However Daoists analyze attitudes, perception, and perspectives, they always come back to the primacy of life over fame, wealth, and power. Such a fundamental attitude helps to free the person from mental and physical stress, anxiety and suffering; it aids in the attainment of psychological health and well-being.

Li Xinqing similarly writes that "among the world's religions, Daoism most emphasizes human beings' bodily existence and welfare. According to Daoism, human life is most precious. The highest goal for human life is to nourish, cherish, and prolong life. ... Seeking longevity is a focal point of the Daoist faith. Bodily care and preservation are the purpose of daily practice" (CDC 2007, 350). She articulates three key points about nourishing life (*yangsheng* 养生):

—The practice is first and foremost about cherishing life. Everyone has only one life, so one must know how to guard this life by restraining desires for external things. Preserving life sometimes requires giving up: giving up fame, profit and power in order to safeguard the life itself.

—Nourishing life is about the psychological well-being of mind and emotions. Maintaining a peaceful mind and harmonizing all emotions are basic elements of longevity. This ideal state of consciousness is one of quietude, desirelessness, and peace. Not just a Daoist ideal, this reflects the art of tranquility.

—The practice includes a variety of cultivation techniques, such as, internal and external alchemy, controlled diet, breathing exercises, and the Dao of immortals. Unfortunately this aspect of the tradition is either absent or only mentioned vaguely in the various essays. According to Master Huang, the particularly techniques practiced are a "personal matter and kundao practice according to their own preference under the guidance of various masters in their home temples."[10]

Observations and Reflections

To be a virtuous wife and good mother (*xianqi liangmu* 贤妻良母) has been the age-old ideal of Chinese women, described especially in the Confucian tradition. The prominent Han scholar Liu Xiang 劉向 (79-8 B.C.E.) compiled 125 biographies of virtuous women to evoke and commemorate this ideal. From stories such as these a celebrated and enduring tradition gradually evolved, known as *lienü* 烈女. It extols three distinctive and culturally significant qualities in women: virtue (*de* 德), talent (*cai* 才), and beauty (*se* 色). In addition, ancient China praised three role models that every woman should emulate: Mencius's mother who sacrificed herself to provide a good environment for her son; Yuefei's wife who fought the barbarians on behalf of the Song dynasty; and Hua Mulan who masqueraded as a filial son and fought as her father's proxy for twelve years. These women played important social roles as models of the standard ideal.

Above and beyond this mainstream system, there was also an alternative way of life for women, with its own tradition and history: that of the female Daoist renunciants (see Despeux and Kohn 2003). Following this model, kundao today make a "leap of faith" through commitment and passion. They show great courage and willpower in defying traditional roles and pursuing faith, freedom, and self-realization. Entering the temple and breaking off from pre-ordained female functions creates a spiritual and physical space for women to construct their own life and identity. In the past, Daoist women could spend their lives peacefully in mountain temples: Mts. Qingcheng, Wudang, Nanyue, and Hua all have centuries-old traditions of female Daoists.[11] Today kundao have the unique opportunity to be formally educated. This opportunity is particularly precious for them, given the fact that most come from impoverished conditions with little chance for advanced education.[12]

The kundao training at the new school on Nanyue closely matches traditional Chinese education and is significantly different from contemporary systems. For one, it is broadly oriented toward cultivating the whole person; it

---

[10] Personal interview, July 2006, June 2007.

[11] I have visited five mountains where kundao establishments are prominent today. On Mt. Qingchen, I met one 103 years old; many others ar ein the 70s and 80s.

[12] Out of forty-eight students, only one had a college education. Many of them have not even finished high school.

does not aim merely at conveying knowledge but also involves mental, spiritual, and physical discipline. In this respect it stands in stark contrast to the narrow focus of contemporary Chinese education which sees success only in achieving good test results and is more like a Western liberal arts education. However, it is broader even than this since it extends even to ritual and physical practices. For another, the kundao training is reminiscent of traditional education in the classical six arts. While current Chinese education is almost entirely modeled on Western systems, kundao training is still primarily Chinese. Students are taught many subjects and become proficient in history, theory, music, architecture, art, and business. At the same time, the training is modern, including things like computer skills and business management. Given the concerns about the narrowness of the current Chinese educational system and the loss of Chinese culture, the kundao training may supply a valuable model for educational reform.

Daoist teachings have been criticized or perceived as lacking ethical guidance or relevance to concrete social and cultural circumstances, focusing more on internal peace of mind. This limits the possibility of Daoism as a practical and beneficial social doctrine, particularly in contrast to Confucianism. These kundao essays, however, show clearly how many ethical and normative principles are contained in Daoism that can have great implications not just for individuals but also on a social and cultural level. For example, passages in the *Daode jing* like the discussion of the three treasures and seven qualities of goodness are presented as central points of the teaching—aspects commonly ignored or marginalized in non-religious discussions.

The essays also treat the *Daode jing* as an ethical treatise and apply it to many contemporary moral issues. Their interpretations make Daoism a constructive and living force in the contemporary world. Current trends of returning to traditional culture usually work on the revival of Confucianism. These essays, on the other hand, offer Daoist doctrine as an indispensable conceptual resource for China today. Refraining from criticism of the political and economic system, they strive to reconcile Daoism with present-day reality. They mobilize a Daoist outlook to combat consumerism and engage in attitudes and activities that lead to a good and happy life, showing how one can maintain mental and physical well-being in a profit-driven world. Yet they do not condemn such a world either, but seek ways to benefit from it. Similarly, on the political level, they frequently repeat common government rhetoric, discussing "socialist Daoism" and the construction of a "harmonious society." It is hard to know whether this represents their true views or is just political strategy. In any case, it is clear that the kundao as future masters of temples receive a political education which helps them to avoid conflicts with local officials.

It is also striking that none of the essays deals with gender concerns. Maybe gender is just not an issue in Daoist teachings, and the women find it perfectly natural that they get the same education as monks and are equally trained as future leaders. There appears to be nothing gender specific built into the curriculum. Because their personal self-cultivation practices are private and beyond standardization, it is hard to know how much they are geared specifically to women. Perhaps gender identity and awareness are absent in Daoist temples because these kundao are leaders of institutions and supervisors of male Daoists. This, of course, is quite different from the overall situation of women in China, especially those of lower economic status, which is still quite tough. The kundao on Nanyue have largely escaped lives of heavy labor and continuous care for extended families. Instead, they enjoy their time reading, playing music, and striving for self-realization. Having broken free from the constraints of gender, they reflect little on their personal journeys of female fulfillment and on the broader restraints still faced by women in China.

Lu Xichen who has spent more personal time with this class reports that only three to five kundao are practicing internal alchemy with their home-temple masters. While at school, they do not practice much at all, since without proper guidance the practice could be dangerous or even harmful. In addition, all internal cultivation is personal and kept secret, beyond what one commonly shares with other people. While, therefore, it is not clear what kind and what level of internal alchemy kundao leaders are practicing today, their vision of what Daoism is and what their role should be in a modern society provides a powerful insight into the modern framework of internal practice.

Bibliography

CDC, ed. 2007. *Huangting ji*. Hunan: Nanyue, Chinese Daoist College.

Despeux, Catherine. 2000. "Women in Daoism." In *Daoism Handbook*, edited by Livia Kohn, 384-412. Leiden: E. Brill.

_____, and Livia Kohn. 2003. *Women in Daoism*. Cambridge, Mass.: Three Pines Press.

Schafer, Edward H. 1977. "The Restoration of the Shrine of Wei Hua-ts'un at Lin-ch'uan in the Eighth Century." *Journal of Oriental Studies* 15:124-38.

Skar, Lowell, and Fabrizio Pregadio. 2000. "Inner Alchemy (*Neidan*)." In *Daoism Handbook*, edited by Livia Kohn, 464-97. Leiden: E. Brill.

Daoist Internal Alchemy in the West

Michael Winn

> The Dao is very great, for it offers human beings 3,600 pathways. Each pathway has 10,000 methods to help us become who we truly are.
> —Daoist saying

In 1980, I was introduced to Mantak Chia in his tiny office in New York's Chinatown. A friend had alerted me his energy was "off the charts," and looking for a writer. A 36-year old Thai Chinese Daoist, Chia made his living doing energetic healing. Dr. Young, a Chinese MD with an office next door, sent Chia patients with difficult diseases Western medicine could not cure. Many recovered their health (Young 1984).

I had never met a Daoist. "What do you teach?" I asked Mantak Chia. "Immortality," he replied without hesitation. I looked at him skeptically. I was into Kundalini yoga, at the time still an underground culture. My yoga friends and the popular Indian gurus of the day only talked about enlightenment. "In China we have records of many hundreds of immortals. In the West, they only talk about one: Jesus," Chia added, as if his cultural boast allayed my skepticism.

I took the bait, and signed up for the first class ever offered to Western students, on the Microcosmic Orbit. Chia warned me it was only "kindergarten" in the One Cloud system of Daoist internal alchemy. I later realized the Orbit was the piece missing from Indian Kundalini yoga practice, which directs all *qi* to flow up cakras located in the fire channel of the spine, then out the crown. The Daoist approach re-circulates Heaven-*qi* back down the crown into the water channel in the chest, connects to Earth-*qi* at the perineum, then spirals it back up the spine. The Orbit turns the human body into a refinery of whirling *qi* mixing fire and water *qi*. Within two years I was practicing One Cloud's second formula, Lesser Water and Fire, in which the *qi* moves into a third neutral channel, the Penetrating Vessel in the center of the body. The fire and water *qi* are sexually coupled and an alchemical elixir forms. It created a wonderfully warm glowing feeling in my body, unlike any of the many other spiritual practices I had experimented with.

Thus began a lifelong journey in which I became an adept, teacher, scholar, and witness to the unfolding of *neidan* culture in the West. In addition to documenting One Cloud's Seven Alchemy Formulas for Immortality spread widely in the West by Chia's Healing Tao organization, and other streams of Daoist alchemy in the English-speaking West, I will address two other issues. One: how is Daoist internal alchemy tied to Chinese culture and language? Has the appropriation of *neidan* resulted in different insights or experiences by Western adepts, who may cultivate energy bodies differently from Chinese adepts? Two: are immortals real, or merely a Chinese cultural projection of a deep human desire to survive death? If immortals are real, are Western adepts in contact with them?

Western Growth

In 2008, twenty-eight years after my meeting Mantak Chia, yoga and Indian notions of enlightenment had surfaced into mainstream American culture, with 12 million yoga practitioners and glossy magazines. Numerous Hindu and Buddhist centers of meditation had flourished, died, and been replaced by new ones. Daoist internal alchemy had emerged from its "doesn't exist" status, but was barely visible on the cultural horizon. Its biggest presence was the thousand Healing Tao instructors Mantak Chia had certified globally in at least the first formula of One Cloud's *neidan* system. In 1980, Chia planned to write a single book. I ended up editing or co-writing his first seven books. By 2008 he had published thirty-three books and dozens of videos.

Daoist alchemy has ridden the coattails of surging interest in what might be viewed as external alchemy (*waidan gong*): Chinese medicine, martial arts, taiji quan and qigong as health arts. *Qi Journal* and *The Empty Vessel*, the only magazines to carry articles on *neidan*, had by 2008 a combined circulation of about 35,000. The internet had created numerous on-line Daoist communities; my website forum (HealingDao.com) had over 5 million hits in the last three years. A Hong Kong website with an English encyclopedia on Daoism got a million hits in 2007 (eng.taoism.org.hk).

Oriental healing schools have proliferated. Many are aware Daoist *neidan gong*, or "skill with the internal elixir," is considered the pinnacle of self-realization and healing in China. Why don't they teach *neidan*? The training is not well understood, and its complexity and long progressive work make it difficult to commercialize in the alternative healing market. There is an acupuncture textbook *Nourishing Destiny: The Inner Tradition of Chinese Medicine*, inspired by Zhang Boduan's *Four Hundred Words on the Gold Elixir* (Jarrett 1999). It highlights *neidan*, also translated as "internal medicine," as the highest distillation of Chinese medical principles.

Jeffrey Yuen, a Daoist priest, opened an accredited school in New York that offers "Classical Chinese Medicine" training based on alchemical principles and garnered attention amongst acupuncturists seeking to re-spiritualize "Traditional Chinese Medicine" (TCM) after the Communists sanitized it in the

1950s. These publications, internet sites, and schools suggest the Western appropriation of Daoist internal alchemy, while slow compared to yoga and other Eastern meditation, is steadily growing.

Chinese alchemical literature is fascinating but maddeningly obscure. It wears two masks simultaneously, one promising mystical illumination and immortality, the other promising a spiritual science that systematically bridges the dark gulf between a fragile human mind in a mortal body and the vast eternal life of the cosmos. "Spiritual science" implies a practicality especially attractive to Westerners. Scientific materialism has become a *de facto* standard of truth often pitted against religious faith. *Neidan* offers a bridge between the two.

The Process

Daoist alchemy seeks to reconcile the creative tension between impersonal nature and the personal human. It simultaneously embraces the mystical oneness or primal chaos of Dao, expressed by an all-penetrating primordial *qi*-field, and many individual bodies, each with a unique destiny, arising within that field. External alchemy can help heal individual human bodies, but cannot deliver the experience of oneness or chaos. Death and disease could be seen in this context as unconscious ways to return to oneness. *Neidan* seeks to achieve this return consciously, by embracing the life force at its deepest level of ever-changing process. Western science and medicine could be considered a form of external alchemy: ingenious at transforming matter and producing a surplus of magical technological goods, yet unable to fill human hearts.

Neidan serves to speed the completion of both personal worldly destiny (*ming*) and the realization of one's spiritual essence or inner nature (*xing*) arising from the impersonal origin. What distinguishes Daoist *neidan* from other forms of meditation is that it traditionally involves the creation of a *dan*. This is variously described as an elixir, pearl, or egg in which the adept's worldly and spiritual destiny are integrated. This elixir or pearl is a vessel for the highest authentic essence of a human, a lifetime of wisdom condensed into a single spiritual drop. It's vibrational purity and integration of spirit and matter is what survives death and allows for spiritual immortality. The elixir is progressively cooked or refined internally with different methods and goes through different stages.

In One Cloud's Seven Alchemy formulas, the first popular *neidan* system in the West, primal Water and Fire are caused to merge with each other in an explicitly sexual internal coupling. This union of yin and yang is an alchemical marriage of inner male and inner female. The adept gets "spiritually pregnant" and forms an immortal embryo in the belly center or elixir field (*dantian*). This births an immortal child in the adept's core channel, which progressively moves upward. It matures over many years into a sage or immortal at the solar plexus, the heart, third eye, and crown.

The inner sage may achieve different levels of immortality – human, earthly, heavenly, full celestial, or complete merging with Dao. Different yin-yang forces are coupled at each level; male-female sexual coupling evolves to a purer level, i.e., becomes sun-moon coupling, and continues into humanity collectively coupling its soul forces with planetary and star beings. These levels may be understood as metaphors for the evolution of human consciousness beyond its mortal limitations. After physical death, spiritual immortals merge into the vast ocean of cosmic consciousness but continue to evolve and create within the greater process of Dao. Physical immortality is not the goal; that would be too fixed and thus not aligned with an ever-changing Dao. Soul immortality would be a mid-level achievement that results in conscious re-incarnation on earth, such as is used by Tibetans to preserve their spiritual culture.

Daoist rebirth is a long, gradual process, in which the adept moves inward by stages, refining the polarized and corrupted *qi* of postnatal after-Heaven (physical plane) into the balanced and purified *qi* of the prenatal stage Before Heaven, a middle plane that holds all possible forms waiting to birth. The adept finally penetrates to the pure field of the original energetic trinity of primordial origin. This is the full return to original being, a merger with the cosmic egg or gourd before it cracked open. In some cosmologies, beyond this primal egg lies the Daoist notion of supreme mystery or Unknowable Ultimate (*wuji*), the source from which the primal trinity of the *qi*-field arises.

Language Questions

One of the most bewildering aspects facing Western seekers is that in China there are thousands of qigong forms, meditation and alchemical systems. It is a labyrinth grown over the millennia into many paths—medical, martial, spiritual, and further subdivided into Daoist, Buddhist, and Confucian. It takes years of training to see the myriad methods as expression of a single common deep energetic language. Adepts may guide *qi* using external body or breath movement, shape it by intention or imagination or using an internal alchemical operation. Even when the mind surrenders or empties itself to allow the spontaneous movement of the *qi*-field—it is still a process that uses the language of *qi*.

One can produce many different word combinations in English or Chinese, all comprehensible because of a common grammar and vocabulary. Likewise, one can create many qigong forms and *neidan* methods, each pattern having a unique effect on the body-mind's *qi* field. Even the feeling of dissolving into what appears to be ultimate emptiness is just another way to describe the human experience of original breath (*yuanqi*) where all the contents of manifest experience are dissolved or transformed into their original nature.

This view defines qigong (lit. "skill with subtle breath") as learning to speak a natural energetic language rather than a bodily exercise. Qigong can be likened to a more tangible language that arises to the surface of physicality from *neidan's* deeper grammar of *qi*-patterns. Practicing qigong (which includes taiji, bagua, and xingyi internal arts) or ritual (using invocations and Daoist movement ceremony) is like learning the strokes of the *qi* alphabet. One moves one's body-mind in particular patterns. The *qi*-field governing the meridians and energetic centers of the physical body is activated and "speaks back" to one initially as different feelings of energy. Qigong and internal alchemy are not physical or energetic exercises that one "does" in the ordinary sense of action. Rather they are methods of shaping how one communicates with the greater field. The shape of the inner *qi* patterns being communicated elicits a response from one's outer reality, and together they shape the process of the unfolding of the whole field.

Written Chinese pictographs are visually richer in association than Western alphabets and thus facilitate grasping the multiple meanings of obscure Daoist terms that describe the subtle movement of *qi*. However, these pictographs are still intermediary written images, interpreted by the mind's visual functions, and do not by themselves open communication with the deep language patterns underlying them. If speaking or reading Chinese automatically accessed these deep patterns of *qi*, it would suggest that everyone in China is enlightened, which is doubtful.

Internal alchemy also uses intermediary symbols, but they are neither spoken nor written. This language consists of *qi*-channels and fields in the human body perceived as resonating spheres of sensation, feeling, and spiritual qualities. Alchemy requires close observation of these natural body processes, and sometimes employs images of the seasons, color, sound, or direction as its language symbols. This is known as resonant response (*ganying*). The vibration of the color red, by example, may be used to activate the fire element, the physical heart, its passions, the direction South, the planet Mars, etc.

The assumption of Daoists is that nature can talk back to you. When alchemical symbols and feelings are evoked, they shape silent language patterns of response within an omnipresent *qi*-field. The written symbols of the *Yijing* (Book of Changes), a foundational classic for all Daoists, uses broken yin or solid yang lines. These are used by many *neidan* adepts as a concise shorthand for describing or invoking alchemical processes. Spoken sounds are sometimes used to invoke directional energies. The adept may internally hear a response from natural entities associated with that direction.

In Daoist alchemy, the silent language of *qi* is an embodied experience that directly touches three levels of a human being. Alchemy transforms the adept's intelligence/spirit (*shen*), subtle breath (*qi*), and body or sexual essence (*jing*) into a created reality. These Three Treasures of the alchemist form a continuum, vibrating at different speeds. By analogy, the field (*shen*) becomes a wave (*qi*) which becomes a particle (*jing*), or vice versa. Beyond these three is nonbeing (*wu*), the unknown field of all possible expression. All process happens within the energy body of the alchemist. This internal or microcosmic conversation within the adept is communicated by vibrational resonance to the external macrocosmic field of Nature. Underlying both is an invisible proto-cosmic field. Nature mirrors back the adepts' *jing-qi-shen-wu* patterns, which allows the alchemist to experience herself as harmonics of higher dimensions.

Language, both spoken and energetic, may shape our biology. A fascinating study showed that Japanese speakers processed vowel sounds and intuitive feelings in their left brain, the opposite of Westerners. Westerners raised from an early age with Japanese language also shifted to left brain intuition. *The Alphabet versus the Goddess: The Conflict between Word and Image* posits that Daoist culture, with its right-brained emphasis on femininity, synthesis, holism, simultaneity, and concreteness is an expression of pictographic language (Shlain 1998). This raises the question whether adepts who speak and write Chinese resonate with nature more easily than Westerners because of brain hemispheric patterns. Daoism is the "watercourse way" and appears more feeling-intuitive than Western thinking-conceptual culture. Perhaps Chinese language creates biological pathways that predispose or hardwire one to feel deeper energetic patterns, thus facilitating ability to introspect and sense inner body space.

Daoist Culture

This issue of language raises the question of how far and in what ways internal alchemy is bound to its Chinese and Daoist roots. Rene Goris has schools in Wuhan and Amsterdam that integrate *neidan* with Chinese medicine. His viewpoint that *"neidan* is uniquely Chinese" is held especially strongly in his Heavenly Masters school, the earliest form of temple Daoism that dates back to 2nd century C.E.

> Cultures in the East and West have different root notions of enlightenment. Westerners who seek to learn *neidan* cannot escape the Christian notions of God and heroic individual suffering as the path to salvation. It's enmeshed in their religion, sports, and language. *Neidan* and immortality are deeply embedded as an ideal in the hive or group mind that influences traditional Chinese culture. The Daoist who cultivates immortality is effectively considered to be crazy for being so individualistic in his aspiration.
>
> The legendary Zhang Sanfeng refused to serve the emperor and lived alone in wild mountains for hundreds of years. This showed that his power was greater than that of the Son of Heaven. But his achievement of immortality is not viewed as merely his individual accomplishment. The attainment of supernatural powers or great longevity using *neidan* is instead a validation of Chinese culture and redeems its collective spiritual endeavor. Western practitioners are not embedded in China's group culture, and so cannot really participate in *neidan* as a group process. They are striving for themselves only. (Goris 2009)

Goris contends the many eleventh-century Song dynasty Daoist *neidan* schools—typified by One Cloud's Seven Alchemy formulas—were overly influenced by Buddhist and Confucian ideas of enlightenment that obscure the original simple Daoist notion of *wuwei* or spontaneous natural enlightenment.

The sole attempt to introduce a uniformed Heavenly Masters lineage in the West with formal ordination was the Orthodox Daoism in America movement spearheaded by Charles Belyea (Liu Ming) in California in the 1990s. He attacked other Western Daoists on the grounds that they were all fundamentally still Christian in outlook and thus not authentically Daoist. The group disbanded after nine years when questions were raised about the authenticity of Belyea's claimed lineage, but continues as a meditation circle (see Phillips 2008).

Other Westerners have recently taken ordination in Heavenly Masters temples in China and are promoting its deity-invoking magical practices (Johnson 2008, 40). Their focus on ritual magic may be a more successful strategy for attracting adherents than trying to adapt to Western culture the complex rites of renewal (*jiao*). But its a question whether the methods of the Heavenly Masters or other Daoist magical practices by themselves are part of *neidan*.

The Great Work of all alchemy, East and West, traditionally focuses on humanity's function of harmonizing spirit and matter. Daoist magic uses yin-yang and five-phases theory similar to *neidan*. But it emphasizes personal need and manifestation skills rather than service to cosmic process of Dao and risks manipulation by dark or unconscious selfish forces. An example of this, well known in the Healing Tao community, was a man who mixed Healing Tao alchemy with magical Cabala and Castaneda shamanism. He lost his job, his wife died of cancer, and his children denounced him. He later confessed the forces he tried to control with magic had possessed and nearly destroyed him.

Efforts to transplant the other major uniformed Daoist school, the Complete Perfection (Quanzhen) order, to the West are still in a seminal stage. This school mixed Daoist *neidan* with Buddhist notions of karmic retribution, hell, monasticism, asceticism, vegetarian diet, and celibacy when it was founded in the twelfth century. Their monks' black top shirt with white leggings and hair tied in a top knot is the uniform most widely recognized in China today as "Daoist." Its *neidan* integrates Daoist alchemical operations with Chan Buddhist methods of "facing the wall for nine years."

Chen Yunxiang, a Daoist priest in Ft. Collins, Colorado, offers *neidan* retreats. Like many Quanzhen monks who leave mainland China, he married, has three children, and runs a business. Marriage would not be tolerated in mainland monasteries but is tacitly accepted for priests abroad and may foreshadow changes in the way internal practices and other Daoist beliefs are taught in the West. In 2006, Chen brought the first large contingent of thirty Complete Perfection adepts from Mt. Wudang to Boulder. They performed Daoist rituals and martial arts displays. He hopes to build a Quanzhen temple in the Rocky Mountains (wudangtao.com). When I asked him how many of his Western students were likely to wear the dress uniform of Daoist monks, his reply was "none." Similarly Ren Farong, head of the Chinese Daoist Association headquartered in the White Cloud temple in Beijing, in 2007 made a discreet trip to California to investigate sites for building a Quanzhen temple as a bridge to the West. No land was purchased.

Both efforts signify the changing attitude of Complete Perfection Daoists towards foreigners. An increasing number of them are being initiated as priests. Alan Redman and two English friends were initiated in China and founded the British Taoist Society in the mid-1990s (Towler 2007). Michael Rinaldini from California underwent initiation in 2003 and was empowered to set up ordination in America. Like Redman, the main practices he was taught were chanting Daoist liturgy and a meditation of "sitting and forgetting the self" (Rinaldini 2008). Louis Komjathy, an American scholar of Daoism, was also initiated into the order, and has translated its corpus of sacred texts (2003). His Ph.D. thesis on Quanzhen (2007) details the extensive alchemical operational methods originally taught in the twelfth century, but it is unclear how many of those are actively being used by modern Complete Perfection Daoists. These esoteric secrets are being revealed anew with increasing rapidity. The initiate Wang Liping (profiled in Cleary's *Opening the Dragon's Gate*) in 2008 taught a group of Westerners the secrets of "Opening the Golden Flower" and "Female Alchemy," and opened his future trainings to interested foreigners. His reason for breaking this former cultural taboo? It was suggested to him by a reading in the *Yijing*.

Are Immortals Real?

Beyond language issues, the question of archetypal differences in psyche must also be asked: can Westerners connect to Chinese immortals? This topic is best approached by subjective testimony. As a teacher who has taught over 75 week-long *neidan* retreats, I can report numerous instances where meditators felt they had interactions with divine beings who assumed human form, many explicitly Chinese in appearance. One woman reported an internal experience of a Chinese man repeatedly pressing her to marry or merge with him, claiming he was an immortal. When she finally surrendered, she underwent a powerful spiritual awakening. Another man, long suffering from negative side effects of wrong internal practice, reported a Chinese-looking immortal visited him and began healing his condition. Perhaps the most dramatic encounter is my own, which explains my path:

> In March 1981, a few months after meeting Mantak Chia, I had just begun to practice *neidan*. I was a journalist, staying in the Addis Ababa Hilton in Ethiopia, finishing a story on Black Jews. My next job was to spend a night inside the Great Pyramid. Before I flew to Egypt, I suddenly became nauseous, with regular bouts of diarrhea. This went on for three days and nights, preventing me from eating any food. My body got so hot I often had to jump into a cold shower.

Strangely, I did not feel sick—only that my body was going through the motions of illness. I went to a hospital for blood tests, but nothing was wrong. By the third afternoon I lay on my bed exhausted but fully awake. My hotel room suddenly began to slowly spin. The furniture and walls began to soften and flow in a large vortex around me. An ancient looking Chinese man in a long robe appeared from nowhere, floating above me as if riding on a cloud. He had a long wispy white beard, and eyes that strangely seemed to be looking inward at himself. His skin was so wrinkled I remember thinking, this guy must be 2000 years old!

Speechless, I watched as a laser beam of a dense white light shot out of his navel and into mine. The light felt highly charged and totally solid upon contact. My body immediately exploded. Energy shot up my core and out my crown like the mushroom cloud above an atom bomb. I felt myself raining back down in tiny droplets that formed themselves into a body on the bed. The Chinese man disappeared into nowhere. I lay on the bed, feeling intense bliss, floating in a pool of divine love for hours. All symptoms of my illness disappeared. (Winn 2010)

Years later I investigated my amazing experience with the help of a full-trance channel for a Western immortal, who allegedly lived physically for 2,300 years in the time of Atlantis before ascending. He told me I had been purified by my guardian, a blind Daoist immortal named Jingmingzi as a kind of "medical checkup" before being allowed to spend a night inside the Great Pyramid. At the time of my experience, I had absolutely no belief in immortals. I had never read descriptions nor seen any image of one. It was impossible for me to project the experience out of previous mental impressions. The explanation of this Western immortal felt correct. I now have absolutely no doubt that immortals are real. Later, I would have many communications with beings I felt were immortals, but never again did they appear in human form.

The point of sharing this story is not to convince anyone that my personal experience is an objective or verifiable truth. It is to demonstrate that the field of archetypal forms in the collective Chinese psyche is fully available to Westerners. It affirms, in regard to *neidan*, that any cultural-linguistic boundary is easily transcended when one's energetic reality is shifted. The major schools of Daoism began after their founders were visited by immortal beings of light.

It took me another twenty years of practice to realize that I had been given in my visitation a transmission of the essential purpose of *neidan*. The beam of literally "solid" light emitted from the immortal's elixir field was made of original essence (*yuanjing*). This is primal matter or space itself, the aspect of consciousness that creates form and expresses will. It is part of the original trinity, but has a different function than primordial *qi* or *shen*. The immortal showed me that when humans merge with Dao, they are entrusted with the free will to shape original essence. In this case it was used to purify me and speed up my worldly and spiritual destiny. I was able to enter the Great Pyramid without harm, and was propelled on my *neidan* path.

Western Alchemists

The westward move of organized Daoism was preceded by other trends that saw Daoism as a spiritual philosophy. In America Alan Watts, an English ex-Episcopalian priest, first popularized the notion of Dao with books in the 1950s and 60s. He was Daoist philosopher intellectually, but a Zen practitioner. In love with the Chan Buddhist notion that emptiness has inherent existence and allows one to transcend the wheel of life, Watts disliked the internal meditative operations of Daoist alchemy. Watts blurred the distinction between Daoism and Buddhism in his books, which continues to confuse Westerners today.

Neidan is based on the early Daoist premise that emptiness is not an absolute nothingness in the Buddhist sense, but just an emptying phase within the Dao's process. Emptiness is relative in this view; it functions as the open space at the center of the wheel of life, from which the turning spokes or cycles of Dao manifest as *de* or spiritual powers (Moeller 2004, 151). In this sense Daoist alchemy follows the philosophical view of Laozi that gives equal weight to the *wu* (unnamed or formless) and *you* (named forms) as part of the yin-yang paradox of an ever changing Dao (Hansen, 1992, 225). This equal weighting of spirit and matter within an alchemical continuum of transmutation distinguishes *neidan* from purely transcendentalist approaches seeking an absolute.

The Secret of the Golden Flower (Wilhelm 1962; Cleary 1992), was a translation of an eighteenth-century *neidan* manual (Mori 2002) that first appeared in German in 1929. It was the first book on Daoist alchemical *qi*-circulation as a golden light elixir flowing inside the human body, in an energetic pathway later known as the Microcosmic Orbit. Carl Jung wrote an introduction, but misunderstood the terminology and unsuccessfully imposed Western psychological structures of anima-animus on Daoist yin-yang energy channels.

Jung spent the last fifteen years of his life trying to decode Western alchemical texts as metaphors for psychological processes. Other famous Western thinkers shared his interest in alchemy. Isaac Newton's scientific discoveries were the result of his fascination with alchemy as the mysterious subtle force behind physical gravity. Newton's writings on alchemy far outnumber his treatises that became the backbone of physics. Sir Robert Boyle, father of modern chemistry, was led to his discoveries as a lifelong alchemist. The scientific focus on the transmutation of elemental forces is what defines Western science as a laboratory branch of external alchemy, in the West known as spagyric arts.

Daoist internal alchemy thus did not arrive into a vacuum in the West. *The Forge and the Crucible* documents that myths of alchemy exist in all cultures of the planet and precede the development of religion (Eliade 1962). The most enduring Western influences originate in Egypt. Most famous is the *Emerald Tablet*, an alchemical treatise whose principles any Daoist *neidan* adept could readily accept (Hauck, 1999). The Egyptian schools of alchemy gave rise to

Freemason, Rosicrucian, Theosophical, Gurdjieff, and eventually New Age movements that popularized esotericism in the West. Rudolf Steiner's Anthroposophy spread many alchemical methods which esoterically were identified with Atlantis. These Western schools, with the exception of Gurdjieff's Sufi-like dances, generally lacked a body-centered method of meditation; their primary focus was on invoking spiritual forces external to the body. What was missing in the West was a powerful, body-centered, internal energetic science that went beyond intention, invocation, or prayer as ways to systematically focus invisible spiritual powers. Daoist qigong and internal alchemy are having a significant influence in filling that gap.

Taoist Yoga: Alchemy and Immortality (Lu 1970), a translation of Zhao Bi-zhen's late nineteenth century practice text (Despeux 1979), provided Westerners their first glimpse into the detailed sequence of Daoist internal alchemy operations. Lu Kuan-yü, a.k.a. Charles Luk, coined the term Microcosmic Orbit as a translation for the more literal "small heavenly circuit," a key meditation practice in many schools. Without a teacher or sufficient foundation training in Daoist meditation, his complex text was nearly impossible to implement. But publication of the text signaled to Mantak Chia, who arrived in New York in 1976, that there was Western interest in *neidan*. Chia told me he tried to practice from Lu's text but found it too different from the methods he learned. He had similar problems with Chinese alchemical texts coded to protect non-initiates from access to the mysteries. This is why it is a given in Chinese circles that you need a teacher and a live transmission to begin *neidan* practice.

Another important transmitter of Daoist *neidan* culture is Ni Hua-ching. Raised by Daoist parents in China, he became a traditional doctor and, after World War II, emigrated to Taiwan. In 1976, Westerners invited him to found his Shrine of the Eternal Breath of Tao in Los Angeles (Johnson 2009). But neither his *Internal Alchemy: The Natural Way to Immortality* (Ni 1992) nor his other forty books on Daoism gave concrete *neidan* techniques that were easily useable by Westerners. He belongs to the school of Seclusion that believes alchemical methods should be transmitted only to one or two select disciples (Winn 2008). Ni's philosophical books prepared the ground for acceptance of Mantak Chia's more practical "how to" *neidan* teachings.

The translation of texts such Cleary's *Understanding Reality* (1987), *The Book of Balance and Harmony* (1989), and *Opening the Dragon Gate* (1996), as well as Kohn's *The Taoist Experience* (1993), and Bertschinger's *The Secret of Everlasting Life* (1994) further fueled an appetite for Western teachers of internal alchemy. Robinet's *Taoist Meditation* (1993) and *Taoism: Growth of a Religion* (1997) offered fascinating details of Daoist vision practice and a definitive historical perspective on *neidan* relative to other Daoist religious practices. Robinet, one of Europe's great Daoist scholars, notes amongst the many Daoist traditions in the last two millennia, only the schools of internal alchemy offered immortality and the ecstatic experience of a light body for the living practitioner. The rest focus on healing, meeting personal or ancestral needs, invoking deities or worshipping Heaven and Earth.

These texts in English were immensely helpful to Western seekers hoping to penetrate the secrecy of Daoist esotericism. Students of One Cloud found them helpful in verifying the process and cosmology of the alchemical path they had embarked upon, since the spiritual culture of the West offered little support. Translations of *neidan* texts by Eva Wong such as *Cultivating Stillness* (1992) and *Tao of Health, Longevity, and Immortality* (1998) gave Westerners a good understanding of *neidan* principles. Her *Harmonizing Yin and Yang: The Dragon-Tiger Classic* (1997) offered deep operational insights into the alchemical coupling of prenatal and postnatal forces, but again was useful only for trained adepts who could make those distinctions. Eva Wong later began teaching *neidan* workshops as a lineage holder in the Primordial Limitless Gate school, which traces itself back to Chen Tuan, tenth-century hermit of Mt. Hua.

One Cloud's Alchemy

Mantak Chia was the first Chinese teacher with enough esoteric knowledge and drive to make the Western public aware of *neidan* as a personal pathway to physical longevity and spiritual immortality. He made internal alchemy practical and accessible, no longer a myth in a kung-fu novel or beguiling allusions in mystical poetry about Dao. For the first time, the "hard science" of Chinese operative alchemy was taught openly in Western style workshops and retreats. If you paid, you got the teachings. Chia was bitterly criticized by some Chinese for commercializing these secrets, yet most eventually followed his model.

Chia received his system, the Seven Alchemy formulas, from One Cloud, a Daoist hermit who pursued the secrets of internal alchemy for thirty years in various Quanzhen monasteries with limited success. His abbot finally told him to "go into the mountains to find a true teacher." On Mt. Changbai in northern China, he found a hermit who had left Quanzhen and found a true *neidan* teacher. He transmitted the seven formulas to One Cloud, who practiced and entered into the breatharian state of grain abstention (*bigu*) for several years, living purely on *qi*.

During the Japanese invasion, One Cloud left the mountain and hiked across China to settle in the hills behind Hong Kong's Daoist Yuen-Yuen Institute. There he built himself a small hut with a dark room for meditation and healed local people for a living. Mantak Chia attended high school nearby and was introduced to him by a classmate. One Cloud was a simply dressed man who constantly smiled. His only complaint was that eating bad food after he came down the mountain would cause his early death. He died in 1977 at the age of 96.

One Cloud's formulas resonate with writings attributed to Lü Dongbin, the key figure of the Zhong-Lü school. Some of his practices also resemble operational teachings preserved in the Complete Perfection tradition. But One Cloud's higher formulas, as far as I know, are not held in the Quanzhen order. When I shared them with the vice abbot of Mt. Hua, he gasped and exclaimed: "These are very secret teachings. Very few in China know of them." He had difficulty grasping that they are being openly taught in the West.

Mantak Chia became the first Chinese teacher to overcome linguistic and cultural hurdles and build a large Western school of *neidan*. He was a cross-cultural ice breaker, explosively opening a gap that other Chinese schools would later use to enter Western culture, and support the growth of a wholly new kind of Western Daoist subculture that was not a copy of Chinese *neidan* culture. I posit five major reasons why Chia's Healing Tao organization (Universal Tao overseas) succeeded in transplanting *neidan* to the West.

1. Healing Tao identified sexual energy up front as the key alchemical agent. Chia's emphasis on cultivating sexual energy—solo or with a partner—as a means of enhancing spiritual power clearly distanced him from monastic religious orders in China. The Western "quest for spiritual orgasm" acted as a cultural pheromone and attracted large numbers of seekers dissatisfied with the sexual repression in other paths and religions (Winn 2003). Those hoping for quick sexual thrills soon learned they had years of hard cultivation work to do in integrating their inner male and inner female, the primary fire and water of the early stage of *neidan* practice (Winn 1984). The hope for sexual liberation drew a large base of students, even though many dropped out. As if to punctuate the point of his teachings on sexual vitality, in 2007, at age of 64, Mantak Chia fathered his fourth child with a Thai woman 40 years younger than him.

2. Healing Tao *neidan* results were practical and had the dependability of a science. Chia's mantra, "You do it, you get it" helped Westerners gain confidence to engage in a lengthy, progressive training that evolved from physical body to energy body to spirit body. He used language taken from quantum physics or computing metaphors to illustrate his energetic teachings, which made students more comfortable. The presence of a seven stage developmental structure—One Cloud's formulas—was important to the science-based minds of Westerners. They want to know why they are doing a practice and where it leads before they commit to a path.

3. Chia did away with Chinese cultural taboos on secrecy and lineage dependence. His books released a flood of esoteric Daoist information at the same time it happened in esoteric Tibetan, Hindu, Cabbala, and Christian traditions. Chia transmitted One Cloud's hermit or mountain lineage. He was not subject to the many Chinese cultural restrictions found in organized Daoism. Decisions were made in America, not in China. Chia himself was well suited to cross-religious communication. Raised in Buddhist Thailand by a Christian chaplain mother, he adopted Daoism in high school. He often jokes that you need spiritual allies from all traditions when the moment of death comes.

In Healing Tao, it is the responsibility of each adept to unfold his or her inner truth and destiny. No allegiance to a lineage or prostration before a teacher is necessary, only respect for the teacher. This is very popular with Westerners tired of false religious authorities and dogmas. It also reflects the early Daoist tradition in which Laozi and Zhuangzi were not priests mediating the divine to followers, but individual cultivators sharing their experience of direct relationship with Dao.

4. Chia readily accepted guidance from many Westerners, including myself as editor or writer of his first seven books. Chia taught me *neidan* methods, and after testing them, I found ways to make the highly technical Daoist terms understandable. I presented Chia as speaking in the refined literary voice of a Westerner. This was key to the books' success, which were translated into dozens of languages. Other Western students showed Chia how to dress, gave him feedback on what was culturally acceptable and useful in a workshop. He was a quick learner, but could not have done it without a Western support team.

5. He had enormous persistence. A lead pioneer in bringing *neidan* to the West in 1980, in 2008 Chia still had a grueling teaching schedule on four continents for 200 days of the year. He does not need the money. What drives his extraordinary, tireless effort after three decades? A personal sense of destiny, fueled by simple desire to help others spiritually. "I am happy if twenty percent of my students can catch and hold my frequency," he recently told me. "It takes years of practice, a loving heart, and much work to cultivate immortality."

Daoism is not a missionary religion. China's indigenous higher creed, it assumes Chinese culture is the apex of human development and that foreign barbarians will ultimately seek China's superior level of refinement. *Neidan*, the inner sanctum of Daoism, relies on transmission, not on numerical conversion of souls. The assumption is that worthy souls will be attracted to Daoist teachings; those who don't seek it do not deserve its treasures.

Many Chinese adepts seem too introverted to bother transmitting the kind of yang energy that Mantak Chia had naturally. One Chinese adept put it succinctly: "It is not my personal destiny to teach others". The only imperative in most *neidan* lineages is to teach one truly worthy soul. This custom, combined with strict secrecy, may ultimately threaten *neidan* with extinction in China. When I tell Daoists there that more Westerners are studying *neidan* than Chinese, they simply shrug.

The weight of China's long history is too heavy for Daoists to change their ways. In contrast, the West offers a spiritual culture of openness in which Daoist experimentation can more easily occur. Western interest in *neidan* may eventually stimulate the Chinese to revive their own tradition. Already I've had Chinese seekers emailing me and asking for help with *neidan*, as they cannot find teachers in China.

It is curious that of Chia's thirty-three books, only one small booklet covers One Cloud's second formula, and nothing is published on the last five formulas. This lopsided coverage is not due to secrecy. It is impossible to teach higher alchemy from a book. Students do best with an oral transmission, even if recorded digitally. Oral transmission allows the mind to focus internally while listening to guidance. Reading stimulates and fills the eyes and brain, but does not penetrate to the kidney/*jing* level of psychic substance that must be activated in *neidan*. This is why as a *neidan* teacher of the higher formulas I have focused on audio courses rather than written books. Books offer information "about" *neidan*; skillful oral transmission guides you deep into the inner space.

The subjects of Chia's published books are the ones Western culture is ready to absorb at this point. Westerners mostly need the first formula, which covers the fundamental principles of Chinese medicine. It focuses on harmonizing postnatal health and cycles of *qi*-flow, and becoming grounded in the body. Without a strong body and integrated psyche, one cannot hold the soul and cosmic forces of the higher alchemical formulas.

Western Adaptation of Alchemy

Each human has a unique nature, physically and spiritually. This explains why different forms of alchemy arise. In China, *neidan* is taught differently on every mountain. I noticed my own practice of the Seven Alchemy formulas unfolded in quite different directions from Mantak Chia's. He was attracted to expanding out to the Pole Star. I wanted to go deeper inside my cauldron, the Mysterious Gate of the Dark Female (*xuanguan*), and listen to the music of the spheres. Key insights from my background in Kundalini and kriya yoga, Dzogchen, Celtic-Christian mysticism, and six years training in Western (Atlantean) internal alchemy have all been absorbed into my Daoist *neidan* practice and teaching (Winn 2009). It is impossible to shut out diverse influences if they work; whatever is not discarded must be integrated.

I have observed while teaching *neidan* around the world that each culture responds differently to the alchemical process. Alchemists cook whatever flows into their cauldron from the field around them until it becomes spiritually refined within their own body. That is the micro-macrocosmic dynamic of Daoist cultivation.

Chia originally insisted One Cloud's higher formulas be learned slowly, with a minimum of one year's practice to stabilize energetic shifts before "eating" the *qi* of the next formula. Students who rush through them, stuffing their heads with information, invariably cannot hold onto anything and drop out completely. This emphasis on gradual progress through different levels of enlightenment and immortality is a hallmark of Daoist training, and distinguishes it in China from Chan Buddhist teachings that promise sudden enlightenment. Some Daoists consider a sudden empty mind to be a "yin ghost", if it does not arise from the concrete essence of a tangible, yang and unique human destiny (*ming*). In *neidan*, the true formless spiritual nature (*xing*) must be cultivated within one's worldly destiny, i.e. the spirit being sought must be extracted from matter. The density and resistance of the individual's ordinary heart-mind provides the authentic ground for immortality (Robinet 1997, 250).

What follows is a brief discussion of the major Healing Tao practices, and how One Cloud's formulas were creatively evolved by Western Daoists accommodating energetic needs very different from the Chinese.

Foundation Practice: Inner Smile

One Cloud's internal alchemy begins and ends with a *wuwei* or spontaneous practice, the Inner Smile. The ordinary outer smile tends to be reactive to or manipulative of other people. The Inner Smile is a method of opening the inner heart or soul (*lingshen*) to the *qi*-field. It allows a feeling of deep acceptance from the heart to effortlessly penetrate with gentle radiance into one's biology (its underlying *jing*). This radiant feeling is then spread to one's vital organ spirits (*jingshen*) that control one's *qi*-flow and psychology. Then one's heart spirit smiles outwardly to one's community and natural world which offer a context for one's destiny.

The Inner Smile is the simplest and most basic practice, yet is also used in all the higher formulas. It ultimately becomes the most advanced practice—the adept merges into the mind of Dao, effortlessly smiling from the primordial *qi*-field into all dimensions of nature, humanity, and body. This merger of the adept's personal smiling with the mind of Dao implies that humanity's destiny (as one of Dao's Three Treasures, along with Heaven and Earth) is to elevate the Dao with its purity of heart and ability to feel personal love.

The Inner Smile, I believe, is an evolution of "sitting in forgetfulness" (*zuowang*), the Daoist practice of emptying or "fasting" the heart-mind as formulated most clearly in the eighth century (Kohn 1987). The practice empties the mind of physical density, so the *neidan* adept can more easily concentrate polar forces in order to shape the *qi*-field. One empties the conditional mind so it does not interfere with the soul expressing its will. In this way, *zuowang* allows one's destiny to be more effortlessly completed. Inner Smile is like *zuowang*—you forget the "little" self and gradually dissolve the body into the *qi*-field. The main difference is the Inner Smile stays heart-centered.

Inner heart smiling is a simple and practical method of cultivating unconditional openness and all-pervading spirit (*tong*). By accepting every aspect of self unconditionally, all polarized perceptions of self simply disappear. The boundary between self and other dissolves. A sense of peace and unity spontaneously arises, by opening perception of the deeper non-dual consciousness underlying all yin-yang divisions or apparent distinctions that lead to creative tension.

The Inner Smile typically begins with a yin phase, systematically focusing heart-centered unconditional acceptance on the brain, spine, three elixir fields, five vital organs, their *qi* channels, all other physical tissues. The yang phase embraces everything outside the body, layer by layer: one's aura, the room, village, country, planet, moon, sun, stars, and blackness beyond. The adept then flips their perspective, reversing the direction of the flow of acceptance, smiling through layers of outer world back into the physical body until everything is dissolved into prenatal formless in the elixir field.

For Westerners, the Inner Smile's heart-centeredness and unconditional openness offers a bridge between Daoism and Christ's teaching of unconditional love. Sitting in forgetfulness helps the adept to surrender to the impersonal *qi*-field of Heaven and Earth, but does not necessarily integrate human heartedness. *Zuowang* inspired Chan (Zen) "sitting in emptiness," which can feel too cold or impersonal for some Westerners. The Inner Smile is often interpreted as unconditional self-love grounded first within one's own body and then radiated out. In higher formulas, Inner Smile is used to integrate personal and impersonal forces within the collective human heart. It ultimately dissolves any boundary between lesser self and other, greater Self. The entire cosmos is embraced within the adept's deep field of Self-acceptance.

Formula 1

This formula opens the Microcosmic Orbit, harmonizes the five organ spirits and Eight Extraordinary Vessels. Its principles encapsulate those of Chinese medicine and are used for self-healing. Students may spend several years learning this formula, as it has many practices. The Six Healing Sounds clear vital organ *qi* cycling through the five phases and three burners (heart fire, digestive fire, sexual fire). The Orbit balances the fire and water as they flow in the yang spine and yin chest. These teachings evolved in the West. I discovered in China many other internal methods to circulate the Orbit not taught by One Cloud, some of which work better. Westerners tend to be mental, so I also created new forms of movement qigong to activate the Orbit, which was very successful.

Fusion of the Five Phases or Elements—levels I, II, and III—is emotional and psychic alchemy. One absorbs innate virtues from the prenatal *qi* field and dissolves postnatal negative emotional *qi* trapped in the heart-mind. Refined emotional *qi* is crystallized into a pearl, made of depolarized postnatal *qi*. It divides into five colored pearls as vessels of expression for the virtuous feelings of each organ spirit. The original pearl is circulated through the body in five-phase creation and control cycles to regulate feeling and attain tranquility. Its alchemical value? It is a way to access one's original or primordial *qi* and true feelings as they arise from the Gate of Destiny (*mingmen*) between the kidneys, i.e. before the heart-mind gets conditioned by life's traumas. This is key to cultivating the True Self or Inner Sage in later formulas.

The Macrocosmic Orbit circulates the purified pearl through the Eight Extraordinary Vessels. This opens communication between the trunk, four limbs, and outer world. Adepts learn basic sexual practices at this stage. Males recycle *jingqi* of their semen, females learn to reduce or end blood loss from menstrual cycles. Testicle Breathing, Ovarian Breathing, and breast massage combine with the Orbit to re-circulate sexual energy. If one has a partner, dual cultivation methods for the bedroom are studied.

Westerners had to make major shifts in the Fusion practices to adapt them to their style of emotional and sexual expression, which is often more extroverted and socially uninhibited than in Chinese culture. Original Fusion method internally mimicked Chinese cultural use of "face" to suppress any negative feeling not in harmony with social or "outer group" mind. This emotional *qi* was fused into a pearl, eventually jammed with suppressed negativity. The intent was to control the bodily flow of *qi* to transform negative emotions of the five *shen* or "inner group" mind. This was comfortable for Chinese adepts. But in Westerners this attempt to control had the unfortunate side-effect of empowering the head's mental power at the expense of expressing feelings. Many Western Fusion adepts noted their feelings would "dry up" after an initial period of clarity.

This became an opportunity to integrate Daoist five-organ theory and Western depth-psychology with its notion of shadow, inner parts, family therapy, and Jungian ideas of individuation. It took me a decade of research and careful testing of Fusion process in the teaching environment to make five-*shen* dynamics a workable, user-friendly part of my Healing Tao meditative practices and psychology. It was a shift from qigong to *shengong* (skill with spirit). Ultimately, opening a relationship between the soul (*lingshen*) and the five body spirits (*wu jingshen*) made all the internal alchemy practices more simple, powerful, and less likely to use mentally forced chi patterns.

This westernized Daoist *neidan* fills in the huge gaps in Jung's only partially successful attempt to reconstruct Western alchemy as a process of psychic transformation. Grasping the influence and functions of our body spirits and their *qi*-channels builds a bridge between shamans, psychologists, doctors and neuro-scientists. It clarifies the energetic foundation of the blossoming body-centered Western "energy psychology" movement trying to integrate acupuncture and psychotherapy with methods such as tapping on meridians while focusing on emotional issues (see Feinstein et al. 2005). In return, Western archetypal and shadow theory have helped illuminate the psychological workings of Daoist *neidan*.

The successful Western *neidan* adept at this early stage experiences his body-mind as a process, a collective team of body-spirits consciously utilizing deep *qi*-channels and guidance from the soul to respond to the world, instead of unconsciously reacting to events. The sub-personalities have been identified and empowered to function within a harmonized whole. The attainment of tranquility comes from the *shen* collective consciously and virtuously shaping the emotional and sexual *qi*-flow according to its (Western) need for completion.

Formulas 2, 3, and 4

Originally titled "Lesser, Greater, and Greatest Enlightenment of Water and Fire (Kan and Li)", it was my work to title and clarify them as "Inner Sexual Alchemy," "Sun-Moon Ancestor Alchemy," and "Planetary and Collective Soul Alchemy." This made the training progression clearer for Western adepts. Water and fire are reversed and coupled "vertically" along the body's core channel axis in each formula. The vertical coupling of water and fire is part of a "primal" or soul level trinity, not to be confused with postnatal water and fire of the five-phase emotional *qi* refined in Fusion. In these three formulas the postnatal five-phases are also "horizontally" fused into the central cauldron, which moves from lower elixir field to solar plexus and on to the heart. Reversal means the adept's desires to pursue outer physical life in the state "After Heaven" is reversed as their *qi* begins to dissolve and flows back into the portal of the prenatal opened by the vertical coupling of primal water and fire.

The second Lesser Formula marks the critical shift from postnatal to prenatal, and requires concentrating the sexual forces of the soul to ignite or impregnate the elixir, the spiritual essence in the pearl. This happens within the Mysterious Female or Dark Cavity, the portal opening to the prenatal *qi* field in the mingmen. This ignition produces a very tangible speeding up of the vibration of one's entire body that continues for months.

The third Greater Formula progresses to internal coupling sun with moon, while the fourth couples inner earth with inner sun. My teaching of these formulas was dramatically changed by hints given by my channeled teacher of Western alchemy from Atlantis. I also offer as an option to my *neidan* students the Atlantean alchemical "fire" method of counter-force spinning pyramids to speed up the refining process of the elixir. This illustrates how the West is an experimental cauldron for Daoist *neidan*.

The secret in each Formula is coupling the "true yang" hidden within the yin and "true yin" within the yang. The Lesser Kan and Li Formula completes the sexual polarities of the soul. The Greater Kan and Li completes the bloodline ancestors still trapped in the sun, moon, and seasonal earth cycles of time. The Greatest Kan and Li Formula, finally, completes the astrological and archetypal collective human forces held within planetary *qi*, the broad karmic forces shaping our destiny.

These formulas involve multi-level sexual couplings of polar forces. This reflects nature's need to restore the primordial *qi* lost when the androgynous human split into male and female bodies. The net effect of practicing these three formulas is an accelerated completion of one's soul purpose. This dissolves all fear of death and ends the soul fragmentation driving an unconscious need to reincarnate. This three-tiered enlightenment of the individual's postnatal self is prerequisite to attaining higher immortality in formulas 5, 6, and 7.

Formulas 2, 3, and 4 opens one to receive a new mandate, or higher soul destiny from Heaven.

Formula 5

Originally called "Sealing of the Five Senses," I renamed this "Star Alchemy" to reflect the level of vibration absorbed. The practice seals the senses and mind of the adept inside the upper elixir field. The intent is to open up communication between the adept's inner sage and the great spirit (*dashen*) symbolized by the vastness of star intelligences, the Pole Star and zodiacal sweep of the Big Dipper. Its focus is to complete one's spiritual nature (*xing*). It opens the portal of the central axis of After Heaven into the state Before Heaven. Feeling the power of this channel open was one of my most overwhelming and terrifying *neidan* experiences. It reminded me why adepts need years of training to handle the powerful forces that could burn out the unprepared.

The meditations activate progressively subtler energetic fields that allow the adept to communicate instantly across vast distances. The five vital organ intelligences are trained to resonate with the five great directional spirits or "dragons" of the planet. These directional spirits in turn talk to the intelligences of the planets and they to the vast star quadrants of the zodiac. All three levels of intelligence—Human, Earth, and Heaven—have "a single ancestor," meaning they are born, function, and die within the same primordial *qi* field of Dao.

Once you learn to listen to one pattern within the body, it is only a matter of training to "listen" to the same pattern in other parts of the *qi*-field, even if they are as physically remote star beings. *Qi*-patterns are not limited by physical time or space, but travel at the speed of consciousness, much faster than the speed of light. This is because the patterns do not need to travel across space. The living *qi*-field's triune nature holds the matrix of space, time, and intelligence, including past, present, and future, all in one primordial stream. A similar idea has been recently posited by physicists, as an infinite number of parallel universe co-existing in the same space.

Formula 6

In the "Congress of Heaven and Earth," the adept internalizes the act of cosmic sexual intercourse between After Heaven and the formless state Before Heaven. All the lesser body spirits are sent out of the body, so the inner sage can commune undisturbed with the Three Pure Ones. These are essentially the ruling intelligences of Heaven, Earth, and Humanity. This internal coupling of Heaven and Earth within the adept re-births the essence of humanity as their child. The True Self or sage re-experiences humanity's redemptive possibilities of personal love and immortality. The cosmic coupling also opens deeper communication with the "clear light" of the chaos or original unity of *hundun*, the primordial, heavenly state preceding the creation of yin-yang and five-phase cycles. Postnatal *jing-qi-shen* are consciously integrated with original *jng-qi-shen*.

The endless transformations of original *qi* between the Three Heavens is the true Macrocosmic Orbit.

Formula 7
The final stage is the union of Man and Dao. One Cloud did not claim to master it or teach it. He described it as a human's immortal or true self merging spontaneously into the Supreme Mystery or Non-Ultimate (*wuji*), the portal to the unknowable Dao. This allows functioning simultaneously at the level of all seven formulas.

Conclusion

The appropriation of Daoist internal alchemy by Westerners is proceeding slowly but steadily. Its use as a direct path of spiritual practice has had an elevating influence on external alchemical arts such as taiji quan and Chinese medicine. *Neidan* methods allow adepts to communicate with their internal body spirits and to shape the flow of *qi* within the body of nature at a deep level. It is the most direct path of refining human ability to explore the relationship between matter and spirit, and to heal the split between male and female.

Neidan opens the door to understanding exactly how the human soul, like the brain, is binary in nature. We are divided into yin-yang aspects at many different levels of body and psyche, polarities often in conflict. The purpose of internal alchemy is to speed up the integration of the warring halves of our soul as part of human evolution. When *neidan* practice is successful, physical rejuvenation, the emergence of an authentic self, and some level of immortality may be achieved.

Internal alchemy is China's highest path of self-realization, defined as the process of giving greater reality to a multi-dimensional Self. Alchemy speaks the language of *qi* radiating from the primordial ground of unity-chaos that births all yin-yang and five-phases patterns in the "formless forms" of Before Heaven and in the state After Heaven or on physical earth. Western adepts have used the operative principles of Daoist *neidan* to explore the spiritual nature of space, time, gravity, and consciousness as it relates to Western paradigms of science and Christian notions of unconditional love. Chinese *neidan*, being body-centered and thus accessible, may help rejuvenate the field of Western internal alchemy, whose external laboratory paradigm historically had great influence on Western culture. As Westerners absorb the deep language of *neidan*, they are growing an entirely new spiritual sub-culture that is neither purely Daoist nor Christian-Scientific.

Daoist alchemy views both personal life and the life of the cosmos as processing, an ultimately unknowable Dao, but one in which humans can intervene. This view of Dao does not seek or worship a higher absolute order typical of Buddhism, Hinduism, or Platonic Christianity (Ames 1998). The *neidan* adept's awareness of the impersonal or non-being aspect of nature does not imply passive surrender to it. Rather it serves to stimulate human creativity in alchemically shaping the life force. Walking the razor's edge between the personal and cosmic is ultimately the job of an immortal—to crystallize the elixir hidden within the heart-mind, and use it to create ever greater balance and harmony within the flowing ocean of Dao.

Bibliography

Ames, Roger, and Lau, D.C. 1998. *Yuan Dao: Tracing Dao to Its Source*. New York: Ballantine.

Bertschinger, Richard. 1994. *The Secret of Everlasting Life*. London: Element Books.

Cleary, Thomas. 1987. *Understanding Reality: A Taoist Alchemical Classic by Chang Po-tuan*. Honolulu: University of Hawai'i Press.

_____. 1989. *The Book of Balance and Harmony: Chung He Chi*. San Francisco: North Point Press.

_____. 1992. *The Secret of the Golden Flower: The Classic Chinese Book of Life*. San Francisco: Harper.

_____. 1996. *Opening the Dragon Gate: The Making of a Modern Taoist Wizard*. Tokyo: Tuttle.

Despeux, Catherine. 1979. *Zhao Bichen: Trait'e d'alchimie et de physiologie taoïste*. Paris: Guy Trédaniel.

Eliade, Mircea. 1962. *The Forge and the Crucible: The Origins and Structure of Alchemy*. Chicago: University of Chicago Press.

Feinstein, David, Donna Eden, and Gary Craig. 2005. *The Promise of Energy Psychology*. New York: Penguin.

Goris, Rene. 2009. *How Clouds Become Dragons: A Study of China's Cultural Sciences*. Forthcoming.

Hansen, Chad. 1992. *A Daoist Theory of Chinese Thought*. New York: Oxford University Press.

Hauck, Dennis W. 1999. *The Emerald Tablet: Alchemy of Personal Transformation*. New York: Penguin.

Jarrett, Lonny. 2000. *Nourishing Destiny: The Inner Tradition of Chinese Medicine*. Stockbridge, Mass.: Spirit Path Press.

Johnson, Jerry A. 2008. "Introduction to Daoist Mysticism: *Qi*." *Journal of Traditional Eastern Health and Fitness* 18.1.

Johnson, Mark. 2009. *Life is Divine Play: My Life and Training with Enlightened Masters.* Bloomington, Ind.: Universe Books.

Kohn, Livia. 1987. *Seven Steps to the Tao: Sima Chengzhen's Zuowanglun.* St. Augustin: Monumenta Serica Serica Monograph.

_____. 1993. *The Taoist Experience: An Anthology.* Albany: State University of New York Press.

Komjathy, Louis. 2003. *Handbooks for Daoist Practice,* Seattle: Wandering Cloud Press.

_____. 2007. *Cultivating Perfection: Mysticism and Self-Transformation in Quanzhen Daoism.* Leiden: E. Brill.

Lu, Kuan-yü. 1970. *Taoist Yoga: Alchemy and Immortality.* London: Rider.

Moeller, Hans-Georg. 2004. *Daoism Explained.* LaSalle, Ill.: Open Court Publishing.

Mori, Yuria. 2002. "Identity and Lineage: The *Taiyi jinhua zongzhi* and the Spirit-Writing Cult to Patriarch Lü in Qing China." In *Daoist Identity: History, Lineage, and Ritual,* edited by Livia Kohn and Harold D. Roth, 165-84. Honolulu: University of Hawai'i Press.

Ni, Hua-ching. 1992. *Internal Alchemy: The Natural Way to Immortality.* Malibu: Shrine of the Eternal Breath of Tao.

Phillips, Scott P. 2008. "Portrait of an American Daoist: Charles Belyea/Liu Ming." *Journal of Daoist Studies* 1:161-76.

Rinaldini, Michael. 2008. "How I Became a Daoist Priest." *Journal of Daoist Studies* 1:181-87.

Robinet, Isabelle. 1993. *Taoist Meditation: the Mao-Shan Tradition of Great Purity.* New York: State University of New York Press.

_____. 1997. *Taoism: Growth of a Religion.* Translated by Phyllis Brooks. Stanford: Stanford University Press.

Schipper, Kristofer M. 1994. *The Taoist Body.* Translated by Karen C. Duval. Berkeley: University of California Press.

Schlain, Leonard 1998. *The Alphabet versus the Goddess: The Conflict between Word and Image.* New York: Penguin.

Towler, Solala. 2007. *The Empty Vessel: Journal of Contemporary Daoism.* Eugene, Oreg.: Abode of the Eternal Tao.

Wilhelm, Richard. 1962 [1929]. *The Secret of the Golden Flower.* New York: Harcourt, Brace and World.

Winn, Michael. 2002 "The Quest for Spiritual Orgasm: Daoist and Tantric Sexual Cultivation in the West." Paper Presented at the. Conference on Daoism and Tantra, Boston University. www.healingdao.com/cgi-bin/articles.pl?rm=mode2&articleid=35

_____. 2003 "Magic Numbers, Planetary Tones and the Daoist Energy Body as Musical Instrument." Paper Presented at the Conference on Daoism in the Contemporary World, Boston. www.healingdao.com/cgi-bin/articles.pl

_____. 2008. "Daoist *Neidan*: Lineage and Secrecy Challenges for Western Adepts." *Journal of Daoist Studies* 1:195-99.

_____. 2009a. *Shape Power - Ask the Life Force to Create a Reality You Truly Need: A Brief History of Atlantis' Spiritual Technology*. Asheville: Healing Tao Press.

_____. 2009b. *Taoist Microcosmic Orbit: Advanced Methods of Circulating the Golden Elixir*. Asheville: Healing Tao Press.

_____. 2010. *Tao Inner Alchemy: Sexually Couple Male Water and Female Fire to Complete Your Destiny and Cultivate Immortality*. Asheville: Healing Tao Press.

_____, and Chia, Mantak 1984. *Taoist Secrets of Love: Cultivating Male Sexual Energy*. New York: Aurora Press.

Wong, Eva. 1992. *Cultivating Stillness: A Taoist Manual for Transforming Body and Mind*. Boston: Shambhala.

_____. 1997. *Harmonizing Yin and Yang: the Dragon-Tiger Classic*. Boston: Shambhala.

_____. 2000. *The Tao of Health, Longevity, and Immortality: The Zhong-Lü Tradition*. Boston: Shambhala.

Young, Allen. 1984. *National Clearinghouse for Healing Effects of Taoist Meditation*. New York: Private Publication.

On Being Moved

Kundalini and the Complete Maturation of the Spiritual Body

Stuart Sovatsky

> A coil of lightning, a flame of fire folded.
> She cleans the skin down to the skeleton.
> Old age gets reversed.
> She…dissolves the five [bodily] elements.
> …[then] the yogi is known as Khecar [tumescent tongued]
> Attaining this state is a miracle.
> Shakti [feminine power] and Shiva [masculine power] become one
> and in their union, everything. . . gets dissolved.
> Further, there is nothing more to experience beyond [this]—
> Hence, let me stop speaking of it,
> For it is useless to talk.
> —Numbered couplets related to Kundalini, ca. 1210 (Saraswati 2002)

Vibrant well-being, overwhelming ecstasy, effulgently enlightened consciousness, the summit of human evolution, pathway to an endless eroticism, the Great Procreatrix, the deification, regeneration and immortalization of the body, the somaticizing of spiritual aspirations, the teleological freeing of soul from flesh via the literal unwinding of the mortal coil into its constituent elements, the lost wisdom of the serpent of Genesis and the fuel of all human genius, the energy of the Dionysian revelry, the spiritual side of DNA, Christ's fiery baptism and that of His followers ever since, the seething cobra sheltering Lord Buddha—such are the ancient and modern claimed manifestations of Kundalini, literally, "the mother of all creation and of all yogas."

The Basics

Kundalini practice is traceable for at least five-thousand years, to the archeological relic known as the Pashupati Seal. This depicts an antler-crowned demigod, sitting cross-legged with one heel pressing his androgynous perineum and the other the root of his erect penis. He is mildly breasted, with a *phalam* fruit in one hand and a phallic staff in the other—assumed to be the ultimate attainer himself, Shiva, reincarnated some twenty-eight times, most recently as Lakulisha, the staff-bearing Gujurati saint (ca. 100 C.E.). He in turn was the inspiration of the legendary Goraksha-nath and Matsyendra-nath yogic saints, from whom all modern forms of hatha yoga have emerged.

Kundalini has ancient Vedic references in terms of an inner sunlight, an inner nectar of immortality (*soma*), divine circulating wind (*vayu*), and a "crookedly-shaped" or serpentine (*kunamnama*) potential that the bodily wind of the ancient "long-haired ascetic (*keshin*) churns into serving his spiritual goals to know ultimate reality and its inherent bliss. And, as paths to the Ultimate multiplied over the millenia of Indian history, those that were more inclusive of a positive role for the body (rather than on consciousness itself and meditative and ascetic modes of transcending the body) could be discerned.

Whether Buddhist or Hindu, they became known as tantra, the "expanded teachings" on the "interweavedness" of the evermore subtle vibrational dimensions of reality. While Upanishadic or nondual (*advaita*) paths simplified their focus toward a singular oneness of consciousness, tantric traditions tended to broaden their scope to include cultivating spiritual powers of the mind, the material world, and—a most significantly—of the body. Practitioners strove for extreme longevity and even physical immortality through rituals, sexo-yogic, celibate transmutations, and herbal-mineral preparations (see White 1996). Texts on the practice go back to the fifth century c.e. and tend to come from Kashmir and northern India (see Silburn 1988).

Tantra typically resolved to the reverberations between masculine and feminine qualities, deified as Shiva and Shakti (or Durga, Kali, and other goddesses)—the primordial couple. Their interactions created not only endlessly reproductive and evolving lineages, but also the entire manifest Universe. Between all males and females and within each individual reverberated Shiva's tendency toward absolute and unwavering consciousness with Shakti's wide-ranging dynamic powers, from the most nurturing to the wildly purifying and even antinomian or "transgressive" (of orthodox or conventional) practices (see Kinsley 1997; Bühnemann 2000).

Unwavering auditory meditation upon mantric vibrations revealed deeper beauties and empowering intricacies within the mantras while also adding brilliance and perspicuity to the unwavering consciousness. Important mantras include *Om Namo Bhagavate Vasudevaya, Om Namo Shivaya* and *So-Ham,* as well as *Om Bhur Bhuva Swaha Tat Savitur Varenyam Bhargo Devasya Dhimahe Dhyo Yonah*

Prachodayat. Likewise, visual meditation upon interpenetrating triangles blossomed into an infinity of vibrations as the meditator approached the radiant, inner Source of his or her own consciousness and perhaps of the subatomic structure of the manifest universe itself.

The Body

Of central importance and dating back to the *Taittiriya-Upanishad* are descriptions of a subtle energetic anatomy (*sukshma-sharira*) revealed through body-scanning meditations. This subtle body was seen to pervade the fleshy "food-eating" body (*anna-maya-kosha*), consisting of some 72,000 subtle channels (*nadis*) and spinally-aligned ascending centers (*cakras*). Within these, subtle structures as founded in the generic life energy (*prana*), were seen flowing in various circuits of inhalation, exhalation, and elimination as well as circulating, digestive, breathing, and speaking functions.

The primordial Kundalini energy itself glowed and seethed at the perineum in the "root generator" center (*muladhara cakra*) that governs the earth element. Sexual passion rested in the lower abdomen in the reproductive center (*svadhishthana cakra*) that governs the water element. Willfulness resided in navel-level center (*manipura cakra*) that governs the fire element, while the heart and its surges with moods of devotion, longing, courage, and love connect to the heart center (*anahata cakra*).

Whereas the first three cakras govern the fleshy body, the latter rules the air element and is associated with the nonphysical energy body (*prana-maya kosha*). Above it is the throat center (*vishudhha cakra*), associated with speech and governing the subtle etheric element and the thinking-emotional body (*mano-maya kosha*). Following this, the sixth or third-eye center (*ajna cakra*) rests in the head behind the midpoint of the forehead. It functions as the evermore refined capacity for reflective discernment and subtle judgement in the body of subtlest discriminations (*vijnana-maya kosha*).

The reflective capacity of the third-eye center hovers around a central point of nonduality or, from a tantric perspective, "oscillating duality-nonduality" (*dvaita-advaita*). It is capable of the most refined discernment, extending into psychic powers. The highest of them all, the crown cakra (*sahasrara cakra*) is part of the the causal bliss body (*ananda-maya-kosha*); it is the "thousand-petalled lotus" of endlessly effulgent light and bliss beyond all concepts and intellectualizations, where male and female live in ecstatically commingled union.

Awakening Kundalini

All the practices of hatha yoga—postures (*asanas*), hand gestures (*mudras*), visceral contractions or "locks" (*bandhas*), and breath control (*pranayama*)—help to awaken the dormant Kundalini in the root cakra. Likewise, the vibrational chanting practices of mantra yoga—rosary-like repetitions (*japa*), group chanting (*kirtan*) with an awakened leader via an energetic transmission known as *shaktipat*, and personal mantric prayers over the course of many years can awaken Kundalini.[1] Quiet-sitting meditative practices tend to minimize the complete awakening of this energy, but instead focus upon inner peace, undifferentiated consciousness, compassion, insights into impermanence and the limitations of egoic identifications.

Below is a regime of twenty asanas with cakra meditations and breathing prescriptions sequenced to awaken the cakras for Kundalini arousal.[2]

Yogic Posture (Asana)	**Cakra**	**Breath holding**
Yoga mudra (kneeling foldover)	root	in and out
Paschchimottana-asana (seated forward bend)	root	in and out
Ardha-matsyendra-asana (seated spinal twist)	reprod.	normal breathing
Buddha-padma-asana (lotus pose)	reprod.	out
Lola-asana (uplifted lotus balance)	navel	in
Dola-asana (lotus v-balance with chin-lock)	navel	in and out
Ardha-supta-padma-asana (supine lotus pose)	navel	in and out
Matsyendra-asana (fish pose)	heart	in and out
Viparita karani-padma-asana (reverse lotus)	heart	normal breathing
Hala-asana (plow pose)	throat	normal breathing
Karani pida-asana (knee to ear pose)	throat	normal breathing
Sarvanga-asana (shoulder stand)	throat	normal breathing
Viparita karani (legs up the wall pose)	throat	in and out
Mukta pavana-asana (supine knee-to-chest)	throat	in
Setu-asana (bridge pose)	third eye	in
Bhujanga-asana (cobra pose)	third eye	in
Salabha-asana (locust pose)	third eye	in
Dhanura-asana (bow pose)	third eye	in and out
Sirsa-asana (head stand)	crown	normal breathing
Sava-asana (corpse pose)	crown	normal breathing

---

[1] While the Sikh Dharma of Kundalini yoga taught in the West by Yogi Bhajan has become synonymous with the entire practice, the term embraces all forms of yoga.

[2] The aspirant ideally also follows the *yamas* and *niyamas* character-cultivating first two "limbs" of the "eight-limbed" (*ashtanga*) path that also includes *asana, pranayama, pratyahaya* (sensory withdrawal), *dharana* (concentration), *dhyana* (meditation), and *samadhi* (absorption).

Once Kundalini awakens—or once its common precursor, pranic awakening, occurs—many initially intentional practices emerge spontaneously. Given the requisite level of pranic activation and meditative relaxation, the body spontaneously moves into various yoga postures, mood-enhanced dance movements, intensified breathing patterns, and automatic utterances. At that point, many yoga practices reveal themselves to be innate or endogenous (though typically dormant) in all humans with cognate phenomena visible in numerous charismatic or "inspired" religious and spiritual traditions, worldwide.

Embryonic Beginnings

Kundalini's motherly creativity is first visible microscopically in the nucleus of the fertilized ovum as, literally, the immortalizing chromosomal process of cellular meiosis. The spiraled, bifurcating genetic strands quiver animistically like enthralled lovers, separating and realigning themselves within the nucleus of the fertilized ovum that divides again and again, recreating this same fibril ritual within the nuclear sanctum of each newly reproducing cell. What guides this primordial origination of all bodily life? Kundalini, the "coiled serpentine wisdom-energy." Thus, in contemporary terms, Kundalini might be renamed, "meta-DNA."

As the zygotic cells divide and ball-up, Kundalini quickens embryological development towards a recognizable human form. An elongating groove folds into itself and creates the dorsal proto-spinal cord whose subtle channel, sushumna, will be the favored pathway for adult Kundalini activity while below, a ventral alimentary pouch and proto-organs manifest inside the emergent gut. This is the first step in separating the body's "heaven realm" of neural consciousness functions from the earth, air, water, and fire realms of digestion, circulation, elimination, etc., thus Kundalini creates a bodily home for the soul, literally, the "one who lives" (*jiva*).

Continuing on, sweet-tasting muco-polysaccharides will secrete into the developing oral cavity as it divides from the heavenly cranial vault, causing the tongue to lick itself away from the heavenly hypophysis (proto-hypothalamus, pituitary, pineal) and into the earthy and watery realms of the just-forming mouth.[3]

The anterior end of the proto-spine blossoms into the proto-brain, altogether forming the anatomical armature of Darwinian evolutionary history from invertebrate to vertebrate to homo erectus and the uniquely neo-

---

[3] During Kundalini activity in the highly advanced adult yogi, sweet-tasting nectar (*amritas*) or elixir of immortality (*soma*) will re-arouse the yogi's tongue into the tumescence of "the tongue's ecstatic dance into the heaven-realm" (*khecari mudra*) in mystic rapport with the matured hypothalamus, the "little wedding chamber" (ancient Greece) or "pleasure center" (modern physiology) and also with the "seat of the soul," i.e., the pineal gland.

cortexted homosapiens. Simultaneously, Kundalini manifests a gill-slitted fish-like stage and a tail-bearing and other lower-mammal stages in a mysterious process that biologists call, ontogeny phylogeny recapitulation—a replay of billions of years of evolution in the gestation of every human being.

Equally mysterious, Kundalini manifests a urogenitally androgynous perineum stage that, for the advanced yogi, will later "fertilize" him with the bio-concentrated powers of the entire polarized universe. Thus, the supreme importance given by yogis (and seen in the Pashupati Seal) to the heel-to-perineum "sitting pose that unleashes supernatural powers" (*siddha-asana*).

All the while, fetal movements perform their own profound asana dance, coaxing and vibrating arm-buds and leg-buds into tiny arms, legs and fingers, while also articulating joints, organs, heartbeats and even pouting and smiling, into existence. When the fetus is fully formed, Kundalini sequesters herself at the posterior node of the spine (the root center) and becomes quiescent.

When the fetus attains individual viability, this same Kundalini dimension within the mother's body engenders the throbs of labor contractions and the ensuing downward pushing and birth of the child. Thereupon, spontaneous proto-linguistic developmental sound-making emerges in the newborn as proto-mantric (*bija*) emotion- and larynx-developing utterances. Likewise, neo-natal developmental stretching movements continue to more fully incarnate the neonate via proto-asanas of hatha yoga. The baby's common spellbound staring into space or at some object emerges as one of the earliest of spontaneous meditative concentrations, whose adult version has been aptly called beginner's, pure, or unconditioned mind.

As enculturation proceeds, the child's mouth- and tongue-shaped sounds will be molded into a native language and her movements and musculature into producing the skills and actions expected within the home culture. Although the primordial "pure consciousness" and its capacity to "rest in itself" remains, her operative "ego mind" will be slowly filled with concepts, memories of delight or terror, moods, desire, and so forth, that evermore individualize her.

The power of Sanskrit (and other sacred languages) is based upon its salutary sonic or mantric effects on all dimensions of the maturing body, far beyond the semantic utility of conceptual meaning. Thus, the emphasis upon nuanced pronunciation in all sacred language instruction. For, the mesh of words, concepts and "forms" inevitably reifies a secondary "ego" mind that can become self-obsessed with worded thinking and grow out of touch with the primordial consciousness of "pure feeling-awareness." Thus, mantra and silent meditation become ever more important practices in "remembering" the unconditioned consciousness itself.

As the individuating process continues, the child's glands will grow in congruence with common emotional states—anger, sorrow, joy, love, desire, shame. Likewise, through the events of her life she comes to feel evermore unique, often too unique and overly embedded in her historical conditioning, according to spiritual psychology. The primordial Kundalini remains dormant and is likely to grow evermore unknown within more worldly, ego-based, or materialistic cultures—warnings found in many ancient texts.

Life Energy

Thereafter, the life energy of prana guides physiology and empowers all thought processes, willful movements, and maintenance-level growth. When growth intensifies during puberty or pregnancy, however, prana re-enters a heightened condition of activity as visible in the glow of infants, pregnant women, new fathers, pubescent teenagers, and saints. Lesser modes of this state include the glow of super-athletes, charismatic musicians and leaders, as well as of ordinary people under psychedelic drugs. A miraculous level manifests in ordinary people in heroic moments, such as mothers lifting cars to save a child or fathers enduring life-threatening situations to save their families.

Under special conditions uplifted prana vibratorily goes so far as to foment the reactivation of the dormant Kundalini. In this gradual or sudden process, spontaneous sounding (*anahata-nad*), movements and yoga positions (*sahaja yoga*) will emerge breaking through the enculturated habits of body and mind—and even break through learned, static hatha yoga postures—which, as spontaneously arising yoga, takes on a surreal, that is, super-real, quality. As one of the most advanced of all Kundalini yogis, Jnaneshvar, wrote,

> That is called [Kundalini yogic developmental kriya] action of the body in which reason takes no part and which does not originate as an idea springing in the mind.
> To speak simply, yogis perform actions [asanas, mudras, kriyas] with their bodies, like the [innocent] movements of children. (1987, 102)

For, under the influence of escalating prana, viscera, musculature and various moods of longing or devotional moods (*bhakti*) vibrate the larynx in characteristic overwhelming, trilling fashion as heard in operatic arias, Sufi *qwaali*, Judaic *nigune*, yogic *anahata-nad*, and shamanic and indigenous trance singing. These moods also gyrate and twist the body into ecstatic dance and, most mysteriously, into various time-honored yoga asanas and others unnamed or unknown to the yogi. They follow the same way that neonatal movements occur or, more vigorously, like birth contractions taking hold of a laboring mother's body. Thus, the mystical significance of "forceful" (*ha-tha*) yoga asserts itself, far beyond any egoic modes of agency.

Likewise, the passion of these longings is as compelling as any romantic love affair, revealing another mystical significance of *ha-tha*, literally the union of sun (masculinity) and the moon (femininity) within a singular body. While seated, the heel draws itself into the once-adrogynous perineum of the awakened one, like a flower unfolding in time-lapse photography. The spine becomes tumescently erect, similar to how male genitals arouse at the thought of one's beloved. The diaphragm lifts into the chest (*uddiyana-bandha*) and the anal sphincter throbs and draws upward (*mula-bandha*), like a runner reaching for the finish line. Thus, the most esoteric aspects of the ancient Pasupati seal come to life—the ultimate goal of the enlightened mind and fully matured human body.

Yoga as the union of Shakti and Shiva seems no mere symbolic metaphor to the Kundalini yogi whose whole life becomes enthralled by these energies. Indeed, five to ten hours per day, for decades unto death are consumed by the inner yogic pregnancy. Indeed, the manifestion of the ascetic Shiva as half male and half female could not be clearer as to the primordial, inwardly erotic and outwardly chaste powers unleashed by Kundalini.

Breathing will become heavy or racy (*bhastrika* or *kapalabhati pranayama*) to animate the passionate stretching and longing. Trilling moans and mantric utterances emerge. Altogether, we see why "the Mover" or "the Lord" (*Ishvara*) is the deity named in classic yoga's second step of ethical prescriptions (*yamas*), while in the *Hathayoga Pradipika* (Light on Hatha Yoga), prana is also deified. Indeed, the moral guidelines or character building principles of yoga (*yamas* and *niyamas*), as well as the postures (*asanas*), hand gestures (*mudras*) and breathing practices (*pranayamas*) are all understood as ways of worshipping prana.

That is, they are understood as yogas, methods at one with their goals, for the highest expressions inherent to prana, are acts of worship—prana worshipping prana, movement worshipping the capacity to move—thereby the worshipper becomes, in mind and body, the deity whom she has long been devoutly worshipping. In other words, a naturalistic quickening of the entire human being unfolds, *sui generis*. This is Kundalini, the Mother of all Yogas.

Comparative Methods

It does not feel like the ego is involved in these actions anymore than in embryonic body-manifestation, and one cannot discern any personal agency in their occurrence. This is quite similar to what charismatic Christians call a "manifestation of the Holy Ghost." Other cross-tradition cognates include spontaneous Judaic and Islamic spinal-rocking (*davvening, zikr*), Tibetan *tumo* heat, Daoist unintentional qigong movements, Bushman *thxiasi num*, shamanic and Voodoo trance-dance, Andalusian flamenco, stomach-undulating bellydance, as well as the charismatic quaking and shaking in Quakerism, Shakerism, Pentecostal "Holy Ghost" dancing, and Orthodox Hesychasm.

Raja Yoga and Buddhism's still-sitting during long meditation periods seek the same awakening, but restrain the body in the hope of channeling all energies directly into the erect spine, but thus bypassing the cultivation of numerous expressive and emotional potentials in mobility. Mortifications, severe vigils and flagellation are the most desperate methods. Even Elvis Presley's charismatic gyrations and his teenaged fans pubescent screams can be located at the beginning of this profound continuum.

Indeed, Kundalini phenomena are not only cross-culturally ubiquitous, taken altogether, they point to an innate, somatic dimension of all manifestations of spirituality and religious aspirations. Within our still-dominant Freudian and Darwinian theories of development, I make the case that these and other spontaneous phenomena constitute as-yet-unmapped stages of adult maturation. That is, they are beyond Freud's final stage of genital primacy and Darwin's stage of mature fertility. They are also beyond the ego-developmental stages of recent Western psychology, such as described by transpersonal psychologists Ken Wilber, Jorge Ferrer, and Michael Washburn.

Just as Freud chose to name the fundamental developmental force libido or yearning, so too does the *Bhagavad-gita*, where Krishna says: "I am the passion [*kamo*: desire, yearning] in beings that manifests in the greatest maturation, truth, and goodness" (7.11). According to Freud, this yearning is experienced foremost as sexual desires based in genital puberty, the hallmark of biological adulthood.

Kundalini Yoga merely reopens the matter of human development and sees spine, hypothalamus, hypoglossus, pineal gland, and cerebral lobes as capable of undergoing "puberties" with all the alterations in physiology, identity, and existential life-purpose that are usually part of genital puberty, but now carry a more spiritual emphasis. Indeed, one of the oldest terms for yoga is "releasement beyond the genital thrall" (*shamanica medhra*).

Yet, in their exportation to the West, early teachers such as Krishnamacharya and B. K. S. Iyengar were not prepared to convey these endogenous depths, but modeled their instruction of the ancient asanas (see Sjoman 1996) upon the pedagogy and aesthetics of European ballet and gymnastics, complete with hardwood floors and mirrored walls, and thus the perfection of held positions became the disciplined practice. These positions tapped the outer edges of the Kundalini dimension and thus their singular therapeutic efficacy, but rarely so far as to enter inspired movement or transfixed stillness. Indeed, the concentrated willfulness of the practices quite effectively suppresses the path for the vast majority of practitioners.

Furthermore, to fit modern values, the inwardly "erotic" celibacy (*brahmacharya*), held for thousands of years to be essential to Kundalini yoga, has been largely dispensed with. Only a few modern practitioners fall in love and marry their yoga, with eight to ten hours of its spinal mysteries unfolding every day, decade after decade unto death, infused with the romance of a challenging yet deepening love. As noted in the *Bhagavad-gita*: "He is my true devotee, whose voice is choked with emotion of love for me, whose heart is moved with tears rolling down from the eyes" (11.14).

Indeed, Sri Aurobindo has called *brahmacharya* the foundation of all Indic wisdom traditions and cultural sophistication. He says:

> The secret of that gigantic intellectuality, spirituality, and superhuman moral force which we see pulsating in...the ancient philosophy, in the supreme poetry, art, sculpture, and architecture [of India]... was the all-important discipline of *brahmacharya* ... as also reflected in its role as the first of the four *Ashramas* or stages of the idealized, one hundred-year lifetime (and reincarnating series of such lifetimes). (1973)

Stages of Life

Despite the ideal of celibacy, the vast majority of classical practitioners do not remain celibate yogis after age twenty-five, but enter a second stage called sacred householder's life (*grihasthya ashrama*), which involves marriage and familial creation into the fifties, when one's own children begin to reproduce. Kundalini here takes the form of lineage propagation and the mysterious phenomena of yoga rarely manifest. A subsidiary householder's *brahmacharya* of one sexual union per month is considered within dharmic rhythms suitable for a moderated practice of Kundalini yoga. If the tongue-hypothalamus-pineal puberty should awaken, the couple might engage in the coitus reservatus of erotic yoga (*pariyanga*). According to the South Indian master, Thirumoolar:

> The pleasure of the sex union is endless when breath savoring is the only way. Anointing her body with unguents diverse—bedecking her tresses with flowers fragrant. Do you enjoy the damsel in passion's union? If your desire becomes devotion, prana will shoot up through the Spinal Pathway. Then your enjoyment will be endless. (Thirmuloolar 1993, V:1)

From the age of fifty to seventy-five, practitioners undergo the retired grandparent stage (lit., "forest-dwellers stage;" *vanaprasthya ashrama*), the time when one's grandchildren begin to bear children. The sense of the eternality of lineage spreads forth visibly in both directions as the embodied truth of human life. Thus, Kundalini matures these individuals to a life-long, creative marriage, an achievement that is fraught in the modern West. The powers of interpersonal devotion, forgiveness, apology, fidelity, honesty, and love mature between the spouses as Shakti and Shiva, the creative partnership of the human version of the primordial forces that manifest the entire universe.

Beginning at seventy-five years, the "world-shedding" stage of great-great-grandparenthood (*sannyasa ashrama*) can emerge. Now prana and consciousness, its most revered aspect, are evermore released from adaptation to worldly ways of life and one returns to the unconditioned or pure mind. Followers discern a deepening spiritual wisdom of eternal rather than contemporary truths regarding the nature of love, time, the perishable, and the imperishable. Consciousness and body recognize their different fates, the former as eternally aware and the latter as destined to wither into the primordial elements of earth, air, water, and fire. Death is understood as an entirely positive experience of a deep absorption, the great knowing of the originary source of all by the ever-awake consciousness (*maha-samadhi*).

Five generations of happy, creative marriages comprise the ideal manifestation of Kundalini, through the householder's path. Each family member matures to the point of being equal to the requirements of marriage and family life, with grand, great-grand- and great-great-grand-children and parents all flourishing. A world of such lineages fulfills the greatest possibility of the central maxim of all Indian wisdom traditions: "The world is, indeed, one family."

The joint-family system that incorporates newly-weds and extended families is a structural manifestation of this hoped-for ideal; the extremely low Indian divorce rate is a testimony to and remnant of this increasingly forgotten sociological ideal of a fully-dharmic, highly enlightened society. The energetic foundation of such a social order is Kundalini, from the quivering chromosomes of meiosis, to blush of adolescent puberty and new parenthood through great-great-grandparenthood, and the esoteric *khecari mudra* puberty whereby the pineal orgasm secretes the mystic *soma* or *amritas* (nectar of immortality).

Progress through Renunciation

There is also an alternative to the four-staged path wherein the power of the developmental trajectory begun in the womb predominates over sociological adaptation and family creation. In this second path, known as the naturalistic way without intentions (*nivritti dharma*) or lifelong renunciation, the incarnating movements of the fetus and newborn persist and mature to re-emerge later in life, giving rise to "beyond-reason," developmental yoga. Likewise, the common moments of spellbinding concentration of infants also re-emerge as naturalistic meditative awe and a matured, innocent wonder.

Instead of joining in the family trade and getting married—or leaving all worldly ties behind after some years—followers of this path become renunciants, yogis in the original sense. They may take advantage of Indian civil law which to this day grants "renouncing the world" to pursue the unequivocal absolute of unmodified spiritual aspirations of yoga, meditation, and religious practices as honorable grounds for divorce. Becoming lifelong renunciants, they soon manifest some degree of a bio-spiritual salutary effect upon others known as grace (*shaktipat*) and are often known as "spiritual-power bestowing saints" (*siddha-guru*).

The following schema situates Kundalini manifestations in this system:
<u>Beginning:</u> Sperm-ovum fertilization: zygote, blastula, and gastrula stages develop.
<u>First months:</u> Starting at the embryonic spinal base, Kundalini energy-intelligence guides the formation of the neural groove, the evolutionary funda-

ment of all evermore complex vertebrate bodies, from amphioxus on; gill- slits, tail and other "ontogeny phylogeny recapitulation" vestigial phenomena emerge and vanish; organs form, the heart beats as the causal body, reflective-mind body, neuro-endocrine mind/emotion body, mitochondrial-meridian vital energy body, and food-eating or fleshy body develop.

Middle months: The soul (*jiva*) enters the causal body.

Late months: The fetal body gestates toward fragile sufficiency as Kundalini completes its formation of the body and recedes into dormancy at the spinal base; the more generic prana of vital energy body continues as the flesh body's sustaining force, nourished with earthly foods and oxygen through the umbilical cord.

Birth: First breath, umbilicus cut, eye contact, reaching, neuro-endocrinal developmental utterances related to yogic developmental breathing—a "crying" that can be over-associated with adult anguish; psychomotor developmental movements akin to Yoga postures and hand signs emerge; there is nursing.

First decade: Teething, walking, play; glandular secretions underlying character-building sentiments of moral rules (*yamas* and *niyamas*) begin to fructify in the social and family context; language appropriates mind and tongue, and psychosomatic enculturation occurs; prepubescent pranic activity sustains the child's growth, visible as "the glow of childhood."

Second decade: Childhood prana activity intensifies, fomenting genital puberty or fertility as the embodiment of infinite future incarnations; hormonal-temporal urgencies quicken as gender-oriented desires; intermediate puberty of *yama* and *niyama* neuro-endocrine secretions emerge, with emphasis upon developmentally sublimative first stage of life; basic prepubescent postures and breath control emerge in willful and minimal practice or "spontaneous" forms

Third decade: Karma yoga, the life of responsible action and character maturation; the mind matures beyond childhood's scattered vitality toward sensory withdrawal, the capacity for sustained perception and careful attention; second stage of householder: family-creation of the path or the solitary mystic path is entered; diverse worldly involvements are varyingly dharmic or aligned with the endogenous maturational process; the maturations known as the "good neighbor" or "well-balanced person" emerge; if prana activity continues to intensify through the householder's life, the postgenital puberties quicken.

Fourth decade: Concentration begins: the dawning of awesome awareness of life as endless impermanence; soteriological radiance-secretions of spiritual zeal) and virtue emerge; advanced yogic practice matures the body for more intensified energies; meditation commences: devout and unwavering appreciation of the flow of endless impermanence and the poignant grace of life; the puberties of the linguistic anatomy underlying further meditative and mental maturations begin: tongue-extended "lion-pose" and inward-turned tongue become precursors of the pose where the tongue curls back in delight above the soft palate; this initiates the puberties of the hypoglossal-larnyx, hypothalamus, pituitary and pineal glands; there are activities like speaking in tongues and resounding sacred chantings.

<u>Fifth decade:</u> The desire-self identity matures toward the immortal soul-self identity; the auric glow of spiritual maturity emerges; a subtle pineal secretion-radiance of immortal-time essence and revitalizing hormones occurs; there is the uroboric embodiment of endless impermanence.

At this point, the Kundalini awakens, initiating the puberties of the six cakras and the inner shamanic heat; the eyes and pineal gland undergo puberty (*shambhavi mudra*), leading to an inner vision of the soul's radiances and the matter-time-space-scent-taste-light-bliss continuum emerges as a phenomenon of embodied eternal impermanence; the "delight-gesture of free consciousness" signals the occurrence of cerebral puberty (*unmani mudra*); there is internal or breathless respiration in the celstial ethers; grand-children may be born to householders who enter the third and fourth stages of life.

<u>Ultimate absorption:</u> The fully matured origin-consciousness emerges, first with, then without, future waverings (*sabija / nirbija samadhi*).

<u>25-50 incarnations:</u> Practitioners experience the exceedingly rare full maturation of the ensouled body as an immortal divine light body of extended longevity; complete maturation of all soul-body potentials ensures; there is ultimate liberation into eternal being-in-time.

The Saint

The ultimate result of this process is the saint of high maturity. An example is Hariakhan Baba, the several-thousand-year-old Babaji who both initiated Neem Karoli Baba, known best as the guru of Richard Alpert (Ram Dass), and sponsored the lineage of Paramahansa Yogananda, one of the first yogis to come to the West at the turn of the twentieth century (see Dass 1975; Satyeswarananda 1984). Yogananda attained additional esteem after his death in 1952 when his corpse showed no signs of decomposition, even after some twenty days. According to Los Angeles Mortuary Director, H. T. Rowe's notarized statement:

> The absence of any visual signs of decay in the dead body of Paramahansa Yogananda offers the most extraordinary case in our experience. . . .No physical disintegration was visible in his body even twenty days after death. . . . No indication of mold was visible on his skin, and no visible desiccation (drying up) took place in the bodily tissues. This state of perfect preservation of a body is, so far as we know from mortuary annals, an unparalleled one. . . No odor of decay emanated from his body at any time. . . There is no reason to say that his body had suffered any visible physical disintegration at all. (Yogananda 1977, 575).

According to the late Vinit-muni of Pransali, Hariakhan Baba was also Lakulisha (ca. 150 C.E.) from Kayavarohan who organized the Pashupata sect and is described as the 28th incarnation of Shiva according to several *Puranas*. He furthermore initiated Swami Kripalu and another saint whose corpse showed no signs of rigor mortis before his burial (Kripalu 1982). His image remains embossed in the Elephanta Island carvings (ca. 500-600) near Bombay which purport to show the "practicing [of Kundalini] yoga as the origin and culmination of all life" (Collins 1988, 48).

Followers of his school of Kundalini yoga practiced an ecstatic ritual including wild laughter, sacred singing, "dancing consisting of [all possible] motions of the hands and feet: upward, downward, inward, outward and shaking motion," a sacred "sound produced by the contact of the tongue-tip with the palate . . . after the dance when the devotee has again sat down and is still meditating on Siva," an "inner worship," and prayer (Collins 1988, 137-38). Later practitioners of the Pashupata sect, which spread throughout Hindu, Buddhist, and Jain India for some 600 years, moreover, was noteworthy for its scorn of the caste system and its belief in a deity capable of bestowing redemptive grace beyond the mechanistic dictates of karma. They believed that, as forest-dwelling Kundalini yogis, they transformed the strife of city-dwellers with their *shaktipat* blessings. As many other saints, Babaji thus represented Heaven lived on earth and provided those in his wake with redemption into fully dharmic life.

Bibliography

Aurobindo, G. 1960 [1920]. *The Brain of India*. Pondicherry: Sri Aurobindo Ashram.

_____, and The Mother. 1973. *On Love*. Pondicherry: Sri Aurobindo Ashram.

Banerjea, A.K. 1983. *Philosophy of Gorakhnath*. Delhi: Motilal Banarsidass.

Bharati, A. 1965. *The Tantric Tradition*. London: Rider.

Briggs, G. 1982. *Gorakhnath and the Kanphata yogis*. Delhi: Motilal Banarsidass.

Buddhananda, C., with S. Satyananda. 1978. *Moola Bandha, the Master Key*. Monghur: Goenka Bihar School of Yoga.

Bühnemann, G. 2000. *The Iconography of Hindu Tantric Deities*. Groningen: Egbert Forsten.

Collins, C.D. 1988. *The Iconography and Ritual of Siva at Elephanta*. Albany: State University of N.Y. Press.

Dass, A. and Aparna. 1978. *The Marriage and Family Book*. New York: Schocken.

Dass, B.H. 1975. *Hariakhan Baba, Known, Unknown*. Davis, Calif.: Sri Rama.

_____. 1981. *Ashtangha Yoga Primer.* Santa Cruz: Sri Rama.

Dyczkowski, M. 1987. *The Doctrine of Vibration.* Albany: State University of New York Press.

_____. 1992. *The Stanzas on Vibration.* Albany: State University of New York Press.

Elizarenkova, T. 1995. *Language and Style of the Ancient Rsis.* Albany: State University of New York Press.

Feuerstein, G. 1989. *Yoga, the Technology of Ecstasy.* Los Angeles: Tarcher.

_____. 1998. *The Yoga Tradition.* Prescott, AZ.: Hohm Press.

Foucault, M. 1980. *The History of Sexuality*, vol. 1. Translated by R. Hurley, New York: Vintage.

Govindan, M. 1993. *Babaji and the 18 Siddha Kriya Yoga Tradition.* Montreal: Kriya Yoga Publications.

Haines, R. 1972. *Handbook of Human Embryology.* Edinburgh: Churchill Livingston.

Harper, K. and R. Brown. *The Roots of Tantra.* Albany: State University of New York Press.

Iyengar, B.K.S. 1976. *Light on Yoga.* New York: Schocken.

Kinsley, D. 1997. *Tantric Visions of the Divine Feminine: The ten Mahavidyas.* Berkeley: University of California Press.

Krishna, G. 1970. *Kundalini: The Evolutionary Energy in Man.* Berkeley: Shambhala.

Kripalvanand, S. 1977. *The Science of Meditation.* Kayavarohan: D.H. Patel.

_____. 1982. *Guru prasad.* Sumneytown, Penn: Kripalu Yoga Ashram.

_____. 1989. *Realization of the Mystery: Commentary on the Hathayoga pradipika.* Unpublished manuscript. www.naturalmeditation.net/Design/meditation1RS.html

Muktananda, S. 1974. *The Play of Consciousness.* Campbell, Calif.: Shree Gurudev Ashram.

Mitchell, S. 2000. *Bhagavad Gita: A New Translation.* New York: Harmony Books.

Pradhan, V. G., trans. 1987. *Jnaneshvari.* Albany: State University of New York Press.

Ramanujan, A. K. 1973. *Speaking of Siva.* Baltimore: Penguin Books.

Ranade, R. 1994. *Jnaneshvar, the Guru's Guru.* Albany: State University of New York Press.

Sannella, L. 1976. *Kundalini, Transcendence or Psychosis?* San Francisco, CA: Henry Dakin.

Saraswati, D.S. Radhikananda, trans. 2002. *Dnyaneshwari Once Again.* Pune: Swami Radhikanand.

Satyeswarananda, S. G. B. 1984. *Babaji, the Divine Himalayan Yogi*. San Diego: The Sanskrit Classics.

Silburn, L. 1988. *Kundalini: Energy of the Depths*. Albany: State University of New York Press.

Sivananda, S. 1971. *Kundalini Yoga*. India: Divine Light.

Sjoman, N.E. 1996. *The Yoga Tradition of the Mysore Palace*. New Delhi: Abhinav Publications.

Sovatsky, S. 1998. *Words from the Soul: Time, East/West Spirituality and Psychotherapeutic Narrative*. Albany: State University of New York Press.

———. 1999. *Eros, Consciousness and Kundalini*. Rochester, VT: Inner Traditions.

———. 2005. *Your Perfect Lips*. Lincoln, Nebr.: Universe

———. 2006. "*Grihasthya: Sacred family psychotherapy.*" In *Consciousness, Yoga, and Indian Psychology*, edited by M. Cornellisen. Delhi: Centre for Studies in Civilization.

Thapar, R. 2001. *Early India*. Berkeley: University of California Press.

Thirumoolar, S. 1993. *Thirumandiram, a Classic of Yoga and Tantra*, vols. 1-3. Translated by D. Nataranjan. Montreal: Babaji Kriya Yoga.

Tirtha, S.V. 1993. *Devatma Shakti*. Delhi: S. Shivom Tirtha.

Vasu, R., trans. no date. *The Siva Samhita*. New Delhi: Oriental Book Reprint Co.

Venkatesananda, S. 1984. *The Concise Yoga Vasistha*. Albany: State University of New York Press.

Vishnu, S. V. T. 1993. *Devatma Shakti*. Rishikesh: Vigyan Press.

White, D.G. 1996. *The Alchemical Body*. Chicago: University of Chicago Press.

Yogananda, P. 1977. *Autobiography of a Yogi*. Los Angeles: Self Realization Fellowship.

Western Parallels

The Esoteric Teachings of Hermeticism

Althea Northage-Orr

Hermeticism is a philosophy that attempts to describe how the universe operates on the level of cosmos, earth, society, and individual. Like Daoism, it contains many divergent strains and represents broad patterns of thought rather than rigidly defined systems of logic and dogma. It has many aspects in common with Daoism, and many of the ideas within both systems developed in similar time periods.

This paper presents some common areas of thought and shows the development within Hermeticism of a tradition parallel to that of internal alchemy, which also had set guidelines designed to take practitioners on a path to immortality and transcendence. Similarities include:

—a belief in the existence of a non-personal creative force which is the source of all things;

—a system of ethics based on a few simple strictures against killing, stealing, lying, and sexual misconduct rather than highly elaborated rules;

—the belief that the soul could achieve a transcendent state of being through specialized techniques of purification, meditation, and physical practices;

—and the existence of a system of ritual and physical methods that served the transformation of the mortal human into an immortal being.

Parallel practices, moreover, included dietary guidelines, breathing techniques, visualizations, meditations, chants and incantations, physical conditioning, ritualized sexual practices, as well as alchemical and herbal preparations.

Hermeticism

Hermeticism has been called the "perennial philosophy," because it appears in many different periods and cultures in a variety of forms (see Huxley 1990). As Paul Newell puts it,

> Hermeticists believe that Hermeticism represents the common center of all forms of religion. The general idea is that the esoteric core of religions are the same; the exoteric shells, however differ due to the regional, environmental, historical and other factors at work at the time of their creation and development (www.galilean-library.org, "Hermeticism as a System")

As various religions and philosophies dominated the West, Hermeticism often took on the external guise of these religions while maintaining its core beliefs. Thus, Pythagorean schools taught that the Hermetic philosopher ought to follow the religion of the land to avoid persecution yet privately hold true to his beliefs (D'Olivet 1975, 14-16). Hermeticists accordingly define their teaching not as a religion but as a philosophy. As such, they see it not as a prescription of how to worship or as a definition of the nature of the deity, but as an attempt to explain the nature of the universe and, by inference, as a way to best exist in harmony with it.

Hermeticism appeared in various combinations with Pagan, Christian, and alchemical systems, yet maintained certain basic concepts that form its core. Sometimes it is confusing as to what these core beliefs are. For example, Hermeticism drew upon the magical system of Zoroastrianism without incorporating its essentially dualistic worldview. In many respects it resembles Gnosticism, another dualistic system that relied heavily on early Hermetic sources. It also found its way into esoteric Christianity, but does not have its millenarian tenets. Its practices, moreover, appear strongly in Western alchemy, but the latter can also be Gnostic, Islamic, or Christian. In the modern age, it permeates much of New Age thought and nearly all Western magical traditions.

What, then, are the core beliefs of Hermeticism? A classic definition includes the following:

1. There is an ultimate creative force that serves as the primal cause of the universe. This Monad, the One or the All, is an infinite mind which contains all creation and is immanent in it. It is transcendent, non-personal, and infinite.

2. Creation is an emanation of the All, sometimes referred to as its exhalation. Its purpose is to express the All by evolving through the material world back to a perfected state of being (i.e., the inhalation of the All). This is a process of involution that ends in a reunion with the unitary state, after which the great cycle begins again. Hermeticism is thus cyclical in its worldview and quite different from linear, millenarian thinking with its end of the world and ultimate separation of the damned from the elect (see Cohn 1995).

3. All creation is essentially good, divine in origin and participating in the divine, even if obscured by the imperfections of matter. Matter is only "fallen" in that it has yet to achieve its fully divine purpose. Like a gem that has not yet been faceted to reveal its beauty, creation awaits the revealing touch of humans in the Great Work (Smolley and Kinney 1999, 197).

4. The ultimate purpose of human beings is to identify with the eternal self and thus come to understand the purpose and laws that govern creation, allowing them to both perfect themselves and all creation (Huxley 1990)

5. Creation consists of overlapping layers of manifestation, in which each layer corresponds to and mirrors all others. By observation we can infer much about one level of reality through studying another. As Huxley explains, reality can "be known and understood both by observation and by a direct intuition, superior to discursive reasoning. This immediate knowledge unites the knower with that which is known" (1990, 59). In Hermeticism, knowledge is accordingly an essential way for human beings to perfect themselves.

Since it leaves out references to gods and other supernatural figures, many adherents consider Hermeticism a science that provides a way of understanding the purpose, workings, and laws of creation, as well as a roadmap to perfection of self and world. This is where the alchemical aspect comes in: perfection is not just theoretical but has to be attained through an active process of purification and development.

History

The origins of Hermeticism are unclear—or at least not documented formally in historical sources. Plato and other early thinkers tend to place its genesis into Egypt, locating Hermes Trismegistus, the mythical founder of alchemy, at the court of the pharaohs and making him the teacher of Moses who later carried the ideas into Judaism where it became the inner tradition known as Cabbala. Eric Hornung in *The Secret Lore of Egypt* similarly makes a strong argument for the Egyptian roots of the tradition, pointing out that many Hermetic ideas can be found in early Egyptian writings. Referring to an inscription on a temple statue at Karnak, dated to about 1360 B.C.E., he says:

> These formulations already sound quite hermetic, with their initiation into the wisdom of the Egyptian god Thoth, the later Hermes Trismegistus, and into a 'divine book' that the god wrote and revealed. But the roots of Hermeticism might reach deeper, back to the beginning of the second millennium BCE. (2001, 5)

Other authors cite passages from the *Papyrus of Nu* and *The Egyptian Book of the Dead* to show how hermetic and alchemical ideas of the purification and transformation of the body were embedded in these early texts.[1] Many Hermetic concepts certainly appear in various ancient contexts, such as the early monotheism of Akhenaton, Chaldean astrology and beliefs,[2] certain magical aspects of Zoroastrianism, and the Pythagorean thought of the sixth century B.C.E. Hermetic concepts, moreover, infused the mystery cults of ancient Greece and flowered in Neo-Platonic schools of thought.

Originally a collection of diverse ideas and orally transmitted traditions, Hermetic teachings were formalized in various written sources in the early centuries of the Common Era. Texts such as the *Corpus Hermeticum*, *The Emerald Tablet of Hermes*, and *The Golden Verses of Pythagoras* weave together diverse strains from multiple geographical areas (Persia, Egypt, Israel) and philosophers (Democritus, Empedocles, Pythagoras, Heirocles, Plato, Hippocrates,).[3]

Following this initial standardization, Hermeticism found its way into (or became hidden in) a variety of religious traditions. It made its way into Christianity through Augustine, Boetheus, and other church fathers. It reached Islam through the alchemical and medical tradition as developed by Al Razi, Ibn Sina, Avicenna, and Jabir Ibn Hayyam (Geber), brilliant Arabic physicians who greatly influenced the development of Greek medicine. In the late medieval period, it moved into the alchemical movement—largely underground in the West due to its association with Gnostic, Cathar, and Waldensian heresies. Later it emerged on the fringes of scholasticism where it became an object of study by Albertus Magnus, Thomas Aquinas, Arnau de Villanova, Ramon Llull, and Roger Bacon. It may also found its way into the Templar movement and later formed the basis of the Masonic Lodges. In the papal bull of 1317 John the XXII banned alchemy, leading to even greater secrecy (Constable 1990, 30).[4]

---

[1] For works that make a case for this, see Hauck 1999; Newall 2005; Reed 1966; Smoley and Kinney 1999.

[2] The Chaldeans placed a great emphasis on numbers, the three levels of being, star deities, and numerous correspondences among planets, colors, numbers, and stages of development (Reed 1966, 16, 88). Many of these facets later formed a major part of the Hermetic teachings. For an interesting discussion of early philosophers and their relationship to Hermetic ideas, see Reed 1966; 1990.

[3] The *Corpus Hermeticum* has numerous translations: a classic version is Everard 1978; a good modern one Copenhaver 1992. *The Emerald Tablet*, too, exists in many translations, from the eighth-century text by Jabir ibn Hayyab (Geber) to those by Sir Isacc Newton and Fulcanelli. Excellent working versions with good commentary are found in Burckhard 1967 and Hauck 1999. *The Golden Verses* is a collection of maxims attributed to Pythagoras and ostensibly passed down by his disciple Lysis in the sixth century B.C.E. Its text is first cited in the commentary of Hierocles (ca 430 C.E.). See D'Olivet 1975.

[4] Good sources ono history include Newall 2005 and Yates 1964. See Heindel 1998 for the Rosicrucian connection. Websites include the open directory project at www.dmoz.org/Society/Religion; Spirituality/ Esoteric_and_Occult/Hermeticism; www.geocities.com; www.mastermason.com/luxoccula/hermetic.htm.

This changed again in the fifteenth century, when Italian Renaissance scholars acquired classical Greek texts and eagerly studied Hermetic sources. They placed great emphasis on the tradition, even to the point that Cosimo de Medici ordered the translation of the *Corpus Hermeticum* to proceed before the works of Plato. At this point Hermeticism exerted a strong influence on the development of Renaissance humanism via the works of Pico della Mirandolla, Giordano Bruno, Marsilio Ficino, Paracelsus, and others, including also Roger Bacon, Isaac Newton, Raymond Lully, and so on (Constable 1990, 80-100). Ironically it influenced also the rise of what later became materialism and found its way into medicine and science through the alchemical tradition—giving rise to homeopathy, spagyric herbalism, and the modern system of Anthroposophy, responsible in its turn for biodynamic farming, Anthroposophical medicine, and Waldorf education..

In the Age of Enlightenment, Hermeticism provided a spiritual basis for anti-authoritarian political and masonic lodges that fueled the revolutionary movements of Europe. In the magical revival of the late nineteenth and early twentieth centuries, it spawned numerous lodges and orders such as The Golden Dawn, the O.T.O, the Rosicrucians, and the Theosophical movement. Many of these groups continue today either in their original forms or through groups which claim to be descended from them.[5]

Fundamental Concepts

Like Daoism, Hermeticism expresses itself in multiple theoretical strains. It contains both ecstatic and ascetic aspects and possessed a variety of systems of deity and spiritual beings that changed over time in accordance with dominant religious and cultural patterns. *The Kybalion*, a work of unknown provenance dated to the 1920s that practicing Hermeticists swear by, lists seven basic principles that sum up the heart of the teaching:

1. Infinite Mind: All things are an expression of the universal mind.

2. Correspondence: As above, so below—the microcosm is but a reflection of the macrocosm.

3. Vibration: Everything is perpetually in motion; nothing is ever static or unchanging.

4. Polarity: Everything contains the basic two poles.

5. Rhythm: Everything moves back and forth between the two poles in an eternal cycle of being and non being, arising and dissipation

---

[5] For more, see http://www.oto.org ; www.esotericgoldendawn.com ; www.hermetic-goldendawn.org; www.theosophical.com.

6. Cause and Effect: Every effect has its cause and everything happens according to cosmic principles which are an expression of the universal law.

7. Gender: The masculine and feminine principles are in all things which underlies the generation of all things. (Three Initiates 1940)

Infinite Mind

Infinite Mind is quite similar to Dao. It is the universal life force at the source of all things; a primordial One that manifests in primal, undifferentiated reality as the unknowable, infinite, non-gendered, and transpersonal power from which primordial duality arises. It contains the basic polarities of force and form, male and female, active and passive, light and dark, Heaven and Earth—pairs that are very similar to Daoist yin and yang.

From the mutual interaction of the two polar forces, moreover, just as in the Chinese system, comes the entire world of creation. It unfolds through phases of development that are metaphorically understood in terms of planetary, configurative forces. Physical manifestation can then be understood through the metaphors of the three alchemical levels of being: Salt, Mercury and Sulphur; the four elements: earth, air, fire, and water; and the five bodies, known by various names discussed below. Because all things are an expression of Infinite Mind, they are by nature divine. Creation is inherently good, and there is no opposing principle of evil. All that exists is essentially alive, infused by the creative mind and capable of attaining the perfect state. The latter exists in the mind of the All much as the oak tree exists in potential within the acorn.

Correspondence

The second principle of Correspondence is perhaps one of the most important Hermetic and alchemical ideas: the concept that the individual (microcosm) and the universe (macrocosm) can be understood through a process of observation and inductive thinking (see Three Initiates 1940). It finds its best expression in *The Emerald Tablet of Hermes*:

> That which is Below corresponds to that which is Above,
> And that which is Above corresponds to that which is Below,
> To accomplish the miracles of the One Thing.
> And just as all things have come from this One Thing,
> Through the meditation of One Mind,
> So do all created things originate from this One Thing
> through Transformation. (Hauck 1999, 51)

"That which is below" represents the microcosm, the physical reality of human beings and the earth. "Above" is the macrocosm, the less substantial realms which underlie physical matter which can also be described as the etheric blueprint, the energetic foundation, the configurative forces of heavens, planets, and the various invisible realms and beings. These realms mirror one another and are governed by an immutable, eternal law which Hermetic philosophers called Necessity (D'Olivet 1975, 31). They are different in form but similar in inner nature because they are made up of the same stuff, the *prima materia*, which *The Emerald Tablet* calls the "One Thing."

This relates closely to the Daoist concept of *qi*. While *qi* exists in many forms and on different levels, it remains one thing. Primordial *qi* is an expression of Dao; it finds its form within the human microcosm in varying densities and forms, such as the *qi* that flows in the meridians, the *weiqi* that flows under the skin and protects the body, or the chest-*qi* that regulates the breath and heart. But everywhere and in every form *qi* is always *qi*. Likewise, in Daoist thought Heaven and Earth mirror one another. Imbalance in the human realm manifests as imbalances in the weather and the seasons, thus in the geological and heavenly realms. Imbalances in Heaven are similarly reflected in the health of everything on earth. Everything comes from Dao: heavens, gods, nature, and human beings all exist within it and are answerable to its laws.

"Through the meditation of One Mind" refers to the existence of all reality in the workings of the Infinite Mind, which then acts via its meditation upon the *prima materia* to "accomplish the miracles of the One Thing." This notion is also expressed in *The Golden Verses*:

> Begin thy work,
> First having prayed to the Gods to accomplish it.
> Thou, having mastered this,
> That essence of gods and mortal men shalt know
> Which all things permeates and all obey.
> And thou shalt know that Law have established
> the inner nature of all things alike.
> So shalt thou hope not for what can not be,
> Nor aught that is possible shall escape thee.[6]

Hermetic philosophers believe that anything true will be valid on all levels and under all circumstances. They see truth as provisional, based upon observation and modify it as their understanding develops. They find truth by observing the particular and projecting observed patterns into the cosmic or by taking the cosmic and applying it to the specific. What is observed in the seasons must also be observed in the human; what is observed in the human will be manifest in the operations of the heavens. Using the metaphors of the Seven Planets and the Four Elements they looked at patterns and qualities, which they could then

---

[6] This version is my own, based on the Nicholas Rowe translation (1952). The only changes made were the use of inclusive language and an occasional smoothing out of syntax. So "man" becomes "human", and the phrase "men are children of the gods" becomes "we are children of the gods." This is also very close to the Florence Wirth version popularized by Annie Besant. See **www.sacred-texts.com**.

use to describe the characteristics of individual humans, herbs, metals, health conditions or anything at all. Likewise the Chinese developed the five-phases system of correspondences to describe the qualities of everything. Both contain correspondences that allow the careful observer to determine the best (and worst) time for any action, the energetic qualities of things and their corresponding balancing qualities, the tides of the individual, nature and the heavens.

On the other hand, all that is discerned is also limited by the position and knowledge of the observer. The truth of the child is not the truth of the adult, although what is essential in the former will be retained in the latter. Knowledge is never absolute, but constantly evolving. While broad patterns are discernable, application is at best a chancy thing, determined by the context of the observer and best understood as a provisional attempt at understanding rather than as a fixed rule. In both Hermeticism and Daoism "The Way that can be told is not the eternal Way."

Nonetheless, in Hermeticism humans *can* know about themselves, and by knowing themselves they can infer much about the universe, which in turn can be known by observing the patterns of nature. This knowledge guides people to deeper knowledge and leads to a gradual reunion with the divine over the course of time. Everything mirrors everything else, and humans stand at the center, as if were, between Heaven and Earth. We are limited by our physical state of being but we are still participating in the divine. Smolley and Kinney explain it by saying: "Hermeticists do not so much see man as the creature in need of redemption, but rather as the redeemer of the light of consciousness that has become trapped in the darkness of matter" (1999, 197).

Thus the goal of the alchemist, and ultimately the purpose of creation, is to realize a state of fully spiritualized or perfected matter. On the level of the macrocosm this means the end of creation in the perfection of all things and assumption into the Infinite Mind. Creation then disappears into the formless as the inhalation of the All, only to begin again as the exhalation of the All. On the level of the microcosm, at the same time, the goal is the perfection of Adam, the human, as Adam Kadmon, the transcendent and immortal essential human.

Another important aspect of Correspondence is that it gave alchemists and Hermetic philosophers a tool not only for understanding things but also for creating change. To create a particular change, they could use the principle of resonance—another concept essential to Daoist thought, where it is called *ganying*—and induce change by aligning themselves with energies of the proper correspondence. So, for example, if a physician wished to cure someone of a hot and dry disease, he would choose herbs that had a lunar correspondence, because the moon is cool and moist. Just as in the five phases system of traditional Chinese cosmology, colors, metals, planets, numbers, sounds, notes, and all things had a correspondence. By learning to work with correspondences

Hermetic practitioners could change the vibration of the target and thus transform it.

Vibration
Vibration, first described by the atomist Democritus (4th c. B.C.E.) on the basis of Pythagoras's theory of numbers and musical intervals, is the corollary of Correspondence. Again very much like the Chinese understanding of *qi*, which is said to vacillate at different frequencies and sound in varying intensities (Kohn 2005, 15-16), it means that all things vibrate and are in constant motion. Just as each object's vibratory rate determines how it exists in the world, so this rate is subject to change through applied energy and can be either slowed down or speeded up. Today firmly substantiated in particle and wave theories as well as in the modern understanding of color and light, these ideas formed the basis of laboratory alchemy, centered on the application of heat—a basic form of energy—to create change in matter, moving the solid to the gaseous, the gaseous back to the solid. Hermetic practitioners also used Vibration to develop sound therapies with the help of incantations and chanting that altered the vibratory rate of the person and thereby transformed emotions and create higher states of awareness. Today it is the basis of whole healing systems known as vibrational medicine and plays a key role in sound therapy (see Gerber 1998; Gass 1999).

Polarity and Rhythm
Polarity and Rhythm are closely allied. As all things move and change, they have the rhythm of the pendulum, swinging from one extreme to the other. What goes up must come down; what swings right must return left. The philosopher's task in this context is to rise above the pendulum swing by establishing himself firmly in the objective, detached position of the divine self, a vantage point from which he could view all changes with equanimity—not unlike Zhuangzi talking about the center of the hub at the core of all mentation (ch. 2) and *The Golden Verses* statement: "In all the mean is best."

This feature also allowed philosophers to predict to some degree what was likely to happen, so they could move without expanding needless energy or resisting the inevitable. Similarly, they could ameliorate the effects of events by preparing for them. Because the cosmos contains polarities, human beings can learn to predict when what kind of change will occur. They can thus time alchemy, ritual, and physical practices in accordance with the rhythms of the greater world.

Polarity and Rhythm both emphasize that everything contains the two poles of positive and negative (in the magnetic sense, not "good" or "bad"). They are quite similar to the Daoist forces yin and yang. Just as yang represents energy, light, movement, engendering, and Heaven, the primal pole in the West is masculine and positive; it represents energy, movement, light, i.e., the creative force in its potential and active aspect. Similarly, where yin is dark, structive, concrete, and feminine, the other extreme in the West is the Great Mother, the bringer into being, formation, solidity, and denseness. Yang/active and yin/passive closely match the polarities in the West. In both systems, life takes place between these two interdependent and constantly moving powers.

Gender

Another dimension of Polarity and Rhythm is the principle of Gender. While the physical form has gender and is decidedly male or female, the soul is inherently neither but occupies both aspects. Every woman has a masculine aspect; every man, a feminine part. The masculine aspect is active; it acts upon the feminine. But as nothing is purely yin or yang, none is only masculine or feminine either, and all things are yin or yang, masculine or feminine, only relative to something else. Thus the body is yin/feminine relative to the spirit, and is acted upon by it. The emotional soul is yang/masculine relative to the body, and acts upon it, but is yin/feminine relative to the mind, which ought to guide and act upon the emotions.

Gender also means that there must be an interaction between the masculine and feminine for anything to be created. The masculine must act upon the feminine in a mirroring of the Infinite Mind acting upon the prima materia to bring creation into being. This is reflected in the alchemical transmutation of the self. The active principle of mind, masculine in nature, must act upon the passive unconscious in order to create. This is central to all Hermetic magic; it is the reason why Hermeticism developed so many ways of activating the unconscious through rituals full of color, sound, movement, and images. Imagination is the force that generates change in the self or—if employed powerfully enough—in the external world through its impact on the astral realms.

> Corresponding to the tripartite division of the small world of man [microcosm] into body, soul, and spirit was a cosmic soul which dwelled in the realm of the stars. This cosmic soul reflected the ideas of the higher, transcendental sphere of the divine intellect, and through the influence of the stars these ideas imprinted their eternal 'symbols' on the lower, physical transient sphere. Man thereby has the possibility of manipulating events in the earthly sphere, using magical practices…to effect this middle sphere of the cosmic soul. Contact is established through the fine material of the "sidereal" or "astral body" that invisibly surrounds man. (Roob 2001, 19)

This notion of the generation of effects through the proper use of masculine and feminine principles is what is meant by the alchemical marriage, a key concept also in Daoist internal alchemy. As described in the Western tradition, the union of the two poles results in a fusion that mirrors divine creation and which in turn produces a new, third creation. By marrying the masculine mind to the feminine soul, the eternal self emerges. In laboratory alchemy a similar process occurs. The substance to be transformed must be broken into its component pieces during the dissolution phase which mirrors our descent into matter and into fragmentary consciousness. This process is known as *negrido* or blackening. Next comes the purification phase in which each of the three aspects (matter, soul, and spirit or salt, mercury, and sulphur) must be purified. It is called *albedo* or whitening. The third stage is *rubedo* or reddening. Here the purified substances are transformed and enlivened through the action of fire, a process which on the psychological plane would be the perfection of self through an ecstatic connection to the divine. The final stage is coagulation, the recombination of the pieces into the reconstituted and perfected "gold" or "resurrection body" (Smoley and Kinney, 1999, 187). The eternal emerges from the mortal, freed by transformation even as "through the meditation of One Mind, so do all created things originate from this One Thing through transformation."

Cause and Effect
The Principle of Cause and Effect builds upon the other principles, for it exemplifies the fact that nothing in the universe is random and is an expression of divine order unfolding according to law. "Every effect has its cause" (Three Initiates 1940, 22) means that nothing is meaningless. Of course, from the human perspective meaning is often unclear; our vantage point is too limited to understand the vast chains of cause and effect in the evolutionary unfolding of events. What may seem pointless in an individual life is understandable if one looks to the tide of his or her surrounding society. Individuals receive impulses from their families, societies, the consciousness of the era; they are affected by all these factors.

Events are never meaningless, but always proceed from their causes. Ultimately this sets up a paradox: we are conditioned beings, yet we are also free to act and create. That is the divine power within us, which is exemplified in Hermeticism as the "higher self" or in Daoism as the spirit (*shen*). Hermeticism resolves this by postulating: we are free in direct proportion to the degree to which we are awake. In other words, when we connect with the creative and aware part of ourselves, we can act freely in response to events When we are asleep, unconscious, we are only reactive and conditioned. We are always subject to Necessity for nothing is outside the Law of the Infinite Mind (Dao), but we *can* choose how we respond. If we are unconscious, we are subject to our material and unconscious state; we are acted upon. If we are awake, we are creative and can act upon events.

The degree to which we are awake also determines our ability to see and understand the swing of the pendulum, the tides of events, which in turn gives us a substantial ability to control or ameliorate them. This is reminiscent of the advice of the *Yijing*, which counsels the individual to be wise and in alignment with the current of events. The whole secret is to become aware and conscious enough to rise above the swing of the pendulum, to become one who is causative rather than one affected. This is the true meaning of the lines from the *Golden Verses*: "Fate gives the least of evil to the good."

The idea is that events are what they are, but that the good can make them serve their growth if nothing else, and in many cases they can survive them better than others, because their spirits remain intact. So one must "bear meekly thou thy lot, nor grieve at it; but cure it as thou canst." Thus one will reap the best that can come, even if the local situation is bad. After service in this life, one can go on. In both Daoism and Hermeticism, the next step on the path is called the Inner Planes, matching the celestial administration in Daoism. From this vantage point one can then affect what is happening upon earth, becoming a guide or causative force. Simultaneously one is still affected by higher forces. Only when one has become reunited with the Infinite Mind or Dao does one become part of the ultimate cause and therefore immune to the effects of Necessity.

Deities

In addition to believing firmly in an underlying cosmic power and a set of fundamental principles, Hermeticists as much as Daoists acknowledge an intricate hierarchy of beings, both living and dead, natural and supernatural. As D'Olivet notes:

> Polytheism was not in their opinion what it has become in ours, an impious and gross idolatry, a cult inspired by the infernal adversary to seduce men and to claim for itself the honors which are due only to the divinity; it was a particularization of the Universal Being, a personification of its attributes and its faculties. (1975, 15)

Deities on the highest level in both systems thus represent pure aspects of the Dao or Infinite Mind; they are powerful and transcendent, and possess enormous powers. Just like Daoists venerate the Queen Mother of the West, the Lord King of the East, the Three Ones, the Dipper, the planets, and so on, so Hermetic adepts honor Saturn, Jupiter, and Mars as well as numerous local and tribal deities. They recognize these beings as real constellations of cosmic energy that have an impact on the terrestrial realm.

Beyond the celestial powers, there are also beings such as angels and elementals directly tied to the earth. In Daoism, these correspond to dragons, foxes, and other archetypal entities. Both systems moreover recognize the existence of beings that have moved beyond their earthly existence to a transcendent state; they include, saints, spirit guides, and ascended masters (Tyson 2000, 423-30, 613-15, 663-64; in Daoism, see Kaltenmark 1979, 31). Just as Daoists have various rituals to place the practitioner in contact with or even command these various beings, Hermeticism has whole branches of magic devoted to the such contact as well as rituals for the evocation and conjuration of other-dimensional beings (see Bardon 1981)

Both, too, see practitioners ascend systematically through the hierarchy. Thus Daoists begin by undertaking bodily cultivation, then transform their consciousness, and eventually become immortals and serve in the celestial administration, often starting by managing the realm of the dead, then gradually serving at higher levels of being to eventually become celestial perfected (see Kohn 1990). Similarly, Hermetic adepts progress towards immortality and attain the status of spirit guide or ascended master, i.e., of a being who is still actively concerned with the guidance of humans on earth.

What happens beyond that point is not clear. Classical sources tell numerous stories of people, such Heracles or Asclepius, who set out as mortals and become divine by passing a series of trials on earth. Daoists have similar tales of immortals, such as Lü Dongbin, who undergo increasingly demanding trials before they are taught the necessary techniques. Both traditions have a hierarchy of order, but unlike in Daoism where different entities can metamorphose into all kinds of beings, in the West some never go beyond their state. Humans or angels can thus conjure up and command a *djin* or an elemental because the latter is lower in the hierarchy. Should the human lose control of the magical operation, the elemental can overpower and destroy him. Angels, moreover, always have power over both since they belong to a higher order of being. Yet while they interact, each are a class of their own and humans never become angels or elementals, nor can the latter transfer into the human or angel levels. They are separate strands of evolution rather than evolutionary stages.

The path for human beings in both systems is to transform and purify their physical nature into a higher energetic state so they can become entities of pure energy capable of manifesting in both physical or non-physical form. In Daoism, this is expressed in the notion that one must sublimate essence (*jing*) and transform it into energy (*qi*), which in turn is transformed into spirit (*shen*) that takes shape as the immortal embryo, the yang body or body of light.

Hermetic literature, too, speaks of the creation of an immortal body, although mostly in obscure sources. More often it mentions achieving an immortal body by purifying the self so that at the time of death one becomes a transcendent being. This is somewhat similar to the Daoist immortality method known as deliverance from the corpse, in which the adept transforms into the transcendent body at the moment of death (see Robinet 1979; Cedzich 2001). In addition, just as Daoists' bodies vanish completely when they transit into the immortal realm, there are some Western examples of adepts who avoid death altogether. Thus Enoch of the Old Testament was directly assumed into Heaven; the Blessed Mother in Catholic teaching did not die but ascended body and soul. Jesus, although dead on the cross, obtained a transcendent body in which he to manifest physically so that the apostle Thomas could place his fingers in the wound in his side. And, of course, lack of decay in the exhumed body is one of the parameters for becoming a saint in the Catholic church. Both traditions, therefore, have a vivid history of human beings transcending into the spirit realm in various ways.

The Three Bodies

Hermetic teachings propose three levels of being: salt, mercury, and sulphur. Salt is physical form, parallel to the Daoist concept of essence, the first of the Three Treasures; it is the physical body composed of matter and subject to birth, maturation, aging, and death. The salt level of any entity—plant, mineral, animal, or human—is thus the actual physical substrate.

Mercury symbolizes the etheric or astral body, often associated with the soul or animus and loosely matching the level of qi in the Daoist system; it animates the physical body and gives it heat, warmth, sensations, and so on. Common to animals as well as humans, it represents the animating life force and the emotions.

Sulphur, third, is the transcendent and immortal spirit that occupies and governs the other bodies; it corresponds to the Daoist level of spirit. It is not to be confused with the soul, although the mercury level, too, is light and lively, has an affinity is to alcohol (spirits), and is the animating force of the person. Some philosophers, such as Rudolf Steiner, have clarified the distinction by referring to the astral body as the "animal soul"—animals clearly possessing souls in that they have feelings, sensations, and emotions—and contrasting it with the "sentient soul" or "immortal soul" which emanated at the first moment of creation and continues to evolve through ongoing incarnations on earth. This soul ultimately becomes a directing force to create and gestate the immortal body (Steiner 1994). Any reference to "soul" or "spirit" in Western literature should thus be carefully examined with regard to its exact connotation.

Practitioners of alchemy purify all three levels to refine and recombining them into a new immortal form. They use laboratory alchemy to this end by mutating natural substances into potentized and empowered medicines such as described in the writings of Paracelsus (Waite 1976, 47-58). In their laboratory work they produced concoctions known as spagyric medicines, substances which were purified on one, two, or all three levels. Applied merely on the salt level, such a medicine could cure the physical body. On the salt and mercury levels, it would be distilled with ethanol or "spirits" and emerge as a spagyric tincture. Form this, alchemists could further extract the herb-infused ethanol and then add the purified mineral salts back to again create a spagyric drug. A remedy of this sort acted potently on the astral or etheric body. To refine materials on all three levels, they would draw off the essential oils in a process which later gave rise to aromatherapy. Recombining all three, they produced a so-called magistery, a medicine that directly impacted the sentient soul; it could correct karmic imbalances or problems arising from disharmonies on the cosmic level. Modern vibrational medicine is a direct offshoot of this tradition, employing potentized remedies such as homeopathic medicines, essential oils, nosodes, and flower essences.

Hermetic adepts further applied the same concepts of refinement, purification, and transformation to the spiritual path, working along very similar lines as Daoist practitioners of internal alchemy. To achieve their goal of transforming the physical, emotional/energetic, and spirit bodies, they utilized special meditations, ritual work, and sometimes sacred sex (see Patai 1990).

The Five Levels

A more complex but similar system that integrates the ancient Egyptian model, Hermeticism divides the human being into five levels (see Masters 1991; Steiner 1994). Here the physical body is called the Aufu; it represents the salt or essence aspect, i.e., the physical being which lives, dies, and is subject to decay.

The second body is the Ka; it corresponds to the lower aspect of the mercury or energy level and is known in vibrational medicine as the etheric or ether body. An energetic template for the physical body and its double, it is a finer and subtler aspect of the person that animates the physical part. and endows it with sensation and warmth, generally providing an organizing principle. Not unlike the material soul (po) in the Daoist system, the Ka departs the physical body at death and returns to earth. Disruptions on the etheric level cause cancers and/or other diseases.

This third level is the astral body called the Haidit, the higher aspect of the person on the mercury level; it is the body of emotional experience. Subtler and more volatile than the Ka, it is capable of taking different forms. It is the body of the imagination, of dreams, and of trance journeys, inviting a state in which one can become anything: male or female, animal or divine, master or slave. Whatever the Haidit believes, moreover, becomes manifest in the two lower bodies so that what someone experiences in deep trance will duly manifest in their physical body. Hysterical illnesses and forms of hypochondria are an example of this as is the use of intentional imaging and visualization in modern hypnotic healing. The term "psychosomatic" reflects the same connection.

The fourth and fifth bodies are known as the Sahu and the Khu and both belong to the sulphur or spirit level. The highest and subtlest is the Sahu, said to be the essential soul of the individual, that which was emanated from the All in its pure potential form. This is like the spirit in Daoism and Chinese medicine. Hermetic philosophers believe that the Sahu's purpose is to descend into physical life, gather experiences through the multiple incarnations, and eventually reach fully expressing. Thus the microcosm of the individual soul evolves to its greatest extent and becomes complete and perfected—Adam becomes Adam Kadmon—just as the macrocosm of all creation becomes perfected through the process of evolution. As all creation when fully expressed is the ultimate perfection of the universal mind, so the Sahu—a kernel of ultimate possibility unique in creation—finds its highest expression by building a body of experience that is transcendent, immortal, and fully expressive of its being.

This body, finally, is called the Khu; it built up over many lives, rising and maturing through prior experiences. Only brought into being through the work and effort of the individual, it corresponds in many ways to the immortal embryo gestated by *neidan* practitioners.

In a different vein, the five levels of the person in the Hermetic system can also be compared to the five psychological aspects as defined in Chinese medicine and activated in Daoist practice (see Ishida 1989). The Aufu or physical body here would correspond to the will (*zhi*), the creative life force associated with the kidneys and generative organs that expresses itself in the drive to survive, procreate, and express in physical form. Second, the Ka that at death separates from the body and returns to earth, thus precipitating the decay of the Aufu, is analogous to the material soul (*po*), which similarly returns to the earth at death, lacks sentience, and is associated with breathing and the lungs.

The Haidit, the emotional or astral body, third, is analogous to the spirit soul (*hun*), associated with the liver in both systems. Representing the personality or psyche of the individual, neither the Haidit nor the spirit soul dissolves immediately upon death but undergoes a process of purgation and integration often described in terms of heaven and hell. In some cases, moreover, this aspect of the person does not dissipate readily and has trouble being released from its worldly desires, addictions, and attachments, thus lingering about and haunting the living in its effort to integrate its experiences. In both East and West spirits trapped at this level of disembodied desire are referred to as ghosts and are generally considered displaced, if not actually dangerous. Only after the Ka has assimilated its experiences and moved on, can the Sahu, the spirit aspect, reincarnate, carrying with it whatever consciousness has been built up in the Ka.

The Sahu, then, is analogous to the spirit (*shen*), associated in China as much as in Egypt with the heart and said to be formless and in control of the other aspects. The Khu, finally, is the mediator between body and spirit, water and fire, and represents the ability to take in energies and experiences and configure them into useable materials for the ultimate immortal being. In the Chinese system it corresponds to intention (*yi*), associated with the spleen, the planet Saturn, and the person's conscious focus. The planetary association, moreover, matches Western astrology, where Saturn not only rules the growth of physical form but also has to do with developing experience into karma and thus the creation of the body of ultimate destiny.

Working with all five levels and aspects of the person, Hermetic practitioners strive to build an illumined consciousness in the form of the Khu capable of surviving the dissolution of the three lower bodies and influencing future incarnations, so that the Sahu can continue its development. Once the Khu has achieved sufficient power it is capable of assimilating the energies of the three lower bodies into itself and, like the immortal embryo in Daoism, becomes fully immortal either at death or by bypassing death altogether (Masters 1991).

Preparation

The path of personal perfection through Hermetic teachings and alchemy consists of preparation, purification, and perfection. Its prime source is *The Golden Verses of Pythagoras*, which presents a detailed outline in quite specific terms. According to this, preparation means:

> Pay honor first to the Immortal Gods,
> As order hath established Their Choirs:
> Reverence the Oath.
> The Heroes great and good
> revere thou next,
> and earth's good Geniuses,
> paying to them such honors as are due.

Fabre D'Olivet comments:

> Pythagoras . . . begins his teaching, by laying down a principle of universal tolerance, he commands his disciples to follow the cult established by the laws whatever this cult may be, and to adore the Gods of their country, whatever these Gods may be; enjoining them only, to guard afterwards their faith—that is, to remain inwardly faithful to his doctrine, and never to divulge the mysteries. (1995, 14)

Followers are thus to create the proper priorities in life, putting spiritual dedication to the All first, next honoring the gods, demigods, spirits, and angels. Last of all they should pay honor to the Heroes or living sages. Preparation thus means that one places God or the All squarely at the center of one's being and recognizes that commitment to the spiritual life as one's primary duty.

In addition, followers have to lead a morally good life and follow certain basic ethical principles. This is very similar to the Daoist tradition, which emphasizes precepts together with the engendering of specific virtues (see Kohn 2004). *The Golden Verses* contains various ethical directives that address obligations both to each other and to society as a whole. It also contains rules meant to guide practitioners in relation to their own body, mind, and spirit. It first outlines the necessity to observe filial piety and the bonds of kinship. Having satisfied these obligations aspirants should choose friends who will further them on their virtuous path and to whom they will remain loyal. They should also lead a balanced life, neither being too ascetic nor too indulgent. As the text says:

> Honor thy parents and thy nearest kin;
> of others—make the virtuous thy friends:
> yield to their gentle words, their timely acts,
> nor for a petty fault take back your love.
> Thy belly first, sloth, luxury and rage.
> Do nothing base with others or alone;
> and above all things, thine own self respect..

While this addresses the necessity to establish mental control over physical appetites, intemperance, and the emotions, the following emphasizes the need to find balance, peace, and equanimity and to treat others with respect and compassion. Adepts should be aware that "wealth comes and goes" and that "all must die," remaining always conscious of the constant change of the universe. They should be wary and "let no one's word or deed seduce" them "to do, or say, anything not to thy best good." Beyond this, *The Golden Verses* encourage followers to be moderate in their practices. "Use discretion in lustral rites and the freeing of thy soul," the text states, implying that extremes are to be avoided in favor of the balanced application of oneself in all respects and at all occasions of life.

The text moves on to reiterate the need for taking care of the physical body, nurturing the mind, leading a modest life, and achieving contentment, then turns to the exultation of the spirit. This is reached by undertaking a daily self-examination of one's deeds, thoughts, and practices, asking "How have I sinned? What done? What duty missed?" In response, one should rejoice in goodness and reproach oneself for misdeeds, creating a resolution to do better the next day. Preparation concludes by fixing one's intention firmly upon the Great Work, taking a formal oath, and invoking divine aid in accomplishing it.

> By the One who gave the Tetractys to our soul,
> Fount of Eternal Nature, this I swear:
> Begin thy work first having prayed to the Gods to accomplish it.

Purification

Purification, the second part of the Hermetic path, much like Daoist cultivation, involves a series of specific practices, such as diet, sexual techniques, meditation, and elixirs. Still, there are some important differences.

To begin, in Daoism dietary modification known as abstention from grain (*bigu*, see Arthur 2006)—no grains, only raw food, herbal concoctions, and complete fasting—is an important prerequisite to harmonizing the body's energies and setting the stage for internal cultivation. Similarly the ancient Pythagoreans followed specialized vegetarian diets with some unusual strictures, such as the avoidance of beans.

Hermeticists, on the other hand, do not usually propose dietary guidelines. They did, however, embrace the notion that one can alter one's vibration by eating exclusively certain foods that correspond to the energy that one is trying to create. For example, during an elemental or planetary working, the adept might eat only foods corresponding to that element or planet. Similarly, traditional Western herbalists utilized a practical application of the principle of Correspondence known as the "Doctrine of Signatures." According to this, masters chose foods and herbs based on their correspondences. They would, for example, prescribe solar foods and herbs for a depressed individual or give lunar-powered ones to a woman suffering from infertility.

Hermeticists today still utilize food classifications that equate them with energy centers and match their eating accordingly. Proteins, to give an example, are Saturnian and grounding; they help people in need of this particular trait. All drugs, herbs, and ingested substances have similar cosmic matches and can be very efficacious for certain types of change.

A similar situation prevails with regard to sexual practices. Just as Daoists emphasize the transmutation of sexual essence and often encourage partner practice, there are some Egyptian documents that show related techniques. However, Hermeticism lacks a coherent tradition of sexual cultivation or at least it is not documented. Information tends to be negative in that Hermetic authors on occasion warn against the dangers of sexual practices as transformational techniques. Still, there is some indication that sexual practices played a role in the Cabbala (notably in the work of Isaac Luria). Beyond that, many modern magical lodges employ systems of sexual magic which they claim go back to antiquity, but which tend to imitate Hindu and Tibetan methods. On the whole, therefore, both in terms of diet and sexual cultivation, the Daoist tradition provides much more explicit information and detailed instructions.

This is not the case with regard to meditation. Here both traditions make use of numerous different techniques, beginning with a fundamental focus on breathing and mental concentration. The main difference may be that Daoists place a greater emphasis on visualization while Hermeticists employ more sound techniques. The latter are particularly effective in altering consciousness both by virtue of their vibration and through their magical powers. Sound changes vibration when chanted in pure tones rather than as words with specific intellectual content; it magically controls entities when pronounced precisely and in specifically determined formulas, calling forth deities, spirits, and other forces. Examples include the model used in the "Key of Solomon" and the Enochian system channeled by John Dee in the sixteenth century. Hermeticism have used them for generations with great success.

Western practitioners frequently mixed these practices with visualization of specific deities, mental states, trance journeys, or energetic transformations—all features familiar in the Daoist context. In general, they believed that sensory input could impress specific, change-producing energies upon the unconscious. Applying various modes of sensory reprogramming through meditation was thus fundamental to the Hermetic system.

Again, quite like Daoists, Hermeticists also employed physical techniques, i.e., body meditations that involved specialized postures and movements as well as ecstatic dances and other structured movements, for the alteration of consciousness or modulation of emotions. They often combined these with sound and visualizations, creating a complete sensory drama to transform the self. Already ancient philosophers such as Democritus, Pythagoras, and Crito describe such practices as aids in clearing negative emotions (see Somnji 2002**).** Modern masters, such as George Gurdjieff and Robert Masters, continue the tradition today (see Masters 1991).

Perfection

The ultimate goal that all Hermetic practitioners and Western alchemists had in common was the creation of the elixir of immortality, the quintessence of life and medicinal analogue of the Philosophers' Stone—a substance that would confer eternal being upon whoever consumed it,. Numerous stories tell of rare individuals. such as Nicholas Flamel and his wife Pernelle, who found or created the perfect recipe for the quintessence (Constable 1990, 46-47).

What is more important however is that in the process of this search a whole system of medicines was created that were designed to affect the astral and etheric levels of being. Modern Homeopathy and the Flower Essences of Bach and others are examples of this. While not everyone agrees as to their effectiveness, both systems have many followers. Spagyric medicines and the system of alchemical preparations begun by the Arabic physicians and carried on by Paracelsus continue to be utilized today. Whole companies are dedicated to their production and their efficacy is attested by physicians and patients worldwide.

Hermeticism has touched nearly every aspect of modern life. It is to be found in quantum physics, modern medicine, and metaphysics. It still is found in art, literature, and philosophy. Indeed, its influence is so pervasive that is almost invisible, it is so much a part of our daily consciousness. For those who wish to follow a spiritual path outside the container of western mainstream religions, Hermeticism still offers a powerfully appealing path.

Bibliography

Albertus, Frater. 1974. *The Alchemist's Handbook*. York Beach, Maine: Samuel Weiser.

Arthur, Shawn. 2006. "Life Without Grains: *Bigu* and the Daoist Body." In *Daoist Body Cultivation*, edited by Livia Kohn, 91-122. Magdalena, NM: Three Pines Press.

Baines, John. 2001. *The Secret Science: Hermetic Philosophy Book One*. New York: John Baines Institute.

Bardon, Franz. 1981. *Initiation Into Hermetics*. Wuppertal: Dieter Ruggeberg.

———. 1984. The *Practice of Magical Evocation*. Wuppertal: Dieter Ruggeberg.

Burckhardt, Titus. 1967. *Alchemy*. Long Mead, UK: Element Books.

Cedzich, Ursula-Angelika. 2001. "Corpse Deliverance, Substitute Bodies, Name Change, and Feigned Death: Aspects of Metamorphosis and Immortality in Early Medieval China." *Journal of Chinese Religions* 29: 1-68.

Cleary, Thomas. 1996. *Immortal Sisters: Secret Teachings of Taoist Women*. Berkeley: North Atlantic Books.

Cohn, Norman. 1995. *Cosmos, Chaos, and the World to Come: The Ancient Roots of Apocalyptic Faith*. New Haven, Conn.: Yale University Press.

Constable, George, ed. 1990. *Secrets of the Alchemists*. Richmond: Time-Life Books.

Copenhaver, Brian P. 1992. *Hermetica: The Greek Corpus Hermticum and the Latin Asclepius in a New English Translation, with Notes and Introduction*. Cambridge: Cambridge University Press.

Coudert, Allison. 1980. *Alchemy: The Philosophers' Stone*. Boulder, Col.: Shambhala.

D'Olivet, Fabre. 1975 *The Golden Verses of Pythagoras*. New York: Weiser.

Despeux, Catherine, and Livia Kohn. 2003. *Women in Daoism*. Cambridge Mass.: Three Pines Press.

Everard, Doctor. 1978. *The Divine Pymander of Hermes Mercurius Trismegistus*. San Diego: Wizard's Bookshelf.

Fortune, Dion. 2000. *The Mystical Qabalah*. York Beach, Maine: Samuel Weiser.

Gass, Robert. 1999. *Chanting: Discovering Spirit in Sound*. New York: Broadway Books.

Gerber, Richard. 1988. *Vibrational Medicine: New Choices for Healing Ourselves*. Santa Fe: Bear and Company.

Guthrie, Kenneth Sylvan. 1987. *The Pythagorean Sourcebook and Library*. Grand Rapids, Mich.: Phanes Press.

Halevi, Z'ev Ben Shimon. 1985. *Kabbalah Tradition of Inner Knowledge*. New York: Thames and Hudson.

Hartmann, Franz. 1932. *Paracelsus*. Philadelphia: David McKay.

Hauck, Dennis William. 1999. *The Emerald Tablet Alchemy for Personal Transformation*. New York: Penguin Books.

Heindel, Max. 1998. *The Rosicrucian Cosmos-conception of Mystic Christianity: An Elementary Treatise Upon Man's Past Evolution, Present Constitution and Future Development.* Ann Arbor: University of Michigan Press.

Hornung, Eric. 2001. *The Secret Lore of Egypt: Its Impact on the West.* York Beach, Maine: Samuel Weiser.

Hulse, David Allen. 2000. *The Western Mysteries.* St. Paul, Minn.: Llewellyn.

Huxley, Aldous. 1990 [1946]. *The Perennial Philosophy.* London: Harper & Brothers.

Ishida, Hidemi. 1989. "Body and Mind: The Chinese Perspective." In *Taoist Meditation and Longevity Techniques*, edited by Livia Kohn, 41-70. Ann Arbor: University of Michigan, Center for Chinese Studies Publications.

Jacobi, Jolanda. ed. 1951. *Paracelsus: Selected Writings.* Princeton: Princeton University Press.

Kaltenmark, Max. 1979. "The Ideology of the *T'ai-p'ing-ching*." In *Facets of Taoism*, edited by Holmes Welch and Anna Seidel, 19-52. New Haven, Conn.: Yale University Press.

Knight, Gareth. 1965. *A Practical Guide to Qabalistic Symbolism.* Cheltenham: Helios Book Service.

Kohn, Livia. 1990. "Transcending Personality: From Ordinary to Immortal Life." *Taoist Resources* 2.2: 1-22.

_____. 2001. *Daoism in Chinese Culture.* Cambridge, Mass: Three Pines Press.

_____. 2004. *Cosmos and Community: The Ethical Dimension of Daoism.* Cambridge, Mass.: Three Pines Press.

_____. 2005. *Health and Long Life: The Chinese Way.* Cambridge, Mass.: Three Pines Press.

_____, ed. 2006. *Daoist Body Cultivation.* Magdelena, NM: Three Pines Press

Love, Jeff. 1976. *The Quantum Gods.* Old Brewery: Compton Press.

Masters, Robert. 1991. *The Goddess Sekhmet: The Way of the Five Bodies.* St. Paul, Minn.: Llewellyn.

Mead, G.R.S. 1991. *The Hymns of Hermes.* Grand Rapids, Mich.: Phanes Press.

Newall, Jack. 2005. "Hermeticism." www.galilean-library.org.

Nicholson, Helen. 2001. *The Knights Templar.* Phoenix Mill: Sutton Publishing.

Nott, C.S. 1978. *Further Teachings of Gurdjieff.* York Beach, Maine: Samuel Weiser.

Patai, Raphael. 1990. *The Hebrew Goddess.* Detroit: Wayne State University Press.

Reed, John. 1966. *Prelude to Chemistry: An Outline of Alchemy.* Cambridge, Mass.: MIT Press.

———. 1990. "Chasing the Seductive Gleam." In *Secrets of the Alchemists*, edited by George Constable. Richmond: Time-Life Books.

Robinet, Isabelle. 1979. "Metamorphosis and Deliverance of the Corpse in Taoism." *History of Religions* 19: 37-70.

Roob, Alexander. 2001. *The Gold of the Philosophers: Alchemy and Hermeticism:*. Los Angeles: Tashen.

———. 2005. *The Hermetic Cabinet:: Alchemy and Mysticism:*. Los Angeles: Tashen.

Rowe, Nicholas. 1952. *The Golden Verses of the Pythagoreans*. Fintry: Shrine of Wisdom.

Russell, Richard. 1994. *Alchemical Works of Geber*. York Beach, Maine: Samuel Weiser.

Schumann, Anteleme Ruth, and Stephanie Rossini. 2001. *Sacred Sexuality in Ancient Egypt: The Erotic Secrets of the Forbidden Papyrus*. Rochester, Vt: Inner Traditions.

Schwartz-Salant, Nathan, ed. 1995. *Jung and Alchemy*. London: Routledge.

Scott, Robert 1993. *Hermetica*. Boston: Shambhala.

Seligmann, Kurt. 1971. *Magic, Supernaturalism and Religion*. New York: Pantheon Books.

———. 1997. *The History of Magic*. New York: Pantheon Books.

Smolley, Richard, and Jay Kinney. 1999. *Hidden Wisdom*. New YorkPenguin Group.

Somnji, Richard. 2002. *Emotion and Peace of Mind: from Stoic Agitation to Christian Temptation*. Oxford: Oxford Scholarship Online.

Speeth, Kathleen Riordan. 1989. *The Gurdjieff Work*. New York: St. Martin's Press.

Steiner, Rudolph. 1994. *Theosophy*. Hudson, NY: Anthroposophic Press

———. 1997. *An Outline of Esoteric Science*. Hudson, NY: Anthroposophic Press.

Three Initiates. 1940. *The Kybalion: A Study of Hermetic Philosophy*. Chicago: Yogi Publications.

Tyson, Donald. 2000. *Three Books of Occult Philosophy of Henry Cornelius Agrippa*. St. Pau, Minn: Llewellyn Books.

Waite, Arthur Edward, ed. 1976. *The Hermetic and Alchemical Writings of Paracelsus*. Berkeley: Shambhala.

Waldberg, Michel. 1981. *Gurdjieff: An Approach to His Ideas*. London: Routledge & Kegan Paul.

Wilson, Colin. 1978. *Mysteries*. New York: G.P. Putnam's Sons.

Yates, Frances. 1964. *Giordano Bruno and the Hermetic Tradition*. Chicago: University of Chicago Press.

Index

alchemy, operative: 1, 17-22; elixir, 18, 67, 82, 87, 181; materials of, 17-18, 56-57; mercury in, 56, 224, 232; reversal in, 78; salt in, 224, 232; sulphur in, 19, 224, 232; water in, 9; Western, 13, 18-19, 21-22, 188-189

animals: alchemical, 42, 68, 137; celestial, 32, 128; directional, 66, 133, 135, 137, 153-154; supernatural, 89, 231; chicken, 32; crane, 89; deer, 42; dog, 32; dragon, 66, 68, 89, 135, 137, 23; fox, 231; ox, 42; phoenix, 90, 128; tiger, 66, 68, 89, 133, 137

body: dharma, 96-97; habits of, 4, 209; in India, 205-206; of Laozi, 29, 43, 47-48; levels of, 182, 224, 232-235; in *neidan*, 27-52; and pilgrimage, 33-34; preparation of, 2-4; puberty, 211; techniques of, 3-4; transformation of, 155-157; and trepanation, 101-102

body, alchemical: Divine Water, 66; embryo, 20, 56, 112, 207-208; Golden Bird, 46, 66; Golden Elixir, 75, 109-110, 158; Golden Flower, 188; Golden Fluid, 41, 66, 133; Golden Radiance, 109, 114; Heavenly Water, 156; holy fetus, 37, 91, 112, 133; Jade Fluid, 133; Jade Liquor, 66; Jade Rabbit, 46, 66; nine orifices, 27; pearl, 112, 196; Three Treasures, 39, 84, 112, 171, 183, 194, 232; River Cart, 42-44

body, centers: Ancestral Cavity, 45-46; breasts, 32, 142-143; cakras, 37, 179, 205-206; Cavern Chamber, 30; Door of Earth, 108; Double Pass, 33, 110; Earth Palace, 38; Earthly Axle, 108; elixir fields, 6, 31, 37-38, 41, 79, 91, 143, 153, 197; Essence Chamber, 153; Flowery Canopy, 8; Gate of Destiny, 33, 39-40, 47, 195; Gate of Heaven, 37-38, 43, 79, 87-102, 108, 116; Gate of Mystery, 39; glands, 207; Grotto Chamber, 8; Hall of Light, 8, 27; head, 44, 87-102; Heaven Palace, 38, 89; Heavenly Pass, 108; Heavenly Terrace, 43; Infant's Palace, 153, 155; Jade Chamber, 34; Kunlun, 8, 29, 30-31, 33; mouth, 207; Mysterious Pass, 45-46; navel, 41, 91; Nine Palaces, 8, 30; Niwan, 8, 10, 37-38, 79, 114, 143; Passes, 46; Primordial Cavity, 109; Primordial Pass, 109; Purple Chamber, 8, 31; Purple Elixir, 109-110; Purple Palace, 37; Qi Cavity, 39, 41-42, 155-156; Scarlet Palace, 8, 31, 38, 114; Sea of Blood, 155-157; Sea of Suffering, 33, 37; Spring Cavern, 46; Summit Gate, 93, 95; Three Passes, 42-44, 110, 143; Twelve-storied Tower, 34, 109; Valley Spirit, 45-46; Yang Cavity, 39; Yang Pass, 40; Yellow Chamber, 39; Yellow Court, 9, 31, 38, 41, 68, 114

body, cultivation: breathing, 4, 45, 55, 113, 154, 175, 183, 195-196; diet, 4, 219, 237; Eight Brocades, 6; exercise, 4, 55, 206-210; hatha yoga, 208; karma yoga, 214; Kundalini, 21, 203-218; longevity, 4; *neigong*, 108, 110; *pranayama*, 206, 210; qigong, 4, 21, 47, 180, 182-183, 189, 196; Six Healing Sounds, 195; yoga, 2, 203-218

body, fluids: blood, 6, 18, 19, 36, 39, 44, 47, 66, 130, 151, 153-154: essence, 1, 151; Red Dragon, 142-143, 153-155, 158; saliva, 5, 20; semen 130, 161-162; various, 37, 47, 66

body, organs: five 7, 14, 27-28, 48, 66, 76, 89, 100-101, 196, 198; heart and kidneys, 6-9, 16, 20, 36-39, 56, 65-69, 100-101, 109, 112-114, 153, 195, 234

body, points: Bubbling Spring, 46-47; Iron Rampart, 43; Jade Pillow, 43-45, 48, 143; Narrow Strait, 43-44, 109-110, 143; Ocean of *Qi*, 5, 8, 33; Tail Gate, 42-44, 143; Wind Pond, 43

cosmology: After Heaven, 198-199; archetypes, 187; Atlantis, 187-188, 194; Before Heaven, 16, 64, 130, 198-199;

243

beings in, 231; body in, 37, 47, 69; and colors, 7, 14, 108-109, 227; correspondences in, 127; creation, 78, 127, 181, 219, 220, 226, 229; Dipper, 112, 198, 230; directions, 137, 198; elements, 224, 226; evolution, 78; five phases, 14-15, 27-28, 195-196, 226; general 13, 64, 126-127, 129, 152, 163, 182, 198-199, 220, 223-224; Great Clarity, 31; Great Purity, 115; Heaven and Earth, 3, 12, 16, 20, 28, 30, 42, 64-66, 69, 79, 90, 110, 126, 135, 152, 159, 168, 190, 198-199, 224-226; microcosm, 109, 224-225; Milky Way, 38; Non-Ultimate, 33; Penglai, 31,159; Phoenix Pavilion, 115; planets, 226, 230; Pole Star, 198; Pure Land, 100-101; pure yang, 67-69, 90; Purple Capital, 95; stars, 198, 230; sun and moon, 3, 8, 29, 31, 126, 152, 209, 215-216; Three Heavens, 115; Water Bureau, 42; yin-yang, 9, 13-16, 27, 47-48, 65-67, 126, 133,, 152-153, 158, 181, 194-195, 197-199, 224, 228

Dao: and body, 10, 29; gods of, 31; of internal alchemy, 48, 56; in life, 164, 170-171; of Middle Oneness, 12; and mind, 194, 230; oneness with, 11-12, 48, 77-78, 159, 167-169; theory of, 79-80, 126, 144, 150, 188, 200; and transcendence, 55; transmission of, 60, 151; work with, 79-80

Daoists: Bai Yuchan, 6, 62, 64, 74-76, 79-80, 83-84, 108, 117; Cao Heng, 121, 123, 125, 129, 131, 139-140, 143; Chen Daoxuan, 134, 138; Chen Nan, 61, 74, 123, 128; Chen Pu, 59-60, 90; Chen Tuan, 64, 73, 97, 190; Chen Yingning, 110; Chen Yunxiang, 185; Chia, Mantak, 179-180, 186, 189-193; Cihang Daoren, 96; Cui Xifan, 59-60; Deng Yougong, 111; Dong Dening, 82; Five Patriarchs, 61, 63, 74, 137; Fu Jinduo, 147; Fu Jinquan, 122, 144, 145, 147; Fu Shan, 143; He Longxiang, 146, 148, 150; Huang Zhi'an, 165, 176; Li Daochun, 123, 129; Li Ruohai, 132-134, 138; Li Song, 60; Li Xinqing, 175; Lin Lingsu, 105; Liu Chengying, 172; Liu Chuxuan, 62; Liu Haichan, 42, 59-60, 62, 73; Liu Huayang, 90; Liu Ming, 185; Liu Ruozhou, 105; Liu Xiyu, 64; Liu Zhongyu, 107; Liu Yiming, 81, 144-145, 158; Liu Zhongzhen, 168; Lü Kun, 148; Lu Xixing, 122-123; Luo Gongyuan, 56; Ma Danyang, 62; Master An, 133; Min Yide, 144, 145; One Cloud, 179, 181, 184, 190-193; Qin Yehe, 132; Qiu Chuji, 63; Ren Farong, 185; Seven Perfected, 62-63; Shen Defu, 125; Shi Jianwu, 59-60, 64; Shi Tai, 61, 74; Shiguzi, 133; Sima Chengzhen, 11-12; Sun Buer, 63; Sun Dianqi, 122; Sun Guangxin, 104; Sun Jiaolun, 132-134, 138; Sun Ruzhong, 123, 127, 132-134, 138; Sun Simiao, 5, 124; Tan Chuduan, 62; Tan Qiao, 107; Tao Hongjing, 112; Wang Changyue, 146; Wang Chongyang, 43, 62, 142; Wang Chuyi, 62; Wang Jia, 135; Wang Qianyi, 90; Wang Wenqing, 106, 117; Wang Yungu, 132; Weng Baoguang, 58, 92; Wengzhong, 32; Wu Shouyang, 135, 137; Wu Yun, 68; Xiao Zhitian, 169; Xue Shi, 143; Xue Zixian, 61, 74; Yang Xintai, 174-175; Ye Fashan, 56; Yixing, 56; Yu Taichen, 126-127; Yu Yan, 59; Yuen, Jeffrey, 180; Zeng Liyan, 167-168; Zeng Zao, 56, 59, 124; Zhang Boduan, 61, 64, 73-76, 78, 81-83, 91, 127; Zhang Jixian, 105; Zhang Yuanhua, 87-88; Zhao Bichen, 35-36, 38, 46; Zhao Daoyi, 142, 88; Zhao Yizhen, 93-94; Zhen Yixing, 56; Zhu Wenbin, 90

deities: Ancestral Master, 114-117; in body, 7-8, 10, 30-31, 66; Buddha, 45; Dark Emperor, 114, 116; Dark Female, 193; demons, 105, 135-136; Dionysus, 18, 204; divine parents, 9, 127, 130; Dongwang gong, 30-32, 230; elementals, 231; Five Thunders, 110; General Zhou, 115; Generals Gou and Bi, 108; Golden Mother, 95; Great Harmony, 31; Great Simplicity, 31; Great Unity, 31; Guanyin, 96; Heavenly Lords, 124; Heavenly Worthy, 114; Heracles, 231; in Hermeticism, 230-232, 235; Hundun, 169, 199; hungry ghosts, 136; Indian, 204; Jade Maiden, 31; Krishna, 211; Laozi, 31, 84, 115; Maitreya, 100-101; Mazu,

95; Moses, 221; Mysterious Female, 197; Northern Emperor, 111-112; Officer Wang, 128; Pangu, 29; Perfect Warrior, 111-114, 116-117; Primordial Princess, 154-155; Purusa, 29; Shakti and Shiva, 203-204, 210; Three Corpses, 106; Three Ones, 8; Thunder Generals, 105-119; Thunder Lord, 104, 128; Xiwang mu, 30-32, 145, 230; Yellow Emperor, 126; Yingming, 31; Yuefei, 176; Ziwei furen, 124

dynasties: Han, 14, 54, 124; Ming, 121-140, 148: Qing, 81-82, 90, 141-160, 164; Tang, 4, 9-10, 21, 55-56; Tang-Song, 53-54; Song, 34, 42, 104-119, 123, 142, 149; Yuan, 34, 88, 99; Zhou, 5, 15

ethics, 2-4, 9, 83, 171, 124, 128-129, 135-136, 142, 146-150, 159-160, 165-166, 170-173, 219, 228, 235-236; goodness, 171, 221; moderation, 160-170; precepts, 173; virtue, 170, 176, 188; in yoga, 210

family: 128, 132-134, 172, 213; ancestors, 137-138; and monastics, 149, 164

immortality: 18, 68, 151, 179, 190, 204, 207; ascension to, 18, 67, 87-10, 126, 154, 232; and death, 87-88, 93-94, 100-101, 139, 212-213, 215-216, 231; as salvation, 159; transcendence, 167; trials of, 19, 58, 231; transformation, 91, 228

immortals: Eight, 57; Jinmingzi, 187; Lü Dongbin, 57-59, 62, 73-74, 90, 142-143, 231; reality of, 186-187; Wei Boyang, 96; Wei Huacun, 165; Zhang Daoling, 112, 115, 165; Zhang Sanfeng, 123, 184; Zhongli Quan, 57-59, 62, 67, 73-74, 90

masters, Indian: Hariakhan Baba, 216: Kripalu, 216; Neem Karoli Baba, 215; Ram Dass, 215; Thirumoolar, 212; Yogananda, 215

masters, Western: Hermes Trismegistos, 18, 221; Luria, Isaac, 237

medicine: 5, 13, 27-28, 32, 40-41, 44, 46, 66, 143, 180, 238-239; herbs, 75, 232-233, 237, 238; Homeopathy, 238; and science, 179, 190, 196; TCM, 44, 180; tinctures, 233

meditation: 1, 9-12, 45, 55, 76, 134, 152-153, 155, 168, 181, 219; concentration, 5, 9, 12, 75, 82, 214; and death, 100; Inner Smile, 194-195; insight, 10; macrocosmic orbit, 196; mantras, 204-205; Microcosmic Orbit, 5-6, 40, 42, 46, 48, 143, 157, 179, 195-196; observation, 9-10,168; quietude, 75, 152; sounds, 100; trance, 12; visions in, 186-187; visualization, 1, 5, 6-9, 19, 34, 76, 92, 96-97, 99-100, 108-118, 128, 142-143, 183, 205, 219, 233, 237; *zazen*, 11; *zuowang*, 1, 9, 11-12, 194

metaphysics: cause and effect, 229-230; of Dao, 167-168; emptiness, 79-80, 18; *ganying*, 108, 183; Gnosticism, 220, 222; harmony, 165, 170, 177; infinite mind, 223-225, 228; nonaction, 81, 84, 163, 171-172; nothingness, 167; numerology, 35; Philosophers' Stone, 18-19, 238; simplicity, 3, 99, 174; Tree of Life, 21; weakness, 175; *wuji*, 199; *youwei*, 163, 174, 188

mountains: 135, 165, 176; Changbai, 190; demons in, 111; Hua, 133, 176, 191; Huagai, 105; Keng, 43; Luofu, 123; Nanyue, 165, 176; Qingcheng, 56, 60, 176; Song, 94; Wudang, 176, 185

neidan: fire and water in, 9, 16, 20, 81-82, 96, 98, 112, 179, 181, 191, 197; firing times, 41; fusion 195-196; seven returns, 84; term, 54, 56; unity, 47-48

psychology: contentment, 10, 169, 236; desires, 3, 11, 79-80, 82-84, 169, 175, 197; destiny, 39-40, 41, 75, 77-78, 81-85, 144, 151, 181, 191-194, 234; dreams, 91, 233; emotions, 6, 10-11, 15, 29, 41, 47, 125, 128-129, 170, 174-175, 195-196, 205, 208, 214, 227-228, 236, 238; faith, 164, 167, 170-173, 176; inner nature, 41-42, 73-86, 144, 150-151, 232; intention, 56; mind, 73-86, 183, 208; self, 194, 196, 199, 215, 227; senses, 80; soul(s), 7, 74-76, 91, 182, 192-194, 196-197, 203, 207, 214-215, 219, 228-229, 232-234, 236; spirit, 1, 10-11, 20, 68, 76, 92, 99, 183, 195, 232, 234

qi: and astral body, 234; and destiny, 83-84; embryonic, 90, 97-98; emotional, 195-196; field, 182-183, 194; flow, 4,

17, 29-30, 42-44, 47-48, 76-77, 143, 179, 193-194, 196; guiding of, 1, 4-6, 9, 19, 33-35, 54, 110, 132, 151, 188, 196; language of, 182-184; luminous, 38; and medicine, 76, 170; organ, 7, 16, 39, 64-66, 89, 106, 113, 115; personal, 129; postnatal, 46, 182, 195; and prana, 205-206, 209-210, 212, 225; primordial, 9, 64, 69, 78-79, 126, 129-130, 182, 187, 195, 225; in ritual, 107-110; and sex, 121, 129-130; and spirit, 92; timing, 65; transformation of, 1, 37, 73, 75, 77-78, 82-83, 110, 142, 155, 195-199, 231; true, 109, 130; and vibration, 227; in women, 152-154, 157

qi-channels: 27, 35-36; Belt, 35-36, 46; Conception, 34-35; extraordinary, 195; Governing, 33, 35, 38, 40, 42; *nadi*, 21; penetrating; 6, 21, 35-36, 47, 179

regions, China: Anhui, 121; Beijing, 146, 164-165, 186; Gansu, 144; Henan, 58, 87, 155; Hubei, 105, 134; Hunan, 62, 165; Kaifeng, 134; Ningxia, 144; Shandong, 62-63, 132; Shaanxi, 62; Shanxi, 144; Sichuan, 56, 60-61, 73, 104-105, 144-145; Wuchang, 134

regions, world: Egypt, 188, 221-222, 233, 237; India, 29; USA, 179

religions: Chan, 188; Buddhism, 2, 3, 5, 10-11, 13, 32, 35, 37, 53, 56, 73, 80, 83, 93-94, 134, 149, 182, 199, 204, 210, 216; Cabbala, 185, 191, 221, 237; Christianity, 3, 184, 191, 193, 195, 199, 220, 222, 232; Confucianism, 2, 27, 53, 73, 74, 123, 137-183; Hermeticism, 219-239; Hinduism, 180, 191, 199, 203-218, 237; Islam, 210, 220, 222; perennial philosophy, 220; practice in, 209, 210; Rosicrucians, 21, 189; shamanism, 185, 196, 233; spirit-writing, 90, 147, 150; tantra, 34, 100-101, 203-218; Theosophy, 189, 223; Tibetan Buddhism, 93, 100-102, 191, 193, 237; Zoroastrianism, 220, 222

ritual: 104-119, 166, 173, 185, 219; mudras, 94, 113, 206; ordination, 185; petitions, 115; registers, 105, 107; talismans, 106, 110; thunder, 104-119; vulgar, 118

rulership: Huang Chao, 53; Huizong, 33, 105; Song Taizu, 105; Wang Anshi, 53; Chinggis Khan, 63; Medici, 223

scholars: Bertschinger, Richard, 189; Boltz, Judith, 118; Bourdieu, Pierre, 3; Cleary, Thomas, 189; Darwin, Charles, 211; David-Neel, Alexandra, 100; Dee, John, 238; D'Olivet, Fabre, 230, 235; Freud, Sigmund, 211; Goris, Rene, 184; Gurdjieff, George, 189, 238; Hornung, Eric, 221; Huxley, Aldous, 221; Iyengar, B. K. S., 211; Jung, Carl, 188, 196; Kohn, Livia, 189; Krishnamacharya, 211; Li Yuanguo, 123; Lu Kuan-yü, 189; Lu Xichen, 166, 177; Masters, Robert, 238; Mauss, Marcel, 3; Needham, Joseph, 139; Ots, Thomas, 47; Pregadio, Fabrizio, 111; Robinet, Isabelle, 189; Rowe, H. T., 215; Rowe, Nicholas, 225; Steiner, Rudolf, 189, 232; Van Gulik, Robert, 139; Wang Yier, 164; Watts, Alan, 188; Wile, Douglas, 139; Wong, Eva, 190

schools: Complete Perfection, 41, 43, 62-63 73, 185-186, 190-191; Eastern, 122-123; Golden Elixir, 73-74; Healing Tao, 180, 185, 191-192, 196; Heavenly Masters, 105, 112, 115, 124, 184-185; Highest Clarity, 1, 8-9, 12, 55, 164; Limitless Gate, 190; Longmen, 63, 144-146; Northern, 61, 62-63; Numinous Treasure, 111; Pashupata, 204, 216; Pure Tenuity, 93; Sanlun, 9; Southern, 6, 61-64, 91; Tiantai, 9; Tongshan she, 95; Twofold Mystery, 11-12; Western, 35; Wu-Liu, 35; Xiantian dao, 95; Zhong-Lü, 42, 55, 57-60, 64-69, 74, 78, 191

sex: avoidance of, 17; and bedchamber arts, 122, 124, 129-130; criticism of, 129-130, 190; discrimination, 170; Duo-cultivation, 121-140; energy, 6, 183; liberation, 191; practices, 55, 121-140, 203, 219, 237; zither bed, 130-131

society: 128, 132-136, 141, 149-152, 160, 185, 211-213; administration, 172-173; commerce, 172; competition, 171; Daoist Association, 165; Daoist College, 165-166; ecology, 169, 171; finances, 134, 138-139; fortune-telling, 15; kundao, 163-178; local culture, 147;

merchants, 125; printing, 147; and Western *neidan*, 179-200; yoga adaptation, 211

space: 135-138, 165; altar, 136-137; chamber, 135-138; furnace, 17, 41, 56, 136, 149, 197; platform, 136

stages: in alchemy, 73-75, 77, 142, 145, 155, 181-182, 191, 195-197, 231, 237; and colors, 229; of life, 126, 208, 212-213, 214-215; in yoga, 206, 213

symbolism: 9, 19, 33-34, 183; bellows, 131-132; mountain, 33-34; Taiji, 46; water, 174-175

temples: Baiyun guan, 146, 164, 186; Beiji guan, 87; Chongfu gong, 94; Erxian an, 146; management of, 171-174; Portrait Hall, 87; Shaolin si, 155; Yousheng yuan, 117

texts: *Baiwen pian*, 42; *Baopuzi*, 8, 17-18, 135; *Baosheng biyao*, 143; *Beidi leigong fa*, 104; *Bhagavad-Gita*, 211; *Caizhen jiyao*, 123; *Chen xiansheng neidan jue*, 60, 89, 90-91, 93, 97-99; *Chisongzi zhangli*, 115; *Chongyang jiaohua ji*, 62; *Chongyang quanzhen ji*, 62; *Chongyang zhenren jinguan yusuo*, 142; *Chongyang zhenren shou Danyang ershisi jue*, 62; *Chunyang dijun shenhua miaotong ji*, 142; *Corpus Hermeticum*, 222-223; *Cuigong ruyao jing*, 60; *Cuixu pian*, 62; *Cuixu pian*, 89, 123; *Cunshen lianqi ming*, 5; *Dacheng jieyao*, 89, 94-99; *Dadan zhizhi*, 34, 38, 110; *Dadong zhenjing*, 30; *Danfang xuzhi*, 60; *Danjing jilun*, 89, 91-94, 97-99; *Daode jing*, 7, 11-12, 46, 54, 68, 70; *Daode jing*, 73, 78-79, 93, 163, 167, 169, 171, 173-174, 177; *Daode jing* commentaries, 7, 113; *Daofa huiyuan*, 46, 108; *Daoshu shier zhong*, 144; *Daoshu*, 40, 56, 59, 65, 124, 142; *Daoyuan yiqi*, 121, 123, 127, 129, 131, 134, 138-139, 143; *Dung honglong*, 143; *Duren jing neiyi*, 33; *Emerald Tablet*, 18, 222, 224-225; *Fahai yizhu*, 108, 116; *Golden Verses*, 222, 225, 227, 230, 235-236; *Guanzi*, 27, 54; *Guifan*, 148; *Haiqiong Bai zhenren yulu*, 62, 77; *Haiqiong chuandao ji*, 62; *Haiqiong wendao ji*, 62, 79-80, 83; *Hathayoga Pradipika*, 210; *Huainan yesou*, 90; *Huainanzi*, 27-28; *Huandan fuming pian*, 61; *Huangdi neijing lingshu*, 46; *Huangting ji*, 167-178; *Huangting jing*, 29, 38, 40, 109, 165; *Huanjin pian*, 60; *Huanyuan pian*, 61; *Huashu*, 107; *Huixin ji*, 144; *Huncheng ji*, 59; *Hunyuan pian*, 43-44; *Hunyuan shengji*, 43; *Jinbao neilian danjue*, 61; *Jindan jieyao*, 123, 139; *Jindan sibai zi*, 61; *Jindan xinfa*, 34; *Jindan zhenchuan*, 127, 128-130, 132-134; *Jindan zhi*, 144; *Jinguan yusuo jue*, 43; *Jinping mei*, 147; *Jinque xiansheng jiashu biwen*, 116; *Jinxian zhenglun tushuo*, 40; *Jiyizi zhengdao bishu*, 145; *Kunjue*, 45-46; *Kunyuan jing*, 151; *Kybalion*, 223; *Laojun nei riyong miaojing*, 19-20; *Laojun wai riyong miaojing*, 2-3; *Laozi bianhua jing*, 29; *Laozi huahu jing*, 29; *Laozi ming*, 29; *Laozi zhongjing*, 8, 30-31, 113; *Leimen yuanshuai fa*, 108; *Liangzhu zhixuan pian*, 76, 79, 80, 84; *Liji*, 27; *Lingbao bifa*, 59, 88-89; *Lingbao guikong jue*, 93, 99; *Lizhi zhenxian tidao tongjian*, 87, 105, 142; *Lun heche*, 110; *Luofu cuixu yin*, 123; *Lüshi chunqiu*, 28; *Neiguan jing*, 10; *Neijing tu*, 43, 110; *Neixun*, 148; *Neiye*, 27; *Niwan Li zushi nüzong shuangxiu baofa*, 145; *Nü jindan fayao*, 145, 151, 156; *Nü jindan koujue*, 38; *Nü jindan*, 38-39, 45, 154; *Nü sishu*, 148; *Nüdan cuoyao*, 154, 156; *Nüdan fa*, 144; *Nüdan hebian*, 38, 146, 148, 150-152, 154, 156, 158-159; *Nüdan shize*, 148; *Nügong lianji huandan tushuo*, 157; *Nügong quebing*, 143; *Nügong zhengfa*, 157; *Pomi zhengdao ge*, 59; *Qiaoyang jing nügong xiulian*, 154; *Qinghua biwen*, 76; *Qinyuan chun danci*, 59; *Sandong xiudao yi*, 104-105; *Sanfeng danjue*, 123, 126, 128, 136, 138; *Sanfeng ge*, 56; *Shangcheng xiudao bishu sizhong*, 143; *Shangqing Tianxin zhengfa*, 111, 115; *Shanhai jing*, 43; *Shiyi ji*, 135; *Songshi*, 105; *Suling jing*, 38; *Taiji liandan mijue*, 33; *Taiping jing shengjun bizhi*, 7; *Taiping jing*, 55; *Tang Lü Chunyang zhenren sitang ji*, 58; *Tianxian zhengli qianshuo*, 135-136; *Tiangong xiaomo huguo jing*, 105; *Tibetan Book of the Dead*, 93-94, 100; *Upanishads*, 204; *Vedas*, 204; *Wanli yehuo pian*, 125; *Weisheng shilue*, 41; *Wenyang lingdan tu*, 35; *Wulei koujue*, 108; *Wuzhen pian*, 61, 74, 78, 82-83, 91-92, 127, 143; *Wuzhen pian* commentaries, 58, 81; *Xiaodao lun*, 29; *Xingming fajue mingzhi*, 35-36, 45-46; *Xingming guizhi*, 35, 38-40, 41; *Xinyin miaojing*, 94; *Xishan qunxian hui zhenji*, 60, 89; *Xiuxian bianhuo lun*, 75; *Xiuzhen biannan*, 144, 151, 158; *Xiuzhen shishu*, 6, 59, 61, 75, 77; *Xiwangmu nüxiu zhengtu shize*, 145, 157; *Xiyou ji*, 147; *Xuantian jizou lingwen*, 114, 116; *Xuanwei xinyin*, 122, 126-128, 130, 137, 139; *Yangsheng bilu*, 42; *Yangxing yanming lu*, 124; *Youlong zhuan*, 43, 48; *Yueling*, 27; *Yuqing jing*, 104; *Zhen longhu jiuxian jing*, 6; *Zhen'gao*, 112; *Zhengdao bishu*, 122; *Zhonghe ji*, 123; *Zhong-Lü chuandao ji*, 42, 59, 77, 88-89; *Zhouyi cantong qi*, 73, 96; *Zhuangzi*, 9, 11, 45, 54, 169, 227; *Zituan danjing*, 124; *Zouchuan hunlian fashi*, 113; *Zuowang lun*, 11-12

thinkers: Aurobindo, 211; Bodhidharma, 155; Boyle, 188; Cheng Xuanying, 11; Democritus, 227; Dong Zhongshu, 27-28; Ge Hong, 1, 8, 17; Geber, 222; Heidegger, 168; Heshang gong, 7; Liu Xiang, 176; Mencius, 176; Newton, 222; Paracelsus, 223, 232; Plato, 221-222; Pythagoras, 220, 227, 237-238; Sima Guang, 43

time: 65, 197; calendar, 1, 15, 17, 29, 65; hours, 36-37, 65, 143-144; seasons, 197; solar nodes, 15; three years, 145

women: alchemy, 35, 141-160; attributes, 174; body, 48, 155-157; differences, 144, 150-155, 160, 197, 228; today, 163-178; segregation, 135

Yijing: 1, 13, 15-17, 27, 56, 68, 70, 81, 109, 152, 164, 230; Eight Trigrams, 16, 109, 112-113; hexagrams, 15, 27-28; Kan and Li, 16, 34, 37, 67, 112, 113, 152, 155, 197-198; Qian and Kun, 16, 42, 68, 152-153, 156, 164